D1447451

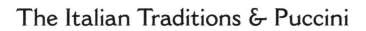

The Italian Traditions & Puccini

MUSICAL MEANING & INTERPRETATION

Robert S. Hatten, editor

The Italian Traditions

& Puccini

COMPOSITIONAL THEORY AND PRACTICE
IN NINETEENTH-CENTURY OPERA

Nicholas Baragwanath

INDIANA UNIVERSITY PRESS

Bloomington & Indianapolis

This book is a publication of

Indiana University Press
601 North Morton Street
Bloomington, Indiana 47404-3797 USA

iupress.indiana.edu

Telephone orders 800-842-6796
Fax orders 812-855-7931
Orders by e-mail iuporder@indiana.edu

Manufactured in the United States of
America

Library of Congress Cataloging-in-
Publication Data

Baragwanath, Nicholas.
The Italian traditions and Puccini :
compositional theory and practice in
nineteenth-century opera / Nicholas
Baragwanath.
p. cm. — (Musical meaning and
interpretation)
Includes bibliographical references and
index.
ISBN 978-0-253-35626-0 (hardcopy :
alk. paper)
1. Opera—Italy—19th century.
2. Puccini, Giacomo, 1858-1924—
Criticism and interpretation. 3. Music
theory—Italy—History—19th century.
4. Composition (Music)—History—
19th century. 5. Music—Instruction and
study—Italy—History—19th century.
I. Title.
 ML1733.4.B37   2011
782.10945'09034—dc22
                              2011008988

1 2 3 4 5 16 15 14 13 12 11

In Memory of Meta Lilian Baragwanath

CONTENTS

Although it focuses on his life and operas, this book is not primarily about Giacomo Puccini (1858–1924). It concerns the Italian musical tradition of which he remains, by common consent, the last great representative. What, precisely, "tradition" might mean in this context forms the main subject of the book.

The methods of musical training current in Lucca during Puccini's formative years had remained essentially unchanged since the eighteenth century. In many respects they differed profoundly from conventional modern teachings. Nineteenth-century Italian accounts of rhythm and its relation to phrase structure, for instance, bear little resemblance to the German tradition represented by Koch (1787), Hauptmann (1853), and Riemann (1884), which continues to underpin contemporary theory. Similarly, the modern understanding of musical "form," based on a notion of abstract templates that may be traced to such sources as Reicha (1824–26) and Marx (1837–47), began to influence Italian publications only toward the end of the nineteenth century. The study of harmony and counterpoint, as undertaken by Rossini, Verdi, and Puccini (principally through playing and singing), was entirely at odds with modern approaches to similarly named disciplines. In the broadest sense, these teachings comprised a body of guidelines and rules that had evolved over centuries to meet the demands of the church, the court, and the opera industry by allowing trained professionals to produce compositions and performances in the appropriate styles effectively in a remarkably short time. The pedagogical tradition gradually faded away during Puccini's lifetime, together with the practices and industries that gave rise to it, and is now largely forgotten.

It was replaced—or, some might argue, superseded—by an alternative and in many ways antithetical tradition, the legacy of which continues to inform attitudes and approaches today. Music history still belongs to the victors of this century-long struggle for cultural supremacy. (To describe it in blander, more objective, and less provocative terms as part of a general process of cultural transformation would be to deny the conscious intent with which it was carried out and to provide alibis for both the historical agents and their commentators.) The new tradition could be said to have begun with the birth of Romanticism and German artistic self-consciousness, and in particular with the formulation of a new philosophy or "metaphysics" of instrumental music around the turn of the nineteenth century, in the writings of Achim von Arnim, Johann Forkel, Ernst Theodor Amadeus Hoffmann, Novalis, the brothers August Wilhelm and Friedrich Schlegel, Ludwig Tieck, Wilhelm Wackenroder, and others. The battle lines were already drawn by 1834, when Austrian music philosopher Raphael Georg Kiesewetter laid claim to the future of music on behalf of the German nation in his blatantly one-sided *Geschichte der europäisch-abendländischen oder unserer heutigen Musik* (History of Western-European, or Our Modern, Music). By reducing the entirety of music history to a succession of Hegelian "Epochs," determined through the actions of superior males in touch with the *Zeitgeist* and spiraling toward some absolute liberated consciousness, he sought to depict Beethoven's instrumental style as the foreordained culmination of an inexorable process of historical development. Within this vast dialectic of inspired innovations and outdated former novelties, Kiesewetter acknowledged the hegemony of the Italian tradition only until the year 1760, conveniently categorizing it into epochs defined by Palestrina (1560–1600), Monteverdi (1600–40), Carissimi (1640–80), Scarlatti (1680–1725), and Leo and Durante (1725–60). Evidently, the Neapolitan schools from 1680 to 1760 had yet to give way to Bach and Handel in terms of historical significance. The fateful turning point, Kiesewetter maintained, after which European music became "Our" music, occurred with the operatic reforms (1760–80) of honorary-German Christoph von Gluck, who corrected some of the worst abuses of the Italians and paved the way for the "golden age" of Haydn and Mozart (1780–1800).[1] These two "classic" composers in turn created the conditions for the next radical world-historical breakthrough toward the Ideal, in Beethoven's further emancipation of music (German, instrumental) from the word (Italian, operatic). Kiesewetter's inclusion of Rossini's name in the title of his final chapter, which would otherwise have been called "The Epoch of Beethoven: 1800 to 1832," testified to nothing more than a grudging acquiescence to the inescapable reality of Franco-Italian opera's status as representative of a mainstream of European music. To pass over the most celebrated international composer of the age without mention would have revealed too obvious a prejudice, even for his purpose. The promised commentary on Rossini amounted nevertheless to just a couple of sentences, commending his partial assimilation of some of the achievements of the Austro-German orchestral tradition.[2]

Considered within the context of its own times, Kiesewetter's overtly partisan reading of history may be understood to reflect the optimism and enthusiasm that accompanied the drive toward German self-determination and the associated ascendancy of Romantic ideas such as the "spirit of the people" (*Volksgeist*). In the lead-up to the revolutions of 1848, this kind of celebratory cultural nationalism was regarded as a developmental force for freedom and progress. The magnificent, exciting, and newly configured instrumental traditions from Bach to Beethoven appeared worthy of assistance in their struggle to overcome the stuffy conservatism and, worse, continued popularity of a formula-ridden and historically (or philosophically) obsolete opera industry.

Such was the opinion of Young-German firebrand Richard Wagner, who advocated a more explicit variety of cultural imperialism for the good of less advanced peoples like the French and Italians. In a Parisian article of 1840, entitled *Über deutsches Musikwesen* (On the Essence of German Music), he took up and intensified Kiesewetter's identification of "Our Music" with the European mainstream by making the claim that to annex and nationalize foreign traditions was, for *German* artists, to render them *Universal*:

> The German genius would almost seem predestined to seek out among
> its neighbours what is not native to its motherland, to lift this from its nar-
> row confines, and thus make something Universal for the world. Naturally,
> however, this can only be achieved by him who is not satisfied to ape a for-
> eign nationality, but keeps his German birthright pure and undefiled; and
> that birthright is Purity of feeling and Chasteness of invention. Where this
> dowry is retained, the German may do the grandest work in any tongue and
> every nation, beneath all quarters of the sky. Thus we see a German raising

the Italian school of Opera to the most complete ideal at last, and bringing
it, thus widened and ennobled to universality, to his own countrymen. That
German, that greatest and divinest genius, was *Mozart*. . . . He made the foreign art his own, to raise it to a universal.[3]

A similar point of view was graphically expressed in Josef Danhauser's well-known painting of the same year, *Liszt at the Piano,* in which a
drawing room full of Romantic artists—including Liszt at the keyboard,
his mistress Marie d'Agoult at his feet, Alexandre Dumas (*père*), George
Sand, and Victor Hugo—are portrayed as worshipping at the altar of the
all-conquering German tradition, as represented by a floating, luminous,
deified bust of Beethoven.[4] Observing the scene from the shadows in a
similarly awed but far less enraptured manner are two musicians of the
purportedly outmoded and outclassed Italian tradition, Paganini and
Rossini, who appear to comfort one another in mutual resignation to their
subordinate place in the new musical order.

Much the same basic claim determined the overall historical framework of Leipzig professor Franz Brendel's *Geschichte der Musik in Italien,
Deutschland und Frankreich von den ersten christlichen Zeiten bis auf die
Gegenwart* (History of Music in Italy, Germany, and France from the
Earliest Christian Times to the Present, 1852), which appears to have been
intended to update and supplant Kiesewetter's earlier study. Not only did
it affirm the success of Mozart in wresting opera from the Italians, purg-
ing it of substandard elements, and returning it to the world in Ideal form,
stamped with a German seal of quality, but it also promoted Wagner and
his theories as the latest breakthrough (*Aufschwung*) in the world-artistic
dialectic.[5] Brendel's *Geschichte* was continuously in print until 1903 and,
together with its guiding principle of a nationally determined "universal"
tradition, provided the foundation for many subsequent music histories,
including Hugo Riemann's widely read *Geschichte der Musik seit Beethoven
(1800–1900)* (History of Music since Beethoven, 1800–1900, 1901).

During the same period, a proliferation of more specialized studies
began to adapt and (according to their own rhetoric) "improve" age-old
Italian (and French) theories and practices according to the norms of
the Austro-German instrumental tradition. Moritz Hauptmann, for instance, another Leipzig professor, made a conscious attempt to subvert
and refashion the traditional Italian teachings on rhythm he had received
through composition lessons with Francesco Morlacchi, a student of Zin-

garelli in Naples and Mattei in Bologna. That, at least, was how the Italians received his theory (as will be documented in chapter 3). In *Die Natur der Harmonik und der Metrik* (The Nature of Harmony and Meter, 1853), Hauptmann inverted the central Italian concept of the primacy of free expressive melodic rhythm (*ritmo melodico*) over the regular pulse of the accompanying harmonic rhythm (*ritmo armonico*)—perfectly encapsulated in the oft-cited observation that Chopin maintained a strict pulse with his left hand at the piano, while allowing the right hand considerable freedom—by insisting that "the rhythmic phrase finds its artistic meaning first of all in meter."[6] Henceforth in the German (universal) tradition, the rational divisions of meter, or the "harmonic-metric," provided order and therefore aesthetic value to the allegedly irrational and chaotic "melodic-metric."

Early twentieth-century theories of analysis and composition, such as those of Guido Adler, Heinrich Schenker, and Arnold Schoenberg, were equally committed to consolidating and furthering the dominance of German music.[7]

One consequence of this century of composition and associated scholarly activity, subsequently aided and abetted by the migration of Austro-German scholars to the United States and elsewhere, was that the ancient Italian traditions, unable to compete either with the new instrumental repertories or with an influx of disarmingly intellectual musicological publications, and undermined, moreover, from within by a fifth column of Germanophile progressives in Florence and Milan, gradually dwindled to a meager canon of historically second-rate (but stubbornly popular) "masterworks."[8] Lost to European art were not only an enormous number of perhaps deservedly forgotten operas and opera composers but also an entire musical culture, a way of thinking about and making music that represented, in a profound sense, the antithesis of much that Austro-German Romanticism had come to stand for. However magnificent the tradition of instrumental masterpieces from Bach to Brahms may be, the persistent claims to universality made on its behalf (compounded, of course, by relevant social and economic factors) contributed to the erosion and eventual disappearance of other European musical cultures.

This book sets out to explore some of the Italian traditions of compositional theory and practice in more detail—to establish a framework for further studies—through a survey of contemporary and historical sources that underpinned the training received by composers throughout the nineteenth century. It aims to distil from the extant documentary evidence a coherent theory that reconstructs the once commonplace fundamentals, methods, and formulas that were taught at the Italian conservatories and to explore their significance to composition through a variety of case studies from Rossini, Bellini, and Donizetti to Verdi, Boito, and Puccini. The disproportionate emphasis upon Puccini's training and early compositions throughout the book is intended to underscore the longevity of the Italian traditions and their closeness to our own times. Puccini's music is taken to serve as a prism, through which may be glimpsed some of the archaic practices he inherited through generations of maestros. For this reason many of the commentaries and analyses that follow may be considered deliberately one-sided, facing only the past and ignoring the obvious progressive elements of Puccini's music, as if to observe the "sacred flame" of the Italian tradition—to borrow a poetic metaphor coined by Giovanni Pacini—by the glow of its dying embers.

The reconstruction of compositional theory and practice is by no means comprehensive. If it were, it would have to begin with the process for selecting the subject matter or text for the opera and then take into account such factors as the construction of the libretto, the dramaturgical conventions that determined the overall layout of scenes and events, and the revisions and changes that usually followed each run of performances. These stages of the composition process are here overlooked in favor of a theory that is limited to the production of what Philip Gossett describes as the essential creative phase of the opera, the "continuity draft" (*abbozzo*), after which composers regarded their work as substantially complete. "Composers of nineteenth-century Italian opera considered this phase of their preparation critical," he maintains. "Once the skeleton of an opera was prepared, they considered the creative work finished."[9] This stage of the process may be taken to commence at the point when composer and librettist agreed upon the completed versified libretto and work could begin on the *abbozzo:* a complete draft of the entire opera on two or more staves, concentrating on the vocal and bass lines with occasional indications for details such as scoring and harmonization and sometimes incorporating earlier fragmentary sketches. The interpretation advanced in the following chapters draws upon material relating principally to this level of the composition process: the setting of individual phrases, their relation to larger periods, and the layout of pieces or *pezzi*. It does not attempt to take into account later stages that deal with issues such as orchestration, revisions and alterations, performance, or reception.

The main Italian "schools," as they were understood from Martini (1774–75) to Florimo (1881–83), are surveyed in chapter 1, together with some of the primary source materials used in the writing of this book. Chapter 2 discusses the nature of training provided at the conservatories of Lucca and Milan, in preparation for the more detailed survey of Italian traditions of compositional theory and practice in chapters 3, 4, and 5, in terms of rhythm and versification, harmony and counterpoint, and form and structure. Chapter 6 explores the relation of sung "practical counterpoints" to exercises in singing and melodic writing (*solfeggi*) and the significance of both to real composition (*composizione ideale*).

For help in preparing this book and for many fascinating and fruitful conversations over the years I owe a special debt of gratitude to David Ledbetter, a scholar of rare knowledge and insight. My thanks go also to the following friends and colleagues, all of whom read the manuscript entirely or in part and provided expert guidance and support: Andrew Davis, Robert Gjerdingen, Anthony Gritten, Robert Hatten, Douglas Jarman, and Giorgio Sanguinetti. The writings of Richard Taruskin significantly influenced my approach to music historiography in this book. The many other scholars whose work has inspired and guided me are acknowledged in the text and endnotes.

Others to whom I would like to offer thanks include my friend and former boss, Martin Harlow, for doing his utmost to ensure that this book was not written entirely on weekday evenings, Sunday afternoons, and snatched quarter-hours; Mavis Fox, Geoff Thomason, and the staff of the Royal Northern College of Music library, Alberto Bivash of the Biblioteca del Conservatorio di Musica San Pietro a Majella in Naples, and Alfredo Vitolo and Cristina Targa of the Biblioteca della Musica di Bologna for fielding my requests for ever more obscure Italian esoterica; Deborah Burton, for providing me with photocopies of material derived from her extensive archival researches; John Deathridge, James Hepokoski, Alexandra Wilson, and Simonetta Bigongiari of the Centro Studi Giacomo Puccini in Lucca, for support and encouragement during the early stages of the project; Sarah Hibberd, for reminding me that France

also existed in the nineteenth century; Vyacheslav Borukhson, for technical support; Vladimir and Lyudmila Osmakov, for building me a grape-
and-cucumber-lined *byesyedka* overlooking the Caucasian Mountains
in which to complete the book; and finally Svetlana Baragwanath, for
always managing to look suitably agog when held captive during lengthy
one-sided conversations on the history of music theory.

Funding in support of this project was very gratefully received from
the Arts and Humanities Research Council (UK), for six months of research leave, and from the Royal Northern College of Music Research
Committee, for trips to Italy.

Unless otherwise stated, all translations in this book are my own. The guiding principle has been to capture the most accurate meaning regardless of the flow of the prose and to preserve as closely as possible the formulations, terms, and (often) ambiguities of the texts. All significant quotations in English are accompanied by the corresponding passage in the original language, either in the text or in the endnotes. Italian terms that relate to important concepts are included throughout in brackets to allow the reader to cross-reference their usage in different sources. Owing to the scope and complexity of the material, it has not proved feasible to include a simplified glossary of terms. For definitions and translations, readers should refer to the index of concepts in this volume.

Many of the primary sources are practical guides written by maestros who were evidently more accomplished at dealing with musical notes than with words. Given also the idiosyncrasies that developed over generations in different places at different times, and the generally casual use of composers' jargon, it is perhaps hardly surprising that the meaning of basic terms can vary widely across the traditions. The same words may be used, even in the same text, to signify utterly different meanings. This presents a formidable obstacle to scholarship. The most problematic of such terms are discussed briefly below.

ACCENTO or "accent" could be used in a conventional sense to refer to a stressed musical beat, often corresponding to a syllabic accent. In such cases it usually indicated the initial, *subsidiary* accent of a line of verse, since the final, *principal* accent was referred to as the "common accent" (*accento comune*) or "inflection" (*desinenza*). *Accento musicale* or "musical accent," in contrast, was a specific term that signified the various means through which a vocal melody could express the emotions embodied in the words. It was premised on an analogy with the "accent" of speech.

MOTIVO may be translated literally as "motive" and understood to encompass a similar variety of meanings as the English word. But only very occasionally, and usually in the final quarter of the nineteenth century, did it signify what would now be commonly understood as a musical motive: that is, a short melodic or harmonic cell that underlies the construction of larger units. *Motivo* nearly always referred to an opening melody of at least four measures and may be most accurately translated as "principal theme (or subject)." The term that corresponded most closely to the modern concept of a musical motive or cell was *disegno* or "design," after the *dessin mélodique* described in Reicha's *Traité de Melodie* (1814); but *disegno* could also be used synonymously with *ritmo,* as explained below.

MOVIMENTO (or *muovimento*) was one of the most overused words in Italian writings on music. Although, in a simplistic sense, it could be translated as "movement," this would not take account of its diverse applications to various musical parameters. Its precise meaning must be determined according to context. It could, for instance, refer to the overall tempo of a piece as the "movement" of its affect, such as adagio or allegro, or to a regular pattern of intervals (*movimento regolare*) that was used as a type of fixed voice (*canto fermo*) to generate harmonic-contrapuntal structures, or to the concept of a dynamic impulse within the orchestral accompaniment (*movimento armonico*), shifting from weak to strong accents and corresponding to a given verse rhythm.

RITMO or "rhythm" could be used in the everyday sense to signify the divisions of a regular pulse that generated a time signature, but only rarely and usually in rudimentary books for beginners. Far more commonly it referred to a concept for which modern music theory has no clear equivalent. For this reason, it has been mostly left in the original Italian throughout this book. Its occasional translation as "phrase rhythm" is intended to capture something of the idea of a repetitive rhythmic pattern, cutting across bar lines and made up of both a melodic design (*ritmo melodico*) and accompanying harmonic impulse (*ritmo armonico*), that is determined by, but does not necessarily correspond to, the musical setting of a line of verse. The singular form of the term, *ritmo,* could be used to refer to the musical rhythm of either one individual line of poetic verse or, somewhat confusingly, to a series of several such verses, in much the same way that the singular word "verse" can be used to signify both an individual poetic line and an entire stanza. In this sense, "rhythm" (*ritmo*) was effectively synonymous with "phrase" (*frase*), which could also signify an individual setting of a line of verse or a series of such settings.

Because the term *ritmo* was most often applied to this concept of a flexible poetic verse rhythm, the terminology used for basic concepts of time and meter could be extremely confusing. Lucchese maestro Marco Santucci's attempt to clarify his terminology in the following (typical) sentence serves to illustrate the possibilities for misunderstanding: "The measure [*misura*] in music has as its object the *tempo*, which is commonly known as the *battuta*."[1]

MISURA translates most literally as "measure," meaning the basic pulse within the unit of the measure. But it could also be used as a synonym for *battuta*, which could mean either a single "measure" or an individual "beat" within a "measure," depending on context.

More confusingly still, *misura*, when indicating an underlying rhythmic pulse, could also be used synonymously with *metro* or "meter," a term borrowed from poetry to describe the regular patterns of syllables and feet that made up a verse. Santucci frequently used both terms together, as in the phrase "meter [*metro*] or alternatively measure [*misura*],"[2] while De Vecchis wrote of "meter [*Metro*] or rather verse [*Verso*]."[3] In general, because of the centrality of opera and vocal music to the Italian traditions, discussions of "measure" tend to presuppose an identity with poetic "meter."

TEMPO or "time" could signify a time signature, as in "duple time." More often it referred to the overall tempo character of a piece, in much the same way as *movimento* or the modern term "movement." Consider, for instance, Luigi De Macchi's definition of a measure in his *Grammatica musicale* (ca. 1830), in which *tempo* applied only to the designated speed of the piece: "The beat [*Battuta*] or measure [*Misura*] is a complex of one or more figures or equivalent pauses, formed by a given value expressed and determined by a sign that is found after the key signature and is called the *tempo*."[13] Amintore Galli, professor of complementary harmony and counterpoint and music history at the Milan Conservatory from 1878 until 1908, defined "tempo" as follows in his *Piccolo lessico della musicista* (Brief Lexicon for Musicians, 1902): "*Tempo* is synonymous with *misura,* and indicates also the movement of the hand in signifying the same *misura;* it expresses also one of the parts that divide up the Symphony, Suite, Quartet, Sonata, etc."[4]

THE HELMHOLTZ SYSTEM Where it is necessary to identify the precise register of a pitch, the Helmholtz system is used, as follows:

C–c–c^1 (Middle C)–c^2–c^3

The Italian Traditions & Puccini

ONE

Musical Traditions in Nineteenth-Century Italy

I. THE ITALIAN SCHOOLS

The Italian musical tradition was not a unified whole but an aggregate of diverse regional traditions. There were a number of recognized musical centers and institutions, within which individual maestros passed on their own compilations and interpretations of earlier teachings to successive generations. Although the distinctions between them became increasingly blurred during the period of the Risorgimento, it is nevertheless possible to identify specific lineages in pedagogy, theory, and practice throughout the nineteenth century. These traditions were proud to trace their origins back to the Renaissance, post-Josquin, as Padre Giovanni Battista Martini (1706–84)—pedagogue, antiquarian, *maestro di cappella* at the church of San Francesco, and prominent member of the Accademia Filarmonica in Bologna—noted in his overview of the main Italian "schools."[1] There was the Scuola Romana deriving from Giovanni Pier-Luigi da Palestrina (1525–94), Giovanni-Maria Nanini [*sic*] (ca. 1543–1607), his younger brother Giovanni-Bernardino (ca. 1560–1618), Orazio Benevoli (1605–72), and Francesco Foggia (1604–88). Developing in parallel was a Scuola Napolitana involving Rocco Rodio (ca. 1535–1615), Alessandro Scarlatti (1660–1725), Leonardo Leo (1694–1744), and Francesco Durante (1684–1755). The Scuola Veneta (called Scuola Veneziana by later authors), which encompassed Padua and Verona as well as Venice, could boast a similarly exalted heritage in Adriano Willaert (ca. 1490–1562), Giuseppe [*sic*] Zarlino da Chiozza [*sic*] (1517–90), and Antonio Lotti (1666–1740). The Scuola Lombarda included musicians not only from Milan and the surrounding towns of Lodi, Brescia,

1

Cremona, and Vigevano, but also, according to Martini, from the cities of Modena and Parma in neighboring Emilia-Romagna. It traced its foundations to Costanzo Porta (1528–1601), Pietro Ponzio [sic] (1532–96), Orazio Vecchi (1550–1605), and Claudio Monteverde [sic] (1567–1643). Martini sought the origins of his own Scuola Bolognese in Andrea Rota (1553–97), Girolamo Giacobbi (1567–1628), Giovanni Paolo Colonna (1637–95), and his former maestro, Giacomo Antonio Perti (1661–1756). These historical lineages were taken up and elaborated in Lichtenthal's influential music dictionary of 1826, which divided their memberships into separate lists of composers and singers and added a Scuola Fiorentina that ended with Boccherini.[2] Building upon the foundations of both Martini and Lichtenthal, Francesco Florimo provided more detailed descriptions of the six Italian schools as they were conceived at the end of the nineteenth century and put forward specific dates: the first and most ancient school, la Napolitana, was formed in 1480; the second, la Bolognese, began in 1482 and lasted until Mattei (1750–1825) and Cherubini (1760–1842); the third, la Veneziana, stretched from 1527 to the Russian-based maestro and singing teacher Catterino Cavos (1775–1840); the fourth, la Lombarda, was founded in 1485; the fifth, la Romana, which included Boccherini and Clementi, traced its origins to 1540; and the sixth, la Fiorentina, lasted only from ca. 1580 to the career of Giovambattista Doni (1593–1647). The schools were distinguished, he claimed, not so much by their approaches to counterpoint as by their sentiments, expression, and effects.[3]

By the beginning of the nineteenth century, the Roman and Venetian schools had all but faded away as significant centers of compositional pedagogy, surviving only through the activities of a few isolated maestros such as Bonaventura Furlanetto (1738–1817)[4] or Pietro Raimondi (1786–1853). The remaining schools continued to be defined as much by their characteristic pedagogical approaches as by their music. The Neapolitan tradition was represented primarily through the teachings of Fedele Fenaroli (1730–1818) and his colleagues, as listed later in this chapter. The Bolognese tradition, associated with Padre Martini and the church of San Francesco, which encompassed maestros from Parma, Piacenza, and Correggio, continued to flourish through the teachings of Martini's students Giuseppe Sarti (1729–1802), Luigi Sabbatini (1732–1809), and especially Padre Stanislao Mattei (1750–1825), who took over as Martini's successor in 1776. As professor of counterpoint at the Liceo comunale di musica in Bologna from its foundation in 1804 until his death, Mattei was personally associated with a "chief school" (*capo-scuola*) of Italian music, having taught over 150 students by 1812.[5] What Martini described as the "Lombardy school" was effectively supplanted by the foundation of the Milan Conservatory in 1807, which established its own pedagogical traditions based on the teachings of its first director, Bonifazio Asioli (1769–1832). For the purposes of this book, it is necessary to mention also two radically contrasting Tuscan traditions of the nineteenth century: the conservative "Lucchese school" of Marco Santucci (1762–1843), Giovanni Pacini (1796–1867), and Michele Puccini (1813–64), which drew upon older Neapolitan and Bolognese teachings (as described in chapter 2), and the progressive "Florentine school" of Abramo Basevi and colleagues, discussed more fully below, which sought inspiration from the latest French and German theories and practices. All of these nineteenth-century traditions may be grouped into two broad overlapping categories on the basis of their approaches to harmony and counterpoint: first, the antiquated Neapolitan *partimento* tradition, promulgated primarily through editions of Fenaroli (1775), and second, newer (late eighteenth-century) northern Italian traditions that eschewed the old thoroughbass methods in favor of Ramellian concepts of fundamental harmonic roots and the equivalence of chordal inversions.

II. AN INTRODUCTION TO THE PRIMARY SOURCES

The Italian schools and their associated traditions consisted not only of composers and scores and musicians and performances but also of a body of theory, knowledge, and practice that was partly memorized, partly written down, and passed from generation to generation.[6] Much of this information has been documented through a vast store of research and scholarship on the various elements that made up the tradition, from studies on impresarios, theaters, and librettists to accounts of costumes, staging, and vocal delivery.[7] Attempts to explain nineteenth-century Italian opera in terms of the conventions, guidelines, and formulas that underpinned the training of composers, singers, and instrumentalists have tended to concentrate on one particular aspect of compositional theory or practice, usually in relation to the music of Rossini, Bellini, or Verdi.

The only survey to attempt a degree of comprehensiveness is Wedell (1995), which, drawing in part on Bernardoni (1990), explored a number of early nineteenth-century theoretical approaches and their potential relevance to Verdi's operas. Sanguinetti (1997) provides an invaluable overview of Italian writings on music theory published between 1850 and 1950. In terms of more focused accounts of versification and musical rhythm, the researches of Lippmann (1973–75) and Moreen (1975) have proved influential, informing many later studies. New light has recently been shed on the study of harmony and counterpoint in Italy through increasing interest in the Neapolitan *partimento* tradition, especially by scholars such as Cafiero, Gjerdingen, Rosenberg, Sanguinetti, and Stella. On issues of form and structure, a rich seam of debate and scholarship followed the introduction—in Powers (1987)—of Basevi's (1859) "usual form for duets" (*solita forma*) as a catchword for a range of conventional practices and expectations. Similarly important was the identification of the "lyric prototype" as the most common pattern for operatic melodies of the *primo Ottocento*, in sources ranging from Lippmann (1966) through Kerman (1982) to studies by Balthazar and Huebner.[8] For the most part, it seems fair to suggest, such studies on compositional theory and practice in nineteenth-century Italy have tended to venture into the written historical source materials only as far as their specific aims and research questions required, concentrating primarily on observations and analyses of sketches and scores.

Any attempt to reconstruct the compositional methods of the Italian schools through their pedagogical traditions must rely to a disproportionate degree on the extant documentary sources, together with analyses of the music. A great deal depends on the interpretation of texts. It is crucial that key terms and concepts are accurately defined within their historical contexts and that authors' intended readerships are identified, in addition to any underlying agendas and prejudices. This introductory chapter begins the task, through a brief overview of sources.

The teleological approach to music history—according to which both writings and compositions are bound up in an inexorable process of evolution and development, like links in an ever-progressing chain—should be applied with caution to the Italian opera traditions of the *Ottocento*. Many of the texts in regular use at the time of Puccini's studies were already over a century old. The age of a published treatise was not regarded as a significant measure of its worth. Indeed most maestros preferred to teach as they themselves had been taught, from standard eighteenth-century sources that were widely revered as classics, such as Fedele Fenaroli's *Regole musicali per i principianti di cembalo nel sonar coi numeri e per principianti di contrappunto* (Musical Rules for Beginners at the Keyboard in Playing from Figures, and for Beginners in Counterpoint, 1775). The Lucca Conservatory was especially conservative in this respect, through its close affiliation with the church. Besides, a majority of more contemporary treatises, especially those with the word "compiled" (*compilato*) in the title, consisted of little more than collections of earlier teachings. The same rules, exercises, and examples appeared again and again throughout the nineteenth century, from straight reproductions, with or without additional commentary, to new realizations of basic exercises and formulas. In this respect, Puccini's training differed little from that available at the time of Rossini, and perhaps even before. His studies in Lucca even involved some of the same lessons that Rossini would have received at the Liceo comunale in Bologna, as published later in Mattei (ca. 1824–25 and ca. 1827). Such conservatism helps to explain some otherwise surprising chronological juxtapositions in the following chapters, which challenge the common musicological assumption that a publication on music theory must relate most significantly to the compositional practice of its own time. Textbooks such as Fenaroli (1775) were just as integral to composition lessons in the 1870s in Lucca as they were in eighteenth-century Naples.

Of course, composers did not learn their craft entirely, or even predominantly, by reading treatises and other publications. Harmony and counterpoint were taught primarily as "practice" (*pratica*) rather than "theory" (*teorica*). The study of *armonia* involved realizing individual lines of music in several parts at the keyboard, while *contrappunto* was mostly sung and played (as explained in chapters 4 and 6). One-to-one lessons with a maestro or small-group classes at a conservatory were regarded as the basic means of acquiring the necessary knowledge and skills. The maestro was central to the training process. One of the main harmony textbooks in use during Puccini's time at Milan, Lauro Rossi's *Guida ad un corso d'armonia pratica orale per gli allievi del R. Conservatorio di musica in Milano* (Guide to a Practical Oral Course of Harmony for the Students of the Royal Conservatory of Music in Milan, 1858), even acknowledged the importance of spoken guidance in its title, by referring to an "oral" course (not to be mistaken for a misspelling of "aural") and by preceding each lesson with an explanatory "Note for the Maestro." Copying and emulating classic and contemporary works was also considered an essential part of training.

Unfortunately, these pieces of evidence have gone largely unrecorded. Centuries of busy practice have left relatively few traces of the basics of the craft that underpinned a career as an opera composer. Indeed, it was customary for treatises to consist primarily of music examples, with only minimal written commentary intended to prompt the maestro to provide more thorough spoken explanations. Countless apprentice exercises have survived in the form of pastiche compositions (usually fugues or short liturgical pieces), but less advanced lessons that might offer insights into compositional methods were seldom retained. This is hardly surprising. Those assignments that were not played or sung were written on *cartelle,* varnished linen boards that could be wiped clean and reused.[9] In addition, music, like any profession, was founded upon the selling of specialized skills that had to be guarded and kept at a distance from the general public. Italian opera composers of the nineteenth century seldom revealed even the most cursory details of their compositional practice to critics and audiences. To describe too fully the means of constructing a beautiful *cantilena* might have proved damaging to the entire profession. Now that the living tradition has long since passed away, however, such insights into the dark recesses of the creative process may, paradoxically, serve to shed light on the very ideals of art and beauty that were formerly to be found only through their concealment. Exploring the inspired use of these "tricks of the trade" by composers such as Bellini, Verdi, and Puccini in the following chapters is intended to enhance, rather than to diminish, an appreciation of the artistic worth of their operas.

Even a partial reconstruction of compositional theory and practice as taught at the Italian conservatories throughout the nineteenth century must take into account a vast quantity of documentary evidence. The primary sources used in the writing of this book were for the most part known to Puccini from his earliest years and formed the basis of his musical training. Over generations of service as maestros, his ancestors had acquired the largest and most comprehensive library of books and manuscripts on music in Lucca, and he effectively inherited this library at the age of five, following the death of his father.[10] Together with the library of the Seminary of San Martino, these constituted the core of teaching materials at the Lucca Conservatory. The contents of the Puccini family library will be discussed in more detail in chapter 2 and elsewhere, as appropriate. For now, it may be useful to provide a summary outline of the main documentary evidence used in this book, with an overview of how it will be interpreted.

The sources can be divided into six categories:

1. Documents pertaining to the Neapolitan and Bolognese schools of composition, stemming from the teachings of Francesco Durante, Giovanni Battista Martini, and their colleagues.

2. Successors to these teachings in the form of numerous treatises on harmony, counterpoint, and related disciplines, written specifically to cater to students at the newly founded conservatories of the nineteenth century.

3. A relatively small number of publications that aspired to comprehensiveness in terms of the skills and knowledge needed for composition. They generally included discrete sections on harmony, counterpoint, and "composition properly so-called." Appended to this category are musical dictionaries and encyclopedias.

4. Historical surveys and biographical studies, insofar as they relate to compositional theory and practice.

5. Polemical dissertations and monographs on various topics, such as melody, meter, and aesthetics. These often overlap with the previous category by incorporating historical surveys and biographical information.

6. Innovative, speculative, or analytical theories of music that distanced themselves from received traditions. Often published as journal articles, these began to gain ground during the 1840s and thus coincided with the general mood of national reappraisal that accompanied the move toward Italian unification. Drawn from contemporary German and French publications, they marked a profound change in the Italian traditions, since they were concerned primarily with theoretical systems rather than the practical training of musicians.

1. The Neapolitan and Bolognese Pedagogical Traditions

In the early eighteenth century a method of training was consolidated for the benefit of young musicians at the conservatories in Naples, who normally began studies at the age of twelve, to enable them to compose and to accompany at the keyboard quickly and effectively in a variety of artistically (and, of course, financially) rewarding styles.[11] It has become known, after its most characteristic feature, as the *partimento* tradition. Most sources tend to point to Francesco Durante as the leading author of this method, sharing credit with his teachers Gaetano Greco and Alessandro Scarlatti, although its origins are to be found in earlier seventeenth-century thoroughbass practices.[12] Its essentials may even be found in sixteenth-century sources, such as Petrucci's fourth book of *frottole* (1505) or the second volume (on formulas for improvisation) of Tomás de Santa María's *Libro llamado arte de tañer fantasia* (Art of Playing the Fantasia, 1565). The significance of this Neapolitan didactic tradition has only recently come to light. Overshadowed since its demise in the late nineteenth century by rival Austro-German and French traditions, it is usually portrayed, if at all, as a localized phenomenon at odds with the mainstream of European music theory. The extensive *Cambridge History of Western Music Theory* (2002) contains, for instance, only one brief mention of this tradition—citing the *partimento* as an aid to improvisation (548). It would probably be closer to historical truth to claim the Italian tradition as the "mainstream" during the eighteenth century.

The *partimento*—most often an unfigured bass line that provided a linear guide to the realization of a keyboard piece—was only one among several disciplines within the system of musical training devised by the Neapolitan conservatories. Together with written-out components such as fugues and *disposizioni* (realizations of bass lines in open score in two or more parts, often involving imitation and other contrapuntal procedures), and sung elements such as *solfeggi* (short compositions for one, two, or three voices and bass that cultivated skills in melodic writing and embellishment), it occupied one of the stages in a progressive course of instruction in harmony (played or sung) and counterpoint (played, sung, or written). As the overview of the method in chapter 4 demonstrates, it was in essence a variant of Baroque thoroughbass practice, profoundly at odds with Rameau's influential theories of fundamental chord-roots and inversions.

The vast resource of *partimenti* is gradually being transcribed, studied, and made available online by the "Monuments of Partimenti" project hosted by Northwestern University under the direction of Robert Gjerdingen (2005). It includes parallel-text translations of important *regole* (rules) by maestros such as Durante (1730s?), Fenaroli (1775), and Furno (1817?). The best introductions to the tradition are Gjerdingen's monumental study of *Music in the Galant Style* (2007a), the special issue of the *Journal of Music Theory* (2007) edited by Gjerdingen and containing articles by Holtmeier, Sanguinetti, Gjerdingen, Cafiero, and Stella, and the 2009 issue of *Rivista di Analisi e Teoria Musicale* 15, no. 1 (Lucca: Libreria musicale italiana), edited by Stella, entitled "Composizione e improvvisazione nella scuola napoletana del Settecento," and containing articles by Cafiero, Gjerdingen, Paraschivescu, Sanguinetti, Stella, and Sullo. A concise historical survey of the tradition and summary of scholarship—including landmark publications such as Fellerer (1940), Borgir (1987 [1971]), Christensen (1992), Cafiero (1993), Rosenberg (1995), and Sanguinetti (1997)—may be found in Gjerdingen (2007b).[13] A comprehensive and authoritative study by Sanguinetti is expected to be published soon.

The principal musicians associated with this didactic method all worked as maestros at one or more of the Neapolitan conservatories. A representative list of authors, corresponding to primary sources given in the bibliography, would include the following: Alessandro Scarlatti (1660–1725), Nicola Fago (1677–1745), Francesco Durante (1684–1755), Nicola Porpora (1686–1768), Leonardo Vinci (1690–1730), Leonardo Leo (1694–1744), Nicola Sala (1713–1801), Fedele Fenaroli (1730–1818), Giacomo Tritto (1733–1824), Giovanni Paisiello (1741–1816), Giovanni Furno (1748–1837), and Niccolò Zingarelli (1752–1837).

By the early 1800s these maestros were firmly established as "classic" authors of the method, their exercises and *partimenti* forming a core of teaching materials for the new conservatories. Evidence of their influence in provincial towns such as Lucca at that time may be found in Pellegrino Tomeoni's brief overview of the rules for "basses, *partimenti*, or sonatas" in his *Regole pratiche per accompagnare il basso continuo* (Practical Rules for Accompanying the Thoroughbass, 1795).[14] Some idea of how the Neapolitan tradition was then perceived may be gleaned from an account related by Haydn's biographer Giuseppe Carpani, in a letter of May 21, 1809, that was later published as part of his *Le Haydine* (1812). Because there are so few published sources for readers to turn to for information on the tradition, and given its significance to the training of nineteenth-century opera composers, a fairly lengthy quotation is given below, in a contemporary English translation:

The following sketch of the music of the Neapolitan school was given to me some years ago [in 1803] by a tall abbé, wedded to his violincello, and a constant frequenter of the theatre of San Carlo, where I believe he has not missed a single performance for forty years:

"Naples has had four schools of vocal and instrumental music: but only three exist at this day, which contain about two hundred and thirty pupils. . . . It is from these schools that the greatest musicians of the world have proceeded; which is very natural, for our country is fonder of music than any other. The great composers whom Naples has produced lived at the beginning of the eighteenth century.

It is proper that we should distinguish the composers who have occasioned revolutions in music in general, from those who cultivated only one species of it.

Among the former, we shall place before every other Alessandro Scarlatti, who must be considered as the founder of the modern art of music, since it is to him that we owe the science of counterpoint. He was a native of Messina, and died about 1725.

Porpora died in poverty about 1770 [sic], at the age of ninety. He has written many works for the theatre, which are still regarded as models; and his cantatas are even superior.

Leo was his pupil, and surpassed his master. He died in 1745 [sic], at the age of forty-two. His manner is inimitable. . . .

Francesco Durante was born at Grumo, a village near Naples. The glory of rendering counterpoint easy was reserved for him. The cantatas of Scarlatti, arranged as duets, I consider as his finest works.

At the head of the musicians of the second order, we shall place Vinci, the father of all who have written for the theatre. His merit consists in uniting great expression to a profound knowledge of counterpoint. His best work is the *Artaxerxes* of Metastasio. He died in 1732, in the flower of his age; poisoned, as it is said, by a relative of a Roman lady, for whom he had an attachment.

Giambattista Jesi, was born at Pergola, in the March of Ancona, from which circumstance he was called Pergolese. He was brought up in one of the schools of Naples, under Durante, and died in 1733, at the age of twenty-five. He was a true genius. . . .

Hasse, called *the Saxon,* was a pupil of Scarlatti, and was the most natural composer of his time.

Jomelli was born at Aversa, and died in 1775. He has displayed a comprehensive genius. . . . He was too fond of the instruments.

David Perez, who was born at Naples, and died about 1790, composed a *Credo,* which, in certain solemnities, is still sung in the church of the Fathers of the Oratorio, where people still go to hear it as original. He was one of the last composers who maintained the rigor of counterpoint. . . .

Traetta, the master and companion of Sacchini, in the Conservatory of Saint Mary of Loretto, pursued the same career as his pupil. He had more art than Sacchini, who is considered as having more genius. . . .

Bach, born in Germany, was educated at Naples. . . .

All these professors died about 1780.

Piccinni has rivalled Jomelli in the noble style. . . .

Paisiello, Guglielmi, and Anfossi are the most celebrated of his disciples. But notwithstanding their works, the decline of music at Naples is evident and rapid. Adieu."[15]

Apart from such careless, eyebrow-raising assertions as "Bach . . . was educated at Naples"—which almost certainly refers to Johann *Christian* Bach, who spent some time in Bologna with Martini—the main points of interest here are the sentences concerning the "revolution" in the "science of counterpoint" brought about by Alessandro Scarlatti as "the founder of the modern art of music" and concerning Durante, for whom "the glory of rendering counterpoint easy was reserved."[16] Passing over the backhanded compliment praising Durante's arrangements of Scarlatti as his best compositions, such extravagant claims surely refer to the new method of training, to be outlined in chapter 4, which served as one of the foundations of Italian operatic composition for almost two centuries.

The compilation of rules and exercises in Fenaroli (1775) was intended to preserve the original teachings of Durante. It remained the central resource for instruction according to the Neapolitan methods and was continuously in print until 1936.[17] Nicola Sala's *Regole del contrappunto pratico* (Rules of Practical Counterpoint, 1794) was also widely available, especially through a French translation published as part of Choron (1808), which will be discussed more fully in chapter 3. For the most part, nineteenth-century composition students received the Neapolitan method secondhand, through compilations and newer (yet hardly innovative) publications. Many examples and teachings from the old eighteenth-century rulebooks were included, often without acknowledgment, in numerous treatises "compiled" by professors at the Italian conservatories, such as Pietro Ray's *Studio teorico-pratico di contrappunto compilato pe' suoi allievi dal maestro P. Ray professore di composizione e vicecensore del Conservatorio di musica in Milano* (Theoretical-Practical Study of Counterpoint Compiled for His Students by Maestro P. Ray, Professor of Composition and Vice Principal of the Conservatory of Music in Milan, 1846). There were few genuine additions to the tradition, exceptions being perhaps *Bassi imitati e fugati divisi in tre libri* (Basses for Imitative and Fugal Treatment, Divided into Three Books, 1836) by Pietro Raimondi, a distinguished student of Giacomo Tritto, who is remembered chiefly for his three oratorios that combine contrapuntally into one, and *Trattato d'armonia: seguito da un corso di contrappunto dal corale al fugato e partimenti analoghi divisi in tre fascicoli* (Treatise on Harmony: Followed by a Course of Counterpoint from the Chorale to the Fugato and Related *Partimenti* Divided into Three Fascicles, 1883) by Pietro Platania.[18] Most treatises used for teaching, including Selvaggi's *Trattato di Armonia* (Treatise on Harmony, 1823) and Michele (father of Giacomo) Puccini's *Corso pratico di contrappunto* (Practical Course of Counterpoint, 1846), were essentially compilations drawn from old rulebooks by such authors as Durante, Fenaroli, Mattei, and Sala, which were passed through the generations from maestro to student. Guarnaccia (ca. 1851) was effectively a heavily revised edition of Fenaroli's *partimenti*.

Baron Giuseppe Staffa (1807–77) was a student of Giacomo Tritto who, after writing seven operas, went on to preside over the music section of the Academy of Sciences, Letters, and Fine Arts in Naples and to direct the orchestra at the Teatro del Fondo. He attempted to record the ancient method for posterity in his *Metodo della Scuola Napolitana di composizione musicale* (Method of Musical Composition of the Neapolitan School), published in two parts: *Parte prima: Trattato d'armonia* (1849) and *Parte seconda: Trattato di composizione* (1856). It inspired a weighty response in the form of Raffaele Napoli's *Esame critice del trattato di armonia e composizione sul metodo della scuola di musica napoletana pubblicato da Giuseppe dei baroni Staffa* (Critical Examination of the Treatise on Harmony and Composition According to the Method of the Neapolitan School of Music Published by Baron Giuseppe Staffa, 1857). Staffa's omission of an expected central treatise on counterpoint was in a sense rectified by the publication of the *Compendio di contrappunto della antica e moderna scuola di musica napolitana* (Compendium of Counterpoint of the Ancient and Modern Neapolitan School of Music, 1850) by Giovanni Battista De Vecchis, *maestro di musica* at the Royal Abbey of Montecasino, which relied heavily on the teachings of his own maestro, Niccolò Zingarelli. It is of particular interest for its account of the relationship between practical counterpoints, *solfeggi*, and actual composition (*composizione ideale*), and for its survey of aesthetics and orchestration. A curious account of the pre-Neapolitan traditions of the ecclesiastical style and a testament to the profound conservatism of the Lucchese musical establishment may be found in Luigi Nerici's *La Scuola di Canto Fermo* (The Cantus Firmus School, 1857).

By the 1860s there was an increase in calls for the replacement of the old-fashioned, practical Neapolitan method by more up-to-date theoretical systems of musical training, primarily those from Germany. Professors in Naples, such as Michele Ruta (1876, 1877a–b, 1884), sought to defend the efficacy of the old *partimento* techniques, whereas the progressives of the Accademia del Regio Istituto musicale in Florence favored the more "scientific" German study of harmony, as championed by De-Champs (1879). Evidence that a relatively unaltered version of the Neapolitan method continued to be taught in Milan as late as the 1880s survives in the form of numerous publications on *partimenti,* among which may be mentioned Girolamo Bonomo's *Nuova scuola d'armonia: metodo elementare di partimento* (New School of Harmony: Elementary *Partimento* Method, 1875), Giuseppe Gerli's *L'allievo al primo corso d'armonia applicata al pianoforte: esercizi elementari progressivi in tutti i toni, bassi numerate, preceduti dalle relative scale e dalle cadenze semplice composte e doppie nelle tre posizioni che servono d'introduzione allo studio di partimenti dei classici d'ogni scuola, no. espressamente composti per la scuola d'armonia teorica e pratica del R. Conservatorio Mus.le di Milano* (For the Student on the First Course of Harmony Applied at the Piano: Progressive Elementary Exercises in All Keys, and Figured Basses, Preceded by the Respective Scales and by Simple, Compound, and Double Cadences in the Three Positions That Serve as an Introduction to the Classic *Partimenti* of Each School, Specifically Composed for the School of Theoretical and Practical Harmony at the Royal Musical Conservatory of Milan, 1877?); and, surprisingly, given the progressive harmonic views of his teacher Alberto Mazzucato, Amintore Galli's deliberate homage to Fenaroli, *Partimenti: regole musicali per quelli che vogliono suonare coi numeri e per i principianti di contrappunto* (*Partimenti*: Musical Rules for Those Who Wish to Play from Figured Basses and for Beginners in Counterpoint, 1886).

The main nineteenth-century sources for instruction according to the Bolognese method, elements of which may be discerned as early as the imitative contrapuntal works of Italian disciples of Adriano Willaert (ca. 1490–1562), were exercises, *partimenti,* and *contrappunti* by Martini's favorite student, Stanislao Mattei. At the end of his life he oversaw the publication of a course of lessons entitled *Pratica d'accompagnamento sopra bassi numerati e contrappunti a più voci sulla scala ascendente, e discendente maggiore, e minore con diverse Fughe a quattro, ecc.* (Practice of Accompaniment upon Figured Basses and Counterpoints in Several Parts upon the Ascending and Descending Major and Minor Scales, with Diverse Fugues in Four Parts, etc., ca. 1824–25). Further collections of his teachings were compiled and edited after his death by his erstwhile student Luigi Felice Rossi and issued primarily through two publications: an extended version of the second part of the original *Pratica d'accompagnamento,* entitled *Contrappunti da due a otto parti sopra la scala ascendente e discendente in ambo i modi coll'aggiunta di parecchi contrappunti a 4 parti finora inediti* (Counterpoints in Two to Eight Parts above the Ascending and Descending Scale, both Major and Minor, with Several Additional, Unpublished Counterpoints in Four Parts, ca. 1827); and *Bassi numerati per accompagnare: Ridotti ad intavolatura a due violini e viola* (Figured Basses for Harmonizing [at the Keyboard]: Reduced to Open Score for [Cello], Two Violins, Viola, 1850 [1829?]). Although both books of exercises were undated, the second of them appears to have been cataloged (erroneously) as "*Trattato di contrappunto pratico* (1827)" in the Puccini family library. This explains why that date has been assigned in this book to Mattei's *Contrappunti da due a otto parti.* The date of the *Pratica d'accompagnamento* (ca. 1824–25) is taken from the most recent entry in the *New Grove Dictionary.* The original 1883 entry listed three volumes of exercises by Mattei dated 1788, 1829, and 1830, which explains why an original date of 1829 has been suggested for the 1850 edition of the *Bassi numerati.*[19]

Luigi Cherubini, from his arrival in Paris in 1785, and especially through his course of harmony and counterpoint at the Paris Conservatory between 1822 and 1835, taught a slightly different version of the Bolognese method, founded on his studies in Milan with Giuseppe Sarti during the 1780s. It was subsequently published in Paris as *Marches d'Harmonie pratiquées dans la composition produisant des Suites Régulières de Consonances et de Dissonances* (n.d. [1835?]) and reissued in 1880 by the firm of Ricordi for the interest of "harmonists" in Milan as *Andamenti d'armonia praticati nella composizione i quali producono successioni regolari di consonanze e dissonanze* (Harmonic Progressions as Practiced in Composition Which Produce Regular Successions of Consonances and Dissonances).

A clear and thorough overview of the Bolognese system of instruction, from rudiments to advanced performance and composition, may be found in the three parts of Luigi Sabbatini's *Elementi teorici della musica colla pratica de' medesimi, in duetti, e terzetti a canone accompagnati dal basso, ed eseguibili sì a solo, che a più voci* (Theoretical Elements of Music with Practice of the Same, in Duets and Trios in Canon Accompanied by the Bass and Performable by Either One or More Voices, 1789–90). Each "theory" lesson of the first part, involving introductions to mundane elements such as clefs, rhythmic notation, trills, etc., was delivered by *singing* didactic texts set to short canons. The "practice" of the second part consisted of attaching sung counterpoints to a series of scales and "leaps" (*salti:* regular patterns of intervals), employing a mixture of didactic rhymes, vocalization on the vowel *a,* and sol-fa according to both the ancient mutation methods of Guido d'Arezzo and the modern seven-note system, as explained in chapter 6. The course of instruction was rounded off by a series of *solfeggi,* which consolidated skills in composition and vocal performance. De Vecchis confirmed that similar methods were adopted by the Neapolitan school: "The first musical Compositions that all Maestros provide for Beginners to do are the *Solfeggi.*"[20]

2. Textbooks for the Conservatories

The foundation of new conservatories in Italy during the nineteenth century, modeled initially on the Neapolitan schools and later on international institutions such as those at Paris, Leipzig, and Brussels, provided the catalyst for a sharp increase in the number of treatises (*trattati*) published for the use of students on various courses. The following short survey can scarcely do justice to the magnitude of the literature, and thus it mentions only representative works.

In keeping with the Neapolitan model, training at the conservatories was usually divided into three successive stages: rudiments, harmony, and figured bass; counterpoint and fugue; and finally "composition." Of the three, this last, most significant, stage was the least well documented. It appears to have been based largely on one-to-one sessions with a maestro and the emulation of existing works. This helps to explain why published *trattati* were most commonly concerned with either harmony or counterpoint, divided into basic and advanced levels and ranging from a few pages of instructions to vast collections of *partimenti* and fugue subjects. They seldom dealt with more specialized aspects of composition, such as text-setting or form. It should also be noted that, unless specifically stated otherwise, Italian writings during the nineteenth century nearly always assumed that the music under discussion was operatic or vocal.

Although the Neapolitan traditions featured heavily in *trattati*, they were often tempered by more speculative theories, borrowed in particular from the writings of Rameau. Conservatory treatises remained nevertheless geared primarily toward vocational training. Most of them had some mention of the "theoretical-practical" nature of the guidance in their titles, underlining the fact that they were not speculative theories for understanding musical practice, but rather manuals designed to impart practical skills. They were intended to help students make music rather than think (too much) about it. Counterpoint was learned primarily through *singing* and was thus frequently taught in conservatories by professors of voice (see chapter 6); harmony was learned through *playing* at the keyboard and was accordingly taught most often by masters of accompaniment. "Theoretical" or *written* elements supported the study of both. Teaching harmony and counterpoint primarily through textbooks and written exercises, as encouraged by Rameau's theories and by later German publications, was usually referred to as the "scientific" study of music.

For this reason, Italian nineteenth-century didactic books on music generally lacked the kind of systematic rigor necessary for the production of clear and coherent theories. To mold the unruly particulars of a living tradition into a comprehensive scheme of neat universal categories required an abstraction of theory from practice, as may be understood to have occurred in, for instance, Adolph Bernhard Marx's four-volume *Die Lehre von den musikalischen Komposition* (Training in Musical Composition, 1837–47), whose logically ordered system of form types seems to have been conceived more for the clarity of the academic curriculum at the University of Berlin than for the practical training of composers. Similarly focused on theory, Hugo Riemann's *Musikalische Dynamik und Agogik* (Musical Dynamics and Agogics, 1884) offered little by way of instruction for those who might have wished to compose in the manner of, say, Wagner or Brahms. Italian treatises, by contrast, were mostly as unwieldy and unsystematic as the practice they reflected, apart from occasionally elaborate classifications of chord types and orderings of harmony examples according to interval. Interpreting them according to a separation or abstraction of theory from practice can lead to misunderstanding. In particular, there can be a temptation to judge books on theory as part of an interlinked, "organically" developing musical tradition in their own right, detached from practice. The tendency to regard, for example, Kirnberger's writings on meter and rhythm (1776) as precursors to Reicha's comments on phrase structure (1814), which were then taken up by Asioli (1832), betrays a naive reliance on straightforward chronology and ignores the possibility that Kirnberger and Asioli may have been describing essentially the same concepts at different times, derived from a common historical source, while Reicha drew on an alternative set of ideas. Italian treatises of the nineteenth century should not be viewed primarily as belonging to some kind of intellectual dialectic, a logical flow of thought through which ideas interact and react, for the simple reason that they often attempted to explain the same old lessons. Some were merely better at explaining than others. That is why classic works such as Carlo Gervasoni's *La Scuola della Musica, in tre parti divisa* (School of Music, Divided into Three Parts, 1800) remained in circulation long after later books that dealt with similar topics were forgotten.

The obvious starting point for a survey of nineteenth-century Italian treatises is the foundation of the Milan Conservatory in 1807, together with the publication of two new textbooks for its students by Bonifazio Asioli (1769–1832), the founding principal (*censore*) and professor of composition. His *Principj elementari di musica adottati dall'I. R. Conservatorio di Milano per le ripetizioni giornaliere degli alunni compilati da B. Asioli* (Elementary Principles of Music Adopted by the Royal Conservatory in Milan for Daily Repetition by the Students, Compiled by B. Asioli, 1809) and *Trattato di armonia adottato dal Regio conservatorio di musica di Milano* (Treatise of Harmony Adopted by the Royal Conservatory of Music in Milan, 1813) were continuously in print until at least 1875 and formed the basis of numerous similar guides. Although now largely forgotten, Asioli's publications were among the most widely known and respected in Italy throughout the nineteenth century. Composer and theorist Geremia Vitali, writing in 1850, described his teachings as a "species of cult" at the Milan Conservatory.[21] The entry in the *Dizionario Ricordi della Musica e dei Musicisti* (Ricordi Dictionary of Music and Musicians, 1959) claims: "As a teacher he had a notable influence upon many generations of musicians through his vast erudition. His *Elementary Principles of Music* (1809), reprinted many times in Italy and abroad, is still in use."[22]

Following studies with the organist Luigi Crotti, at the age of ten Asioli was sent to Parma to train under maestro Vincenzo Merighi (sometimes spelt Morigi; 1795–1849). Two years later, and after a few months' study in Venice, he returned to his hometown of Correggio to become *maestro di cappella* in 1786, only to take up a better-paid position with a noble family in Turin the following year. In 1799 he was appointed *maestro di camera e di cappella* to the court in Milan, from which position, and on the strength of Haydn's recommendation of him as teacher to Karl (Carlo) Mozart in a letter of April 23, 1806, he eventually became the first principal and professor of composition of the Milan Conservatory.[23] With the Austrian occupation of Milan in 1814, Asioli was forced to return to Correggio, where he continued to publish pedagogical works.

Evidence of Asioli's influence is unmistakable in many sources, such as Niccolò Cattaneo's *Grammatica della musica ossia elementi teorici di questa bell'arte* (Musical Grammar, or Theoretical Elements of This Fine Art, 1828) and Luigi Picchianti's *Principj generali e ragionati della musica teorico-pratica* (Theoretical-Practical General Principles and Explanations of Music, 1834), which, although originally published in Florence, was issued by Ricordi in Milan two years later. Some treatises even assumed a mantle of authority by adopting the phrase "compiled after the norms of Asioli," as in the case of Luigi De Macchi's *Grammatica musicale. Teoria dei principj elementari di musica compilata dietro le norme di Asioli e di altri rinomati autori da Luigi De-Macchi* (Musical Grammar. Theory of the Elementary Principles of Music Compiled According to the Norms of Asioli and Other Renowned Authors, ca. 1830), also written for use by students at Milan. A similar influence may be detected in the only published treatise to come out of Lucca during the nineteenth century, Giovanni Pacini's *Corso teorico-pratico di lezioni di armonia* (Theoretical-Practical Course of Lessons in Harmony, 1844a).

By midcentury Asioli's dominance of the market was under attack. Foreign influences had begun to make their mark on conservatory training, especially through publications emanating from Paris, such as Anton Reicha's *Traité de haute composition musicale* (Treatise on Fine Musical Composition, 1824–26) and François-Joseph Fétis's *Traité du contrepoint et de la fugue, contenant l'exposé analytique des règles de la composition musicale, depuis deux jusqu'à huit parties réelles* (Treatise on Counterpoint and Fugue, Containing an Analytical Account of the Rules of Musical Composition, from Two to Eight Real Parts, 1825) and *Metodo elementaire e ristretto di armonia e di accompagnamento del basso* (Elementary and Condensed Method of Harmony and Bass Accompaniment, 1836). During a review of the curriculum at the Milan Conservatory in 1850, an attempt was made to supplant Asioli's guides in the form of Vitali's polemical pamphlet *Della necessità di riformare i principj elementari di musica di Bonifazio Asioli* (On the Need to Reform the Elementary Principles of Music of Bonifazio Asioli). Unfortunately, Vitali appears to have been motivated more by professional jealousy than by pedagogical principles, and his intended coup achieved little, primarily on account of his lack of a viable alternative. The main thrust of his argument proposed that conservatories should make use of a variety of textbooks, not just those based on Asioli's methods, so as to reflect the variety of compositional practices. Vitali's critique is of interest not so much for its feeble attack on Asioli as for its observations on the essentially disorderly, unsystematic, and practice-driven nature of the operatic tradition at that time:

> Observing the works of composers, one sees in reality that they were not guided by any unity of purpose. As has already been observed elsewhere, sometimes the melody takes precedence over the harmony, at other times the harmony over the melody; sometimes the expression of the affects is at the forefront, at other times the delight of the senses is not the only thing sought after; sometimes the melodic line governs the accompaniment, at other times the accompaniment obstructs and overwhelms the melody; sometimes an opera is made up almost entirely of recitative, at other times this is almost an incidental insert that makes way entirely for the cantabile; sometimes the verbal images are too limited, at other times they are so verbose that they cannot escape a sense of boredom.[24]

The treatise that did eventually rank alongside Asioli's textbooks at Milan, by following them in numerous details, was Rossi (1858), in which old eighteenth-century Neapolitan traditions continued to form the cornerstone of the method of training. Ten years later, Rossi, as director of the Conservatory (1850–72), chaired the next big shake-up of the curriculum through a review intended to modernize the courses and to bring them into line with international competitors. This led to a fresh bout of unsuccessful attacks on the dominance of Asioli's sixty-year-old treatises, such as Melchiorre Balbi's *Rudimenti musicali compilati secondo il nuovo sistema proposto dallo stesso e confrontati col presente di B. Asioli adottati dal R. Conservatorio di Milano* (Rudiments of Music Compiled According to a New System, in Opposition to the Present One by B. Asioli in Use at the Milan Conservatory, 1868).

When Puccini came to enroll at Milan in 1880, the textbooks for the preliminary courses were extremely conservative, adhering closely to Asioli's norms. Although he would have had little use for such basic guides, being registered in the advanced composition class, they do nevertheless provide a background to some of the key terms and concepts that underlie compositional practice at a higher level. Among the basic textbooks in use at that time were those by Giuseppe Gerli, teacher of complementary theory and *solfeggio* from 1859 to 1884. Set texts for the first courses included his *Dialoghi illustrati d'Armonia, che insegnano la dottrina degli accordi, la scienza della modulazione e la teoria di armonizzare melodie, etc.* (Illustrative Dialogues on Harmony, Which Teach the Doctrine of Chords, the Science of Modulation, and the Theory of Harmonizing Melodies, etc., 1870) and *L'allievo al primo corso d'armonia* (1877?). Other professors at Milan also published materials for their courses, seemingly in competition with each other, although the differences in approach were relatively superficial. Among these may be mentioned Amintore Galli's *Elementi di armonia* (Elements of Harmony, 1877) and *Trattato di contrappunto e fuga* (Treatise on Counterpoint and Fugue, 1879), Federico Parisini's *Trattato elementare d'armonia* (Elementary Treatise on Harmony, 1879a), and *Principii elementari di Musica* (Elementary Principles of Music, 1879b), and Alberto Giovannini's *Corso preparatorio allo studio dell'armonia proposto agli alunni del R. Conservatorio di musica in Milano da Alberto Giovannini professore del conservatorio stesso* (Preparatory Course for the Study of Harmony Outlined for the Students of the Royal Conservatory of Music in Milan, ca. 1882).

As Puccini was embarking on his career as a composer in Milan, the city continued to experience an unprecedented influx of "modernizing" influences from abroad. This revolution in musical life did not, however, filter through immediately to the teaching materials at the Conservatory. Traditional books such as Platania (1883) and De Sanctis (n.d. [1887?]) continued to appear, supplementing the courses in harmony and counterpoint. By the turn of the twentieth century, on the other hand, foreign influences, especially from Germany, had begun to usurp the old methods of training. A new and comprehensive textbook of harmony for the Milan Conservatory, Guglielmo Andreoli and Edgardo Codazzi's *Manuale d'Armonia* (Manual of Harmony, 1898), contained elements that were indistinguishable from the kind of treatise being published in large numbers elsewhere in Europe. The adoption of a theoretical approach to the study of composition, sharply opposed to the practical guidance that formed the basis of training for composers up to the time of Puccini, is especially evident in such Milanese works as Vincenzo Ferroni's *Della forma musicale Classica: brevi appunti ad uso delle Scuole di Composizione* (On Classical Musical Form: Brief Notes for the Use of the Schools of Composition, 1908).

Finally, it is important to distinguish between genuine treatises for the conservatories and publications directed at amateurs and dilettantes, of which there were many throughout the nineteenth century. A representative example may be found in the writings of Giusto Dacci, who spent most of his career at the School of Music in Parma. Building upon the approach adopted in his *Trattato teorico-pratico d'armonia semplice e composta* (Theoretical-Practical Treatise on Simple and Complex Harmony, 1872), he outlined a radical program for unifying the three traditional disciplines into one curriculum at a conference at the Milan Conservatory in 1881, and went on to publish his *Trattato teorico-pratico d'armonia, istrumenzione, contrappunto e composizione diviso in 4 libri* (Theoretical-Practical Treatise on Harmony, Instrumentation, Counterpoint, and Composition, Divided into Four Books, 1881). Not finding the success he had hoped for, it was substantially condensed and reissued as *Trattato teorico-pratico di lettura e divisione musicale pei dilettanti. Estratto dal trattato completo dello stesso autore* (Theoretical-Practical Treatise of the Literature and Divisions of Music for Dilettantes; Extracted from the Complete Treatise by the Same Author, 1886).

3. Comprehensive Manuals of Composition

Most Italian treatises dealt with the rudiments of music, harmony, or counterpoint and rarely strayed into areas of "composition proper" such as text-setting, expressive devices, or form, which appear to have been left largely for the maestro or professor to explain. Information on these disciplines must be gleaned from isolated monographs and a small number of publications that aspired to comprehensiveness by combining the various elements that together constituted the craft of composition.

Given the comments made earlier on professional discretion in the opera industry, it is worth asking why these comprehensive guides were written. In the main, they were published by professional musicians seeking to remedy what they perceived as faulty teachings, to clarify basic concepts by attempting to unite significant theories with practice, and to set down a pedagogical method for posterity. They could also be used to curry favor with wealthy dedicatees and to make money from sales to amateurs and dilettantes. In each case, they were never intended to replace the essential face-to-face lessons with a maestro. Indeed, established maestros appear to have regarded them as useful yet elementary supplements to the real study of composition.

Among the best known such comprehensive treatises are those belonging to the German tradition, mainly on account of their perceived significance to the Viennese classical style: Johann Kirnberger's *Die Kunst des reinen Satzes in der Musik* (The Art of Strict Musical Composition, 1771–79) and Heinrich Christoph Koch's *Versuch einer Anleitung zur Composition* (Introductory Essay on Composition, 1782–93). Although they relate to a very different, north German tradition, both works nevertheless serve to corroborate a number of concepts and practices that appear to have been widespread throughout Europe in the eighteenth century and remained essential to Italian opera throughout the nineteenth.

Kirnberger spent most of his life in northern Germany and Prussia, studying for a brief spell with J. S. Bach. He devoted much effort to propagating what he considered to be Bach's compositional methods through his publications. His main work, *Die Kunst des reinen Satzes,* was published over a period of eight years: the first volume, concerning harmony and counterpoint, appeared in 1771, while the second was issued in three installments in 1776, 1777, and 1779. Although the second volume dealt for the most part with counterpoint, its first installment, which Kirnberger later expanded upon in his *Anleitung zur Singkomposition mit Oden in verschiedenen Silbenmassen begleitet* (Introduction to Vocal Composition Accompanied by Odes in Different Syllabic Meters, 1782), is used in chapter 3 to provide supporting evidence for a historical reconstruction of Italian notions of rhythm and phrase structure as they relate to melody. Koch spent most of his career as a violinist in the court orchestra of the small provincial town of Rudolstadt. It is hardly surprising that his *Versuch einer Anleitung zur Composition* (1782, 1787, and 1793) is concerned primarily with a tradition of dance music and other instrumental genres, although it too offers testimony in support of this interpretation.

Other "foreign" manuals of composition that are used to contextualize the Italian traditions in this study include Belgian theorist Jérôme-Joseph de Momigny's three-volume *Cours complet d'harmonie et de composition* (Complete Course of Harmony and Composition, 1803–1806) and *La seule vraie théorie de la musique* (The Only True Theory of Music, 1821; translated into Italian in 1823), and Anton Reicha's *Trattato della melodia considerata fuori de' suoi rapporti con l'armonia seguito da un supplement su l'arte di accompagnare la melodia coll'Armonia quando la prima dev'essere predominante* (Treatise on Melody: Considered Apart from Its Relationship with Harmony, Followed by a Supplement on the Art of Accompanying Melody with Harmony, Where the Former Is Dominant, 1830 [1814]).

Long recognized as an important source of information on Italian methods of composition is Francesco Galeazzi's two-volume *Elementi teorici-pratici di musica con un saggio sopra l'arte di suonare il violin analizzata, ed a dimostrabili principi ridotta, opera utilissima a chiunque vuol applicar con profitto alla musica e specialmente a' principianti, dilettanti, e professori di violin* (Theoretical-Practical Elements of Music, with an Essay on the Art of Playing the Violin Analyzed and Reduced to Demonstrable Principles, A Most Useful Work for Whoever Wishes to Apply Themselves Profitably to Music and Especially for Beginners, Dilettantes, and Teachers of the Violin, 1791 and 1796). According to Fétis's *Biographie universelle des musiciens,* Galeazzi (1758–1819) trained primarily as a violinist in his native Turin before settling in Rome, where he sold compositions, taught the violin, and held a number of minor appointments, such as music director at the Teatro Valle. As the longwinded title betokens, his

Elementi teorici-pratici hedged its bets in the marketplace by appealing not only to budding composers (such as its wealthy dedicatee) but also to beginners, amateurs, and teachers of the violin. It is important to note that it does not appear to have been aimed at apprentice or professional musicians. Both volumes are divided into two parts. The first contains "An Elementary Grammar" and "An Essay on the Art of Playing the Violin." The second begins with a historical survey entitled "Theory of the Principles of Ancient and Modern Music" and concludes with a detailed treatise on composition, "On the Elements of Counterpoint." This last part, especially the section on "Melody," offers a clear account of Italian categories of musical periods and their "conduct," which, in conjunction with later writings on the same topic, contributes significantly to the discussion of musical forms in chapter 5.

Although aimed at a similar amateur market, as confirmed by a welcoming introductory note "From the Author to Dilettantes of Music," Carlo Gervasoni's *La Scuola della musica, in tre parti divisa* (The School of Music, Divided into Three Parts, 1800) provides a useful source of information on Italian approaches to form and genre and to the assimilation of Ramellian theory. Gervasoni (1762–1819) studied literature, music, mathematics, and physics in his native Milan with the intention of entering the church, but spent most of his career as *maestro di cappella* in the small town of Borgo Val di Taro, near Parma. The first part of *La Scuola della musica,* "On Musical Theory," comprises a survey of general elements such as rhythm, melody, and harmony, while the second part, "Introduction to the Practice of Music," offers instructions on how to sing for different voice types and on how to play the various instruments, devoting only a few pages to each. Both parts were translated in Choron's posthumously published *Manuel complet de musique vocale et instrumentale, ou Encyclopédie Musicale* (Complete Manual of Vocal and Instrumental Music, or Musical Encyclopedia, 1836–39). The third part, "On Musical Composition in General," is the most significant for the present study, since it deals with issues that inform several separate discussions. Gervasoni's *Scuola della musica* remained influential and widely known well into the 1840s.[25]

The most comprehensive treatise of all must be Alexandre-Étienne Choron's 1,500-page, six-volume *Principes de composition des écoles d'Italie. Adoptés par le Gouvernement Français pour server à l'instruction des élèves des Maîtrises de Cathédrales* (Principles of Composition of the Italian

Schools. Adopted by the French Government to Serve as Instruction for the Students of the Cathedral Choir Schools, 1808). It is an extremely important source of information on the eighteenth-century methods of composition that formed the basis of training in the conservatories, especially since it was the result of a deliberate attempt to record only the practical aspects of the method, disregarding all superfluous theory. This book can truly claim to record something of the training that a novice composer would have received through lessons with an Italian maestro. According to an obituary published in 1835,[26] Choron (1771–1834), having been forbidden by his father to contemplate a musical career, indulged his passion for music by teaching himself through whatever books he could find, including Rameau's. At the age of twenty-five, he became convinced that such theorizing was of little use, since it was detached from the real practice of composition. Accordingly, he set out to learn *only* the practical aspects, studying such teachings as those of the Bolognese school (Giovanni Martini and his student Luigi Sabbatini in particular) under maestro Barnaba Benosi (ca. 1745–1824) and an unidentifiable Abbé Rosé. This resulted in a collaborative book with Vincenzo Fiocchi on Neapolitan *partimento* methods, especially those of Fenaroli, entitled *Principes d'accompagnment des écoles d'Italie extrait des meilleurs auteurs* (Principles of Accompaniment of the Italian Schools According to the Best Authors, 1804). Choron's later *Principes de composition des écoles d'Italie* (1808) owed much to Neapolitan maestro Nicola Sala's *Regole* (1794), although the exercises in counterpoint and the compilation of *partimenti* in the first volume, "Harmony and Accompaniment," were ascribed to the usual names, such as Fenaroli, Cotumacci, and Durante. The next four volumes followed a fairly conventional format for an Italian treatise: "Simple Counterpoint," "Invertible Counterpoint," "Imitation," and "Fugue and Canons." The sixth volume, on "Musical Rhetoric," set out practical instructions for crucial aspects of "composition" such as text-setting, the disposition of phrases and periods, and rhetorical devices.

Choron's may be the most voluminous treatise, but the most central to this study is Asioli's magnum opus, *Il Maestro di composizione, ossia seguito del Trattato d'armonia* (The Master of Composition, or Continuation of the Treatise on Harmony, 1832). It consists of three books, each accompanied by a separate volume of examples: "Harmony," "Counterpoint," and "Composition." As a summation of Asioli's teachings at the

Milan Conservatory, it goes into a level of detail rarely encountered in Italian treatises. It is perhaps no coincidence that it was published posthumously, in fulfillment of the author's last wishes. Although it draws many of its examples from operas composed at the time of Rossini, Bellini, and Donizetti, it was much used as a source of reference throughout the nineteenth century. There is evidence that Verdi used Asioli's treatises as part of his studies with Vincenzo Lavigna,[27] which is hardly surprising, considering that Lavigna was tutor of theory and *solfeggio* for "complementary studies" (for students who were not primarily composers) at Milan from 1822 until 1836. Indeed, Asioli's influence was so all-encompassing that there appears to have been little need for other comprehensive treatises until much later in the century. Picchianti (1834) was in many respects a condensed summary of Asioli's methods, incorporating newer material (from Reicha, in particular). Uberto Bandini, who joined Amintore Galli as teacher of complementary harmony and counterpoint at Milan from 1888 until 1891, published a *Scuola di armonia, contrappunto e composizione* (School of Harmony, Counterpoint, and Composition, 1888), but this was largely a compilation of earlier sources simplified for less advanced students.

The terms and concepts outlined in these composition manuals have been substantiated in this book by reference to contemporary music dictionaries and encyclopedias. Among the most authoritative is the four-volume *Dizionario e bibliografia della musica* (Dictionary and Bibliography of Music, 1826) by Peter (Pietro) Lichtenthal (1780–1853), a physician from Vienna who spent most of his life in Milan.[28] Although it relied heavily on earlier German and French dictionaries, it nevertheless helps to corroborate a number of points. Especially useful for clarifying terminology with reference to the French tradition is Massimino Vissian's *Dizionario della musica ossia Raccolta dei principali vocaboli italiani-francesi co' loro significati, preceduto da un trattato italiano e francese sui principj elementari della musica* (Dictionary of Music, or Collection of the Principal Terms in Italian and French and Their Meanings, Preceded by a Treatise in Italian and French on the Elementary Principles of Music, 1846). Amintore Galli's *Piccolo lessico del musicista* (Brief Lexicon for Musicians, 1902) provides an overview of key terms as understood at the end of the nineteenth century. It receives additional authority from the fact that Galli was Puccini's tutor in music history at the Milan Conservatory.

4. *Biographies and Histories*

Biographical information has been drawn from standard sources such as Fétis's *Biographie universelle des musiciens et bibliographie générale de la musique* (Universal Biography of Musicians and General Bibliography of Music, 1866–75) and Choron and De LaFage (1836–39). For information on some of the less prominent Italian figures, the most useful books have proven to be, in addition to contemporary journal articles, Giuseppe Bertini's *Dizionario storico-critico degli scrittori di musica e de' più celebri artisti di tutte le nazioni sì antiche che moderne* (Historical-Critical Dictionary of Composers and of the Most Celebrated Artists of All Nations, Both Ancient and Modern, 1814–15), Carlo De Rosa's *Memorie dei compositori di musica del regno di Napoli* (Memoirs of Musical Composers of the Kingdom of Naples, 1840), Francesco Regli's *Dizionario Biografico dei più celebri poeti ed artisti melodrammatici, tragici e comici, maestri, concertisti, coreografi, mimi, ballerini, scenografi, giornalisti, impresarii ecc., che fiorirono in Italia dal 1800 al 1860* (Biographical Dictionary of the Most Celebrated Melodramatic, Tragic, and Comic Poets and Artists, Maestros, Instrumentalists, Choreographers, Mimes, Ballet Dancers, Scenographers, Journalists, Impresarios, etc., Who Flourished in Italy from 1800 to 1860, 1860), Giovanni Masutto's *I maestri di musica Italiani del secolo xix: Notizie biografiche* (Italian Musical Maestros of the Nineteenth Century: Biographical Notes, 1882–84), Carlo Schmidl's *Dizionario universale dei musicisti* (Universal Dictionary of Musicians, 1887–90), Francesco Florimo's monumental four-volume *La Scuola musicale di Napoli e i suoi Conservatorii* (The Neapolitan School of Music and Its Conservatories, 1881–83), and Alfredo Colombani's *L'opera italiana nel secolo XIX* (Italian Opera in the Nineteenth Century, 1900). Shorter surveys include Amintore Galli's *La Musica ed i Musicisti dal secolo X ai nostri giorni* (Music and Musicians from the Tenth Century to Our Times, 1871). There are also numerous monographs on individual composers, such as Filippo Canuti's *Vita di Stanislao Mattei* (Life of Stanislao Mattei, 1829) or Antonio Coli's *Vita di Bonifazio Asioli da Correggio* (Life of Bonifazio Asioli from Correggio, 1834). Andrea Sessa's *Il melodramma italiano, 1861–1900: Dizionario bio-bibliografico dei compositori* (The Italian *Melodramma*, 1861–1900: Bio-Bibliographical Dictionary of Composers, 2003) provides a useful summary of the leading musical figures of the second half of the nineteenth century.

It was common for authors in the nineteenth century to preface discussions of music with historical backgrounds designed to support their
claims. These were typically selective, inaccurate, and romanticized. The
opening sentence of Giovanni Pacini's *Cenni storici sulla musica e Trattato di contrappunto* (Historical Surveys on Music and Treatise on Counterpoint, 1834) gives some idea of their tone: "Music was born with the
world." Such surveys do, however, provide useful evidence on the identity
of schools and lineages.

Insights into the curriculum at the Lucca Conservatory have been obtained primarily from two histories that were based on research originally
carried out by Puccini's father, Michele, and published after his death
by his students: Domenico Cerù's *Cenni storici dell'insegnamento della
musica in Lucca, e dei più notabili maestri compositori che vi hanno fiorito*
(Historical Survey of Music Teaching in Lucca, and of the Most Notable
Masters of Composition Who Flourished There, 1871) and Luigi Nerici's
Storia della musica in Lucca (History of Music in Lucca, 1879). Additional
historical information on musical life in Lucca may be found in "Avvocato A. G. [Carlo Andrea Gambini?]" (1844), Nerici (1872), Landucci
(1905), Damerini (1942)—one of a series commissioned by the Mussolini
government to celebrate the Italian conservatories—Bonaccorsi (1950,
1967), and Battelli (1990). Information on the curriculum of the Milan
Conservatory may be found in Salvetti (2003a) and Lodovico Melzi's
*Cenni storici sul R. Conservatorio di musica in Milano, dal 10 gennaio 1873
al 10 novembre 1878* (Historical Survey of the Royal Conservatory of Music in Milan, from January 1, 1873, to November 1, 1878, 1878), Lodovico
Corio's *Ricerche storiche sul R. Conservatorio di musica di Milano* (Historical Researches on the Royal Conservatory of Music in Milan, 1908),
and Federico Mompellio's *Il R. Conservatorio di musica "Giuseppe Verdi"
di Milano* (1941). As Puccini's tutor of poetic and dramatic literature at
Milan, Corio's *Pietro Metastasio: studio critico* (1882) is also of interest for
its account of versification in opera.

5. Monographs and Dissertations

The direction of Italian opera during the nineteenth century was subject
to public debate in numerous monographs and dissertations. A typical
example may be found in Andrea Majer's *Discorso sulla origine progressi*

e stato attuale della musica italiana (Discourse on the Origin, Developments, and Current State of Music in Italy, 1821), which mounted a conservative defense of tradition as part of a backlash against the popularity of Rossini's reforms. Similarly reactionary in outlook were many accounts written by little-known maestros that dealt with particular aspects of music theory, such as Giuseppe Baini's *Saggio sopra l'identità de' ritmi musicale e poetico* (Essay on the Identity of Musical and Poetic Rhythms, 1820). Baini (1775–1844) espoused an even more extreme form of conservatism than was usual at that time. During a life devoted to the service of the Papal Chapel in Rome, he carried out some of the first archival researches on Palestrina and attempted (unsuccessfully) to establish a school of singing founded on ancient methods.[29] He was almost certainly the "learned priest" who in 1831, according to Berlioz, "told Mendelssohn that he had heard mention of 'a young man of great promise called Mozart.'"[30] More directly connected to Puccini's studies in Lucca is Marco Santucci's paean to tradition and tirade against foreign influences, *Sulla melodia, sull'armonia e sul metro: Dissertazioni di Marco Santucci, canonico della Metropolitana di Lucca, dedicate alla studiosa gioventù* (On Melody, Harmony, and Meter: Dissertations by Marco Santucci, Canon of the Municipality of Lucca, Dedicated to His Young Students, 1828). As the first teacher of Michele Puccini, Santucci was responsible for imparting to the Lucca Conservatory the teachings he had received as far back as 1779 as a student of Fenaroli at the Conservatorio di Santa Maria di Loreto in Naples. A connection to the Bologna school is also evident, through Pacini (1834), written expressly for music students in Lucca. Pacini (1796–1867) first settled in the town in 1821 as *maestro di cappella* to the Duchess Marie-Louise de Bourbon, and he was later instrumental in establishing the *liceo* that eventually became the Istituto musicale "Giovanni Pacini," where Puccini received his first lessons.

The period of the Risorgimento saw a marked increase in the publication of discussions of musical aesthetics, such as Raimondo Boucheron's *Filosofia della musica o estetica applicata a quest'arte* (Philosophy of Music, or Aesthetics as Applied to That Art, 1842). An informed, technical brand of music criticism was also flourishing, as witnessed in Niccolò Marselli's *La ragione della musica moderna* (The Explanation of Modern Music, 1859), which contains among the most detailed contemporary descriptions of set pieces in Verdi's operas, and in Abramo Basevi's better-known

Studio sulle opere di G. Verdi (Study on the Operas of G. Verdi, 1859), which appeared originally as a series of articles in the progressive Florentine journal *L'Armonia* (1857–58) and is discussed more fully below. Alfredo Soffredini's *Le opere di Verdi: studio critico analitico* (The Operas of Verdi: A Critical Analytical Study, 1901), compiled from earlier journalistic articles in the *Gazzetta musicale di Milano,* also belongs to this category.

6. Speculative Theories and Musical Periodicals

Composition textbooks of a type familiar today, offering detailed theoretical explanations of harmony, form, and so on but appearing detached from the practice they purport to represent, became common in Italy only at the very end of the nineteenth century, primarily through the influence of German theorists such as Hugo Riemann and Salomon Jadassohn. While the main German treatises were not translated into Italian until after 1900, they were nevertheless available in the conservatory libraries from the 1880s. The translation of Leipzig professor Ernst Richter's textbook on simple and double counterpoint (1872) that appeared as *Trattato di contrappunto semplice e doppio* in 1873 was a rare exception, arriving by way of St. Petersburg.

Speculative or "scientific" theories were, of course, published in Italy well before this, in increasing numbers from the 1840s onwards and especially in periodicals. At the maverick end of the scale were books such as Melchiorre Balbi's *Grammatica ragionata della musica considerata sotto l'aspetto di lingua* (Annotated Grammar of Music Considered in Terms of Language, 1845). It was constructed on a facile analogy according to which the sum total of notes available for composition constituted an "alphabet" for music. Subsequent chapters pursued the theory in terms of musical "conjunctions," "prepositions," and other grammatical functions, and concluded with an entirely new system of syntax. A more considered theory, based on recent studies of acoustics, appeared in *La scienza dell'armonia spiegata dai rapporti dell'arte coll'umana natura—Trattato teorico pratico* (The Science of Harmony Explained by the Connections between Art and Human Nature—Theoretical-Practical Treatise, 1856) by Raimondo Boucheron (1800–1876), *maestro di cappella* and organist at Milan Cathedral. The 1860s and 1870s witnessed a proliferation of such innovative, idiosyncratic theories, including Francesco Luvini's *Trattato completo d'armonia: con una nuova classificazione degli accordi e delle dissonanze basata sui centri armonici* (Complete Treatise on Harmony: With a New Classification of Chords and Dissonances Based on Harmonic Centers, 1869), Amintore Galli and Alberto Mazzucato's interesting *Arte fonetica: istituzioni scientifico-musicali* (Phonetic Art: Scientific-Musical Foundations, 1870), and Nicola D'Arenzio's *L'introduzione del sistema tetracordale nella musica moderna* (The Introduction of a Tetrachordal System in Modern Music, 1878). Dwelling on abstract theory, they shared a detachment from the real practice of musical composition and performance. Particularly representative in this respect was Bartolomeo Grassi Landi's *Descrizione della nuova tastiera cromatica ed esposizione del nuovo sistema di scrittura musicale invenzione des Sac. B. Grassi Landi* (Description of a New Chromatic Keyboard and Exposition of a New System of Musical Script Invented by Father B. Grassi Landi, 1880), which proposed a new form of notation based on the semitone, and his later *L'armonia considerata come vera scienza ossia Dimostrazione delle leggi fisiche dell'armonia* (Harmony Considered as a True Science, or Demonstration of the Physical Laws of Harmony, 1881), which proposed a new form of notation based on vibrations and divisions of a monochord.

The gradual rise of speculative, theoretical, and (most significantly) German-style approaches to the study of music theory and composition in Italy may be traced back to the progressives and modernizers of the 1840s and 1850s, particularly in Florence and Milan, and to the various journals and periodicals through which they promoted their agendas. Three music journals of great importance were established in northern Italy: in 1842 the *Gazzetta musicale di Milano*; in 1847 *L'Italia musicale* (Milan); and in 1853 the *Gazzetta musicale di Firenze*. All three journals were supported by music publishers, and each reflected the concerns and point of view of the supporting company.[31] Each number typically consisted of four pages, the first generally reserved for major articles on issues such as music history, aesthetics, theory, anecdotes, memoirs, and current events, and the remainder devoted to concert reports, reviews, correspondence, and advertisements. The *Gazzetta musicale di Milano* was published by the firm of Giovanni Ricordi from 1842 to 1862 and from 1866 to 1902. The journal's editors were not maestros. Giacinto Battaglia (1842–46) was a journalist, theatrical critic, and polemicist. Alberto Mazzucato (1846–58) trained as a mathematician but also studied music in Padua, later becoming conductor of the orchestra at La Scala and director of the Milan Conservatory. Filippo Filippi (1858–62) was educated in law. Much of the journal was occupied with reviews and notices, but there were also articles on composition and pedagogy by occasional contributors such as Boucheron, Cattaneo, Pacini, and Lauro Rossi. *L'Italia musicale* was set up in Milan by the firm of Francesco Lucca from 1847 to 1859, primarily to promote the sale of works by foreign composers such as Auber, Halévy, Flotow, Gounod, and especially Meyerbeer. It was one of the first journals to champion Austro-German instrumental music as an antidote to the alleged "decadence" of the Italian traditions.[32]

The journals that proved to have the greatest impact upon the development of music theory, pedagogy, and composition in Italy were those associated with the Florentine progressives.[33] Their three main journals were all published by Giovan Gualberto Guidi: the *Gazzetta musicale di Firenze* (1853–55), its successor, *L'Armonia* (1856–59), and *Boccherini* (1862–80). From the start, they were dominated by the extraordinarily prolific contributions of Abramo Basevi. Educated in medicine but evidently more interested in composition, he turned his formidable energies to music criticism following the failure of his second opera, *Enrico Odoardo,* at the Teatro della Pergola in 1847. On the basis of writing style, it seems very likely that he was the primary author (together with Ermanno Picchi) of an unsigned series of satirical articles that served to strengthen the *Gazzetta musicale di Firenze*'s self-styled mission as an "organ for the reform of music in Italy." These anonymous diatribes launched a bitter invective against the antiquated methods and attitudes of the maestros, followed by similar attacks on the outmoded conventions of the contemporary libretto (see Anon. [X.] [1854c], Anon. [X. *antiscettico*] [1854d], Anon. [X.] [1854e], Anon. [1854f], and Anon. [1855b]). Basevi also published an enormous quantity of signed articles from November 1853 onwards, as listed in the bibliography, culminating in a call-to-arms for progressives entitled "Decadence or Resurgence?" (1855c). The relentless critique of the old traditions continued in the new journal *L'Armonia,* which was by this time under the exclusive direction of Basevi, through articles stressing the need for reform, promoting the superiority of German instrumental music over Italian opera, and offering advice to librettists and maestros on ways to avoid some of the worst failings of the old traditions. *L'Armonia* was subsequently dominated by the six installments of Basevi's account of "Ancient and Modern Mel-ody in Italy" (1856f), the serialization of his *Studio sulle opere di G. Verdi* (1859a), and explanations by Basevi and others of Wagner's theories. On March 15, 1859 (6, no. 5), *L'Armonia* put out a public call for views on what it called the crisis of contemporary opera, in which not even Verdi was spared from criticism.

The main theoretical publication to emerge from the activities of the Florentine circle was Basevi's *Introduzione ad un nuovo sistema d'armonia* (Introduction to a New System of Harmony, 1862), which eschewed es-tablished Italian traditions of composition in favor of newer theories by Fétis, Choron, and Boucheron.[34] Its "new system" concerned primarily the notion of inversional equivalence, familiar nowadays through Ri-emann's function theory, which gave rise to a system of key relations in which fifths above the tonic were mirrored by fifths below, together with mixed-mode equivalents.[35] Although its impact was initially limited, Basevi (1862) set the pattern for the kind of speculative, theoretical, and nonpractical textbooks of harmony that were eventually to dominate the Italian conservatories. The start of its influence may be traced to an extended series of critical reviews published by his Florentine colleague Baldassarre Gamucci in the journal *Boccherini* (1877–78). This successor to *L'Armonia* had found a more effective means to continue the assault on the Italian opera traditions: by ignoring them. Although *Boccherini* featured a few essays on Meyerbeer and Wagner, it was occupied for the most part with instrumental music and especially the quartet reper-tory, as exemplified through the 1874 serialization of Basevi's analyses of Beethoven's Six Quartets, op. 18.

Not to be outdone by their northern colleagues, Neapolitan maestros made four separate attempts to establish an independent music journal, each time entitled *La Musica*. The first (1855), directed by Pasquale Triso-lini in collaboration with Michele Ruta, was characterized by a conser-vative defense of the Italian traditions. Ruta in particular adhered to the old-fashioned teachings of Saverio Mercadante, with whom he had studied composition from 1841 to 1847 at the Collegio di musica S. Pietro a Majella in Naples.[36] The second *La Musica* (1857–59) was dominated by its founder and editor, Baron Giuseppe Staffa, whose "scientific" lean-ings contrasted strangely with his attempts to record the teachings of the Neapolitan traditions for posterity. The third and fourth versions of *La*

Musica (1876–78 and 1883–85) provided something of a counterbalance to the radical changes taking place further north in Florence and Milan. Michele Ruta, director, principal contributor, professor at the Naples Conservatory from 1879, and critic at the *Corriere del mattino,* published a series of important articles aimed at students and amateurs setting out traditional Neapolitan notions of music pedagogy and theory (1876, 1877a, 1877b, and 1884). Ruta's summaries provide eloquent evidence of the continued relevance during the 1880s of what might be described as ancient Italian teachings on a variety of aspects of composition. Together with articles by Giovanni Benzo (1883a and 1883b) on the crisis engulfing contemporary opera, by Tommaso Persico (1883a, 1883b, and 1883c) on hopes for a national resurgence through the "young school" (*giovane scuola*) of Boito and Ponchielli against the influence of Wagner, Goldmark, and Massenet, and by Giovanni Michele Bovio (1885) on the merits of Donizetti's style, Ruta's publications in *La Musica* may be taken to embody a protracted last rites for the Neapolitan school.

III. PUCCINI AND THE END OF THE GREAT TRADITION

Whether Puccini represented the end of the Italian tradition as a conservative "national" composer or as a progressive follower of "international" trends is a question that has occupied the critical reception of his works since the earliest contemporary reviews. In general, whereas his *italianità* has been met with popular acclaim and scholarly doubt, his *internazionalità* has been largely accepted by scholars but not by the public, for whom Puccini's music continues to embody the quintessence of Italian opera. Alexandra Wilson (2007) recently characterized the dichotomy as "The Puccini Problem" in her insightful study of the social, cultural, and political contexts surrounding the reception of his works at the turn of the twentieth century. In particular, through a comprehensive survey of source materials relating to the construction of a "national identity" for Puccini and his operas and to conflicting perceptions of their "modernity"—a catch-all term signifying (German- and occasionally French-inspired) innovations in musical technique—she explored the ways in which his music was portrayed as "both the antidote to and the embodiment of the degeneration widely felt to be afflicting contemporary Italy."[37] As in most recent studies, however, the connections between the composer's musical language and the preceding Italian tradition, which necessarily underpinned the arguments of both sides in the debate, were mostly taken for granted.[38] The "Italianness" of Puccini's music was regarded as self-evident.

The apparent reluctance to engage with the musical traditions of Italian opera may be explained partly through a reaction to widespread scholarly attitudes that dismiss Puccini out of hand for his supposed sentimentality, commercialism, and reactionary musical and theatrical style. To counter such views, commentators and analysts have typically been cast in the roles of apologists, forced to apply a variety of approaches to the task of validating and legitimizing Puccini as a Great Composer with a fully merited place in the canon. This agenda has manifested itself in various ways. Linda Fairtile and Jürgen Maehder have focused attention on compositional process through the transcription and study of materials such as sketches and successive revisions. Dieter Schickling has provided the basis for a complete critical edition by compiling an authoritative catalog of works. Analyses by Deborah Burton, Michele Girardi, and Helen Greenwald have set out to demonstrate the operation of tonal and motivic structures over long stretches of the operas, complemented by dramatic associative meaning. Postmodern strains of Puccini scholarship, while pointing out the weaknesses of earlier approaches, have preferred to see his operas as battlegrounds of ideas on feminist theory or colonialism, implicitly taking them seriously as works of art with something significant to say on such themes. A number of efforts have been made to bolster Puccini's modernist credentials by emphasizing his evident familiarity with contemporary developments in the music of Richard Strauss, Debussy, and Stravinsky,[39] his cordial meeting with Schoenberg in 1924, and the admiration he has inspired in such figures as René Leibowitz and the avant-garde composer Sylvano Bussotti. In a 2010 monograph, Andrew Davis argues convincingly for a modernist interpretation of musical and dramaturgical features in *Il trittico* and *Turandot*. As a consequence of this broad scholarly project, however, Puccini's connections to the Italian musical tradition have been played down or confined to casual asides, such as marginal biographical notes on his musical ancestors.

This is by no means to suggest that there was at any time a pure, self-contained Italian tradition untouched by foreign influences. By the time Puccini enrolled at the Milan Conservatory in 1880, progressive ideas from abroad had long since been assimilated into theory and practice. Indeed, it was in the pages of the *Gazzetta musicale di Milano,* the house journal for the publishing firm of Ricordi, that the need for reform was first mooted (see, e.g., Perotti [1844]) and that Giovanni Simone Mayr enlightened Italian musical circles on the nature of the contemporary repertory of symphonic, chamber, and other instrumental genres to be found beyond the Alps, through the seven installments of his seminal article, "Cenni intorno allo stato e coltura progressiva della musica in Germania" (A Survey Regarding the State and Progressive Cultivation of Music in Germany, 1844–45).[40] Over the next decades a group connected to the school of music attached to the Accademia delle Belle Arti in Florence, evidently influenced by the general mood of national reappraisal that accompanied the Risorgimento, took it upon themselves to promote Austro-German instrumental music as a means to effect what they saw as a necessary revitalization of the Italian tradition.[41] In addition to publishing polemical and analytical articles in radical journals such as those mentioned above, they helped to familiarize the public with this new instrumental repertory through the foundation of an *accademia filarmonica* and a *società del quartetto.* Similar developments were proceeding at such a pace further north in Milan that by 1860 the curriculum at the Conservatory had to be completely overhauled in order to take account of these new instrumental genres, which could likewise be heard in the city through performances by incipient quartet and symphonic societies.[42] At around the same time, recent Conservatory graduates Franco Faccio and Arrigo Boito established the Avveniristi (Futurists) in Milan, an avant-garde group of musicians affiliated to the primarily literary cultural movement known (later) as the "disheveled ones," or "Bohemians" (*scapigliati*), which sought to rejuvenate Italian culture through an appropriation of foreign influences, notably from German Romanticism. The Avveniristi embarked on a brief but influential series of ventures from 1863 to 1868, including the premieres of three "reform" operas, the launch of a progressive journal, *Il Figaro,* and the publication of numerous polemical pamphlets and poems.[43] As the final stages of the political unification of Italy approached, they succeeded in making the transition from revolutionaries to respected pillars of the mainstream musical establishment. Faccio, already a successful conductor, went on to accept a position at the Milan Conservatory, teaching complementary harmony and counterpoint from 1868 to 1877, and Boito eventually became director of the Parma Conservatory.

The legacy of the Florentine progressives, the Milanese Avveniristi, and other reformers decisively shaped the course of music in Italy and the teaching of composition at the conservatories. These musical radicals of the Risorgimento not only fostered an increasing interest in innovative instrumental genres, such as chamber music or the Lisztian symphonic poem, but also encouraged the application of contemporary French developments and Wagner's theories on "the music of the future" to Italian opera, the final symbolic bastion of a specifically national musical culture. Boito, in particular, incorporated chromaticisms and interval cycles derived from works such as Liszt's *Faust* Symphony (1857) into his reform opera *Mefistofele* (1868) and launched a wholesale assault on the traditional Italian system of dramatic versification, in emulation of Wagner's theories on "musical prose." Throughout the 1860s and 1870s, he railed against the conventional correspondence between verse meters and operatic phrases, standardized since the time of Metastasio, which he regarded as the primary cause of "the tedious singsong of symmetry, the great quality and the great defect of Italian prosody, which almost inevitably leads to poverty and commonplace rhythm in the musical phrasing."[44]

Puccini's first opera, *Le Villi* (1883–85), bears witness to the influence of these decades of reform in its "Romantic" subject matter, its extended orchestral interludes, its loosening of traditional verse structures, and, not least, in its quotation (in m. 15) of the head motive of the Last Supper theme from *Parsifal*. Girardi (2000) has provided a comprehensive catalog of such modernisms in Puccini's early works, from the unresolved modulation marked "alla Wagner" in a sketch for the song "Ad una morta,"[45] through the Wagnerian echoes in the Mass of 1880, to the many influences from French operas referred to in his letters (*Carmen, Mignon, Faust, Hérodiade,* etc.).

A similar story of the "modernization" of Italian opera in the late nineteenth century has been told many times and in many contexts.[46] But what exactly were these foreign influences meant to renew? Which musical formulas, methods, and practices were the progressives in Florence, Milan, and elsewhere so keen to replace? What did Basevi mean, for instance, when he castigated his contemporaries for following an outdated

"recipe for composing the easiest, catchiest melodies," which consisted
of "an old rhythm," a copied "conduct," and "almost fixed rules, such as
those that recommend leaps of the ascending fourth, the major sixth, the
third, the descending fifth etc."?[47]

This book sets out to provide some answers to questions such as these,
in its attempt to demonstrate that the musical reforms that took place over
the course of the second half of the nineteenth century, although undeniably effective in introducing progressive foreign influences to Italy, left
many of the foundations of the original tradition intact. Composers were
not always inclined, for instance, to match the freedom and irregularity of
the new style of versification ushered in by Boito's reforms with similarly
asymmetrical phrase structures. Irregular verses were frequently molded
onto an old-fashioned, conventional succession of regular underlying
"rhythms" (*ritmi:* short phrases determined primarily by poetic meter). In
addition, traditional contrapuntal constructs based on ancient teachings
such as the "rule of the octave" (*regola dell'ottava*) or the "regular motions of the bass" (*movimenti regolare del basso*), to be discussed in detail
in chapter 4, continued to appear alongside more progressive chromatic
harmonies.

Puccini's attitude toward the great stylistic divide that confronted
him from the very beginning of his career, between the antiquated Italian schools of his ancestors and newer, more fashionable Austro-German
traditions of symphonic and chamber music, as well as Wagnerian opera,
may be gauged from an imaginary (and, one hopes, facetious) "biographical entry" or "obituary" for himself, which he scribbled in a notebook in
1882 during his second year of study at the Milan Conservatory:

> Giacomo Puccini: This great musician born in Lucca in the year . . . and
> it could well be said the true successor to the renowned Boccherini. Good-
> looking and with a vast intellect, he brought to the field of Italian art a breath
> with a power almost like an echo of transalpine Wagnerism.[48]

Why would Puccini define himself as a "true successor" to Boccherini, an eighteenth-century Lucchese cellist and composer noted for
instrumental music, rather than, say, Pacini or Verdi? How many conservatory students of the 1880s, especially budding opera composers, would
have measured their artistic worth against such an outdated, unfash-
ionable, and seemingly irrelevant figure? The explanation surely rests

on Boccherini's status as a symbol of Lucca's musical heritage, which, for Puccini, was intensified through personal connections. During the 1750s Boccherini not only studied at his old school, the Seminary of San Martino, but he also owed his early career to the patronage of Giacomo senior, the first maestro of the Puccini dynasty. Unless dismissed as an attempt at humor through understatement or incongruence (i.e., the disparity between a contemporary opera composer and a *galant* cellist), which seems unlikely, the sentence can only be understood as a declaration of allegiance to a specific, provincial Italian musical tradition with roots in eighteenth-century practice. It is important to note also that the reference to German Wagnerism is comparative: it serves to contextualize the power of the "breath" or influence the future composer will bring to "the field of Italian art." Far from describing this "breath" as Wagnerian in nature, Puccini's formulation is typically ironic, suggesting that no influence he could ever hope to have on *Italian art* could be as powerful as a mere echo from beyond the Alps. Heard the other way, with the echo of German music rebounding northwards, it could also imply a desire to resist foreign influences. In this sense Puccini's lighthearted self-characterization may be understood to reveal a nationalist and, at the same time, pessimistic view of the future of Italian art, similar to views expressed by Verdi at around the same time, in opposition to the imperialist ambitions of "Wagnerism." Like other musicians with allegiances to the ancient Italian schools, he could only look on impotently as centuries of glorious tradition were swept aside in the name of progress. Milanese singing teacher Francesco Lamperti captured something of the conservative attitude to this transformation in a passage added to the 1891 English translation of his *Guida teorico-pratica-elementare per lo studio del canto* (Theoretical-Practical-Elementary Guide to the Study of Singing, 1864):

> In former times the great German composers came to Italy to study the pure Italian melody, and, as Dante says, 'The song that is felt in the soul' [Quel canto che nell'anima si sente]. Nowadays composers go to Germany to learn a sort of mathematical and scientific music, which, though beautiful as symphonic music, is totally unsuited to opera.[49]

Some twenty years later, in August 1912, while attending what was widely considered the most sacred ritual of the cult of German art—a performance of *Parsifal* at Bayreuth—Puccini took the opportunity to provide a journalist with an explicit and unequivocal account of his allegiance to the Italian traditions:

> I am not a Wagnerian; my musical education was in the Italian school. Even though, like every other modern musician, I have been influenced by Wagner in the way I use the orchestra for illustration and in the thematic characterization of persons and situations, as a composer I have always remained, and still remain, Italian. My music is rooted in the peculiarity of my native country.[50]

TWO

Studies in Lucca and Milan

I. COMPOSITION AS CRAFT

It was obvious, inevitable even, that Puccini would pursue a musical career. His ancestors had occupied positions as *maestri di musica* in Lucca since 1739, and no one, least of all Puccini himself, appears ever to have questioned the assumption that he would continue the family tradition. Like most professional composers in Italy before him, he spent his entire childhood receiving specialist musical training. There was little need for much other education beyond the basics. Such thorough apprenticeships, which had all but died out in the rest of Europe, remained possible in Italy because music was still regarded as a profession or craft, as opposed to a vocation or "calling." Just as maestros in the service of the church were required to furnish whatever music the clergy and congregation demanded of them, so too were professional opera composers expected to please their audience and whoever controlled the industry, whether impresarios, theaters, or, especially after 1850, publishers.[1] Personal expression, particularly if unconventional, was a luxury that few could afford. Music was judged primarily for its artistic entertainment value, for the effectiveness of its delivery, and for its comprehensibility. By Puccini's time the composer was no longer quite so much in thrall to the whims of star singers, owing to the increased emphasis and prestige accorded to the "work" rather than the "act" of music, but the opera audience remained the final arbiter of musical taste.

Such attitudes served to differentiate the Italian musical traditions of the nineteenth century from those that held sway elsewhere in Europe, especially in Germany. Yet this crucial distinction is habitually overlooked in critical assessments of Puccini, which tend to judge his achievement according to "norms" that were far from normal in Italian musical life.[2] The disparaging or downright negative assessment of his work in much scholarly literature may be understood to be grounded on a set of values against which Puccini, like numerous other non-Germanic composers, would always be found wanting. The framework for modern musicology and music criticism was forged in nineteenth-century Germany. Scholars have for the most part kept faith with this inheritance. The attitudes that underpin academic judgments on Puccini are in general related to those that surfaced with the birth of Romanticism and German artistic self-consciousness. Some light may be shed upon these attitudes through the terms *Kultur* and its antithesis, *Zivilisation*. The former signifies the deepest foundations of a culture, *das rein Geistige* or purely spiritual, as encapsulated in the guiding idea of Hegel's *Aesthetics:* "In art we have to do, not with any agreeable or useful child's play, but with the liberation of the spirit from the content and forms of finitude . . . with an unfolding of the truth which is not exhausted in natural history but revealed in World-History."[3] The latter term, *Zivilisation,* implies superficial "civilized" or "cultivated" attitudes, including cosmopolitan tastes and entertainments. *Zivilisation* stood for the culture of the prerevolutionary aristocracy and the values of the Enlightenment. In musical terms, it suggests an essential link between the musician and the consumer. *Kultur* comprised the specifically Romantic and Germanic discourse of *Innigkeit* or self-discovery. As sociologist Norbert Elias puts it:

> In German usage, *Zivilisation* means something which is indeed useful, but nevertheless only a value of the second rank, comprising only the outer appearance of human beings, the surface of human existence. The word through which Germans interpret themselves, which more than any other expresses their pride in their own achievements and their own being, is *Kultur.*[4]

Kultur was associated strongly with *Bildung,* the intellectual formation of the individual. It celebrated the uniquely personal and especially the artist's subjectivity, leading to a producer-oriented system that soon coalesced into the cult of the genius. Much the same ideology continues to inform modern notions of art and artistic activity as "creativity" from within. The music of *Kultur* was primarily the "absolute spirit" of instrumental music, whether expressed through the symphony orchestra, the chamber ensemble, or the "endless (orchestral) melody" of Wagner's operas. Its aim was not so much to please, or to sound agreeable or beautiful, as to elevate and transcend, to reveal deeper levels of being. There was also a distinctly nationalist element that came to the fore during the nineteenth century, with *Kultur* being associated with German sincerity and strength of purpose and *Zivilisation* with Italian and French superficiality. Their "civilized" music was associated with polite mannerism, the base ambitions of performers, and the frivolous tastes of audiences. The public became the enemy, unable to understand the message of the genius. Popularity was often associated with sentimentality and "feminine" frippery. Success was considered vulgar.

An instructive illustration of this clash of attitudes and values may be found in Hector Berlioz's reminiscences of a visit to the opera in Milan. Although the events he described took place in 1832, his reflections upon them and subsequent conclusions on the general musical tastes of the Italians were written at some point between 1848 and 1865, by which time he was widely regarded as an honorary member of what Franz Brendel was to christen the "New German school." Berlioz's account typifies the high-minded, deferential attitude toward "genius" and toward innovative, provocative instrumental music that characterized Romantic notions of *Kultur*. He seemed incapable of understanding how music, for the Italians, could be enjoyed as a sensual pleasure dissociated from profound (or rather profoundly challenging) intellectual or spiritual content. Similarly, their resistance to change, indeed, their aversion to any unfamiliar music that required concentration (including his own), struck him as catering to the lowest common denominator: the preferences of the audience. Since Berlioz's account is so revealing of this ideological divide, as well as being entertainingly written, it is quoted here at length:

> Donizetti's *L'elisir d'amore* was being given at the Cannobiana. I found the theatre full of people talking in normal voices, with their backs to the stage. The singers, undeterred, gesticulated and yelled their lungs out in the strictest spirit of rivalry. At least I presumed they did, from their wide-open mouths; but the noise of the audience was such that no sound penetrated except the bass drum. People were gambling, eating supper in their boxes, et cetera et cetera. . . .

It appears that the Italians do sometimes listen. I have been assured by several people that it is so. The fact remains that music to the Milanese, as to the Neapolitans, the Romans, the Florentines, and the Genoese, means arias, duets, trios, well sung; anything beyond that provokes only aversion or indifference. It may well be that such antipathies are mere prejudice, due above all to the feebleness of their orchestras and choruses, which prevents them from appreciating any great music outside the narrow circuit they have ploughed for so long. It may also be that they are capable to some extent of rising to the challenge of genius, provided the composer is careful not to disturb entrenched habits of mind too rudely. . . . Nevertheless, in general there is no denying that the Italians as a nation appreciate music solely for its physical effect and are alive only to what is on the surface.

Of all the nations of Europe, I am strongly inclined to think them the most impervious to the evocative, poetic side of music, as well as to any conception at all lofty and out of the common run. Music for the Italians is a sensual pleasure and nothing more. For this noble expression of the mind they have hardly more respect than for the art of cooking. They want a score that, like a plate of macaroni, can be assimilated immediately without their having to think about it or even pay any attention to it. . . . Add that they are bigoted and reactionary to a degree no longer known even at the Academy, and that the slightest innovation in melody, harmony, rhythm, or orchestration throws them into a perfect fury of resentment, to the point that when Rossini's *Barber of Seville* first appeared, Italian though it is through and through, the Roman *dilettanti* of the time were ready to lynch the insolent young composer for presuming to go beyond Paisiello. . . .

Having given the Italian musical sensibility a long and unbiased scrutiny, I conclude that their composers write as they do because the natural taste of the public wills it, with the rider that the natural taste of the composers shows every sign of sympathizing.[5]

Modern musical opinion would tend to side with Berlioz. His arguments, considered progressive at the time of writing, are now very familiar. But there was an opposing point of view that is seldom acknowledged. It concerned the notion that music should be pleasing, fulfilling, or entertaining, in a variety of contexts from church to theater, as opposed to educational, demanding, and revelatory. To pursue this idea further, anyone who has tasted Italian cooking at its best might be inclined to take issue with Berlioz's dismissive comparison, which could only have arisen (especially for a Frenchman) from a wholesale acceptance of the Romantic worship of music as the deepest, most metaphysical of the arts. In any case, just because a recipe (culinary or musical) may have remained essentially unchanged for centuries, this did not mean that every serving of it was of equal quality. Even a simple dish, exquisite in the right hands, could turn out surprisingly badly if poorly prepared. In musical terms, the Italians appear for the most part to have been indifferent to originality, progress, and development—Berlioz's "conceptions at all lofty and out of the common run"—because they valued far more highly the guarantee of entertainment, sensual enjoyment, and intellectual stimulation offered by an established maestro and a familiar genre. They weren't interested in "rising to the challenge of genius," especially given the ticket prices at the best theaters.

Puccini, in common with other composers of the Italian opera traditions, was content to remain within time-honored conventions, or at least not to stray too far from them, in order to please his audience and to assist in its appreciation. He worked in complicity with his public, attempting to fulfill its expectations through a well-crafted, often sophisticated, and generally artistic and entertaining reworking of established traditions. As the values of *Kultur* began to gain ground, however, he too came under pressure to innovate and to test the audience.

Far from being a natural modernizer, Puccini was earmarked practically from birth for a career not only as an old-fashioned *maestro di musica* but also as a preserver of the traditions of Italian music. Both his background and his training set him apart from Romantic attitudes that celebrated spontaneous, individual, uncompromising genius. He represented the fifth generation of a musical dynasty that had dominated musical life in the small Tuscan town of Lucca since the 1730s, when his ancestor Giacomo (1712–81) traveled from the nearby mountain village of Celle to study first in Lucca and then in Bologna with Giuseppe Carretti and Padre Martini, subsequently managing to secure the positions of organist at Lucca's San Martino Cathedral and director of the municipal Cappella Palatina.[6] Portraits of the subsequent maestros of the Puccini dynasty took pride of place in the living room of the family home off the via di Poggio. There, hanging on the wall, as daily reminders to the young Giacomo of the expectations placed upon him by his heritage, were paintings of Antonio Benedetto (1747–1832), who, following studies with Padre Martini, succeeded the elder Giacomo as cathedral organist in 1772; of Antonio's son Domenico (1772–1815), who studied in Bologna with Padre Mattei and in Naples with Paisiello; and, perhaps most significantly, of his late father, Michele (1813–64), who studied with Marco Santucci in Lucca, Giuseppe Pilotti in Bologna, and Niccolò Zingarelli (Bellini's maestro) in Naples. When once confronted with the possibility that young Giacomo might lack the talent and dedication to continue the family tradition, his mother is said to have responded: "If he doesn't become a worthy composer like his father and his ancestors, he'll still be something! The important thing is to continue the generation of musicians."[7]

Such family dynasties underpinned the training of musicians until well into the nineteenth century, when they began to be supplanted by institutionalized learning through the new conservatories. Even then it remained common for composers to receive their earliest training within the family. Amilcare Ponchielli, for instance, was tutored in the basics by his father, a village schoolmaster and organist, before entering the Milan Conservatory in 1843 at the age of nine.[8] Alfredo Catalani also studied with his father and other local musicians before beginning full-time studies at the Conservatory in Lucca in 1863 at the age of nine.[9] Even Pietro Mascagni, whose father was a baker, managed to receive lessons from a local organist and a baritone in Livorno sufficient to enable him to be accepted as a composition student at the age of thirteen by Alfredo Soffredini. A representative survey of seventy-nine Italian composers who flourished between the years 1600 and 1900 reveals that around 50 percent of them belonged to musical families while 30 percent descended from what might now be called middle-class parents who could afford to employ private local tutors. The remaining minority were similarly reliant upon early training from local maestros, whether they came from lowly origins (including Donizetti, Verdi, and Mascagni) or aristocratic backgrounds (including Boito and Franchetti).[10]

Puccini's early training was fairly typical in this respect. He began rudimentary musical studies before the age of five with his father, Michele, organist at the San Martino Cathedral and director of the Istituto musicale in Lucca.[11] After 1864 his training continued under his late father's student, Fortunato Magi (1839–82), who also inherited the title of professor of harmony and counterpoint at the Istituto and who was, coincidentally, his uncle on his mother's side. At that time Puccini sang in the choir and attended lessons at the seminary of the church of San Michele in Foro, just a few yards away from his home off the via di Poggio. Three years later, in 1867, he transferred to the larger and more prestigious Seminario di San

Martino a few blocks away, where he took elementary courses in "grammar" and also sang in the choir. By all accounts something of a lazy young scamp, Puccini was forced to repeat his final exams and completed the curriculum one year late in 1873.[12] He had started music lessons the year before with another local maestro, Carlo Giorgi, upon Magi's promotion to a position in Sarzana in 1872.[13] Puccini entered the Istituto musicale relatively late, at the age of fifteen in 1874, as an organist under the tutelage of another of his father's students, Carlo Angeloni. Already reasonably advanced, he managed to complete the course after six years rather than the usual eight, graduating in spring 1880. By the time he enrolled at the Milan Conservatory that November for a further three years of study, he was, by Lucchese standards, already a fully trained musician.

The Italian traditions embodied in the curriculum at Lucca were very conservative. They remained firmly wedded to the practical thorough-bass rules of the Neapolitan *partimento* method, notwithstanding the influence of Ramellian notions of chord roots and inversions. Prolonged and rigorous training in a species of harmony and counterpoint, differing profoundly from modern notions of these disciplines, was regarded as an essential prerequisite for composition. Verdi's suggested course of instruction for students, as outlined in a letter of 1871 to Francesco Florimo that followed his decision to decline the offer of the directorship of the Naples Conservatory, bears witness to this emphasis on craft and technique:

> Practice the fugue constantly, tenaciously, to satiety, until your hands are strong enough to bend the notes to your will. Thus you will learn to compose with confidence, will dispose the parts well, and will modulate without affectation. Study Palestrina and a few of his contemporaries. Then skip until you come to [Benedetto] Marcello [1686–1739], and direct your attention especially to his recitatives. Go to very few performances of modern operas, and don't let yourself be fascinated by beauties of harmony and instrumentation.[14]

No one seems to have seriously questioned the efficacy of this archaic method of training or to have suggested a genuine alternative until the 1850s, when a few figures in Florence and Milan began to take up the cause of Austro-German instrumental music. Such progressive ideas took decades to have any noticeable effect in conservative provincial towns such as Lucca. Maestros continued to teach according to the ways that they themselves were taught. If they harbored any doubts at all, they seldom expressed them. When Rossini, for instance, asked his teacher, Padre Stanislao Mattei, why his lessons were occupied so exclusively with contrapuntal exercises—the same ones, incidentally, that were taught at the Lucca Conservatory until at least the 1870s (see chapter 4)—the maestro replied: "This is the way it has to be done."[15] Verdi adopted precisely the same attitude to teaching when, in 1844, his father-in-law, Antonio Barezzi, sent a young musician from his hometown of Busseto to study with him in Milan. After one month of lessons, the student, Emanuele Muzio, sent home the following account to Barezzi:

> I have finished the books on harmony by Fenaroli. Now I am doing a general review. . . . [Verdi] doesn't want hidden consecutive fifths and octaves (it is well understood that any discovered are excommunicated); nor does he want all the melodic parts like a scale, with no leaps; nor to have them all ascend together in parallel motion; and none of these parts, in whatever key, should ever pass this note: [two leger lines above the stave]. The conditions are few, but the difficulty is to put them into practice. . . . Now, having finished the exercises on the scale, I am studying something else. Instead of that, I put eight consonances under the individual notes of the scale, first note against note, then two against one, etc. This is really counterpoint.[16]

Although the original Italian is clumsily formulated and occasionally ambiguous, Muzio was describing the classic "rule of the octave" (*regola dell'ottava*) method of harmonization, as set out by Fenaroli and countless other maestros. Once the basic harmonizations of the scale had been covered ("having finished the exercises on the scale"), the student could progress to simple counterpoint, involving the addition of progressively more complicated melodic designs (known variously as *attacchi, chiavette,* or *disegni*—see chapter 4) to the notes of the scale in both soprano and bass, or, as Muzio puts it, "under the individual notes of the scale." Although the reference to "note against note, then two against one" appears to indicate species counterpoint in the manner of Fux, the fact that these patterns were added to a scale makes it clear that Bolognese exercises in practical counterpoint were being described, as set out in Mattei (ca. 1824–25 and ca. 1827). Example 4.12 in chapter 4 reproduces several such exercises. In essence, they involved the addition of one-, two-, three-, four-, or eight-note simple counterpoints to the scale in bass or soprano. This method of teaching corresponds very closely to Puccini's earliest lessons in Lucca, as set out in his father's *Corso pratico di contrappunto* (1846). After a further month of scale-based exercises, Muzio mentioned the next stage in the training process, confirming at the same time Verdi's conventional reliance on the teachings of his own maestro:

> I have already started on Corelli's celebrated Opus Five, the most beautiful, most difficult, and longest. This morning I began the imitations. Maestro used the same studies which he did under Lavigna, but which he has improved upon.[17]

By "the imitations" Muzio referred to the addition of what modern musicology would call "short imitative melodic cells" to a scale-based pattern of melodic attachments (*attacchi*), which formed the foundation of more advanced fugato exercises upon a given *partimento* bass. Several examples of such exercises are given in chapter 4 (4.13–4.18). Corelli's sonatas and concertos, dating from the early 1700s, continued to be used as pedagogical models for harmony and counterpoint well into the nineteenth century because they relied so heavily on standard cadences and repetitive patterns of the sort covered in exercises.[18] The Puccini Museum in Celle di Pescaglia, Lucca, possesses a number of manuscripts that contain exercises of figured bass realizations based on Corelli's Trio Sonatas, op. 4 (1694), presumed to have been written by Puccini's younger brother, Michele, at roughly the time he was studying in Lucca, ca. 1880.[19]

II. THE ISTITUTO MUSICALE IN LUCCA

The history of musical training in Lucca may be said to have begun in earnest in 1818, when the two main churches, the San Martino Cathedral and San Michele in Foro, which had for centuries been the principal patrons of music in the town, decided to overcome their reliance on imported talent by annexing music schools to their seminaries.[20] Their sudden interest in maintaining control over music education appears to have been inspired by the start of construction on a new theater, which opened two years later as the Teatro del Giglio. Scandalized, it seems, by the thought that exposure to operatic music might corrupt their young scholars and debauch their congregation, the church fathers sought to uphold moral standards by preserving the purity of the liturgical musical traditions.

From its very inception, accordingly, institutionalized musical training
in Lucca was reactionary to the core and implacably opposed to progressive influences.

Despite these defensive moves by the church, the Teatro del Giglio
flourished from the outset, hosting major opera companies throughout
the nineteenth century and staging popular works by Bellini, Verdi, and
others. After the incorporation of Lucca into the state of Tuscany in 1847,
the performances were not quite as lavish as they had been under Duke
Carlo Lodovico, but the latest repertory was nonetheless appreciated by
the townsfolk. Apart from the gas lamps, which were installed in 1872, and
a few other modernizations (including electric lights) in 1911, the theater
remains substantially unchanged to this day.

This duality of musical life in Lucca, between the changing fashions of the theater and the conservative traditions of the church, was to
make its mark on Puccini. While evidently drawn to the cosmopolitan
lights of the stage, he remained deeply attached, at least in terms of technique, to the old teachings. It was, after all, his great-grandfather Antonio
Benedetto who ensured that the new church music schools had sufficient
teaching materials to open in 1818, by combining the Puccini family library with the smaller collection of the Seminario di San Martino to
form the most important music resource in Lucca. A catalog drawn up
at that time for use by new students may still be seen in the library of the
Istituto musicale Boccherini.[21] It lists many of the major works of western music theory from Vicentino (1555) and Zarlino (1573) to Fenaroli
(1775), Galeazzi (1791, 1796), and Asioli (1809). The original collection
was subsequently expanded by Puccini's father, Michele, upon his appointment as director of the Istituto in 1852 so as to include more recent
didactic books by such authors as Mattei (ca. 1827), Reicha (1830), Asioli
(1832), and Pacini (1834).[22] This collection formed the cornerstone of his
son's education.

Lucca's church music schools might have remained as obscure and
insignificant as the provincial organists and choir masters they produced,
had it not been for the arrival in 1835 of an internationally acclaimed composer, Giovanni Pacini, who made it his mission to unite the seminaries
into one high-quality institution.[23] His vision guided the curriculum and
ethos of the new Conservatory, from its inception through the directorship of Michele Puccini to the studentship of Michele's son, Giacomo.

During the 1820s, Pacini had enjoyed a remarkably successful career as an opera composer, especially in Naples and Milan, and was at that time widely regarded as the main rival to Rossini in Italy. By the mid-1830s, he had begun to be overshadowed by Bellini and Donizetti. It is often assumed that acquiescence in the face of such competition explains his decision to retire to the provincial town of Viareggio and to devote his energies to founding a music school.[24] This much was confirmed by Pacini himself in his autobiography: "I had to withdraw and devote myself to study—Bellini, the divine Bellini, and Donizetti had surpassed me."[25] But his withdrawal from composition was short-lived. The biggest successes of Pacini's opera career occurred during the next decade, beginning with the production of *Saffo* in Naples in 1840. Even as his career was eclipsed once again by the ascendancy of Verdi, his new operas continued to enjoy international acclaim well into the 1860s. Given this continuing professional success, and regardless of whether or not he considered his work as inferior to that of Bellini or Verdi, the question remains: Why would Pacini have chosen to take upon himself the many bureaucratic burdens of setting up a music school, when he could easily have either continued to focus on his opera career or followed Rossini's lead and enjoyed a long and unproductive retirement?

An answer may be found in a series of publications dating from the time of his decision to establish specialist music schools in Viareggio and Lucca. His historical survey of music (1834), for instance—a short book written specifically for the budding musicians of the Liceo musicale in Viareggio and the Lucchese seminaries—is guided by reverence for the Italian musical traditions and by the perceived need to preserve their teachings for future generations. This was to be achieved through the staff and students of the new Conservatory in Lucca, whose task it would be to safeguard the tradition. The zeal of his mission appears to have been shared by the maestros, including his most esteemed colleague, Michele Puccini, together with his many students. Indeed, it can hardly have gone unnoticed in the Puccini household that when Pacini delivered the funeral oration for Michele in 1864, he specifically identified young Giacomo as the next in line to take up the stewardship of the teachings and practices of the Italian traditions.[26]

Pacini's understanding of the Italian traditions was not so hidebound as to exclude contemporary Italian opera. On the contrary, he identified

the old methods as alive and flourishing, particularly in the works of
Rossini. In answer to rhetorical questions such as "How does one sing
the praises of this Genius? How does one analyze him?" Pacini embarked
upon a detailed survey of the Italian traditions, tracing the foundations
of Rossini's success to lineages of teachings by well-schooled maestros.
Underpinning the entire edifice was the old ecclesiastical style, which he
described as the "sacred flame" of the tradition, passed on through the
generations by maestros such as the following:

> Maestro Padre Mattei, student of the celebrated Maestro Padre Martini,
> Furlanetto, student of the great Valotti, Minoja, Asioli, Basili, Santucci,
> Raimondi, Quilici, those who, like custodians of the sacred flame, passed on
> the true principles, based on ecclesiastical music, to posterity.[27]

This is a curious list with which to support such grand claims. Perhaps unsurprisingly, Pacini reserved places of honor for his own teach-
ers: Padre Stanislao Mattei, with whom he studied harmony and counterpoint in Bologna, and Bonaventura Furlanetto, erstwhile director of
St Mark's in Venice, with whom he studied composition. Otherwise,
Pacini seems to have intended the list to encompass representatives from
each of the main Italian musical centers. Padre Mattei represented the
Bolognese school, from which emerged Donizetti and Rossini. Francesco
Antonio Vallotti (1697–1780) was associated with a Padua school, as was
Giuseppe Tartini (1692–1770), whose name is conspicuously absent, even
though he worked alongside Vallotti. The next three names in Pacini's
list all occupied the chair in composition at the Milan Conservatory:
Bonifazio Asioli (1808–14), Ambrogio Minoja (1814–25), and Francesco
Basily (1827–37), a student of Mattei. (The short tenures of Vincenzo
Federici and Gaetano Piantanida were passed over without comment.)
Pietro Raimondi was associated with a Roman school of counterpoint,
even though, like Mercadante and Spontini, he studied in Naples with
Giacomo Tritto. The remaining two figures, Marco Santucci and Massimiliano Quilici, were instrumental in the foundation of the Istituto
musicale in Lucca and were presumably included in order to establish,
for the benefit of the young students, the importance of Lucca as a musical center.

Pacini's historical survey of the Italian traditions was as vague and
piecemeal as his list of maestros.[28] It began not with a composer but with

the poet credited with perfecting the art of *poesia melodrammatica,* Pietro Trapassi (1698–1782), otherwise known by his Hellenized pseudonym, Metastasio. The first composer to warrant a mention was the Neapolitan Leonardo Vinci (1690–1730), who was credited with introducing a "better taste" and "a more suitable [*conveniente*] form for arias," meaning presumably the ternary *da capo.* After declaring that Vinci's reforms were enhanced by Pergolesi's individual brand of "expressive melody," Pacini abandoned any semblance of coherent chronology in a move that was evidently intended to impress upon the young readers the synchronicity of the tradition and the elevated provenance of their textbooks: "In the same era as Leonardo Vinci there was Durante, the student of Scarlatti, Niccolò [*sic*] Sala, and Fenaroli." Shifting closer to the present, Pacini considered the best representatives of the Italian traditions to be Niccolò Jomelli, Niccolò Piccinni, and Antonio Sacchini. Shamelessly plagiarizing the entry on "Italy" in Dr. Lichtenthal's musical dictionary,[29] he reported that "the first perfected the vocal aria around 1757, the second gave the correct form to the duet during the same era, and the third contributed ways to perfect melody toward 1770." Even though this summary probably seemed as helpful then as it does now, Pacini deemed it sufficient to conclude: "You know therefore with absolute precision the rules pertaining to composition and to good performance, as the most beautiful Italian geniuses competed to capture beauty and true good taste in music." Finally, the students were exhorted to study the classic works contained in the library, including "Martini, Sabbatini, Fenaroli, Rousseau, Arteaga, Gervasoni, the musical dictionary of doctor Lichtentall [*sic*], and many other distinguished authors."

Pacini would have found Lucca a fertile ground for the cultivation of this educational project. Not only was the town's musical life steeped in ancient church traditions, but its most prominent musician at that time, Marco Santucci, appears to have shared, if not partly inspired, Pacini's reactionary views. Santucci had studied in Naples with Fenaroli before arriving in Lucca as *maestro di cappella* in 1790.[30] Seven years later he succeeded Pasquale Anfossi as maestro of the church of San Giovanni Laterano in Rome, but he continued to maintain strong connections with Lucca, being elected in 1808 to the position of *canonico della metropolitana* and taking on apprentice composers such as the young Michele Puccini. Fenaroli evidently thought very highly of his former student. In a letter of January 18, 1811, regarding his fifth book of *partimenti,* he wrote: "Only you, who belong to my school and understand a lot, can teach how to harmonize them."[31]

Santucci set out his manifesto for musical training in a series of three dissertations, published together as *Sulla melodia, sull'armonia e sul metro* (On Melody, Harmony, and Meter), which sought to uphold the "true" Italian traditions in opposition to the pernicious influence of "Gothic irregularity" (*gotiche irregolarità*) and the "complexities and sometimes barbarous chords of foreign harmony."[32] Although the book was dedicated to the young students of the Lucchese seminaries, it contained hardly any tuition, being more a polemical statement of conservative resistance to change. Indeed, Santucci's respect for tradition was so intense that it prevented him from making any contribution to music theory for the benefit of his students, higher authorities having already pronounced on the subject: "How many learned and masterful authors on music theory have already written? Among the Italians, Zarlino, Tevo, Tartini, Martini, and Count Riccati; and amongst the foreigners, Rameau, Fux, D'Alembert, and Rousseau are the most celebrated names."[33] Indeed, Santucci tended to append a list of associated maestros to every musical practice, as if to reinforce its authority with the weight of tradition. These lists almost always led toward fellow students of Fenaroli, usually Domenico Cimarosa or Niccolò Zingarelli.

With the support of the relevant authorities and prominent local musicians such as Santucci, Pacini's incipient *liceo,* which had been running unofficially within the seminaries of Lucca since at least as early as 1835, was incorporated through a municipal document signed by Duke Carlo Lodovico di Borbone on July 10, 1838. While Pacini assumed the directorship, the founding faculty was made up of the following local maestros: Eugenio Galli (*solfeggio* and counterpoint), Matteo Quilici (rudiments), Massimiliano Quilici (*bel canto* and accompaniment), and Giuseppe Rustici (piano).[34] The title of Royal Musical Institute (Reale Istituto musicale) was officially sanctioned on August 14, 1842, again by Duke Carlo, with Pacini confirmed in his position as director and professor of composition.[35] This helps to explain why the date of foundation of the Conservatory is nearly always given as 1842, even though it is clear that the school was up and running with the same staff as early as 1838. The new title also came with an expanded constitution and set of rules, setting out a full curriculum. These suggest that the Reale istituto was originally modeled on the conservatories of Naples and was therefore closer in outlook to a charitable institution or orphanage than a fee-paying school. It stipulated that a small number of local children, who were deemed talented enough and worthy of support, would be admitted in order to train as professional musicians.

Pacini found it increasingly difficult to balance the demands of the Reale istituto with an international career, and in 1852 he ceded the positions of director and professor of composition to his favorite Lucchese maestro, Michele Puccini. The change of leadership was timed to coincide with a formal amendment to the constitution on June 4, made necessary in any case by the recent return of Lucca to Tuscany. Henceforth, the school was known as Istituto comunale (or Liceo musicale). Michele served as director until his death in 1864, after which the aged Pacini was forced once again to take over. Twenty-four days after he too had passed away, on December 30, 1867, the Istituto comunale changed its name to the Istituto musicale "Giovanni Pacini," in honor of its founder. It is now known as the Istituto musicale "Luigi Boccherini," having been renamed as part of the celebrations surrounding the bicentennial of the birth of that great eighteenth-century Lucchese maestro, on February 19, 1943.

During Giacomo Puccini's time as a student at the Istituto musicale, eight years of study was the norm. Four years of rudiments were followed by a further three years of advanced studies, the whole course being rounded off with a final year of "composition." The curriculum consisted almost entirely of musical training with only the most basic instruction in other subjects. From Article 13 of the "Rules," it is possible to discover something of what Puccini would have covered in his final year:

> The Professor of Composition shall deliver his course in one year, and shall cover the following topics: the expression of the text in vocal melody, the phrase in comparison with the different poetic meters, the construction of periods, the nature of the human voice, the manner of composing arias, duets, trios and other concerted pieces, and the use of the chorus.[36]

The underlying ideology of the curriculum remained heavily influenced by the churches and by the conservative traditions championed by Santucci and Pacini. Writing in 1871, just before the young Giacomo Puccini was to begin his studies, local maestro Domenico Cerù confirmed

that strict counterpoint and the old ecclesiastical styles were taught rigor-
ously within the Istituto musicale, in order that students should "succeed
in writing better than the hack maestros of recent times."[37] He justified
this approach by pointing out that musicians destined for a career in
church music had little need for familiarity with "the German school,"
by which he appeared to mean progressive instrumental traditions of the
nineteenth century as opposed to Protestant church music. It was indeed
the case that the main musical appointments in Lucca remained within
the gift of the churches. The most senior musician in Lucca during Puccini's years of study was neither Carlo Angeloni nor Fortunato Magi, but
rather Luigi Nerici, *maestro di musica* at the Seminario Arcivescovile di
San Martino and *maestro di canto ecclesiastico* at the Seminario Decanale
di San Michele. He more than shared Pacini's vision of the "sacred flame"
of the Italian traditions. In a speech delivered in Lucca on June 30, 1869,
and published as *Dell'origine della musica moderna* (On the Origins of
Modern Music, 1872), Nerici reinforced the status of "our celebrated Lucchese Gasparini, Gemignani [sic], and Boccherini" by affording them
pride of place within a questionable historical survey from antiquity to
the present, culminating in the modern school of Rossini, Verdi, and, last
but by no means least, Pacini. What Nerici defined as the "chief school"
of Italian music was essentially the Bolognese and Paduan branches of
the *partimento* tradition (Vallotti, Martini, Mattei), traced back to their
Neapolitan roots: "the most renowned composers and *capiscuola* were
Durante, Monteverde [sic], Leo, Scarlatti, Anfossi, Jommelli, Vallotti,
Martini, Mattei." His parting words to his audience left little doubt as to
the importance of the church in Lucchese musical life:

> And here I shall finish, in the hope that I have demonstrated through this
> history that the art of music, the most beautiful of the arts, was born in Italy
> together with the Church, was brought up and nourished by the Church, and
> since becoming an adult has wandered throughout the world carrying the
> song and the name of Italy to foreign peoples.[38]

III. SCARPIA AND THE *PARTIMENTO* CADENCE

Elementary student exercises of the sort recommended in old books of
regole were rarely considered worthy of preservation within conservatory archives. In any case they were more often played or sung than

written down. It is, however, possible to find evidence of Puccini's training in the *partimento* tradition within the music of his operas. He appears to have drawn inspiration from even the most basic pedagogical
exercises.

One of the foundations of the Neapolitan method of training, its first
lesson, so to speak, involved the three basic *partimento* cadences: simple,
compound, and double. They were usually taught in rudimentary form
over a tonic-dominant-tonic bass, as may be seen in books of *regole* dating
at least as far back as Durante (1730s?), although their precise attributes
could differ depending on the individual maestro.[39] According to Sanguinetti, the three cadences were generally ordered according to the number
of separate beats required by the dominant:

> The simple cadence uses only the dominant triad (or seventh) and oc-
> cupies one beat; the compound cadence uses a 4–3 suspension and takes up
> two beats; the double cadence needs four beats and consists of the formula
> $\frac{5}{3}\frac{6}{4}\frac{5}{4}\frac{5}{3}$. The performer can choose any of these cadences in one of the three
> positions.[40]

Example 2.1 presents a version of the teachings copied by Michele
Puccini from Sala (1794), which would have been used in harmony and
accompaniment lessons in Lucca during the 1870s. Realizations of his
original figured-bass indications have been added in small note heads
on an upper stave, corresponding closely to those given in the original
source.[41] As can be seen, the simple cadence (*cadenza semplice*) encompassed only root position triads, to which the compound cadence (*cadenza composta*) added a suspension, involving either the root, third, or
fifth of the triad as the suspended (tied) note. Implicit within Puccini's
figures for the compound cadence was the use of the three (hand) positions at the keyboard, which determined whether the root, third, or fifth
of the triad appeared in the soprano voice. The double cadence (*cadenza
doppia*), omitted from example 2.1, added a further suspension to the
cadenza composta. In Neapolitan theory these cadences were regarded
also as basic tonal structures, consisting of an opening tonic, a central
dominant, and a closing tonic. The space between the opening tonic and
dominant could be filled in various ways, for instance, through passing
notes and consonant skips, giving rise to variants called "cadential progressions."[42] One such progression supplemented the basic cadences with

Cadenze semplici

Cadenze composte

2.1. Michele Puccini, *Corso pratico di contrappunto* (1846), 1.

what would now be called a dominant preparation, such as the one shown in example 2.2, which was dubbed the "mixed cadence" (*cadenza mista*) by Tartini, since it appeared to him to combine the notes of both perfect and plagal cadences.[43] Staffa's Neapolitan method (1849) contained page after page of exercises involving this "cadence of natural tones" (*cadenza de' tuoni naturali*), as he called it, encompassing every key and incorporating almost every conceivable variety of suspension pattern.[44] Derived from the "First Lesson of Counterpoint," according to the teachings of Bellini's maestro, Niccolò Zingarelli, these "cadences of natural tones" were repeated by students over and over again in the three positions until fully assimilated and learned by rote.[45] Example 2.3 sets out a reduced version of the same exercise. It repeats only the first two chords of the cadence and omits the final chord of resolution (in this case E♭ major)

2.2. A "cadence of natural tones" (*cadenza de' tuoni naturali*), "mixed cadence" (*cadenza mista*), or "compound cadence" (*cadenza composta*) with preparation.

in order to concentrate on the essential suspension pattern. To the eye trained in modern notions of tonal harmony and counterpoint, there are, however, a couple of anomalies apparent in example 2.3. The suspended soprano note E♭ of the cadence in first position is prepared by a dissonant seventh, just as the note G of the cadence in second position is prepared by a dissonant ninth. Such licenses would not be tolerated in counterpoint classes nowadays. Yet they were an integral part of the Neapolitan tradition, as confirmed by perhaps the most trusted authority throughout the nineteenth century, Fenaroli, through a musical example very similar to that given in the opening measures of example 2.3. It relates to his guidance "Concerning Dissonances, or the Suspension of the Fourth": "Note that the fourth can also be prepared by the minor seventh and by the diminished fifth. To prepare the fourth by the minor seventh, the *partimento* [i.e., bass] should rise a fourth; that is, [as if] from the fifth to the first degree of the scale."[46] By the same token, the additional dissonance belonging to the cadence in second position is merely a doubling at the third, while the suspended ninth of the cadence in third position is specifically allowed by Fenaroli: "The ninth can be prepared by the third and by the fifth. . . . To prepare it by the fifth, the *partimento* [bass] should rise a fourth or descend a fifth."[47]

Regardless of such arcane discussions over the rules concerning dissonance, by the nineteenth century these old-fashioned cadence formulas were of practical use for only the most conservative ecclesiastical styles. Having to learn them, especially through repetitive exercises as set out in Staffa (1849) and De Vecchis (1850) and as exemplified in example 2.3, must have seemed inordinately tedious and pedantic. This may help to explain why Puccini based the finale of act 1 of *Tosca* upon repetitions of similar *cadenze composte* (example 2.4). The association with outmoded church rituals and, by implication, Baron Scarpia's hypocritical

2.3. An exercise in compound cadences in the three positions.

lip-service to religion must have been obvious to any musicians who had passed through the Neapolitan training regime. In this finale, Puccini goes beyond any mere pastiche of ecclesiastical style by reducing an entire tradition of church music to its most basic and fundamental pedagogical exercise, widely known as "the first lesson of counterpoint." The mindless repetitions of the cadence formula, devoid of feeling or purpose and varied and distorted in response to Scarpia's vocalized thoughts, serve to underline the character's specious and self-serving faith.

IV. THE CONSERVATORIO DI MILANO

Given that the curriculum so steadfastly maintained at Lucca during the 1870s would have seemed antiquated even to Rossini, let alone to an aspiring young composer keen to make a splash in the modish world of opera, it is hardly surprising that Puccini chose to undertake further studies at the Milan Conservatory upon his graduation. Milan, together with Florence, had by that time emerged as one of the undisputed centers for progressive music in Italy. Not only was the city alive with numerous societies promoting concerts of new and seemingly new orchestral and chamber music,[48] but it could also boast the most prestigious opera house in Italy, La Scala, as well as the most powerful and influential publishing firm, Ricordi. Since the 1850s, moreover, the Conservatory had gone out of its way to forge strong links with both institutions, thereby offering unparalleled opportunities for young composers to enter the profession.

The Milan Conservatory was founded by decree of Eugène Napoleon on September 18, 1807, in emulation of, and in competition with, the Neapolitan conservatories.[49] According to Article 6 of its first constitution, there were to be offered free of charge twenty-four studentships, lasting a minimum of ten years, for those applicants who could pass the follow-

2.4. Puccini, *Tosca,* act 1, R80, mm. 9–18 (Milan: Ricordi, 1900).

ing five requirements: students should be over the age of ten, should be sane and of good health, should possess some aptitude for one of the arts, should be able to read and write, and should belong to honest and decent parents who could prove their need for support. On April 23, 1808, the first appointments were announced, including, as director (*censore*) and professor of composition, Bonifazio Asioli, master of chamber and chapel at the Milanese court.

The political unrest that forced the Conservatory to close in 1848 and 1849 instigated a radical reconceptualization of its mission. On July 2, 1850, a committee was established to reform the statute, led by the new *censore,* Lauro Rossi, and the professor of singing, Alberto Mazzucato. Their reforms were adopted almost immediately. In an attempt to bring the Conservatory into line with international rivals such as Paris, Brussels, and Leipzig, they radically increased the number of students and abandoned the charitable status of the institution, transforming it into a public *liceo* with the following staff: three professors of singing; two professors each of composition, accompaniment and harmony, elements and literature of music, piano, and violin; and one professor for each of the remaining instrumental disciplines. The syllabus was broadened to include a range of other subjects, including Italian literature and geography; religion; philosophy of music; history; declamation; French; deportment, mime, and ballet; and "civilized values and honest living" (*i precetti di civilà e dell'onesto vivere*). The maximum length of studies was set at ten years for composers, seven for singers, and eight or nine for the various instrumentalists. Regional dialects were forbidden, and there was a strict dress code.[50]

In 1878, shortly before Puccini's arrival, it was decided that the composition course—for first study composers, not for those taking composition as part of their complementary studies—should be divided into three distinct "schools," each directed by two professors. These schools were intended to form a progressive program of study that could be compressed depending on individual requirements. The complete course would consist of three initial years of harmony, three years of counterpoint and fugue, and four years of "composition proper" (*composizione propriamente detta*). In practice, few composition students took the full ten years to complete the course.[51] Upon enrollment in November 1880, Puccini struck a deal with the authorities to compress the final composition course into three years rather than four.

The main staff members of the Conservatory during Puccini's studentship and their periods of tenure were:

> Chair of composition: Antonio Bazzini (1873–82); Amilcare Ponchielli (1882–86); Cesare Dominiceti (1881–88)
>
> Professors of harmony and counterpoint: Michele Saladino (1876–1912); Angelo Panzini (1877–86)
>
> Complementary studies—theory and *solfeggio:* Giacomo Treves (1850–88); Giuseppe Gerli (1859–84); Eduardo Perelli (1876–85); Alberto Giovannini (1881–86)
>
> Complementary studies—harmony and counterpoint: Giuseppe Gerli (1864–85); Gaetano Coronaro (1876–94); Amintore Galli (1878–1908)
>
> Complementary studies—history of music: Amintore Galli (1878–1906)
>
> Complementary studies—poetic and dramatic literature: Lodovico Corio (1877–1911)

Puccini would hardly have required (or welcomed) further tuition in the disciplines of harmony and counterpoint. His technical assurance was already sufficiently evident in the entrance exam, which he found a "pushover" (*sciocchezza*), as well as in compositions dating from his time in Lucca, such as the Preludio a orchestra of 1876. Milan offered instead a gateway into the musical world beyond Lucca, beyond even the rest of Italy. There Puccini could become familiar with the latest international developments, could make professional contacts such as his fellow Lucchese, Alfredo Catalani, and could hear the views of progressives such as Franco Faccio and Arrigo Boito. He appears to have been rather gifted at such "networking" activities.

As for his studies, he applied himself just enough to fulfill the requirements of the course, concentrating primarily on the main end-of-year composition submissions—despite assurances to the contrary in letters to his mother.[52] He even joked of submitting the same work twice to different tutors. This may have been only a partial confession that served to disguise graver misdemeanors. Could it be mere coincidence that many of the fugues and pastiche works completed in examinations at Milan derive from model subjects and *partimenti* contained in his father's course of counterpoint? They are in any case written in the archaic style characteristic of Lucca. A Fugue in E minor, for instance, which Dieter Schickling dates between 1881 and 1883 on the evidence of examiners' markings on similar papers, appears as number thirty-nine in Michele Puccini's list of model fugue subjects.[53] If Puccini's "Milan" student works were indeed mostly written during his studies in Lucca, this would help to explain why he subsequently donated them to the library in Lucca rather than Milan.

This is by no means to suggest that Puccini learned nothing at the Milan Conservatory. On the contrary, as many commentators have noted, his first professor of composition, Antonio Bazzini, played a crucial role in introducing him to a broader range of composers and especially to the latest currents in instrumental music. Nevertheless, the master could hardly have been more different from the student. Bazzini had spent most of his career at the cutting edge of the progressive movement in Italy, which, as described in chapter 1, sought to distance itself from the formula-ridden opera tradition and to embrace instead a more international style, centered around chamber and symphonic music. Puccini must have appeared, by contrast, a typical product of the old school, steeped in defunct church traditions and hopelessly behind the times, aspiring to compose only opera.

Bazzini had made his name primarily as a virtuoso violinist, as leader of a successful string quartet, and as a composer of short character pieces. He toured Europe from an early age and lived in Germany from 1841 until 1845, where he performed as soloist in the premiere of Mendelssohn's Violin Concerto. Until 1864 he resided in his native Brescia, but spent most of the time away on tour or in Paris. The Bazzini String Quartet, which performed his own compositions as well as the Viennese classics and contemporary German works, was a mainstay of many Società del Quartetto concerts throughout northern Italy. His one attempt to gain entry to the lucrative world of opera, *Turanda* (1867), ended in complete failure. During the 1870s, he continued to promote Austro-German instrumental music and to emulate the latest styles. There can be few Italian works more closely tied to the "music of the future" than his symphonic poem *King Lear* (1874), later transcribed for piano by his friend Hans von Bülow. But the style of this and similar works by Bazzini seems to owe more to the Romantic *Charakerstücke* of an earlier age than to the more uncompromising avant-garde represented by Liszt and Wagner.

Upon the death of Stefano Ronchetti Monteviti in November 1881, Bazzini was called on to assume the directorship of the Milan Conservatory. As a result, after only one year of study, Puccini had to transfer to a newly appointed professor, Amilcare Ponchielli. The change was fortuitous. Ponchielli would have been identified by Bazzini as more closely aligned with the young Puccini's background and interests. He represented the last bastion of the old schools at the Milan Conservatory, having been turned down for a professorship in complementary harmony and counterpoint in 1868 owing to pressure from the progressives of the Quartet Society, including Abramo Basevi and Bazzini (who favored Franco Faccio for the post). Following the success of Ponchielli's opera *La gioconda* in 1876 and especially upon its return to La Scala in 1880, his appointment in 1881 proved unstoppable, carried forward also by what appears to have been an upsurge in nostalgic nationalism prompted by the influence of foreign music, which increased in strength throughout that decade and culminated in the revealing and disproportionate adulation bestowed upon Mascagni's spectacularly successful *Cavalleria rusticana* (1890). While it is impossible to determine exactly what Puccini learned from Ponchielli during the final two years of his three-year course, it seems fair to suggest that for the most part it was not Austro-German

instrumental music. Based on his first opera, *Le Villi* (1883–85), on graduation from Milan Puccini was a technically fluent but stylistically limited
young composer, who relied on an uneasy alliance of traditional operatic
formulas and instrumental effects gleaned from Romantic *Charakter-
stücke*. His most assiduous and effective period of learning appears to
have been largely self-directed, during the decade between *Le Villi* and
his first masterpiece deserving of international acclaim, *Manon Lescaut*
(1893). Puccini's second opera, *Edgar* (1889), occupies the central point
in this search for an individual and artistically (commercially) successful
voice.

THREE

Lessons in Dramatic Composition I: Rhythm

I. RHYTHM WITHOUT MEASURE, ACCENT WITHOUT BEAT

In nineteenth-century Italian usage, the word for musical rhythm, *ritmo,* encompassed a far broader range of concepts and meanings than its modern counterpart. It could, for instance, be used to refer to fluid subjective movements of the individual mind or "soul" in terms of emotions and feelings, especially of the sort induced through the sentiments of poetry or music and manifested in the ebb and flow of a reading or performance. Owing to the overwhelming dominance of vocal music in the Italian traditions, it could also signify the various meters and accents of verse, denoting either the musical "rhythm" of one individual line of poetic verse or, somewhat confusingly, a succession of several such verses, in much the same way that the singular word "verse" can now be used to mean both an individual poetic line and an entire stanza. In this sense, as mentioned earlier, melodic "rhythm" (*ritmo*) was effectively synonymous with "phrase" (*frase*), which could also signify an individual setting of a line or two of verse or a series of similar such settings. A closely associated but essentially independent system of harmonic rhythm, regulated by a succession of weak and strong impulses within the instrumental accompaniment, was considered to supplement these vocal verse phrases. Only rarely, and usually in rudimentary books for beginners, was *ritmo* used to convey the idea of a regular pulse subdivided symmetrically into the beats and measures of a time signature.[1]

A leading article entitled "A Glance at the State of Studies in Musical Aesthetics," which appeared anonymously in the Milanese journal *L'Italia musicale* in 1853, bears witness to this crucial distinction between regular measure and poetic-musical rhythm. Taking issue with Moritz Hauptmann's recently published theory of harmony and meter—which remains fundamental to modern theory and practice in its insistence on the conceptual primacy of regular meter—it emphasized the essential identity of poetic verse and musical rhythm, neither of which, it claimed, were wholly bound by the artificial construct of the measure. This was merely an approximate means of notation in accordance with established systems. The regular divisions of the bar line were a way to capture and "contain" on the page the more or less free and unruly flow of the melody or poetry, as delivered or conceived. They did not, in themselves, constitute rhythm:

> Rhythm is the bond that unites music so closely with poetry, since the harmony of verses depends upon rhythm, which, in the ultimate analysis, does not differ from musical rhythm. . . . The *measure* signifies the relations of rhythm to time, which essentially contains it, but not always in accordance with the absolute rigor of rule by which it is subjugated in our musical system.[2]

An associated article published in 1854, probably by the same author, sought to clarify these definitions more precisely for the benefit of the journal's readership. It reiterated that rhythm was not to be confused with the regular beats of what would now be called the tempo. Bar lines, time signatures, and their divisions were seen to be little more than elements of a separate and inadequate system of notation, far removed from the "primordial" element of rhythm, which was essentially free from such constraints:

> Melody and rhythm are thus closely united. The former is the meaning developed by a succession of sounds; the latter is the form and the proportions of that succession. Melody is the life principle and the soul of music; rhythm is its breath. . . . A few [musical treatises] have confused it [rhythm] with the *beat,* and have even gone so far as to say that the beat generated the rhythm; not considering that rhythm is an essential, primordial element, preceding all systems. The beat is only a mundane component, resulting from certain metrical and rational divisions of the tempo, which is modified by standard degrees of slowness or quickness; it is only a conventional element and relates to music in the same way that the laws of versification relate to poetry. And yet it is said today [e.g., by Hauptmann] that the beat is so integral to our musical system that it appears to be as important as an essential element. Melody flows forth from the composer's fantasy, informed

by the beat, laid out according to its form, [and] subject to the alternating
succession of strong and weak beats. But this is not to say that melody cannot momentarily depart from this game.[3]

Ritmo was regarded as something quite different from the orderly
arrangement of regular beats and measures that served as the means to
record its outlines in written form. But neither could it be explained entirely by comparison with the meters of poetry. Verse rhythms, however
expressive and flexible, still had to scan onto an underlying succession of
strong and weak impulses. This fundamental concept of a union of two
separate rhythmic systems was touched upon in the Neapolitan journal
La Musica of 1883, as part of an article which, although purporting to deal
with the issue of accompaniment in relation to melody, actually sought
to lambast the utterly different rhythmic techniques of Wagnerian orchestral melody:

> *Rhythm,* as beaten with uniform insistence in the accompaniments of
> the past, caused less harm to the work of art than that which gives rise to the
> muddled abuse of rashly conceived complexities. This [uniform rhythm],
> although monotonous and trivial, rendered the melody free to trip lightly
> over the top and to dominate the whole, bound only by the natural laws of
> *tonality, harmony, and rhythm.*[4]

This chapter will explore contemporary theories and methods for
mapping verse meters onto musical phrases through the interpretation
of poetic syllables and accents as note values and for scanning the resulting melodic rhythms onto an accompanying framework of strong and
weak impulses. It will also cover the practice—evident in the music of
Puccini, among others—of using such rhythmic phrases to structure
longer sections of melody even when they differed from the meter of a
given text. Polymetric stanzas, for instance, employing a variety of verse
types, could be set to a series of phrases founded on a rhythmic realization of a single, regular poetic line. While the interpretation of phrases
through verse meters has become something of a commonplace in recent
studies of opera, ideas concerning the incongruence of text and *ritmo* or
a "counterpoint" of different *ritmi,* which may or may not coincide with
the actual words, as evident in Asioli's (1832) separation of rhythm into
melodic design and rhythmic impulse or Staffa's (1856) analytical demonstration of the two systems (explained with reference to example 3.3

below), have received very little attention in the literature.[5] This may be explained partly by the considerable disagreement that existed among Italian nineteenth-century writers as to the means for putting into practice the notion of a fundamental identity of poetry/verse and melody/rhythm. The survey of theories and methods that follows takes account of this diversity of opinion as well as the influence of alternative ideas from abroad.

The ambiguity that surrounded Italian definitions of rhythmic practice throughout the nineteenth century could be traced in part to an earlier division of poetry into the regular "metrical" verse of ancient Greece and Rome and the more elastic "harmonic" verse of modern times, which was not governed by fixed, quantitative correlations between rhythmic durations and syllables and accents.[6] Lichtenthal's dictionary described the ancient "metrical" form of *Ritmopea,* as it was (mis)understood at the beginning of the nineteenth century, in terms of an application of fixed rhythmic durations to poetic syllables:

> In ancient times, when music was still very simple and intended only for singing, musical rhythm was strictly regulated by the rhythm of the sung verses. All syllables were either long or short. One long syllable was twice the duration of a short syllable; the union of several long or short syllables formed the musical feet, and the union of these formed the rhythm.[7]

In a musical setting, a modern "harmonic" poetic text could assume, in Fabbri's words, "clear metrical features, fixing the discretionary and vague qualities of each of its syllabic durations and restricting the freedom of their articulation overall by specifying it with notation."[8] But the resulting musical rhythm would constitute only one among countless possible interpretations. Literary stresses could be compressed into shorter durations or stretched over longer spans. Elisions in the text (the merging of adjacent vowels from two separate words) could be ignored, altering the meter. Melismatic settings made it difficult to distinguish "true musical syllables," in Choron's terms, from elaborations and extensions of them.[9] It was this underlying freedom of contemporary verse that writers in the late eighteenth century were keen to find ways to regulate and control, as witnessed by the debate between Stefano Arteaga and Vincenzo Manfredini during the 1780s,[10] which was informed by Giovenale Sacchi's earlier attempt to define precisely the relation of verse meter to musical rhythm through a "universal theory of versification."[11] Because this speculative theory sought to merge rhythm for dance (*tempo nel ballo*) and for instrumentalists with that for vocal music, it postulated a reduction in the number of types of poetic feet to just four species (anapestic, dactylic, iambic, and trochaic), which generated four corresponding species of rhythm through their regular repetition. A few scholars continued this search for a general theory of rhythm founded on an analogy with the regular metrical feet of Greek and Latin poetry, including Hiller (1779), Burney (1789), Venini (1798), Forkel (1788–1801), Bonesi (1806), and Baini (1820), but the resulting theories were altogether too rigid to be of practical use. Unable to offer supporting music examples, discussions of "ancient" meter and regular feet soon disappeared in Italy. Baini's essay of 1820 was already an anachronism.[12]

As attested by the passage from *L'Italia musicale* (1854) cited above, such "Enlightenment" attempts to rationalize compositional practice and to establish uniform procedures for translating poetic meters into musical rhythms failed to take hold in nineteenth-century Italian traditions.[13] Indeed, at the turn of the twentieth century, Amintore Galli continued to maintain the distinction between a repetitive pulse, whether composed of feet or accents, and *ritmo,* which he defined as "an aesthetic ordering of a succession of musical values (figures), which are repeated identically or similarly one or more times. There is the rhythmic accent, which is repeated isochronously, and there is the rhythmic design, which is being spoken of here."[14] In defining the strong and weak beats of the measure through an analogy with breathing, which also, separately, underpinned the "musical figure" or "rhythmic design" founded upon the verse meter, Galli was careful to keep the two concepts apart:

> The breath is the prototype of the musical measure and the generator of the phrase rhythm, comprised of two physiological instants: inhalation and exhalation, the *thesis* (strong accent) and the *arsis* (weak accent), the *downbeat* and the *upbeat* of the musical measure.[15]

Although a basic pattern of syllables and accents derived from a standard Italian verse type could, in theory, be scanned with reasonable accuracy onto a series of note values, it would remain an approximation, an abstract representation of a mode of expression far too complex to be encapsulated by such a formula. In this context, it might be relevant to mention that melodic composition was taught primarily through exercises in *vocalizzi* and *solfeggi,* which were intended to be *sung* by the students (see chapters 4 and 6). The concerns that evidently dissuaded most Italian maestros from representing poetic meters through simple musical formulas, in the manner of Sacchi (1770), appear to have been similar to those that continue to inform the transcription of oral musical traditions: musical notation seldom proves nuanced enough to capture every expressive fluctuation. As Johann Hiller commented, in a discussion on ornamentation in vocal performance drawn directly from Mancini (1774): "The material is often so intricate that it can only be grasped through intuition and never fully expressed by words. Likewise, even notation cannot represent it well, or if so, only with imperfections."[16] For much the same reasons, in the Italian traditions (as represented by the survey of historical accounts below), the nature of *ritmo* was often discussed in words, but seldom illustrated by formulas in notes. The importance of rhythmic freedom in the delivery and perception of vocal melody, and its association with such crucial factors as meaning, sentiment, and expression, appear to have discouraged Italian writers from specifying too precisely, especially in notated abstractions or generalizations, the musical equivalents of regular poetic verse meters that, as modern scholars from Lippmann (1973–75) and Moreen (1975) to Gossett (2006) and Giger (2008) have noted, served to underpin the setting of an operatic phrase in the nineteenth century.[17] Students at the conservatories would learn the basic rules of versification and "the expression of the text in vocal melody and the phrase in comparison with the different poetic meters," according to the official regulations of the Lucca Conservatory mentioned in chapter 2, but when it came to applying them, they appeared to rely upon mental constructs of the resulting "rhythms" (*ritmi*) and observations of existing practice. Some sources did provide general accounts of relations between poetic feet, meters, and musical rhythm—for instance, Baini (1820) or Ritorni (1841)—but more detailed practical guidance, as found in Reicha (1830) or Asioli (1832), was usually provided in the form of extracts taken from scores and interpreted by analytical annotations.

The essential freedom of vocal rhythm from the beats of a regular pulse and the bar lines depicted on the page was rationalized through the notion of *accento musicale,* which may be translated quite literally as

the (speech) accent of music. It referred to the expressive nuances generated through a variety of devices that together determined the contours
and fluctuations of the vocal phrase. Just as in speech, the meaning of
words may depend to a large extent upon the mode of delivery of the
speaker, through variables such as intonation, speed, and smoothness or
abruptness; so too was vocal melody considered to have its own "accent,"
through which the text was expressed.

Amintore Galli's lexicon (1902) defined *accento* quite simply as the
"inflection of the voice," adding that it was "synonymous with expression."[18] But a glance at earlier writings on the subject suggests that, far
from being considered merely as an aspect of vocal delivery, *accento musicale* was a more integral factor that dictated a number of compositional
decisions. Luigi De Macchi, for instance, offered the following all-encompassing definition in his musical grammar (ca. 1830):

> Q. What is meant by *Accento musicale*?
> A. It refers to the phrase rhythm that regulates the entire phrase or pe
> riod; the several parts of a period controlled by the strong and weak beats of
> the measure; the increase and decrease of force; the smoothness or jagged
> ness; the slowing down and speeding up; the loud and soft; in sum all that
> can give color to the phrase.[19]

It is not immediately clear whether these features were intended to
relate to the composer's choice of setting or to the singer's style of performance. Much of De Macchi's description could be taken to refer to
what would now be called *rubato,* the expressive molding of parameters
such as rhythm and volume left to the discretion of the singer. Giovanni
Pacini's more detailed definition (1834) leaves little doubt, however, that
accento musicale related not just to aspects of performance but also to devices used by the composer to capture the appropriate expression of the
text. This definition was most likely the one taught to the young Puccini.
It was, after all, written by the recently deceased founder of the *istituto
musicale* that subsequently bore his name. As Pacini explained:

> The *Accento,* according to the usual understanding, or, better put, ac
> cording to nature, is none other than a modification of the tempo of the
> vocal part, which must maintain the appropriate key and comply with the
> syllables, the words, and the feeling that make up a period or speech. For
> this reason, three things must be considered: firstly, the note agreeing with

the syllable, whether low or high, short or long; secondly, the relation of the word to the following words through the connecting or breaking up of the unit of meaning; thirdly, the expression should agree with the given sentiment that is made clear by the self-contained period, whether it is pathetic, grave, cheerful, angry, fearful, or whatever.[20]

In other words, the composer could enhance the expression of the text at a local level by deviating from the phrase rhythm corresponding to the verse meter, but only in accordance with the guidelines that regulated harmony and scansion, and only so long as the passage concerned remained true to the "dominant affect" (pathetic, grave, etc.; explained in chapter 5) that controlled the musical setting of the period as a whole. Without a suitable application of *accento musicale,* the close association of musical and poetic accents in nineteenth-century Italian traditions meant that four regular lines or distichs (two lines) of verse could give rise to four identical rhythmic phrases. This was tolerable only in songs with a popular style, although it could also occur in works by unaccomplished composers, as was often pointed out by progressives such as Basevi and Boito in their criticism of the rigidity of the Italian system of versification. By the late nineteenth century, the combined influences of Wagner and French opera, with their looser rules of prosody, had done much to weaken the close pairing of operatic melody with standard verse meters.[21] The old *ritmi,* subject to the expressive distortions of the *accento musicale,* continued nevertheless to inform melodic composition as late as Puccini, even in the setting of irregular polymetric verses (as case studies later in this chapter set out to demonstrate).

Pacini's division of vocal melody into units of meaning (*sensi*), rather than the more usual phrases (*frasi*), with which they may or may not coincide, could be traced at least as far back as Galeazzi's discussion of the melodic period in terms of "clauses" (*clausole*) and "meanings" (*sensi*).[22] Verdi frequently used the term "*senso*" in letters to librettists to refer to the normal correspondence between sense and syntax in lyric verse, which allowed for meaningful units of text to map onto individual musical phrases and to reflect, in words, the musical momentum toward a regular series of cadences at the ends of lines or distichs.[23] Owing to the strict requirements of Italian prosody, however, it was possible in opera libretti for grammatical clauses to straddle two or more lines of verse; in such cases a word essential to the meaning of a line or distich could belong to a separate musical phrase. Take, for instance, the opening seven-syllable lines of Roberto's final aria in Puccini's *Le Villi:* "It returns to happy days / In grief, my thought" (*Torna ai felici dì / Dolente il mio pensier*). Any adjustment to the setting of the first line must take into account the opening word of the second (*Dolente*), if the meaning is to be made clear. When altering a passage in accordance with the demands of the *accento musicale,* consequently, a composer had to ensure that any modifications applied to the *sensi* of the verses and phrases.

The essential difference between measure, as regular pulse, and poetic-musical *ritmo,* as conceived and represented in performance and composition by the irregularities of the *accento musicale,* was summarized as follows in the journal *L'Italia musicale* (1854):

> The modifications and anomalies introduced into the beat by the *ritmo* are not rare. The pauses, the interruptions, the rests, the *accelerando* and *ritardando,* to which composers and performers resort so frequently, are incontrovertible proof of this. Experience has shown that the performance of a piece of music strictly in time with a metronome is not possible. And this occurs because the *ritmo* has its foundation in melody, of which the movement is a manifestation [meaning the expressive movement associated with the given sentiment of the text and as encapsulated by the dominant overall tempo].
>
> *Ritmo* pertains to all the arts that have movement as their principle. There is as much *ritmo* in prose as there is in verse; as much in measured music as there is in plainsong; there is *ritmo* in the voice, in gesture, in the sentence of a speaker or actor; just as it is in the strophe of the poet, so it is in the steps of a dancer.[24]

Much the same holistic concept underpinned the generation of a musical verse rhythm as the foundation of melody. Grounded upon traditional poetic recitation and expressive speech gestures,[25] this part of the process of composition was essentially paperless. One such creative moment appears to have been captured in an account by Giuseppe Giacosa of a meeting with Verdi in 1884, at a time when the maestro was preoccupied with the composition of *Otello.* Regardless of whether or not this account is considered to be genuine—it was added as an afterthought, four years after the original recollection was published, and has all the hallmarks of a manufactured myth—it gives an indication of what Giacosa, in 1893, accepted as a conventional method. His use of the word "accent" refers to the free and expressive delivery of the text, as discussed above in relation to the *accento musicale,* while the term "cadences" signifies the characteristic inflections of the rhythm toward the ends of lines or distichs, to be explained more fully below through the notion of *cadenza regolare:*

> Verdi would sometimes clutch the libretto and read several pieces aloud. Boito and I looked at each other, our gazes expressing our great admiration: the voice, the accent, the cadences, the force, the anger expressed in that reading betrayed such an ardent kindling of the soul, magnified so immeasurably by the sense of the words, that the source of the musical idea was clearly revealed to us. With our own eyes we saw, as it were, the flower of the melody blossom.[26]

II. RULES OF VERSIFICATION, LIPPMANN'S RHYTHMIC-MUSICAL TYPES, AND TWO CASE STUDIES

In spite of the fundamental disparity between rhythm as conceived in poetry and music and as notated in beats and measures, underlying the expressive freedom of the *accento musicale* was an assumed correlation between conceptions of phrase, rhythm, and poetic meter that was founded upon a fixed and relatively unyielding system of standardized verse types. The rules that governed Italian dramatic poetry were consolidated in the early eighteenth century through the reforms of Apostolo Zeno and countless libretti for *opere serie,* especially those penned by the most celebrated dramatic poet of the age, Pietro Metastasio. With good reason Pacini began his historical survey of the *melodramma* of his own times (1834) with Metastasio, rather than with a composer, since the operatic tradition was significantly conditioned by the standardization of verse types encouraged by the popularity of this poet.[27] By the mid-eighteenth century the single-meter or isometric aria had become more or less stable, consisting most often of two stanzas of four seven- or eight-syllable lines, and allowing occasionally for a combination of five- and seven-syllable verses (explained below). In writings, too, there was a marked tendency to regularize the meters and poetic forms and to reduce their number to a few archetypes.[28]

Although mixed meters and variable arrangements of stanzas did occur in *opera buffa* around the turn of the nineteenth century, in gen-

eral the period 1820–60 was characterized, according to Fabbri, by "iso-
metrical squareness (which determined above all the regular meter of the
verse) and the prevalence of binary schemes."[29] The regular, standardized
Metastasian verse types tended to give rise to phrases and periods that
were arranged symmetrically into pairs or groups of four, six, or eight
rhythmic units. Boito's reaction against what he saw as the tyranny of this
system of versification led to an increase throughout the 1860s in the use
of miscellaneous meters and oddities such as three- or nine-syllable lines.
Verdi's correspondence with Antonio Ghislanzoni during the 1870s demonstrates a similar propensity to experiment beyond established norms.
The main Metastasian verse types continued nevertheless to form the
foundation of the theory and practice of *fraseologia* and *periodologia* (as
explained in chapter 5).[30] For this reason, summaries may be found at the
beginning of numerous studies of Italian opera. Since a basic knowledge
of them is essential to the discussion that follows, reproduced below is
one of the clearest and most succinct summaries—Pierluigi Petrobelli's
single-page "Note on Italian Prosody":

> An Italian poetic line is measured by, and named after, its number of syl-
> lables and the position of its final accent. The syllable-count designations are
> as follows: *quinario* (five syllables), *senario* (six syllables), *settenario* (seven
> syllables), *ottonario* (eight syllables), *novenario* (nine syllables; very rare in
> nineteenth-century prosody), *decasillabo* (ten syllables), and *endecasillabo*
> (eleven syllables). A line is called *tronco* (truncated) when the accent falls on
> the last syllable of the final word: *andrò, pietà, amor*. It is *piano* (plain)—by
> far the most frequent category—when the accent falls on the penultimate
> syllable of the final word: *pensièro, fidùcia, beàto*. It is *sdrucciolo* (slippery)
> when the accent falls on the antepenultimate syllable of the final word: *sòr-
> gono, intrèpido*.
>
> The standard for measuring a line's syllable length is the *verso piano*. This
> means that a line ending with a *tronco* word must, for the purposes of assess-
> ing line length, have a syllable added to it, while one ending with a *sdrucciolo*
> word must have a syllable subtracted from it. Thus "Le memorie d'un tempo
> che fù," which has nine syllables but ends with a *parola tronca*, is described
> as a kind of ten-syllable line, a *decasillabo tronco*. Similarly, "suoni la tromba,
> e intrepido," which has eight syllables but ends with a *parola sdrucciola*, is
> described as a kind of seven-syllable line, a *settenario sdrucciolo*.
>
> A further feature concerns the position of the main accents in the lines.
> Lines with an equal number of syllables may differ according to the position
> of the main accents. The distinction is important in order to differentiate

between *versi semplici* (simple lines) and *versi doppi* (double lines): a *verso doppio* is built from two shorter lines with identical accent structure. Thus "O Signore, dal tetto natìo" and "Vieni d'amore—in sen ripara" both contain ten syllables, but the first is a *decasillabo* (accents on the third, sixth, and ninth syllables) whereas the second is a *quinario doppio* (accents on the fourth and ninth syllables).

More terminology concerns the various rhyme schemes and broad groupings of types of verse. *Rima alternata* is *abab cdcd; rima baciata* is *aa bb cc dd.* In poetry for musical drama, there is a clear distinction between *recitativo* and set "numbers" (arias, duets, choruses, ensembles). Whereas for the set numbers the structure of the poetic text is ruled by a principle of symmetry (they are built on two or more verses, all on the same type(s) of verse and rhyme scheme), the standard meter for *recitativo* is *verso sciolto: settenari* and *endecasillabi,* freely alternated without rhyme scheme except at the end of a section, which is usually marked by a *rima alternata* or *rima baciata,* with the last line usually a *verso tronco.*[31]

To this could be added a brief note on the most common poetic feet (*piedi poetici*) that make up a line of verse. These "feet" are two- or three-syllable units that normally include one stressed syllable and either one or two unstressed syllables. The most common foot in Italian poetry is the trochee (*trocheo*), or stressed-unstressed, as in "*pia*no."[32] There is also the unstressed-stressed iamb (*giambo*), as in "di *me*." The three-syllable feet include the anapest (*anapesto*), as in "non più an*drai,*" the dactyl (*dattilo*), as in "*ti*mido," and the amphibrach (*anfibraco*), as in "chi *par*la." Counting syllables in Italian prosody is complicated by factors such as *elision* (combining adjacent vowels from two different words into diphthongs or triphthongs), *dieresis* (not combining adjacent vowels from two different words into diphthongs or triphthongs), *syneresis* (combining adjacent vowels within a single word into diphthongs or triphthongs), and *apocopation* (shortening of a word through the omission of its final syllable or letter).[33]

In the nineteenth century, the process by which the different types of verse could be mapped onto musical rhythms (or phrases) was, as mentioned above, often explained in the most general terms through the ancient notion that the accented syllables received long notes and the unaccented received short notes, usually in the ratio 2:1—"according to the rules of prosody, which assign to the long syllables twice the value of the short," as Asioli put it in 1832.[34] The "principal inflection" or "com-

mon accent" (*desinenza* or *accento comune*), on the penultimate syllable
of a normal plain (*piano*) verse, could receive twice as much value again.
In practice, the placing of the *desinenza* was the main concern, while the
beginnings of phrases were generally treated more flexibly.[35]

But this was not, by itself, intended as a practical method for composers. Owing to the standardization of Metastasian verse and the single-
meter stanza, setting text to music required not a painstaking alloca-
tion of syllables to rhythmic values but rather the identification of an
appropriate, underlying *ritmo*. Once the lines of verse had been mapped
(mentally) onto this basic pattern, the composer was free to engage more
creatively with the music, by varying, for instance, the correspondence
of the words with the underlying rhythm in accordance with the expressive demands of the *accento musicale*.[36] *Ritmo* may thus be understood in
nineteenth-century Italy, in this regard, as a repetitive rhythmic pattern,
cutting across bar lines and substantiated by both a melodic design (*ritmo
melodico*) and a harmonic impulse (*ritmo armonico*), to borrow Asioli's
terms, which was determined by, but did not necessarily correspond to,
the musical setting of a line of verse.

Since the vagaries of the *accento musicale* and the lack of fixed quanti-
ties to syllables and accents made it difficult for Italian maestros to generalize as to the rhythmic patterns that might correspond to standard
verse meters, contemporary accounts were occupied instead with rules
of versification, broad recommendations on the placement of accents, and
specific individual examples drawn from the repertory. In general, musicians rarely seemed equal to the task of explaining clearly in print either
the concept or the practice of representing poetic meters through musical
rhythms. The complexity of the issue was compounded by the arrival of
alternative theories from abroad, such as that of Reicha (1830). By 1844 the
ambiguity surrounding the term *ritmo* was such that Niccolò Cattaneo
opened a debate in the pages of the *Gazzetta musicale di Milano,* inviting
maestros and professors to formulate a clear and comprehensive definition.[37] Vagueness nevertheless persisted in theoretical descriptions of
ritmo. An article published in 1884 by Neapolitan maestro Michele Ruta,
for instance, which was intended to offer guidance to aspiring singers
on aspects of musical construction, defined the vocal phrase in terms of
three aspects: melody (poetic meter), harmony (cadences), and aesthetics

(sentiments), but gave only a vague indication as to how the connection with verse rhythm was to be realized:

> From the melodic aspect the phrase is the servant of the poetic verse. It does not therefore have a determined duration but can comprise one incise, which can be prolonged for one, two, or more measures; but the most common are those that unfold in a first measure in order to rest in a second.
>
> It is considered from the harmonic aspect in terms of the cadences or semi-cadences that serve to provide motion and rest to the phrase. From the aesthetic aspect the phrase is the expression of that beautiful ideal which, in its unfolding and reproduction, depicts the sentiments that inform a given melody.[38]

Ruta's "incises" can be mapped closely onto the "rhythmic-musical types" of eighteenth- and nineteenth-century Italian opera identified by Lippmann (1986 [1973–75]), which were drawn from observations and analyses of a large and representative sample of the repertory. The overview presented in example 3.1 shows that his main "types" of rhythm were likewise prolonged for one, two, or more measures, most commonly unfolding in a first to rest in a second. In reducing numerous particular settings over centuries to a small number of generalized abstractions, Lippmann's rhythmic-musical types have proved an invaluable tool for the interpretation of operatic melody.[39] Their application to individual case studies was, however, far more nuanced and varied than the selective summary in example 3.1 might suggest. They were intended to assist in the interpretation of individual melodies, rather than to establish fixed universals. In general, Lippmann categorized them according to whether they began with a downbeat (type I), an upbeat (type II), or with no particular accent (type III). There were subcategories according to whether the rhythmic-musical types contained caesuras (type B) or not (type A).[40]

Care should be taken to interpret them according to contemporary norms rather than conventional modern notions derived from German theorists such as Hauptmann and Riemann. As the survey of historical sources below sets out to demonstrate, each of Lippmann's rhythmic-musical types corresponds in all important respects to what nineteenth-century Italian musicians would have called a *ritmo* or, depending upon

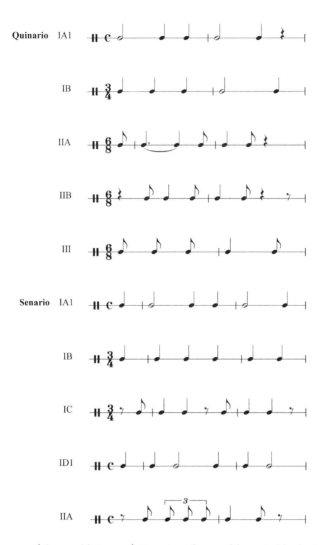

3.1. (*above and facing page*) Overview of some of the main "rhythmic-musical types" from Lippmann, *Versificazione italiana e ritmo musicale* (1986 [1973–75]).

the particular parameter they wished to highlight, a phrase, incise, clause, sense, or member. In contrast to the modern understanding of rhythm, bar lines were not regarded as intrinsic to the *ritmo,* even though, owing to the underlying succession of strong and weak impulses, they normally (but by no means always) coincided with the main accent of a verse.[41] Bar lines belonged essentially to the system of notation through which

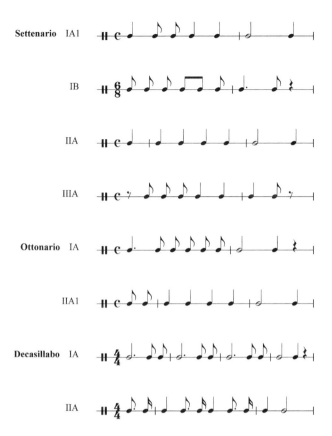

the outlines of the *ritmo* were recorded. The principal and subsidiary accents of the verse type could be scanned onto the musical beats in any number of ways, subject to the overall tempo and character of the piece. For this reason the modern idea of a strict hierarchy of beats, in which the first or third beats of a common-time measure are always regarded as more or less "accented" in comparison with the others, should be applied with caution. In Italian nineteenth-century writings, the final accent of the verse meter (*desinenza* or *accento comune*) took precedence and determined the relative strengths of the others. The main accent of the first rhythmic-musical type of example 3.1 ("Quinario IA1"), for instance, familiar, in halved note values, from the allegretto of Beethoven's Seventh Symphony, falls on the first half note of its *second* measure. This means that the ensuing final quarter note constitutes a weak "resting point" (*riposo*), a dissipation of the energy of the phrase, even though in Hauptmann's terms it falls on an accented beat of a common-time measure. Similarly, the modern concept of "strong" and "weak" measures, integral to the theory of hypermeter, did not apply in the same way to the *ritmo* (as evinced by Asioli's attempt to reconcile the regular beats of the pulse with verse meter through the notion of the *ritmo armonico,* discussed below). To describe the "Quinario IA1" in example 3.1 as a "strong" measure followed by a "weak" measure, according to modern norms (but contra Riemann's mature theory), would contradict just about every published nineteenth-century Italian account of rhythm that did not borrow its ideas from progressive German theories. Each of the generalized *ritmi* in example 3.1 may be understood, regardless of its number of measures, to increase in momentum and energy toward its *desinenza,* situated here in every case on the first beat of the final measure, and to decrease in intensity and fall away immediately afterwards through a cadence of some sort (a term derived, significantly, from the Italian verb *cadere,* "to fall"), followed by a resting point (*riposo*).

Once the underlying rhythmic shape of an individual phrase had been determined, through the mental construction of a *ritmo* or "rhythmic-musical type" corresponding to a particular text and similar in outline to those given in example 3.1, it could be repeated to provide a basic overall pattern for an extended phrase or period. Lippmann gave several examples of how such repetitions could generate four-phrase periods of music.[42] Moreen's study of text forms and musical forms in Verdi (1975) described a similar process through the notion of "regular cadence" (*cadenza regolare*), in which the lines or distichs of text were arranged so that their sense and syntax was always directed toward a final (melodic) cadence.[43] Verdi himself specified that in order to be suitable for melody, a text should accommodate a regular series of cadences at the end of a line or lines, never in the middle. In such settings the main verse accents (*accenti comuni*) were normally placed on the first beats of measures, spaced every two or four measures. A common procedure was to map two lines of text onto a single musical phrase, such that the "regular cadence" occurred at the end of every second line. Musical phrases could also contain one or four lines (or, very rarely, three). This formulation avoided the need to specify the precise rhythmic pattern applied to each poetic line, since it concerned only the placement of the main verse accent and its associated poetic meaning.

Puccini, Edgar *(1889), act 1,* ℛ21,[44] *mm.*
3–11, "Questo amor, vergogna mia"

The opening aria for the character Frank, "Questo amor, vergogna mia," offers an example of an unusually straightforward setting by Puccini, in which verse, phrase, and *ritmo* effectively coincide within a conventional four-phrase section of melody. The aria concerns Frank's desire to break free from the curse of his irrational love for the other secondary character of the opera, the mezzo temptress Tigrana. Its first stanza, taken below from the revised 1905 edition, comprises four standard eight-syllable lines, or *ottonari,* with a normal pattern of accents on the third and seventh syllables (indicated below by *italics*). Together, these four lines, known as a *quartina* or quatrain, constitute the opening section, or *motivo principale,* of the first period of the aria (as described more fully in the analysis in chapter 5, example 5.10).

Questo a*mor,* vergogna *mi*a, (8)	This love, my shame,
io spez*zar,* scordar vor*rei*; (8)	I would like to scorn and forget;
ma d'un *or*rida ma*lì*a (8)	but, through a terrible spell,
sono *schia*vi i sensi *mi*ei. (8)	my senses are enslaved.

The layout of accents suggests a rhythm with an anapestic upbeat as the most suitable choice—despite this being one of "the most annoying rigmaroles in our poetic meter," according to Boito[45]—while the overall sentiment of regret and lament calls for an appropriately slow tempo and affect, such as andante lento. A basic conception of a rhythmic formula thus presents itself (example 3.2 [a]), scanning naturally onto each line of the text and corresponding to a variant of Lippmann's rhythmic-musical type "Ottonario IIA1" from example 3.1.[46] The slurs in example 3.2 (a) serve to mark out the series of eight syllables or note values that are to be repeated, while the accent symbols signify the main inflection of the verse (*desinenza*). The inclusion of signs for crescendos and decrescendos, as well as rests to indicate the resting points (*riposi*) that separate the phrases, are intended to capture something of the idea of inhalation and exhalation, as expressed by Galli; they relate to the notion of a dynamic impulse leading to and from the main accent. It should be emphasized that example 3.2 (a) is not intended to represent any sort of analytical re-

3.2.

a. An anapestic *ottonario-ritmo.*

b. Melodic and harmonic designs added to the same *ritmo.*

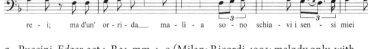

c. Puccini, *Edgar,* act 1, R21, mm. 1–9 (Milan: Ricordi, 1905; melody only, with analytical symbols).

duction. It is rather a generalized abstraction, in the manner of Lippmann, of one particular conceived rhythmic realization of the verse meter of the text. Although a general *ritmo* such as this could underpin the setting of an entire stanza, the vocal part seldom adhered to it slavishly. In the case of Frank's first aria, however, the correspondence is relatively close.

Before the selected *ritmo* could be put into effect, it required additional musical means. It could be realized only through the superimposition of melodic and harmonic designs, in the form of what were often referred to, after Gervasoni (1800) and Asioli (1832), as a melodic phrase rhythm (*ritmo melodico*) and a harmonic or accompanimental rhythm (*ritmo armonico*). Detailed discussions of these formulaic pitch structures are reserved for the next chapter, although it is worth mentioning here that the simplest such melodic designs involved the arpeggio and, most commonly of all, the scale, either complete or in segments. These could be harmonized most readily by using the fundamental chords of the key: the triads on the tonic, dominant, and occasionally subdominant. While undoubtedly effective, recalling Picchianti's observation that "four or five notes are fully sufficient to form correct and interesting phrases and periods,"[47] such rudimentary melodic and rhythmic designs inevitably became something of a cliché in Italian opera. Example 3.2 (b) shows the application of a melodic phrase rhythm (*ritmo melodico*) based on the first five notes of the F major scale to the anapestic *ottonario* verse meter of example 3.2 (a). This should not be regarded as some form of casual "Schenkerian" reductive analysis; it represents, rather, the application of a melodic archetype, integral to the teaching of harmony and counterpoint throughout Italy during the nineteenth century, to a similarly abstract *ritmo*. As will be explained more fully in the following chapter, this melodic design may be traced back to the teachings of Durante and beyond and was labeled, at least by Tartini, Martini, Zingarelli, and Michele Puccini, the "harmonic" (as opposed to "arithmetical") division of the scale (*divisione armonica*).[48] Each phrase in example 3.2 (b) also receives an identical harmonic rhythm (*ritmo armonico*) that progresses from dominant to tonic upon weak and strong rhythmic impulses, notwithstanding the persistence of a tonic pedal point throughout this extract.

From example 3.2 (b) it is apparent that the first and third, and second and fourth, phrases share similar *ritmi melodici*. This is a fairly common, but by no means the only possible layout for a setting of four phrases. It corresponds to what Huebner (1992) termed an arrangement of "balanced phrases" within the opening formal unit, or "thematic block," of the "lyric prototype" ($a^1 a^2 b a^3$).[49] In many nineteenth-century writings, the first phrase in a melody such as this would have been referred to as the "design" (*disegno*) and the second as its "response" (*riposta*). It would not have been seen as a period (*periodo*), owing to its lack of a final perfect authentic cadence. Of interest also is the utter subordination of the *ritmo armonico* to the requirements of the melodic design. This predominance of melody and its *ritmo*, characteristic of nineteenth-century Italian opera, contrasts with conventional modern notions of the primacy of harmony. Each phrase in example 3.2 (b) ends with what today would be called an imperfect authentic cadence in the tonic, regardless of whether it is a "design" or a "response," or whether it is opening or concluding. These cadences do, however, manifest different degrees of rhetorical finality, in accordance with a number of eighteenth-century guidelines (for instance, the discussions of "clausulae" in Werckmeister's 1702 *Harmonologia musica* or Walther's 1708 *Praecepta der musicalischen Composition*), depending on whether they conclude melodically with the fifth or third note of the scale. This contrasts starkly with the emphasis placed on the choice of harmony at the point of cadence in later German theory. Heinrich Koch's *Versuch einer Anleitung zur Composition* (1782–93)—which, together with Joseph Riepel's *Anfangsgründe zur musicalischen Setzkunst* (1752–68), may be regarded as the foundation of modern phrase theory—specifically warned against the practice evident in example 3.2 (b). Koch advised that if two successive phrases were to end on the tonic, they should contain the same material, as a form of statement and reinforcement; otherwise, the effect would be static.[50] As will be seen in chapters 4 and 5, in the Italian traditions the key in which a phrase or period ended was considered of relatively limited importance.[51]

The actual vocal line of Frank's aria, "Questo amor," is given in example 3.2 (c), with indications of the phrases and their main accents. Despite the addition of minor embellishments, its structural dependence on the *ritmo* formula described above and the accompanying melodic and harmonic designs is readily apparent. Puccini, adhering to a standard notational convention, differentiated between the "resting points" in the middle and at the end of each two-*ritmo* phrase, in such a way that the final "syllable" received either its full quarter note value or only an eighth note, followed by a resting point.[52] There are only two occasions when the *ritmo* is altered significantly in deference to the *accento musicale*. In the opening measure, the words "This love," which embody the central poetic theme of the aria, require a more consequential upbeat; accordingly, the initial two eighth notes of the underlying rhythm are expanded to fill the measure. At the climactic point of the melodic unit in m. 8, which occurs in typical fashion in the third phrase, upon the equally central words "a terrible spell" (*orrida malìa*), the rising melodic design is subject to the expressive devices of syncopation and melodic variation in order to interpolate a high note.

Giuseppe Staffa's 1856 Analysis of the Two Rhythmic Systems in Donizetti, Don Pasquale (1843), act 3, no. 13, *"Via caro sposino"*

A rare instance of a contemporary Neapolitan (as opposed to Milanese) analytical demonstration of the dual rhythmic systems of Italian opera occurs in the section "On Rhythm" (*Del ritmo*) in the second volume of Staffa's *Metodo della Scuola Napolitana di composizione musicale* (1856). It is reproduced faithfully in example 3.3 (a), incorporating neither Donizetti's original text nor the conventional syllabic notation of the vocal melody. Staffa may have presumed his readership to be sufficiently familiar with the words and their dramatic context, which concerns a farcical plot to discourage the wealthy old bachelor Don Pasquale from seeking a wife, in order that his nephew Ernesto may retain his inheritance and marry the penniless but pretty and resourceful young widow Norina. In this duet Norina teases Don Pasquale mercilessly, having contrived to arrange a false marriage with him in the guise of a demure "Sofronia," who turns out to be a big-spending, hard-living, promiscuous nightmare. Upon finding out that he is not, after all, married to "Sofronia," the Don gladly gives up all thoughts of marriage for himself and consents to the union of the young couple.

As is obvious from example 3.3 (a), Staffa's analysis treats the vocal part and the accompaniment separately, employing two different systems to account for their rhythms. The slurs and "2" symbols appended to the piano part, culminating in a final "4," relate to the weak and strong beats of a regular "harmonic rhythm" or *ritmo armonico* operating within a unit of two measures. The vocal part is, by contrast, subdivided into phrases that are labeled with the figures "3" and "7," neither of which correspond to the actual number of measures covered, whether applied to the original $\frac{6}{8}$ time signature or to Staffa's revised $\frac{3}{8}$. These analytical figures can be understood only with reference to a "melodic rhythm" or *ritmo melodico* that corresponds to a verse meter functioning independently from the bar lines on the page. By restoring the missing text to the extract, according to the Ricordi edition of 1843, example 3.3 (b) shows that each vocal

3.3.

a. Giuseppe Staffa, *Metodo della Scuola Napolitana di composizione musicale* (1856), 9: rhythmic analysis of Donizetti, *Don Pasquale,* act 3, no. 13, "Via caro sposino."

phrase comprises a *senario-ritmo,* with principal verse inflections (marked by accent symbols) coinciding with the strong or first (*1.*) impulse of the harmonic rhythm every second measure. Staffa's "3" indicates that the common accent (*accento comune*) of each *senario* line falls on the third measure of an imagined ⅜ meter, encircled by resting points (*riposi*) encompassing one additional measure. On paper, consequently, each phrase marked "3" in example 3.3 (a) comprises *four* or *five* measures of ⅜ meter, depending upon whether or not the upbeats to each phrase are included: one initial measure that overlaps with the resting point of the preced-

b. Staffa's analysis interpreted in terms of *ritmo melodico* and *ritmo armonico*.

ing phrase, three central measures that contain the actual *ritmo* and its common accent, and one final measure that marks the resting point. In practice, the surrounding caesuras did not count as an integral part of the *ritmo:* hence Staffa's "3," emphasized by the additional slurs within the phrases, which was intended to approximate the idea of a flexible poetic rhythm mapping onto the pattern "one, two, *three*—rest—one, two, *three*—rest." A similar explanation underlies the attachment of the figure "7" to the concluding phrase in mm. 14–17. Although, as 3.3 (b) affirms, these four measures encompass two lines of *senario* verse along with their corresponding melodic rhythms, Staffa conflates them into one double rhythm (*senario doppio*), in deference to the convention of extending the cadential phrase, and acknowledges only one main inflection on the seventh measure of the imagined ⅜ meter.

III. HISTORICAL SURVEY OF WRITINGS ON *RITMO*

During the nineteenth century, the method outlined in examples 3.2 and 3.3 for setting verses to music—involving the selection and application of more or less standard phrase rhythms (*ritmi*) and accompanying melodic and harmonic designs—appears to have been so generally known by those in the profession that any composer who adhered too closely to its pedagogical models or allowed its workings to show too obviously at the surface of a score ran the risk of being branded a "hack." Abramo Basevi, in his study of Verdi's operas (1859a), based his criticism of the final aria in act 4 of *Macbeth* (1847), "Pietà, rispetto, amore," on just such an observation. After dismissing the aria as "nothing of note" due to its use of a "very old phrase rhythm" (*un ritmo vecchissimo*), he launched into a lengthy denunciation of composers who relied on such devices and in doing so gave a broad outline of what appears to have been a well-known method:

> Concerning this, I should like to mention that phrase rhythm constitutes so great a part of melody that it is unjust to give the name of an *original* composer to one who forms new *principal themes* on very old phrase rhythms, altering only the notes. The much vaunted *ease* of many Italian arias derives in large part from the oldness of the phrase rhythms.[53]

Basevi was describing the application of stock melodic formulas (known variously throughout the nineteenth century as *andamenti, moti regolari, movimenti, progressioni, salti,* or *successioni,* to be explained more fully in chapter 4) to stock rhythmic designs of the sort described briefly above, in order to generate an entire phrase or period that could function as a principal theme, or *motivo.* The *ritmi* he mentioned did not refer to rhythms in the modern sense, as successions and divisions of regular beats, but rather to phrase designs based on verse meters that could be repeated and varied to form a phrase or period of music. By *motivi* he did not mean what would now be called motives, or short rhythmic-melodic cells, but rather entire opening themes typically lasting eight or more measures. In the remainder of his critique, Basevi described the application of received melodic and harmonic designs to the underlying *ritmo,* as well as hinting at a standardization of formal patterns:

> Would you like a recipe for composing the easiest, catchiest *melodies*? Take an old phrase rhythm from the most obvious examples. It doesn't take too much to adapt new notes to it; especially since, when looking for an accommodating progression, there are almost fixed rules, such as those that recommend leaps of the ascending fourth, the major sixth, the third, the descending fifth, etc., etc., and when you also copy the conduct or *form* of the piece from one already in vogue, as from a pattern, without taking the trouble to introduce any modifications. For the harmonies, you have those of the key of the piece [i.e., tonic and dominant], and where you wish to make other graceful modulations, there are appropriate rules. It is in this manner that many pieces of music claiming the title of "new" are created.[54]

The aria thus castigated begins with a classic *quartina* (four lines) of seven-syllable verse, or *settenari,* which are set to an allegedly standard march-like phrase rhythm that corresponds broadly to Lippmann's rhythmic-musical type "Settenario IIA" from example 3.1.[55] Especially irritating to Basevi must have been Verdi's choice of a correspondingly simple accompanying melodic design: an arpeggio descending from the tonic note.

In terms of the procedure for correlating regular lines of verse with musical phrases, this method, based on standard *ritmi,* was most fully explored in Asioli (1832). But Basevi could have known it from a variety of sources. Evidence of similar concepts and practices can be found in many publications dating back to the eighteenth century (and beyond). That these teachings were not confined to Italy at that time is, moreover, borne out in the work of a group of theorists working closely together in Berlin, including Johann Georg Sulzer, Johann Peter Schulz, and, in particular, Johann Philipp Kirnberger, whose writings were later to form the basis of what Riemann defined as the *Akzenttheorie.* Although Kirnberger appears to have had little contact with Italian musicians, many aspects of his theory echoed their methods, such as his discussion of "Tempo" and its related sentiments in volume 2 of *Die Kunst des reinen Satzes* (1776), which resembled Italian accounts of the *movimento* and *Affetto dominante* (as defined in chapter 5). His description of metrical organization relied on a concept of "Rhythmus" that corresponded in all important respects to the Italian phrase rhythm, or *ritmo.* It can hardly be regarded as coincidence that Kirnberger, in Berlin in 1776, described a type of melodic rhythm based on the verse meter very similar to that alluded to by countless Italian writers, including Basevi in Florence some eighty years later.

When Kirnberger wrote of meter in terms of regular patterns of accents, akin to the modern understanding of measure and time signatures, he associated it primarily with short pieces of dance music. But he also spoke of meter through an analogy with speech and in association with vocal music, according to which its patterns of accents were said to correspond to "the length and brevity of the syllables."[56] In such cases Kirnberger employed the terms "phrase," "rhythm," and "musical verse form" synonymously.[57] His description is very close to the concept of *ritmo* as described in relation to example 3.2 above: "The *Rhythmus* of a composition is very similar to the versification of a lyric poem. Individual melodic phrases represent the lines, and larger sections of several phrases are musical strophes."[58] Even more explicitly: "such phrases, also called rhythmic units [*Rhythmus*], can be of different lengths; they can be of one to four, five, and even more measures in length, just as there are long and short lines in poetry."[59] Guarding against any confusion of this phrase rhythm with the idea of a regular pulse defined by the bar line, Kirnberger made clear that "the beginning of a phrase, and hence its end as well, is not restricted to any point within the measure; they can fall not only on any beat but also on any small part of the beat. However, to compose in the easiest and most comprehensible way, one begins either on the downbeat or the upbeat."[60] These and numerous other passages demonstrate beyond a doubt that Kirnberger considered the *Rhythmus* as a regular pattern of syllables and syllabic accents, essentially unbounded by bar lines, which was determined by the musical equivalent of a line of poetry. Even Heinrich Koch, whose phrase theory seldom ventured beyond the North German pedagogical tradition of using short instrumental dance movements as paradigms for composition, acknowledged the essential relationship of musical meter and poetic verse in a footnote to volume 3 of his *Versuch einer Anleitung zur Composition* (1793): "Although knowledge of the syllabic meter is not absolutely necessary for knowledge of the rhythmic pulse, the two things are so similar that one does indeed explain the other."[61]

Unfortunately, Italian writers were seldom so lucid. Francesco Galeazzi's discussion of the musical phrase and its relation to the various *ritmi* typifies the terminological confusion that has, to this day, hampered an understanding of the practice. As might be expected, he assumed the eighteenth-century norms of equating the divisions and cadences of the musical period with the syntax and punctuation of speech, but so casually that the reader must have been left bewildered by the profusion of synonymous terms:

> A *cantilena* will be carried out very poorly if the *ritmo* is ignored. That is the thing that the poets would call the meter [*Metro*], or possibly the measure [*misura*], and which the practitioners call *Tempo*. To give the beginner an idea of what is meant by *Tempo*, we shall say that the musical piece or *Cantilena* is a species of discourse, and that it has accordingly its periods, clauses, and prosody, and in terms of tessitura it is a species of rhetorical art.[62]

No wonder Carlo Gervasoni, in the third part of his *Scuola della musica* (1800), sought to clarify the concept by introducing two seemingly new terms that, considered together, were intended to describe the musical phrase as a counterpart to the meter of a poetic verse: the "melodic phrase" (*frase melodica*) and the "harmonic phrase" (*frase armonica*).[63] These became the prototypes for Asioli's later division of *ritmi* according to similar melodic and harmonic considerations. They were to be understood not as two distinct varieties of phrase but rather as dual aspects of an abstract rhythmic unit (similar to those in example 3.1) that could be realized only through the superimposition of melody and harmony. The "melodic phrase" encompassed the pitch design, conditioned by the verse accents, which served to generate a section of melody based on a particular verse type. In conformity with the phrase rhythm, its length could vary from less than a measure to four measures or more. It mattered little whether it remained in one key or modulated, although the melodic cadence (*termine*) with which it finished needed to demonstrate an appropriate degree of either closure or openness. The "harmonic phrase" served merely to support this rhythmic-melodic unit with a suitable progression of chords articulating a framework of strong and weak rhythmic impulses. Gervasoni offered little further advice on the precise nature of the harmonic phrase, other than to observe the usual layout of half-cadences and perfect cadences within a period of music, which, he stipulated, should end with a noticeable rhetorical pause or gap. This corresponds with Verdi's concept of "regular cadence" (*cadenza regolare*), often mentioned in letters to librettists, which associated the verse inflection (*desinenza*) of a given poetic meter and the meaning of the text (*senso*) with an associated, regular series of (melodic) cadences.[64]

Many of the teachings on methods of phrase setting found later in Asioli (1832) were also evident in the sixth book, "On Musical Rhetoric," of Alexandre-Étienne Choron's *Principes de composition des écoles d'Italie* (1816). Choron began by defining the musical note (*son musicale*) as equivalent, indeed identical, to a syllable.[65] In a subsequent section ("On the Phrase and the Period of Music") this analogy was pursued to the point where the intonations of speech, combined with the rhythms associated with syllabic accents, "give birth to the phrase, to the period, to the musical discourse."[66]

3.4. Alexandre-Étienne Choron, *Principes de composition des écoles d'Italie* (1816 [1808]), 6:4.

More specific instructions followed on how to translate these poetic accents into music. The first lesson involved the identification of the "true musical syllables" from among the many notes that served merely to decorate a melody. This concept is extremely significant, since it explains why the number of actual notes in a phrase seldom corresponds to the number of syllables belonging to its underlying verse meter. Through an aural analysis of the passage given in the first two measures of example 3.4, Choron made the claim that the listener did not hear all nine of its notes, but only the three-note outline presented in the final two measures of the example: "Each of these notes [in 2.] is, as I shall go on to say, a true musical syllable."[67] An awareness of the relationship between the fundamental musical syllables and subsequent processes of elaboration, through such doctrines as the *accento musicale* and the *melodia variata* (as in Rossi 1858), was considered crucial to successful text-setting.

Choron's discussion of the relation between grammar, prosody, and the musical phrase was complicated somewhat by a focus on the French language, as demanded by his intended readership. Drawing upon his earlier writings on the versification theories of Antonio Scoppa—which attempted, crudely summarized, to impose upon French verse forms some of the regular structures of the Italian—he maintained that prose or verse was equally suitable for musical setting,[68] provided that the musical phrase corresponded in length and expressive meaning to the spoken phrase.

> The only rule that applies to this matter is that the resting point of the musical phrase corresponds to that of the spoken phrase; that the meaning of the first be suspended when that of the second is suspended; and that it is finished when that of the other is finished.[69]

In addition to establishing the identity of poetic syllables with the underlying framework of a melody, and the line of prose or verse with a musical phrase, Choron defined a type of phrase rhythm similar to

Kirnberger's *Rhythmus* and Gervasoni's *frase melodica,* which he called, unsurprisingly, *Rhythme.* This applied likewise to the "symmetry, the regular ordering" of the "poetic strophe,"[70] but not just in terms of its individual lines: in Choron's account, the *Rhythme* that underlay the succession of musical phrases could also incorporate two lines, in the form of a couplet or distich. The resulting series of phrases, either regular, if set to verse, or free, if set to prose, determined the larger unit of the period of music. Here, however, Choron's terminology took on something of the ambiguity more characteristic of Italian writings on the topic. His argument appears confused by the use of the term "phrase" to signify both the setting of an individual line or two lines of text—which he called a "simple phrase" (*phrase simple*)—and the larger unit perhaps more accurately designated as the period—which he called a "composite phrase" (*phrase composée*). When "phrase" was employed to mean the overall period, its smaller component units, or "simple phrases," were designated instead as "members" (*membres*) or, more confusedly still, phrases of one member.

According to Choron, the composite phrase of several members came in two types: free or symmetrical. The *phrase symétrique* was made up of regularly proportioned *membres* and was thus the only type that could give rise to the period (*periode*). The best arranged periods comprised four regular *membres,* which, in French prosody, should each consist of "four measures or musical feet" (*quatre mésures ou pieds musicaux*).

Condensed into some kind of coherent, synthetic summary, Choron's observations outline a method for setting text to music in which the line of verse, together with its principal inflection, was translated into a basic phrase rhythm (*Rhythme*) that was substantiated by a melodic framework incorporating appropriate cadence types. As Choron put it:

> I shall observe in the meantime that the musical period has obvious connections with the poetic strophe which is made up of verses of different meters, but disposed similarly: that this symmetry, this regular ordering, without being one of the necessary conditions of its structure, offers new pleasures and means of effect. The different *membres* of the period are made up of main verse accents that are more or less final-sounding. These main verse accents are found always on the strong beat.[71]

Given also the establishment of four regular phrases as the foundation for a normative period of music, this formulation corresponds to the methods set out in a number of later Italian treatises. It is important to

note, however, that in the Italian traditions there were no standard templates for a period of music, such as the modern notions of the classical
"sentence" (*Satz*) or the "antecedent-consequent period."[72] The structure
of the Italian operatic period was not predetermined according to an
abstract scheme but was rather generated by more local considerations,
including the contours and cadence types of the melodic design, its accompanying harmonic design, and the necessary number of repetitions
of the phrase rhythm, which was often extended, fragmented, and varied
in preparation for the final cadence. In contrast to modern phrase theory,
the overall pattern of harmonic arrival points and their relation to the
tonic was subordinate to the units determined by rhythm, melody, and
the meaning of the text. A number of common patterns did, however,
emerge during the first half of the nineteenth century, in reflection of the
standardization of types of verse and stanza. They are discussed in the
context of the modern theory of the "lyric prototype" in chapter 5.

Choron's relatively comprehensive account drew upon concepts and
practices that featured in many publications throughout the nineteenth
century, with varying degrees of clarity. All agreed in asserting the theoretical identity of poetic verse and musical phrase. The Belgian theorist
Jérôme-Joseph de Momigny's rather immodestly titled *La sola e vera teoria della musica* (The One and Only True Theory of Music, 1823) stated,
for instance, that "musicians call *phrases* what should be called *verses* or
stanzas,"[73] and extended the analogy to characterize musical phrases
through a process of respiration involving upbeats and downbeats, and
to explain the divisions of a melodic period through a hierarchy consisting of a complete stanza, two-line units called couplets or distichs
(*distici*), single lines of verse, half lines of verse or hemistichs (*emistichi*),
and cadences.[74]

Giuseppe Baini's *Saggio sopra l'identità de' ritmi musicale e poetico*
(Essay on the Identity of Musical and Poetic Rhythms, 1820), despite its
encouraging title, bore little relation to contemporary operatic practice. It
was based on a comparison between two notional types of rhythm: *ritmo
musicale*, meaning primarily the regular beats and measures of dance music, and *ritmo della versificazione*, which was associated with the meters and
poetic feet of both the "metrical verse" of the ancients and the "harmonic
verse" of modern times. In terms of the application of one type of rhythm
to the other, Baini, a Vatican priest and scholar of Palestrina famed for his

conservatism, largely followed the outmoded ideas of Sacchi (1770) and emphasized the importance of regular, repetitive ordering: "They resemble one another in number, in proportion, in symmetry, in the indefinite continuation of the returning equally spaced musical and poetic accents, and in the uniform repetition of the similarly proportioned verse feet at the uniform repetition of the musical measures."[75] More specifically, Baini distinguished three types of metric organization through which the principal verse types of Italian poetry could be conveyed by a rhythmic unit, based on the number of unaccented syllables within a line of verse and corresponding either to duple time (*di terza in terza*), triple time (*di quarta in quarta*), or quadruple time (*di quinta in quinta*). This method for mapping verse meters onto a regular pulse remained largely theoretical, much as it had in the 1780s, since musical phrases rarely maintained such a uniform flow of poetic feet in practice.

In Lucca, similarly antiquated theories of text setting, such as the quantitative syllabic theories of Tartini (1754) or Arteaga (1785), continued to hold sway. This much is evident from the dissertations on melody, harmony, and meter (1828) by Marco Santucci, a student of Fenaroli who subsequently taught Puccini's own first maestros, Carlo Angeloni and Fortunato Magi, as well as his father, Michele Puccini. Santucci began his dissertation on meter (or measure) by defining the rhythmic pulse in terms of the syllables and accents of prosody:

> The measure may also be considered in relation to the nature of language, which may be adapted to music, and significantly in relation to that property common to both: prosody. For this reason the measure must take note of the precise quantity of long and short syllables, so that the pronunciation of the words is as it should be. The obscenity of setting the long syllables as short and the short as long is, to the hack composer, neither felt nor indeed unusual.[76]

His outline of *ritmo,* though sketchy and incomplete and influenced by theories similar to those of Arteaga and Baini, relates nevertheless to that given in many other sources and elaborated upon earlier in this chapter in relation to example 3.2:

> Let us now consider measure in terms of the phrase rhythm. The rhythm in music is none other than a particular ordering of the succession of notes. The concept of the phrase rhythm may therefore be taken to mean that measure works in the same way as the verses in poetry.[77]

Reicha's Alternative

Although such accounts of rhythm were for the most part unsystematic, if not haphazard, they were at least in agreement as to the fundamental importance of verse meter in the construction of the musical phrase. The same could not be said for Reicha's *Trattato della melodia* (1830 [1814]), which, by detaching rhythm from words and by subsuming the particulars of the *rhythme* (as defined by Choron) under a neat, logical system, substantially altered the generally accepted meaning of the term.[78] The considerable influence of Reicha's theory, as compared to the almost unknown earlier Italian teachings on rhythm and phrase, goes some way toward explaining the absence of an adequate term for *ritmo* in modern music theory. Although some aspects of Reicha's terminology, in Italian translation, did find their way into Asioli (1832)—specifically the *disegno melodico* and the *dimensioni* of musical forms—it is on the whole erroneous to claim that Reicha's theoretical framework and knowledge of the Viennese classics paved the way for Asioli's phrase theory.[79] On the contrary, Reicha's obsession with symmetry—he set great store by his knowledge of mathematics[80]—and the replication of fundamental units at different levels of structure led him to distort terms borrowed largely from Choron in order to fit them into a system fundamentally at odds with the practice of operatic composition. Reicha's theory relates more convincingly to the German pedagogical tradition founded on the emulation of short instrumental dance pieces, as, for instance, informs Koch (1782–93). Through an abstract notion of absolute symmetry, Reicha's treatise posited the idea of a hierarchical uniformity or relativity between smaller and larger units within a piece. A single measure was regarded as a microcosm for meter at higher levels, just as the four- and eight-measure phrases characteristic of dance movements were raised to the status of formal paradigms. Any departure from these "norms" was accounted for as some kind of distortion.

In regard to *rhythme*, Reicha departed radically from the Italian traditions by associating it with units that were *not* tied to poetic meter. Although *rhythmes* could be long or short and could contain even or uneven numbers of between two and eight measures, Reicha held that "nature has particularly favored the four-measure *rhythme,* which is generally

used more than the others."[81] Adapting the melodic divisions formerly
connected with aspects of verse and stanza to more abstract formal units,
he rebranded the individual phrase as a "design" or "figure" (*dessin*, or
disegno in Italian),[82] most commonly two measures in length, which, in
symmetrical pairs, made up the normative four-measure unit called the
rhythme (*ritmo*, in Italian). Two such *rhythmes*, symmetrically arranged,
gave rise to an eight-measure *periode*, which could likewise form an equal
half of a sixteen-measure *coupe* (*divisione*, in Italian).[83] Granting a degree
of variety to this otherwise restrictive pattern of repetitions, Reicha allowed the *periode* to contain two different designs, in the form of a statement and response. According to the ruthless hierarchical recursiveness
of the theory, the multiples of the designs could continue, possibly with
extensions and other deviations from the norm, until they arrived at
the overall "dimension" of the piece. These units, in keeping with the
modern understanding of phrase rhythm, were defined primarily by
bar lines, not by poetic meters. In cases where the *rhythme* started and
ended in the middle of a measure, Reicha made a special note of it as an
exception.[84]

Although Reicha's theory was influential in Italian musical circles
after 1830, its impact was significant primarily for the interpretation of the
"new" instrumental and symphonic styles that were beginning to gain a
following. In terms of the traditions of operatic composition, his theory
was altogether too rigid and too lacking in considerations of versification
to be of practical use. Much of the subsequent confusion surrounding the
concept of *ritmo* can be traced to Reicha's decision to borrow and adapt
terminology that had been associated for generations with verse and poetic meter in order to construct an essentially abstract theoretical system
for describing phrase structure and form in instrumental as well as vocal
music. Matters were complicated further by Asioli's subsequent restoration of Reicha's terminology to the concepts they originally signified and
by the failure of other Italian authors to do so.[85] By the late nineteenth
century, the dominance of German writings on music theory and the
rise of instrumental genres ensured that the Italian method of assigning
musical *ritmi* to poetic meters was almost entirely superseded by more
theoretical notions of meter and hypermeter, which relied on the bar line
as a basic determinant of structure.

Melodic and Harmonic Rhythms, According to Bonifazio Asioli

Although Asioli adopted some of Reicha's terms in the third book of his magnum opus, *Il Maestro di composizione* (1832)—including *dimensioni* for overall formal patterns, *disegno melodico* for the melodic phrase, as well as *ritmo melodico* and *ritmo armonico* in place of Gervasoni's two types of *frase*—his account of vocal phrase setting was drawn largely from older Italian traditions, which assumed the primacy of standard verse meters. Indeed, Asioli (1832, vol. 3) may be regarded as one of the most significant attempts to document a particular theory and practice of phraseology, *contra* Reicha.[86] True, in the preface to the 1834 edition of *Il Maestro di composizione,* his friend and biographer Antonio Coli did stress that Asioli had presented a "new method," but this was misleading sales talk. Italian publications on music during the nineteenth century often made such claims, regardless of their accuracy. Although his more thorough account of verse and phrase may have required some new formulations and terminology, it corresponded in all important details to concepts and practices described in earlier Italian publications. No subsequent author of any note appears to have seriously questioned Asioli's basic teachings on verse, phrase, or *ritmo.*[87] These theories seem rather to have gradually faded out during the late nineteenth century, superseded by progressive (modern) theories from abroad. This is not to suggest that there was an untroubled consensus among maestros on the issue. There were, of course, dissenting voices within the various traditions. Toward the end of the third book, Asioli railed against those who would question his approach: "This comparison between meter and phrase—a comparison that, it seems to me, could not be more true, obvious, and identical—refutes the views, I believe, of a few mediocrities who aim to apply themselves to Music."[88] As usual, these supposedly opposing views concerned only minor issues, such as the unsuitability of short poetic meters for musical treatment or the problems associated with placing certain vowels on accented notes. In answer to this latter point, Asioli did in fact agree with these unidentified critics that it was preferable to place the vowels *a* or *e* on the main accent of the verse, especially if it fell upon a high note, but added: "It is not the fault of Music if an inexpert singer stops to warble pointlessly on the vowels *i, o,* or *u;* and anyway, a good Maestro will avoid these errors in composition."[89]

The main substance of Asioli's teachings on phraseology was set out in the third and fourth chapters of volume 3 of *Il Maestro di composizione,* entitled "On the Harmonic and Melodic Rhythms" and "Comparison between the Musical Phrase and the Different Poetic Meters." Following Gervasoni, he described the musical phrase as determined rhythmically by a line of poetic verse and realized in sound through its dual aspects of melody and harmony. He delivered this same teaching through two seemingly new terms which, unfortunately, suggested misleading parallels with Reicha: *ritmo melodico* and *ritmo armonico.* As mentioned earlier, these signified not two types of phrase but rather the two musical parameters of melody and harmony through which the abstract formula of the phrase rhythm was embodied in sound. Asioli's *ritmo melodico* should not be confused with Reicha's similarly named unit, normally of four measures, which was made up of two symmetrical designs. Nor should the term "harmonic rhythm" be understood to imply changes of harmony, according to modern norms. *Armonico,* in this sense, signified *only* that the rhythm belonged to the accompaniment. It had no connection whatsoever with the choice or progression of chords. A more accurate translation would be "accompanimental rhythm," although this would lack the significant historical resonances of "harmony" in its pre-Ramellian guise *as* accompaniment.

To explain the process through which the melodic phrase rhythm mapped onto the accompanimental or harmonic rhythm, Asioli introduced an additional term, *movimento,* signifying the "rhythmic impulse" that served to connect flexible vocal *ritmi* with a succession of strong and weak beats, at the level of one or two measures or half a measure. It was first introduced in the fourth chapter of volume 1, in association with the similarly named "fundamental movements" (*movimenti fondamentali*) that described stock harmonic-contrapuntal progressions:

> Rhythm, which has so much power over the sense [of hearing] that it may offend even the most boorish ear, when not transgressing its order, is distinguished by two impulses [*movimenti*], of which the first is defined by the sense [of hearing] as *strong* and the second as *weak.* These two rhythmic impulses may be placed across two measures, one measure, or half a measure, according to the type of tempo, whether duple or triple, and according to the designation Allegro, Adagio, Andante, etc. that appears at the beginning of the composition.

The first or strong impulse is that which starts and finishes the phrase or
harmonic rhythm; and the second or weak impulse is that which ends with a
semi-constituent [i.e., diminished chord] or constituent [i.e., diatonic chord]
of the key, which has a tendency to reproduce the first strong impulse; thus it
can be stated that this reproduction, with a few exceptions, decides which of
the rhythmic impulses are strong and which are weak.[90]

Despite Asioli's hint in the last sentence that the inherent tendencies
of chords, or harmonic motion (in the modern sense), determined the
progression from weak to strong impulses—"with a few exceptions"—
there was, in practice, no meaningful or convincing relationship between
the two rhythmic *movimenti* and the harmonies that coincided with them.
The so-called "first impulse" or *primo movimento* served principally to
support the main inflection of the verse meter, whether with tonic, dominant, or any other chord. Later, in volume 3, Asioli persisted in this vague
suggestion of the role of functional chord progressions in generating a
flow of weak and strong rhythmic impulses, in this instance as more fully
developed "cadences" rather than mere "constituents of the key." He went
so far as to claim that in this respect the accompanimental or harmonic
rhythm controlled the phrases of the vocal melody:

The Melodic rhythm, or alternatively the phrase, is a little part of musical discourse that is at all times ruled by Harmonic rhythm, as spoken of
already in the first Book. This [harmonic rhythm], with its two impulses,
the first strong and the other weak, rules with cadences the Melodic phrase
rhythm, which must have the inflection on the first or last impulse; this is
perceived almost by natural instinct and is completely obvious even to the
most musically ignorant person. The inflection goes perfectly in accord with
the penultimate syllable of *verso piano,* the antepenultimate of *verso sdrucciolo,* and the last of *verso tronco.*[91]

Just a few paragraphs later, Asioli was, however, already beginning
to undermine the professed centrality of this supposed regulatory union
of rhythm and harmony. He was forced to concede so many exceptions
to the "variety" of melody that the putative role of "cadences" within the
harmonic rhythm was seriously compromised:

Although the melodic phrase rhythm acknowledges its origins in the
sustaining harmonies and proceeds subject to the cadential impulses of
the harmonic rhythm, nonetheless it is, and always will be, the master, the
life and soul of the musical discourse. It is the principal focus of attention

because of its pleasantness; and, as if despising the uniformity of that which rules over it, it searches incessantly for variety, for instance, by beginning the phrase on the second or first harmonic impulse, or by dividing the various beats of the measure evenly or unevenly, or by even smaller subdivisions of this.[92]

This mutability of weak and strong rhythmic impulses meant that Asioli, retreating yet further from his original claim, had little choice but to abandon the supposition of a neat and logical correspondence of verse phrase, accompanimental pulse, and harmony. In the end he allowed that a melodic phrase rhythm could, on occasion, as a result of expansions, contractions, and other expressive fluctuations in *cantabile* melodies, encompass *three* rhythmic impulses:

> The phrase is sometimes formed arbitrarily of three rhythmic-harmonic impulses, the first of which is strong, the second weak, and the last strong. But such an arbitrary act may not take place in marked and fast tempos—not without offending the sense [of hearing]. It is agreed that it may occur only in medium or slow tempos, in which the disgust will be lessened and made almost imperceptible on account of the slowness of the tempo, and in which from phrase to phrase the harmonic impulses pass indistinctly from first to first, or from second to second.[93]

Subsequent case studies will explore this practice of shifting the underlying accompanimental pulse in more depth. For now, example 3.5 reproduces one of the analyses put forward by Asioli to demonstrate the straightforward, regular operation of the *ritmo armonico*.[94] Recalling his initial argument, it might be supposed that its rhythmic impulses or *movimenti*, labeled by him as *primo* (1.°) and *secondo* (2.°), would be reflected with some sort of consistency in the progression of chords, coinciding perhaps with alternations of tonic and dominant. It is clear, however, that harmony remains entirely subordinate to the dictates of the melodic phrase rhythm. The two phrases of example 3.5 (a) are implicitly harmonized, in typical fashion, by a simple scale, descending two octaves from f[1] to F. In the first phrase a strong tonic harmony in m. 1 coincides with the "weak" rhythmic impulse while the main verse accent in m. 2 (indicated by Asioli as *desinenza piana* or "plain inflection") receives an implied subdominant, leading to a first-inversion tonic on the weak beat. In the second phrase, on the contrary, the harmonic rhythm conforms to expectations by progressing from a "weak" dominant seventh in m. 3 to

3.5.

a. Bonifazio Asioli, *Il Maestro di composizione* (1832), Examples 3: no. 4a, 11.

b. Underlying *ritmo melodico*.

a "strong" tonic in m. 4. Discounting this problematic harmonic aspect, the *movimenti* suggest a close affinity with Verdi's concept of the *cadenza regolare,* occurring in this case every second measure and coinciding with the end of each assumed "poetic line."

According to a straightforward count of the musical notes in example 3.5 (a), the first phrase suggests a ten-syllable plain verse (*decasillabo*) with accents on the third, sixth, and ninth notes, while the second phrase appears to comprise eight syllables (*ottonario*), with accents on the third and seventh notes and a "slippery" or *sdrucciolo* ending. A simplistic analysis of verse meter might interpret these two phrases respectively as a *decasillabo piano* and an *ottonario sdrucciolo.* Taking into account Choron's guidance on "true musical syllables," however, it is evident—not least from Asioli's own annotations—that both phrases in example 3.5 (a) are based on the same underlying eight-syllable (*ottonario*) phrase rhythm, similar to Lippmann's "Ottonario IIA1" (example 3.1) and illustrated in example 3.5 (b). This explains Asioli's interpretation of the final measure of example 3.5 (a) as a *piano* verse inflection (stressed-unstressed) rather than as a straightforward *sdrucciolo* verse (stressed-unstressed-unstressed): the underlying *ottonario* phrase rhythm regulates the entire passage, regardless of such expressive deviations. It functions, in effect, as a "structural" verse meter. Each "true musical syllable" may be altered and varied in accordance with the desired *accento musicale,* but the framework of the *ritmo* remains— even when, as in example 3.5 (a), it corresponds precisely to neither of the actual notated phrases.

Asioli's "Comparison between the Musical Phrase and the Different Poetic Meters"

Having established the identity of poetic verse meter (*metro*) with phrase rhythm (*ritmo*), and the principle of its musical realization through concurrent melodic and harmonic designs, Asioli went on to document in detail each type of verse/phrase, arranged in decreasing order according to length and beginning with the eleven-syllable phrase (*endecasillabo*). Although this part of his book has never before appeared in English translation, its influence is evident in countless studies dealing with Italian opera. Because it is such an important document, the following survey of his teachings on rhythm, illustrated with a few additional examples, includes extensive quotations.

Asioli began by describing a basic method for transferring poetic syllables and accents to musical note values. This generated an abstract notion of a fundamental rhythmic phrase that was regarded as equivalent to the similarly abstract concept of a fundamental verse meter. In practice, of course, the actual notated phrase or written verse, as performed or conceived, could vary in accent and rhythm from one verse/phrase to the next. Although Asioli did not illustrate these rhythmic generalizations with notated formulas, his method nevertheless results in a conceptualized series of "rhythmic-musical types" similar to those identified by Lippmann and summarized in example 3.1. His discussion of particular features in individual melodies presupposed an underlying framework of such archetypal meters/rhythms.

Owing to the complexity of the subject matter, however, Asioli's terminology was not entirely transparent. In essence, he professed an acceptance of the old-fashioned theory of applying longer and shorter note values to the stronger and weaker accents of the verse, in the ratio 2:1. This involved a presumed equivalence of verse syllables with *tempi musicali* and verse accents with *tempi ritmici.* But the meanings of *tempi* in this context were never adequately specified. The former term appears to have described syllables in terms of their relation to the "musical note values" of a particular time signature, while the latter term referred to accents by their "rhythmic durations." This formulaic approach was tempered, however, by what he regarded as the necessity for expressive variety, which meant that the rhythmic values that appeared on the page did not necessarily correspond to the underlying *ritmo* of a given passage of melody (as in the two phrases of example 3.5). Here is the relevant passage:

> It is not given to everyone to be a poet, and perhaps no author of music has ever passed beyond the limits of mediocrity in this genre. It is therefore necessary that the young composer be sufficiently instructed in the rules of versification to understand and profit from the following comparison. The [verse] Meter and the musical Phrase are two identical things in terms of the number of syllables and the note values [of a given time signature: *tempi musicali*], and in terms of the accents or long syllables and the rhythmic durations [*tempi ritmici*]. On the strength of this identity, it can be said that musical Phrases are lines of ten syllables, nine syllables, eight syllables, seven syllables, etc. The long Syllable, following the laws of prosody, is considered to have twice the value of the short. But in the musical Phrase these values are not strictly observed, since the durations are lengthened or shortened according to the ever-present aim of expressive variety, with the sole injunction that they remain firmly placed within the rhythmic tempo. The short syllable is invariably found on the weak beats of the measure. In fast duple tempos it sometimes has the same value as the long, but it maintains its proper value of half in triple, compound-duple, and compound-quadruple time. It very often falls upon even smaller subdivisions of the weak beats, which, one could almost say, surge toward the accent on the long syllable and rhythmic duration in such a way as to render it more lively and marked. Having thus established that any musical tempo is made up of long and short [syllables], we shall turn first to the *Endecasillabo*.[95]

Asioli, "On the Endecasillabo"

Owing to the irregularity of its internal accents, Asioli considered the *endecasillabo* unsuitable for use as a standard melodic *ritmo*. It was appropriate only for the unmeasured melody of recitative—that is, for melody unregulated by a common vocal phrase rhythm and uncoordinated with the impulses of a repetitive harmonic rhythm:

> The *Endecasillabo*, as its name suggests, is composed of eleven syllables, and therefore of eleven musical note values. But since its accents—which fall on the sixth and tenth syllables, or on the fourth, eighth, and tenth

syllables, or on the fourth, sixth, eighth, and tenth syllables—do not appear
uniformly in every verse and do not have to correspond to the regularity of
the underlying harmonic rhythms that always occur at an equal distance,
the *Endecasillabo* gives rise to a number of discrepancies that are dia-
metrically opposed to good construction and to the connections between
rhythmic phrases. This restricts the Musician and the Poet to use it only in
unmeasured melody, that is to say, in the Recitative of the *Dramma*. It is true
that quite a few writers of music have composed and continue to compose
Sonetti, Stanze, etc. [using *endecasillabi*], notwithstanding the difficulty mentioned above, but it is also indisputable that a delicate ear senses in them the
effort required to obtain uniform phrases and the irregularity, incoherence,
and contrived nature of these phrases.[96]

Lyric *endecasillabi* were in practice more common than Asioli suggested,[97] and there was also an alternative pattern of accents upon the
fourth, seventh, and tenth syllables, derived from repetitions of a dactylic
foot and described by authors such as Baini (1820) and Ritorni (1841).[98]
Asioli's criticism appears to testify more to his own preference for the
uniform rhythmic phrases characteristic of the 1830s than to the inherent unsuitability of the *endecasillabo* for melody. This verse type could
be traced to the origins of opera and to the sixteenth-century pastoral,
especially those of Tasso. It was uniquely flexible in the sense that it could
appear in either "complete" or "broken" form. The *endecasillabo* could
comprise a combination of a seven-syllable line and a five-syllable line,
which could be used in "major" broken form (*a maiore*), in this order, or
in "minor" broken form (*a minore*), as a five-syllable line followed by a
seven-syllable line.[99] The free mixture of eleven-, seven-, and occasionally
five-syllable lines that came to be known as the free verse (*verso sciolto*) of
recitative derived from this peculiarity of the *endecasillabo*.

Asioli went on to offer more detailed insights into its setting and
performance, in which he emphasized the flexibility of its underlying
rhythm and the application of expressive devices relating to what was
defined above as the *accento musicale:*

> The measure of recitative is notated in the four quarter notes of common
> time. This tempo is not perceptible, but is merely a visual convention. Triple,
> compound-duple, and compound-quadruple time would seem better suited
> according to the rules of prosody, which assign to the long syllables twice the
> value of the short. The duration of the musical figures depends entirely upon
> the arbitrary declamation of the singer, who must accelerate the motion of

the recitative for urgent, angry, and vehement passions, who must impart a sturdy and grave motion to affects of imperiousness and strength, and who must slow down for the amorous, melancholy, and pathetic passions. In the first of these three different genres of passions the composer will carry the voice toward the high note; in the second he will not depart from the central register and the chest voice; and in the third he will remain in the low register or the bass. He must besides place the accent or long syllable on the first and third quarters, and sometimes on the first half of the second and fourth; he must study the verse well in order to avoid where necessary the two, three, and even four registers of the voice in a single musical tempo [i.e., dominant affect; see chapter 5]; to examine the places where he can use the caesura to improve the declamation, by adding one syllable to the verse and to the musical beat. Finally he will apply the norms of how to express exclamation, supposition, and question marks as set out in the following examples, because one manner of singing and of modulating has gained currency at this time and through convention has become a rule.[100]

Asioli, "On the Decasillabo*"*

In accordance with Asioli's restrictive method for deriving fundamental *ritmi* from verses, the *decasillabo* gave rise to a distinctive anapestic pattern that mapped most readily onto a march-like rhythm. It was related to one of the most characteristic and recognizable varieties of the *ottonario*, likewise beginning with two upbeats (see example 3.1).[101] Asioli's description made clear, however, that the composer was free, indeed compelled, to depart from this underlying pattern in response to expressive demands inspired by the text, which resulted in a variety of different phrases founded upon "the same meter and words." In this way he corroborated the practice of assuming an ideal regular verse meter as what might now be called a "structural" rhythm. This underlying latent succession of regular *ritmi* provided a foundation upon which the vocal melody could engage in all manner of irregularities and expressive fluctuations:

> The comparison between [verse] meter and the measured phrase begins at this point, since, from the *decasillabo* to the *ternario*, the accents prescribed by prosody for every meter go perfectly in accord with the impulses of the harmonic rhythm. Here the composer acquires a limitless ability to vary, shorten, and lengthen the notes and the durations of the syllables; just imagine how so many different phrases can pour forth from the composer's inspired fantasy upon the same meter and words, and how this will produce new and increasing appeal for the listener.

The order in which the ten long and short syllables are arranged in the *de-casillabo* is the same as that of the ten beats or notes that form the *decasillabo* phrase. This begins with two short syllables on the last beat of the measure so that the accent of the third syllable falls on the first rhythmic impulse on the downbeat, then two short syllables fall on the second weak beat of the measure so that the accent on the sixth syllable falls on the second rhythmic impulse on the upbeat. The next two short syllables fall on the last weak beat of the measure so that the new measure begins with the main inflection of the poetic line, or ninth syllable, on the downbeat; this is a firm rule for any main inflection, whether the verse is *piano, tronco,* or *sdrucciolo.* The phrase may also begin on the primary rhythmic impulse on the downbeat, as long as a bi-syllable of one long and one short is at the beginning of the verse; just as it can comprise two musical verses or two phrases by slowing down the melody or making use of the caesura or pauses.[102]

To summarize, according to Asioli, the stressed accents within the *decasillabo* fell upon the third, sixth, and ninth syllables, giving rise to a paradigmatic rhythm characterized by anapestic feet (unstressed-un-stressed-stressed). Several music examples were offered in support of these remarks, including one from "Non più andrai, farfallone amoroso," which closes the first act of Mozart's *Le nozze di Figaro.* In each case Asioli annotated the long or accented syllables with the numbers 3, 6, and 9, respectively, and defined the phrase by means of a slur, marked "Frase." In example 3.6, the *decasillabo* is illustrated by an alternative excerpt, taken not from Asioli but from Leporello's "catalog aria" in act 1 of Mozart's *Don Giovanni.* This has been selected not only to demonstrate a conventional arrangement of accents but also because it features an instance of metric augmentation—one of the devices arising from the composer's "limitless ability to vary, shorten, and lengthen the notes and the durations of the syllables," according to Asioli—in which the note values of the underlying melodic phrase rhythm are doubled. At the composer's discretion, the latent regular phrase rhythm could be halved or doubled so long as it retained its structural integrity. As Asioli put it, "Phrases of even-numbered note values may be shortened by one half, by dividing the value of the notes, just as they may be lengthened by doubling the value, without altering the tempo and without disturbing the rhythmic-harmonic movements."[103] He provided a guide to such metric shifts by way of a chart in volume 1.[104] Example 3.6 demonstrates how the note values of the second phrase (mm. 7–10) have been doubled for expressive

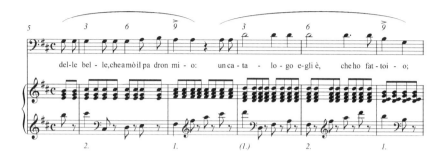

3.6. Mozart, *Don Giovanni* (1787), act 1, no. 4, "Madamina!" mm. 5–10 (with analytical symbols).

purposes, while maintaining the identity of the *decasillabo ritmo.* The symbols for "first" and "second" rhythmic impulses beneath the stave appear to indicate an instance of what Asioli described as a phrase of three *movimenti,* although it might better be understood as beginning with an extended "second" or weak impulse.

Asioli, "On the Novenario"

"No one really knows why the nine-syllable verse is almost excluded from the *melodramma,*" Asioli reflected, "even though melodic and harmonic rhythms may be adapted to it just as much as to the others. The accents or long syllables of the *novenario* are found on the third, fifth, and eighth, so the composer begins the phrase on the upbeat with two short syllables in order that the strong rhythmic impulse falls upon the third syllable, the weak on the fifth, and the strong on the eighth in the second measure."[105]

One of Asioli's accompanying analyses appears in example 3.7. Although his original soprano clef has been replaced by the more familiar treble clef, the annotations have been faithfully reproduced, with the sole exception of a suggested alternative interpretation of accompanying *movimenti* added beneath the stave in square brackets. As can be seen, Asioli highlighted the vocal phrases or "rhythms" with slurs, the verse accents with indications of their corresponding syllables, and the strong and weak impulses of the "harmonic rhythm" with the numbers *1.°* (*primo*) and *2.°* (*secondo*) beneath the stave. Owing primarily to the length of the verse

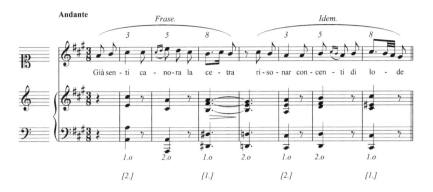

3.7. Asioli, *Il Maestro di composizione* (1832), Examples 3: no. 7, 22 (not attributed).

meter, each phrase appears to comprise three *movimenti*, in the pattern: 1.–2.–1., followed by an additional "resting" measure. This is, however, something of an illusion resulting from an acceptance of the notated $\frac{3}{8}$ time signature. Considered in $\frac{6}{8}$, as indicated by the figures in square brackets, the impulses would fall regularly upon the first subsidiary accent and principal inflection of each line of verse.

Asioli, "On the Ottonario*"*

The *ottonario*, like other even-numbered verses, was governed by a strict pattern of accents which, in its case, always fell on the third and seventh syllables. Subsidiary accents on the first and fifth syllables were nevertheless common, leading frequently to settings that avoided the conspicuous upbeat figure of two notes and began instead on the downbeat. In the following brief account, Asioli, following his own method to the letter, described only a *ritmo* that began with two weak upbeats, similar to that which underlies the aria "Questo amor, vergogna mia" from Puccini's *Edgar* (example 3.2). He mentioned the subsidiary accent on the fifth syllable, but not on the first:

> The essential accents of the *ottonario* fall upon the third and seventh [syllables], so that the composer must begin the phrase two notes before the downbeat in order that the first accent occurs on the strong beat, and must place the three following short syllables in the remainder of the measure so that the seventh falls upon the accent of the primary rhythmic impulse of

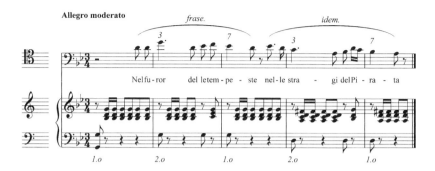

3.8. Asioli, *Il Maestro di composizione* (1832), Examples 3: no. 8, 22 (Bellini, *Il pirata,* act 1).

the next measure. The *ottonario* will therefore be somewhat more harmonious and musical when it also has an accent on the fifth, because this would
coincide with the second rhythmic impulse.[106]

Example 3.8, one of several selected by Asioli in support of the above
passage of text, presents a melody from Gualtiero's opening *cavatina* in act
1 of Bellini's *Il pirata* (1827) that exemplifies this particular rhythmic realization of the *ottonario*. The analytical annotations, reproduced faithfully
from the original, reveal a conventional pattern of accents on third and
seventh syllables coinciding with the weak and strong rhythmic impulses
of the accompaniment. In terms of melodic contour, these two phrases
are guided in a similarly straightforward fashion by the tonic scale in "first
position," descending from g¹ to the octave below. A more sophisticated
example of Bellini's use of the *ottonario* phrase rhythm is discussed in
connection with 3.17 below.

Asioli, "On the Settenario*"*

Owing to its inherent flexibility, the seven-syllable verse was among the
most commonly used in nineteenth-century opera. In theory it possessed
only one fixed accent, on the penultimate or sixth syllable, the others being more or less free. According to Asioli's description,

> *Settenario* verses have the accents sometimes on the fourth and sixth [syl-
> lables], at other times on the second and sixth, or sometimes on the second,
> fourth, and sixth. This last arrangement, which is the most common, is also

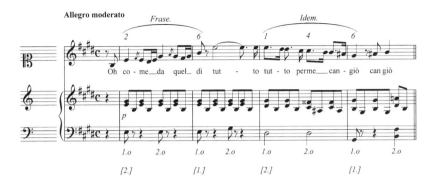

3.9. Asioli, *Il Maestro di composizione* (1832), Examples 3: no. 9, 25 (Rossini, *Semiramide*, act 1).

the most harmonious because the poetic accents occur perfectly in accord with the rhythmic beats, while the short syllables, in the aforementioned manner, coincide with these beats with greater or lesser offense for the listener in proportion to the slowness of the tempo. Moreover, this ceases to matter as soon as the *settenario* is mixed with the *endecasillabo* in the recitative, for the reasons given.[107]

In practice the initial "casual accents" (*accenti casuali*) of the verse, to employ Ritorni's (1841) terminology, could rival the penultimate "obligatory accent" (*accento obbligato*) in perceived importance, even though they were treated with flexibility. The initial accent could appear on any of the first three syllables, although it was more commonly found on the first or second. This shifting casual accent is evident in the excerpt from Rossini's *Semiramide* (1823; example 3.9) that Asioli provided as an example of the *settenario,* in spite of its apparent incompatibility with his account. Seemingly oblivious to the contradiction between commentary and analysis, Asioli marked the beginning of the second phrase of example 3.9 with an unambiguous number "1" to indicate the accent on the first syllable. This may be explained once again through the distinction that was always observed by Asioli, but never adequately explained, between the *idea* of a regular verse meter as underlying or "structural" *ritmo* (as described in his text) and the *reality* of its application (as illustrated by his examples). The two phrases of example 3.9 are both variations of the same basic phrase rhythm or *ritmo melodico,* corresponding approximately to Lippmann's "Settenario IIA" from example 3.1. They

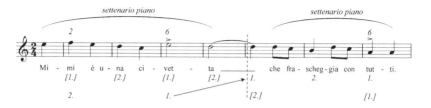

3.10. Puccini, *La bohème*, act 3, R19, mm. 1–8 (Milan: Ricordi, 1896; melody only, with analytical symbols).

map onto three supporting rhythmic impulses (*movimenti*) in the pattern 1.–2.–1., followed by a weak "resting point" (*riposo*), according to Asioli's analysis, or onto a regular succession of impulses operating at the level of the measure, according to the alternative analysis appended in square brackets.

The workings of the *accento musicale* are much in evidence. At the end of the first *tronco* phrase in m. 2, Rossini playfully anticipated the first word ("*tutto*") of the second phrase, in order, first, to simulate the effect of an initial *piano* verse with an engaging syncopation and, second, to supply the requisite first-syllable upbeat that was missing from the line "*tut*to per me cangiò." Rossini employed a similar effect at the end of the second phrase in m. 4 by repeating the final word "*cangiò*," as if to simulate a stuttering, *sdrucciolo* ending. In a manner characteristic of Italian teaching methods, these features received no comment whatsoever from Asioli, other than the syllable numbers added above the stave. The reader was introduced to increasingly complicated examples gradually, as if imperceptibly, and left to assimilate them without further guidance.

The following example (3.10) from Puccini's *La bohème* illustrates the technique of diminishing the note values of an underlying *settenario* phrase rhythm by half. Rodolfo's initial words, which may be translated as "Mimì is a coquette" (or "little owl"), are set to a basic *ritmo* that begins with an upbeat and doubles the note value on the principal verse inflection or *desinenza*. In the following phrase, the music captures something of his emotional state, as he suggests that she "flirts with everyone," by quickening the pace of vocal delivery through a halving of the note values. The two-and-a-half measures of the second phrase amount to precisely

half the five measures of the first, even though Puccini was forced to alter the normal placement of accents to accommodate the anapestic feet
of the verse ("che fra*scheg*gia con *tutti*"). Compressing a vocal phrase in
this way necessitates a change in its relation to the harmonic or accompanimental rhythm. In effect, it gives rise to a metric shift. As indicated
by the symbols for the weak and strong rhythmic impulses or *movimenti*
in example 3.10, the first phrase is perceived at the level of two-measure
units while the second, after the dotted vertical line signifying the shift
in meter, operates at the level of the individual measure.

Asioli, "On the Senario"

In keeping with other verse types containing an even number of syllables,
the accents of the *senario* are firmly fixed. Asioli's description was accordingly unequivocal:

> The *senario* has two accents, one on the second and the other on the fifth
> [syllable]. For this reason the phrase must begin with a short syllable on
> the upbeat, so that the second syllable falls on the rhythmic impulse on the
> downbeat, and the fifth falls similarly on the rhythmic impulse in the fol-
> lowing measure, which, since it coincides with the principal inflection of the
> verse, will always be of the strong type on the first beat in any meter.[108]

Although in theory the strictly regulated *senario* was quite separate
from the looser odd-numbered verse meters, in late nineteenth-century
practice it could, as an underlying "structural" *ritmo melodico,* accommodate lines of five and seven syllables by omitting its initial upbeat or
by adding an additional weak syllable. Puccini occasionally made use
of this particular *ritmo* when confronted, often as a result of his own
contributions to the libretto, with a mixture of odd- and even-numbered
verse types (see, for instance, examples 5.5 or 6.14). Asioli's demonstration of the *senario* through a passage from Bellini's *La straniera* (1829),
given in example 3.11, presents no such complexities. The repetitions of
the *ritmo,* coinciding closely with the actual phrases of the melody, were
indicated as usual by slurs and syllable numbers and the impulses of the
accompaniment by figures beneath the stave. It is interesting to note that
Asioli omitted these figures in the first measure of 3.11, even though the
vocal part contained a complete *senario* phrase, albeit with fermata. Evi-

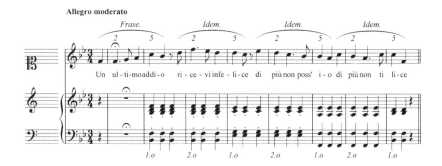

3.11. Asioli, *Il Maestro di composizione* (1832), Examples 3: no. 10, 26 (Bellini, *La straniera,* act 1).

dently, without an orchestral accompaniment there could be no harmonic rhythm. In melodic terms, the phrases correspond to a simple design, which, although varied a little, may be heard to descend after its initial phrase through the octave from f^2 to f^1 by way of four-note segments of the scale: $f^2–e\flat^2–d2–c^2$; $d^2–c^2–b\flat^1–a^1$; $b\flat^1–a^1–g^1–f^1$. Designs such as this were typical of singing exercises or *vocalizzi* based on "melodic attachments" (*attacchi*) to the "third position" of the scale or "movement by step" (*movimento di grado*) and often featured in principal melodies, as discussed below in chapters 4 and 6.

Asioli, "On the Quinario"

In the looser, more prose-like style of operatic text that developed from the 1870s onwards, as typified by the libretti Puccini helped to create in *Manon Lescaut* and *La bohème,* the five-syllable *ritmo* took on an increasingly important role owing to its ability to accommodate a variety of verse phrases. As the shortest serviceable meter, it was also the most flexible. Asioli's description emphasized this versatility:

> The *quinario* has no need of any accents other than that on the fourth syllable; but if it also has an accent on the first or second syllable it becomes much more harmonious because the phrase, instead of beginning with three short syllables on the upbeat, begins on the first or second syllable above the weak rhythmic impulse, so that its inflection on the main accent occurs on the strong impulse.[109]

3.12. Puccini, *Preludio sinfonico* (1882), reduction of mm. 1–16.

In place of Asioli's supporting musical extracts, example 3.12 presents, in reduced score, the opening sixteen-measure period of Puccini's Preludio sinfonico in A major, submitted for his second-year exam at the Milan Conservatory and first performed by students there on July 15, 1882.[110] Press reviews of the concert, keen to stress the progressive credentials of the new generation of composers emanating from the classes of Bazzini and Dominiceti, highlighted their command of orchestral style and drew comparisons with the latest German compositions. As Girardi points out, the symphonic elements of this work and its technical accomplishments demonstrate that "Puccini was capable of competing with composers then active in the flourishing quartet societies."[111] Notwithstanding its chromatic harmonies and appoggiaturas, however, the music of example 3.12 also exhibits a conventional *quinario* phrase rhythm that suggests an affinity with older, specifically Italian traditions of operatic and vocal music. This is especially evident in the placement of eighth-note resting points (*riposi*) at the end of each eight-measure phrase, rather than after every two- or four-measure *ritmo*. Harmonically, too, it rests partly upon an old-fashioned Neapolitan "regular bass motion" (in this case, the progression of the descending third and ascending step), which will be explained more fully in the next chapter. There is even an instance of an imitative entry (*imitazione*) in the fourth measure, familiar from countless Italian student exercises involving the attachment of short melodic designs and their out-of-phase imitations to a fixed voice (*canto fermo*). Taken together, these features may go some way toward explaining any perceived "Italianness" of the melody.

The two eight-measure phrases of example 3.12, which together make up what modern music theory would call an antecedent-consequent period, each comprise four repetitions of a *quinario-ritmo* with a subsidiary accent on the first syllable or beat. These would appear to correspond more closely to the style of regular phrasing typical of Italian vocal, as opposed to German instrumental, music. Each two-measure statement of the phrase rhythm is furnished with a varied melodic design which, after two such statements, concludes with an appropriate type of cadence. The first cadence occurs in the fourth measure, in the form of a four-two chord leading to a weak first-inversion tonic (what Gjerdingen calls the *passo indietro* or "step backwards");[112] there follows a more robust half-cadence in the eighth measure, an evaded cadence (*inganno*) in the twelfth, and a perfect authentic cadence at the end. The striking parallels with Reicha's theoretical model, outlined above, suggest more than mere coincidence. Indeed it is conceivable that a composition student at Milan, such as Puccini, when instructed to write an extended symphonic piece for an end-of-year exam, would rely on just such a "progressive" method associated with instrumental repertory. Not only does the succession of designs, cadences, rhythms, and members in example 3.12 recall the description given in Reicha's *Trattato della melodia* (1830), but it also matches the similar account of melodic structure provided by Cesare De Sanctis (n.d. [1887?]). In recognition of this connection, the phrases in example 3.12 are annotated using De Sanctis's terms, developed from Reicha and illustrated in example 3.16, for designs and their responses.

The tendency of the phrases in example 3.12 to group together into four-measure units (or "*rhythmes*," in Reicha's terms) may be regarded partly as a consequence of the choice of five-syllable meter. On account of its brevity, the *quinario* verse was often perceived in pairs, as lines of "double *quinario*" (*quinario doppio*). This was a common enough occurrence for Asioli to provide a specific explanation:

> It is known that two *quinarj* form a *decasillabo* as far as the number of syllables are concerned, but not in terms of the position of the accents or the

caesura. The *decasillabo* has accents on the third, sixth, and ninth, whereas two *quinarj* have accents on the second and fourth, and seventh and ninth, which alters the harmony of these two meters so much that even the ear most insensitive to accents and rhythms could not fail to notice the scale of difference between them.[113]

An example (3.13) of the *quinario doppio* from the end of Puccini's *Le Villi* (1883–85) serves to demonstrate how an underlying "structural" *ritmo* based on three upbeats leading to a main inflection and succeeded by a resting point (corresponding to Lippmann's "Quinario III") could allow for considerable freedom in terms of the scansion of the actual text. Entire five-syllable lines could be interpolated in the caesura between the statements of the double phrase rhythm, leading to enjambment: a lack of noticeable pauses between lines of verse such that they appear to run together in a continuous flow. In example 3.13, a *ritmo* of *quinari doppi* underpins a theme associated initially with Anna's prayer for Roberto's journey and recalled here to underline his regret, having caused her death through his infidelity. The text, from the premiere of 1884,[114] is a regular stanza of four lines:

O sommo Id*dio*—del mio cam*mino*, (5+5)	Oh almighty God! This is the ultimate aim
del mio de*stino*—questa è la *meta* . . . (5+5)	of my journey, of my destiny.
fa che il per*dono*—la renda *lieta* . . . (5+5)	Grant forgiveness so that happiness returns to her
un solo is*tante* . . . —e poi mor*rò*! (5+5)	for a single instant, and then I shall die!

Each statement of the phrase rhythm that underpins the first three lines encompasses a melodic design based on a *quinario*, together with its sequential repetition at the third below (see, for instance, mm. 13–15). The double *ritmo melodico* likewise progresses through sequential repetitions, rising by thirds through the notes of the tonic triad: $e\flat^2$ in m. 13, g^2 in m. 15, and $b\flat^2$ in m. 17. Puccini's melody reveals a significant disparity between the underlying verse meter and the actual setting of the individual lines of the text. The opening verse, "O sommo Iddio"—closing with tied eighth notes in m. 14 (rather than a more usual quarter note) in recognition of the underlying *ritmo*—is repeated at the beginning of the second statement of the phrase in m. 15, thereby forcing the displaced line "Del mio destin" to be squeezed into the gap or caesura between the

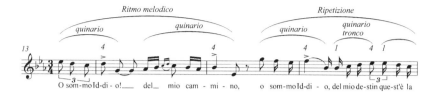

3.13. Puccini, *Le Villi*, act 2, R50, mm. 13–19 (Milan: Ricordi, 1891; melody only, with analytical symbols).

two constituent *ritmi* of the double phrase rhythm as passing notes. A similar interpolation occurs in the third statement of the phrase in mm. 17–19, where the initial *quinario*, "Fa che il perdono," is sounded twice. In effect, the vocal line incorporates two additional five-syllable lines through a process of expressive variation grounded upon the notion of the *accento musicale*.[115]

Asioli, "On the Quaternario and Ternario"

Like the *quinario,* the two shortest verse types in Italian prosody were often to be found in pairs, as components of either a six- or eight-syllable line:

> The *quaternario* and *ternario* rarely occur alone, but often within the *ottonario* and *senario,* because these may be divided into two equal hemistichs, or sections of the phrase, and because the main inflections of the *quaternario* agree perfectly with the rhythms and accents of the third and seventh syllables of the *ottonario,* and those of the *ternario* coincide with the accents and rhythms of the second and fifth syllables of the *senario.* In the following examples, consequently, the phrases of the one are shown to be mixed up with those of the other.[116]

One of Asioli's examples demonstrating the inclusion of the *ternario* within a larger *senario* phrase is given in example 3.14, from Rossini's *Mosè*

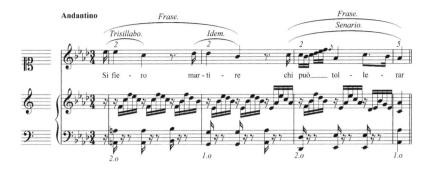

3.14. Asioli, *Il Maestro di composizione* (1832), Examples 3: no. 12, 31 (Rossini, *Mosè in Egitto*, act 2).

in Egitto (1818). It demonstrates, in effect, the application of the caesura as a means of dividing a verse into hemistichs. The double verse (*ternario doppio*) of the first phrase maps onto the regular rhythmic impulses of the accompaniment in the same way as the conventional *senario* of the second phrase, in spite of the seeming absence of a principal verse inflection.

Asioli on Mixed and Irregular Verses

Asioli concluded his comparison between musical phrases and the different poetic meters with a few examples showing how to deal with mixed and irregular verses. In doing so, he was compelled to allude more explicitly than before to the essential separation of the two main levels of melodic *ritmo:* as both a regular underlying structural rhythm based on verse meter, and as an expressive variation on this, "tripping lightly over the top," as the journal *La Musica* put it on May 21, 1883. "The verse and the phrase can take on diverse aspects," Asioli maintained, "such as speeding up their course, combining two phrases into one verse or vice versa, and may even lose the sense of rhythmic impulse and phrase rhythm through slowness. But all this must be directed by the expression of the word."[117] He concentrated in particular on the suitability of blank verse for lyric setting, singling out for attention the frequently encountered division of the eleven-syllable line into components of five- and seven-syllables, explained above through the categories of the "broken" *a maiore* and *a minore* forms of the verse. The only condition he placed on such devia-

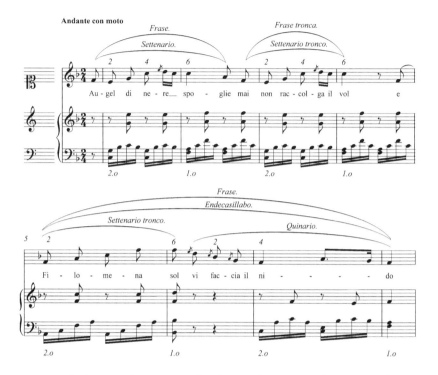

3.15. Asioli, *Il Maestro di composizione* (1832), Examples 3: no. 13, 31 (not attributed)

tions from regular verse meter was that the *ritmo armonico,* the alternation of strong and weak impulses in the orchestral accompaniment, should keep to the "proper steps," or verse inflections. This meant that verses and phrases, especially those of different lengths, could appear detached from a regular melodic phrase rhythm only so long as they agreed with the underlying succession of strong and weak impulses: in effect, this restricted the setting of verses and phrases, however varied and irregular they happened to be, to a regular but mutable underlying meter:

> The instant iridescence resulting from the joining of various meters, or of two unequal hemistichs that form an *endecasillabo,* compel the melodic phrase rhythm, or the phrase, to change character, while the harmonic rhythm follows the proper steps so as not to cause offense to the listener.[118]

Through the extract from a setting of Metastasio's cantata *Il Nome* shown in example 3.15, Asioli sought to clarify how a regular underlying pulse could mitigate the effects of a "change of character" in the phrases of the vocal melody. Having illustrated the relation of the initial verses and phrases in mm. 1–4 to a *settenario-ritmo* with analytical slurs and annotations, he defined the concluding phrase in mm. 5–8 differently, on account of its verse type, as an *endecasillabo,* split on this occasion *a maiore* into two overlapping hemistichs of seven and five syllables. In terms of phrase structure, however, Asioli's symbols for the "first" and "second" impulses of the regular harmonic rhythm, the repetitions of 1.° and 2.° beneath the stave, show that the final four measures of example 3.15 were intended to be understood as a continuation of the same established *settenario-ritmo.* According to this interpretation, the concluding word in mm. 7–8 was simply prolonged through its "missing" fourth to sixth syllables, even though this meant that the principal inflection of its *quinario* phrase ("nido") coincided with a weak impulse (2.°) at the beginning of m. 7 (which should not be regarded in this context as a "strong" measure, according to modern [German] theories of hypermeter). The ambiguity of the analysis may be explained through Asioli's attempt to assimilate diverse aspects of practice into a single didactic system, encompassing phrase structures at various levels determined by verse, melody, and accompaniment. Asioli generally chose to label his examples of mixed verses according to the actual verse meters employed, leaving the symbols for the "first" and "second" rhythmic impulses to attest to their underlying structural *ritmi.*

Later Writings on Ritmo

Despite the occasional ambiguities in Asioli's approach to phraseology and the confusion that accompanied the assimilation of Reicha's alternative theory, subsequent Italian authors continued to rely on the basic teachings on rhythm set out in *Il Maestro di composizione.* Asioli's survey of verse meters and phrases became something of a standard fixture in publications on composition of the mid-nineteenth century. While some, such as Picchianti (1834), contributed to the uncertainty surrounding the term *ritmo* by attempting to combine Asioli's definition with Reicha's system, others, such as Ritorni (1841), more or less paraphrased Asioli as a starting point for further discussion.[119]

By 1844, as mentioned above, the confusion inadvertently provoked by Reicha over the term *ritmo* prompted a quest for clarity in the pages of

the *Gazzetta musicale di Milano*. According to Bernardoni,[120] this quest
was answered most successfully by Geremia Vitali's *La Musica ne' suoi
principj nuovamente spiegata* (Music Newly Explained through Its Principles, 1847), in which *ritmo* was defined according to a compromise between Asioli's concept of a regular phrase rhythm, determined by verse
meter and realized through corresponding melodic and harmonic designs,
and Reicha's emphasis on an abstract notion of symmetry demarcated by
bar lines and cadences. In the following quotation, Vitali merged the idea
of melodic phrase rhythms with a broader and less strictly systematic
concept of symmetry, or "squareness" (*quadratura*):

> And by *ritmo* is meant: an individual part of a melody, the constant regu-
> larity of beats, the homogenous squareness of the phrases, and the whole de-
> velopment of the [poetic-musical] images. . . . I use the term "symmetrical"
> because all the parts that form a musical concept have within themselves a
> certain symmetry of extension and a quality that renders them in confor-
> mity with one another; and in this is found the so-called squareness, one of
> the principal elements of beautiful melody.[121]

Ritmo incorporated yet more meanings over the course of the next
few decades in response to progressive theories, such as those positing
a more or less direct analogy between music and language. An example
may be found in Salvatore D'Anna's *Nuova sistema musicale: Grammatica
riguardante i principi elementari di musica* (New Musical System: Grammar in Regard to the Elementary Principles of Music, 1866), which, recalling ideas of Melchiorre Balbi, put forward a comparison of phrase
and period to verse and language. The essentials of Asioli's teachings
on *ritmo* continued nevertheless to inform Italian treatises as late as De
Sanctis (n.d. [1887?]), conditioned in this case by the theories of Swiss
musicologist Mathis Lussy (1883) as mediated through Amintore Galli's
writings on phonetics and pronunciation (1884). De Sanctis was a Roman composer, organist, and orchestra director who became *maestro di
cappella* at the church of Minerva e di San Giovanni dei Fiorentini during the 1860s and a respected assessor of operas for the Roman theaters.
In 1876 he accepted the chair in harmony and counterpoint at the Liceo
musicale della Reale Accademia di S. Cecilia.[122] Although his explanation
of *ritmo* drew upon an eclectic mix of sources, from Koch, Asioli, and
Reicha to Galli and Lussy, he affirmed the centrality of melodic phrases

3.16. Cesare De Sanctis, *La polifonia nell'arte moderna* (1887?), no. 138, 65.

and harmony to the different species of *ritmo:* "Although rhythm finds itself embodied in melody, harmony is no less important. . . . By *phrase* or *musical period* is meant a succession of notes regulated symmetrically by accents or by rests on strong or weak beats."[123] This assumed identity of melody and rhythm recalls Asioli's notion of a structural phrase rhythm that becomes perceptible primarily through the superimposition of melodic designs. De Sanctis demonstrated this correlation by means of the example reproduced in 3.16. "The first two measures constitute the design or rhythmic motive," he explained; "the phrases and counter-phrases are needed to form a regular musical period. These originate in the repetitions of the rhythmic motive and its response. The phrases may also be subdivided into sections or caesuras, which serve at the same time to form incises."[124] The melody of example 3.16 may be understood to result, therefore, from the repetitions of its basic *quinario* phrase rhythm. Also in keeping with Asioli, De Sanctis pointed out that for expressive purposes composers would often deviate from the mechanical process of duplicating a phrase rhythm, together with its corresponding melodic designs and responses. "Periods may be made up of more rhythmic designs," he suggested, and "rhythms are *mixed* or *alternating* when a phrase is succeeded by another formed of a different group of accents; this is much used in modern music."[125]

IV. SHORT CASE STUDIES FROM BELLINI AND PUCCINI

The practical application of melodic rhythms (*ritmi melodici*) in nineteenth-century Italian opera involved a series of associated formulas for generating pitch structures, such as the harmonic-contrapuntal frameworks derived from the unfortunately named "regular motions" (*moti regolare*) and the repetition and imitation of melodic "attachments" (*attacchi*). The setting of verses also called for an appreciation of the complementary doctrines of the "imitation of feelings" (*imitazione sentimentale*), the "dominant affect" (*affetto dominante*), and the ways in which accepted modes of "conduct" (*condotta*) regulated the disposition of phrases and periods into larger forms. In an attempt to impose some order upon the subject matter, however, discussion of these additional factors has been postponed until later chapters.

To conclude the survey of rhythm, two short case studies from Bellini and two from Puccini's early operas are set out below to suggest some of the ways in which historical concepts and practices, supplemented with more modern techniques of analysis, might be applied as a set of "tools" to assist in the interpretation of operatic rhythm. Central to the method outlined in the following examples are Asioli's symbols of the slur for the phrase rhythm of the vocal part, or *ritmo melodico,* and numbers beneath the stave for the strong and weak impulses of the accompanimental rhythm, or *ritmo armonico.* Although elaborations and embellishments in the vocal melody are occasionally simplified, this does not represent an analytical "reduction" to a more essential level, in the Schenkerian sense, but rather a hypothetical "restoration" of an underlying (mental) framework of traditional guiding melodic lines derived from "practical counterpoints" and *solfeggi* that serve to shape the contour of the melody. These will be discussed more fully in the next chapter. The concluding examples from Puccini seek to explore the continued relevance of similar theories and methods at the end of the nineteenth century, especially in cases that appear to argue against any straightforward correlation of verse, phrase, and rhythm.

Bellini, Norma *(1831), act 1, no. 3, "Casta Diva"*

A classic love triangle provides the dramatic premise or *argomento* for Bellini's masterpiece, played out in front of a backdrop of revolution against a despised foreign power. It was a ready-made recipe for success, in other words, which received a further boost from its association with recent patriotic uprisings in Bologna, Modena, and Parma. Set amidst the romantic and mysterious forests of Roman-occupied Gaul, the story revolves around the druidic high priestess Norma (soprano). Torn between love and duty, she has secretly borne two sons to her sworn enemy, the dashing Roman pro-consul Pollione (tenor). He, however, has come to prefer the more youthful attractions of an initiate to the druidic sisterhood of virgins, Adalgisa (another soprano), and thereby risks incurring not only Norma's considerable wrath but also a nationwide rebellion against Roman rule. Upon discovering her rival, Norma contemplates first infanticide, then suicide, but decides in the end to unleash the rebellion against her Roman betrayer. When Pollione is captured and put forward as a candidate for sacrifice, Norma, in another radical mood swing, is moved to confess her sins and to offer herself in his place. Overwhelmed, he opts to join her in the flames in what could be described as a kind of ecstatic and redemptive "love-death."

At the beginning of the opera, Norma enters at the head of a procession of "druids, priestesses, warriors, bards, eubages, and sacrificers" to enact the sacred lunar ritual of cutting mistletoe with a golden sickle. Her *cavatina*, "Casta Diva," a prayer (*preghiera*) for peace directed at the "chaste goddess" of the moon, is doubly ironic. Norma's appeal to quell the popular clamor for rebellion is motivated by concern not so much for the safety of her compatriots as for their enemy, her lover Pollione; and her calls for the virgin deity to reveal a face "unclouded and unveiled" elicit unavoidable parallels with the concealment of her own guilt, having broken her vows of chastity and led a double life as private Roman mistress and public Gallic virgin. These levels of meaning are superbly underscored by Bellini's setting (example 3.17), which begins serenely but turns toward a restless minor key in m. 23 at mention of the goddess's "fair countenance" and builds to a passionate, desperate outpouring of emotion in mm. 27–28 as Norma, her arms outstretched toward the moon, prays for release and reconciliation—ostensibly for her people, but in reality for herself.

According to the modern system of "letter" analysis, the melody as a whole may be understood to conform to the pattern a^1 a^2 b c. In terms of contemporary theories to be discussed at greater length in chapter 5, alternatively, it may be considered as a single period (*periodo*) divided into three component members (*membri*), corresponding to the categories of principal theme (*motivo*), contrasting passage (*passo caratteristico*), and final cadence (*cadenza finale*).[126] The principal theme in mm. 16–23 takes the first two lines of the *cavatina*'s initial quatrain—reproduced below from the original Ricordi vocal score of ca. 1832—while the contrasting and cadential passages in mm. 23–25 and 25–30 share the last two lines.

3.17.

a. (*above and facing page*) Bellini, *Norma* (1831), act 1, "Casta Diva," mm. 16–30 (Milan: Ricordi, ca. 1832).

Casta *Di*va che in*ar*genti (8)	Virgin Goddess, who casts silver light
queste *sa*cre antiche *pian*te, (8)	upon these sacred ancient plants,
a noi *vol*gi il bel sem*bian*te (8)	turn thy beautiful countenance on us,
senza *nu*be e senza *vel* (8)	unclouded and unveiled.

As may be seen from example 3.17 (a) and its analytical reduction in (b), Bellini exploited the tendency of the verses to separate into two four-syllable lines, or *quaternari doppi,* through their regular accents on the third and seventh syllables. The opening phrase in mm. 16–17, "Casta

Diva," despite mapping onto the same accompanimental framework of rhythmic impulses as the ensuing *ottonario* phrase in mm. 17–19, encompasses only the first four syllables of the verse and thereby imparts a sense of quickening momentum to the pair, in a manner evocative of a liturgical incantation and response. A similar device occurs in the next pair of phrases in mm. 20–23, transposed up a step and with the significant difference that the *ottonario* phrase finishing in m. 23 halves the value of its principal inflection, or *desinenza,* from a dotted half note to a dotted quarter note. This prepares the way for a doubling of the underlying harmonic rhythm to two impulses per notated measure in the "contrasting passage" of mm. 23–25, in response to Norma's disquiet over the personal implications of the request for the "chaste goddess" to reveal her face. The metric shift is illustrated by vertical dotted lines and figures in square brackets beneath the stave of example 3.17 (b).

Embellished with verbal repetitions, the basic *ottonario* phrase rhythm returns at the start of the cadential passage in m. 25. Its principal inflection, on "sem*bian*te," is, however, postponed for a full measure. In a stroke of genius, Bellini avoided the inflection expected to coincide

b. Analysis.

with the high note in m. 27 by supporting it with alternating dissonant harmonies that propel the phrase toward the following downbeat, allowing it finally to cascade with abandon from an appoggiatura high B♭ in a moment of exaggerated emotional release.[127] In technical terms, m. 27 represents a shift in meter within the confines of a single phrase rhythm, as indicated by the faster rate of underlying impulses. These gradually return to the original *ritmo* through textual variations in the final phrase, illustrated by the small notes above the stave in mm. 28–30 of example 3.17 (b). In terms of effect, this passage captures just the kind of fusion of drama, text, and music that the young Wagner claimed to have appreciated.

Bellini, Beatrice di Tenda (1833), act 1, "Oh! divine Agnese!"

Conceived as a vehicle for superstar Giuditta Pasta, Bellini's penultimate opera follows the travails of recently widowed Beatrice di Tenda (soprano) in her lackluster second marriage to the evil duke of fifteenth-century Milan, Filippo Maria Visconti (baritone). Filippo's indifference stems from his lust for Agnese di Maino (mezzo), who is herself in love with the Lord of Ventimiglia, Orombello (tenor). He, in turn, is in love with Beatrice, who cannot return his affections because she is still in love with the memory of her late husband, Facino Cane. The extract in example 3.18 (a) is taken from the opening scene of act 1, in which Duke Filippo, having spotted Agnese across the crowded ballroom of his castle, declares his feelings for her in a *cantabile* aria. The text below is taken from the original Ricordi vocal score of ca. 1833.

gioja mi sei nel *pian*to (7)	you give joy to my sighs
pace nel mio fu*ror* (7)	peace to my fury
se della terra il *trono* (7)	if you were to offer me
dato mi fosse of*frir*ti (7)	the throne of the earth
Ah! non varrebbe il *dono*, (7)	Ah! it would not be worth the gift,
cara, del tuo bel *cor.* (7)	dearest, of your beautiful heart.

The form of the *andante amoroso* as a whole may be represented by the conventional letter symbols a^1 a^2 b a^2 c, in which the principal theme in mm. 6–13 (a^1 a^2) encompasses the first two lines of *settenari*, the contrasting passage in mm. 14–17 (b) takes the next two lines, and the reprise and coda in mm. 18–21 and 21–24 (a^2 c) use the remaining two lines. Example 3.18 (a) reproduces only the final part of the aria, corresponding to the reprise and coda of mm. 18–24. It is of interest here primarily for the way in which a new melodic phrase rhythm for the

3.18.

a. Bellini, *Beatrice di Tenda* (1833), act 1, "Oh! divine Agnese!" mm. 18–24 (Milan: Ricordi, ca. 1833).

coda (mm. 21–24) is derived from the first five syllables of the original seven-syllable verse and the way that this gives rise to a shift in harmonic rhythm despite any concurrent change in the accompanimental patterns. As the reduction in 3.18 (b) demonstrates, the reprise of the principal theme in mm. 18–20 establishes a conventional *settenario* phrase rhythm spanning two rhythmic impulses, notwithstanding the

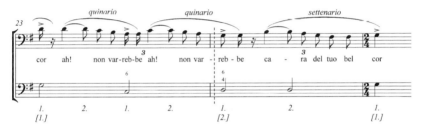

b. Analysis.

verbal repetition and *messa di voce* added to the beginning of the second phrase. At the *poco più lento* of m. 21, the derived *quinario* phrase takes over, to characterize the Duke's flurry of emotions with repetitions of the words "Ah! it would not be worth . . . your beautiful heart." These new *ritmi melodici* proceed over an accompaniment incorporating four rhythmic impulses per measure, with the *desinenza* falling upon every half note. The original *settenario-ritmo* returns only to mark the final cadence in m. 24. On paper, the initial "hypermeter" of rhythmic impulses established by the reprise of the principal theme may be seen to continue to underlie the quicker pattern of *quinario* phrases in the coda, as suggested by the numerals in square brackets beneath the stave of example 3.18 (b). In performance, however, the shift of meter is more clearly perceived than any sense of rhythmic continuity. Indeed, the melody of the coda, encompassing short "rhythms" of four descending steps attached to a broader descent through the scale from the fifth to the tonic of G major—a typical device, explained in chapter 4—serves to emphasize the relationship between the two rhythms: the coda theme (m. 21) represents a condensed, speeded-up version of the principal theme (m. 20).

Puccini, La bohème *(1896), act 1, "Nei cieli bigi"*

The manifest irregularity of the verses in libretti such as those for *Manon Lescaut* or *La bohème* would seem to argue against the relevance of old-fashioned approaches that derive symmetrical patterns of phrases from regular verse meters. As Fabbri notes, "Versification at the end of the nineteenth and the beginning of the twentieth century was highly mobile and flexible, with frequent changes of meter and stanzas of mixed meters. . . . It matched a musical syntax that was not periodic and, while often leaning toward lyrical fragments, no longer culminated in grand, strophic arias."[128] Nevertheless, there are many passages in Puccini's music that could be understood to contain regular periodic structures, determined by an underlying verse meter which, following convention, did not necessarily correspond to the text at any given moment—especially taking into account the traditional distortions, diminutions, and augmentations that were written into operatic phrases in response to the *accento musicale*. Just as Asioli's abstract notion of *ritmo* rarely corresponded in strict terms to the actual setting of an aria, let alone to its performance, so too might the irregular, fragmentary surface of Puccini's music rest upon expressive fluctuations of an essentially stable, traditional verse meter or *ritmo*. Reflecting the increased importance of the orchestra (and perhaps also the influence of Wagner), such underlying *ritmi* might also be seen to feature predominantly in the orchestral melody, allowing the vocal part to declaim a variety of verse meters (as long as their inflections coincided appropriately with the impulses or *movimenti* of the harmonic rhythm). Puccini's correspondence with librettists, like that of other nineteenth-century opera composers, may be understood to concern both levels of *ritmo*. While his requests for specific *maccheronici* verse types—such as the comical "coccoricò, coccoricò bistecca" that eventu-

3.19.

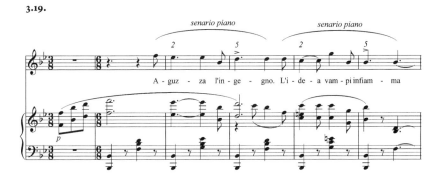

a. Puccini, *La bohème*, act 1, R4, mm. 8–13 (Milan: Ricordi, 1896; analytical symbols added).

b. *Ritmo melodico* of the orchestral theme.

ally became Musetta's *endecasillabo a minore*, "Quando m'en vo', quando m'en vo' soletta"—reflected an awareness of larger-scale aspects of meter, his constant tinkering with details of individual words and lines related to the varied settings of each phrase according to immediate expressive demands.

The different levels of *ritmo* may be perceived through example 3.19, with reference to a theme first heard in *La bohème* at the words "Nei cieli bigi" ("In the gray skies") and associated henceforth with the character Rodolfo. In the passage shown in example 3.19 (a), Rodolfo declaims two regular *senario* phrases over this theme, which appears in full in the orchestra. As example 3.19 (b) shows, however, the "Nei cieli bigi" theme may be considered in itself as an *endecasillabo* phrase, with accents on the fourth, seventh, and tenth syllables and made up of three sequential repetitions of a three-note melodic design, descending by thirds. The six-syllable verses of the text merely "trip lightly over the top" of this more structurally significant *ritmo melodico,* dovetailing with its brief three-note designs (*disegni*). When the same theme appears later in act 1 (R32), it is overlaid with a series of *settenario* verses. Such versatility rested on the establishment of the *endecasillabo* as a fundamental phrase rhythm, above which all manner of what might be called metrical counterpoint could take place. This concept of the underlying "structural" phrase rhythm or *ritmo melodico* offers a useful tool for the interpretation of many of the metric licenses that are featured throughout the score of *La bohème*.

Puccini, Le Villi *(1883–85), act 1,* R14, *"Se come voi"*

Following the premiere of the original one-act version of *Le Villi* at the Teatro dal Verme, Milan, from May 31 to June 3, 1884, Puccini and his librettist, Ferdinando Fontana, began, at Ricordi's request, to expand the opera into two acts for a new production scheduled for the Teatro Regio in Turin. The addition of a large-scale entrance aria for the only female character appears to have been something of a priority, since Puccini and Fontana drafted the verses for Anna's *scena e romanza,* "Se come voi," within a matter of weeks. The score was completed by the end of August.

Example 3.20 (a) reproduces the first of the aria's two main themes, encompassing the four verses of the opening quatrain. As will be explained more fully in chapter 5, it is preceded by an orchestral ritornello and followed by a second main theme (*secondo motivo*), a central "characteristic passage" (*passo caratteristico*), and a closing "cadential period" (*periodo di cadenza*), which forms the opening half of a "large dimension" of the binary or two-part *romanza*. A glance at this first theme suggests that it is highly irregular, even compared with those of Puccini's later operas. There is no obvious pattern of repetitions or symmetrical phrases. Indeed, the overall effect signifies more a loose *scena*-like introduction to the short *secondo motivo* than an independent theme. It is nevertheless analyzed here to explore how verse and *ritmo* may be understood to operate within passages that appear to resist systematic reduction to phrase rhythms.

Fontana, in collaboration with Puccini, created four lyric stanzas of seven-syllable verse:[129]

Se come voi piccina (7)	If I were as small as you,
io fossi, o vaghi *fior*, (7)	oh tiny flowers, I could always,
sempre sempre vicina (7)	always stay close
potrei stare al mio amor. (7)	to my beloved.
Allor dirgli potrei: (7)	Then I could say to him:
"Io penso sempre a te!" (7)	"I think always of you!"
Ripeter gli vorrei: (7)	I would like to repeat to him:
"Non ti scordar di me!" (7)	"Don't forget me!"
Voi, di me più felici, (7)	You, happier than I,
lo seguirete, o fior; (7)	follow him, oh flowers;
per valli e per pendici (7)	through valleys and hills
seguirete il mio amor . . . (7)	you follow my beloved . . .
Deh, se il nome che avete (7)	Ah, if your name [forget-me-not]
menzognero non è, (7)	is not a falsehood,
al mio amor ripetete: (7)	repeat to my love:
"Non ti scordar di me!" (7)	"Don't forget me!"

In terms of both structure and content, this verse may be considered entirely conventional. Addressed to a nosegay of forget-me-nots—a fairly usual stand-in for an absent or unavailable *seconda donna*—it rests upon a simple metaphor in which Anna imagines herself as the flowers in order to accompany her beloved Roberto everywhere and to haunt him with the words "Don't forget me," which is exactly what he does, of course, as soon as he leaves the village. His "obscene orgies" with a "siren" result in Anna's death through grief and provide the motive for her subsequent reappearance as one of the ghostly *Villi*, to wreak vengeance upon him.

Puccini's setting appears at first to shorten the opening *settenario* to a *quinario*, with a *desinenza* on "*voi*" in m. 3. According to the analysis in 3.20 (b), however, the complete verse is stretched out in a leisurely way over three measures. Its true *desinenza* on "piccina" lacks presence because the melody jumps to a lower octave from d^2 to e^1 in m. 3, regaining the upper register only through the rising arpeggio upon the "resting point" of the phrase. In this way it appears overshadowed by the "guiding line" of the melody, which, as restored through a reversal of this octave transposition in 3.20 (b), consists of a simple rising scale to g^2. The second and third verse phrases in mm. 4–8 are subject to radical expressive distortions or *rubati* written into the theme. A quickening of pace at the *desinenza* on

3.20.

a. Puccini, *Le Villi*, act 1, R14, mm. 1–12 (Milan: Ricordi, 1891).

b. Analysis.

"*fior*" in m. 6 is matched notationally not only by the indication *mosso* but also by a diminution of rhythmic values from $\frac{6}{8}$ to $\frac{3}{8}$. As if to compensate, the third phrase expands its central weak syllables over an additional measure, as indicated by the small note heads above the stave in m. 7 of example 3.20 (b). Overall, despite initial appearances, the theme evinces a traditional relationship between its four regular *settenari* and four melodic phrase rhythms, underpinned by a flexible harmonic rhythm that defers to the expressive freedom of the *accento musicale,* incorporated, in this instance, into the notation. Its guiding melodic contour is likewise traditional, ascending and descending through the steps of the G major scale. Although the vocal part departs from the stepwise progression in mm. 9–10, example 3.20 (b) indicates its continued descent by incorporating the orchestral line. This standard compositional formula will be investigated more fully in connection with methods of training at the Italian conservatories in chapter 4 and in connection with the *solfeggio* in chapter 6.

FOUR

Lessons in Dramatic Composition II: Harmony and Counterpoint

I. THE *PARTIMENTO* TRADITION

At the Lucca Conservatory, typically, students entering the final-year composition class would already have received up to four years of primary courses in musical rudiments and a further three years of secondary courses in the disciplines of harmony and counterpoint.[1] These were occupied with a combination of the Neapolitan *partimento* tradition (mainly Fenaroli and Sala) and the associated Bolognese tradition (Martini and Mattei), which was taught primarily through Michele Puccini's compilation of earlier materials (1846), and theories of fundamental bass and harmonic inversion derived ultimately from Rameau, which were incorporated into northern Italian traditions and taught primarily through Pacini (1834 and 1844a).[2] Had these disciplines not been sufficiently mastered, apprentice composers would not have been allowed to progress to "finishing" classes in professional skills such as orchestration, text-setting, and the subtleties of the *accento musicale*. A thorough grounding in the practice of harmony and counterpoint was considered the most essential prerequisite for a successful career in composition.

Until recently, little was understood about the content of these lessons. But over the past decade or so, increasing interest in what has become known, from its most characteristic feature, as the *partimento* tradition has served to shed light on many of the long-forgotten methods of compositional training that students such as Rossini or Puccini would have received. Scholars—in particular Cafiero, Gjerdingen, Rosenberg, Sanguinetti, and Stella—have begun the formidable task of tracing this tradition over the course of two centuries, from its origins in the conser-

vatories of Naples to its eventual disappearance in the early twentieth
century, and in doing so have opened up many new avenues for the understanding of eighteenth- and nineteenth-century music.[3] This chapter
is concerned not so much with the original eighteenth-century traditions
traceable to individual maestros and conservatories as with the more disorderly nineteenth-century reception or continuation of these (and other)
teachings, especially as they relate to opera. For this reason it largely over-
looks the central role of keyboard improvisation and accompaniment in
the tradition, focusing instead on the broader context of Italian teachings
on composition in which the *partimento* is incorporated.

Strictly speaking, the *partimento*—most often an unfigured bass line
that provided a linear guide to the realization of a keyboard piece—was
only one among several disciplines within the system of musical training devised by the Neapolitan conservatories. Together with written-out
components such as fugues and *disposizioni* (realizations of bass lines
in open score in two or more parts, often involving imitation and other
contrapuntal procedures), and sung elements such as *solfeggi* (short compositions for one, two, or three voices and bass line that cultivated skills
in counterpoint, melodic writing, and embellishment), it occupied one
of the stages in a progressive course of instruction in harmony and counterpoint.[4] By means of the *partimento,* core knowledge acquired through
repetitive exercises in cadences, scales, suspensions, regular bass motions,
modulations, and imitative counterpoint was transformed into the applied
skills relevant to the professional world of performance and composition.
As Gjerdingen's definition suggests, its main purpose was pedagogical:

> The term *partimento* began the eighteenth century as a regional variant
> of *basso continuo.* Neapolitan maestros, instead of viewing basso continuo as
> a mechanical process for deriving chords from a numerical shorthand, de-
> veloped their own system for training performers and composers. They used
> basses as cues for the recall and adaptation of various styles or *modi,* which
> in turn were constructed on the framework of numerous schemata taught by
> rote. The power of this system, which helped ensure the success of hundreds
> of indigent boys, lay in its simple method of integrating the craft knowledge
> of small harmonic-contrapuntal schemata into the aesthetic, performative
> experience of a complete musical movement.[5]

Most *partimenti* can be subdivided into component sections that may
be understood to illustrate, in a practical setting, one or more of the basic

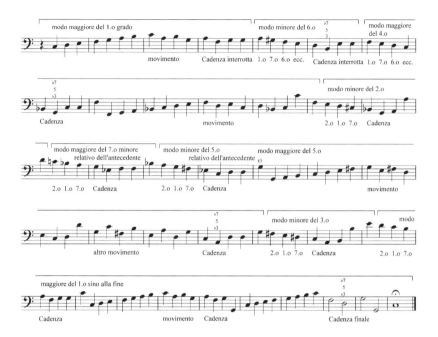

4.1. Giuseppe Staffa, *Metodo della Scuola Napolitana di composizione musicale* (1849), 21: "Esempj Della maniera con la quale deve l'allievo combinare i differenti mezzi di modulazioni, con le cadenze, con le scale, e coi movimenti."

schemata taught through conventional rules and learned by rote. Gjerdingen's 2007 works demonstrate numerous such connections and provide further observations on Durante's exemplars of how to embellish the bass motion of a rising fourth and falling third through an extended *partimento,* designed to test the student's ability to apply this schema in real time at the keyboard.[6] Sanguinetti (2007) provides two similar analyses of *partimenti* by Fenaroli, identifying the fundamental cadences, bass motions, and key changes that underlie each unit within the bass line.[7] Eloquent testimony to its pedagogical function may be found in a short *partimento* entitled "Examples of the way in which the student should combine the different means of modulation with the cadences, scales, and motions" by aristocratic Neapolitan pedagogue Giuseppe Staffa, the major-key version of which is reproduced in example 4.1.[8] Basic rules and principles are clearly identified by means of annotations above the relevant sections. As Staffa's analytical commentaries demonstrate, this type of *partimento* was essentially a compilation of individual lessons melded together into a coherent and aesthetically satisfactory short composition.

Partimenti were not restricted to basic schemata. They were adapted to correspond to the increasingly sophisticated techniques covered over the course of instruction. Fenaroli, for instance, graded his *partimenti* through a progressive series of six books, as described by a pamphlet published in Naples shortly after his death:

> The first one . . . includes scales and cadences, followed by lessons on scales in all major and minor keys. . . . The second book includes examples of dissonances. . . . The third book includes the rules of bass movements and is the last one which offers graded examples corresponding to the printed rules. In the fourth book the students still have to practice all the rules and to find the right accompaniments for all the unfigured *partimenti* included. Eventually the fifth and sixth books (which close the *partimenti*) include diatonic and chromatic fugues, canons, and basses for imitation.[9]

During the eighteenth century the *partimento,* taken to a higher level, could also be considered a type of improvisation at the keyboard which carried its own artistic merit. Sanguinetti's definition places greater emphasis on this performative aspect:

> It is not easy to tell exactly what a *partimento* is. It is a *basso continuo* or thoroughbass, but one that does not accompany anything except itself. It is a figured bass, but very often it has no figures at all. It is a bass, but can as well be a soprano, an alto, or a tenor. Whether tenor, alto, or soprano, it is often the lowest voice, but sometimes it can skip from one voice to another in the texture. It is written, but its goal is improvisation. And, finally, it is an exercise—perhaps the most efficient exercise in composition ever devised— but also a form of art in its own right.[10]

These dual aspects of the *partimento*—as an exercise designed to impart fluency in the application of basic musical schemata in a variety of styles, and as an art of improvisation—were never completely integrated. Already in 1728 Heinichen was grounding his thoroughbass method on a categorical distinction between *Accompagnisten* and *Componisten,* corresponding to a division of the *partimento* into "theory" for composers and "practice" for performers.[11] This distinction was entrenched enough for Fellerer, in his seminal study of 1940, to distinguish two types of *partimento*: the "artistic" (*Kunstform*) and the "pedagogical" (*Schulform*).[12]

By the turn of the nineteenth century in Italy, the emphasis had begun to shift away from improvisation at the keyboard toward written-out exercises that were attached to a variety of lessons. Reduced to treatises for the new conservatories, what began as an essentially oral tradition for the development of skills in improvisation and composition started a gradual process of transformation into the late nineteenth-century study of harmony and counterpoint from printed textbooks.[13] *Partimenti* at the keyboard continued nevertheless to feature prominently in harmony lessons at the conservatories, as may be seen in course guides such as Rossi (1858), Bonomo (1875), Gerli (n.d. [1877?]), Galli (1886), and many others. Counterpoint, at least in the Bolognese tradition as taught at Lucca, Milan, and Paris, likewise remained a practical activity, either sung or played on instruments. The old Neapolitan rules also served to underpin the "preluding" activities of organists and professional piano virtuosos, especially those active in Paris.[14] The Neapolitan basis of the guide to pianistic improvisation by Friedrich Kalkbrenner (1849)—virtuoso, pedagogue, and professional rival to Chopin and Liszt—is, for instance, unmistakable. Drawing presumably upon his earlier studies with the Italian-influenced Charles-Simon Catel at the Paris Conservatory or upon readily available sources such as Choron and Fiocchi (1804), he put forward examples of numerous "improvised preludes" on standard Neapolitan bass motions such as the rising fourth and falling third, the rising fifth and falling fourth, and descending thirds. The Neapolitan *règle de l'octave* was also featured as a basis for preluding, together with its three soprano positions.[15]

While Italian harmony and counterpoint treatises of the nineteenth century depart in various ways from traditional Neapolitan teachings, especially through the influence of foreign theories such as Rameau's "fundamental bass," some of them nevertheless offer generous written instructions and may be considered, in part, to document more fully the processes through which basic rules and formulas (or, in Gjerdingen's terminology, schemata) underpinned more advanced *partimenti* and short compositions. Many eighteenth-century accounts contain only the most rudimentary commentary to support their musical examples, testifying to the centrality of the maestro's spoken guidance in the training process. Textbooks such as Mattei (ca. 1824–25 and ca. 1827) and Asioli (1832, vol. 1), by contrast, contain hundreds of individually annotated exercises to

assist the student on the path toward fluency in performance and composition—in this case derived primarily from the Bolognese school of
the *partimento* tradition and heavily influenced by the northern Italian
reception of Rameau, as well as, in Asioli, newer harmonic ideas by Reicha (1824–26). In general, with the exception of the progressive "foreign"
theories characteristic of Florentine and occasionally Milanese publications from the 1850s onwards, nineteenth-century treatises on harmony
and counterpoint may be separated into two broad, overlapping categories: first, the "original" Neapolitan *partimento* tradition, promulgated
primarily through editions of Fenaroli (1775), and second, newer (late
eighteenth-century) northern Italian traditions that eschewed the old
thoroughbass methods in favor of Ramellian concepts of fundamental
harmonic roots and the equivalence of chordal inversions. The application of these more modern theories to ancient contrapuntal teachings
and to the thoroughbass traditions of the *partimento* was characterized by
Martini (1774–75) as "the Harmonic Principle" (*il Principio Armonico*).[16]
It formed the basis of a protracted debate over the relevance of the fundamental bass to the *partimento,* as witnessed by treatises such as Quadri
(1832) and Staffa (1849) and a series of polemical exchanges in 1858 between Raffaele Napoli, writing in the Neapolitan journal *La Musica* , and
Alberto Mazzucato, writing in the *Gazzetta musicale di Milano.*[17]

Practical and Theoretical Rules of Harmony and Counterpoint

There was a crucial distinction between "practical" and "theoretical" elements in Italian approaches to harmony and counterpoint. The term
pratico referred to methods of learning counterpoint through *singing* and
harmony through *playing,* or occasionally vice versa, while *teorico* signified *written* elements that supported the study of both. When dealing
with historical documents and publications on compositional theory, it is
easy to forget that much of the material was never intended to be studied
on the page; it was for playing or singing. In most cases sung "practical"
counterpoints are readily identifiable by their vocal settings, employing
various combinations of soprano, alto, tenor, and bass clefs in open score
(occasionally with a treble clef indicating a violin) as opposed to the keyboard layout of exercises intended for playing.[18] Teaching harmony and
counterpoint primarily through textbooks and pen-and-paper exercises,

as encouraged by Rameau's theories and by later German publications, was usually referred to during the later nineteenth century in Italy as an aspect of the "scientific" study of music.

In the Bolognese school *contrappunto* was understood primarily as a practical activity, underpinning the study of both performance and composition as well as what would now be called improvisation. It was regarded as nothing less than the foundation of music-making. One of the leading figures of the tradition, Padre Martini's own maestro, Giacomo Antonio Perti, explained its significance in an unfinished manuscript entitled "Exemplars of Counterpoint" dating from the early eighteenth century. The extract below conflates two separate versions of the same paragraph, incorporating later alterations (as well as some editorial clarifications) in square brackets. Despite the opacity and clumsiness of the language, which was never prepared for publication, it serves to corroborate the idea of a practice of "counterpoint" that was inseparable from singing and playing and, in this respect, completely at odds with the modern understanding of the term:

> The art of counterpoint, as it pertains to the practice of music, is the most noble with respect to the other parts [i.e., of the practice of music], which are either vocal or instrumental, because it generates and gives birth to the compositions that the singer sings or the instrumentalist plays. It is not for this, however, that these [other] parts are, I would say, not only useful but indispensable for the contrapuntist, for it is certain that progress in [the art of counterpoint] depends on them. [Presupposing an understanding of the first principles of music], two [things] are, in fact, principally necessary: one is singing, and the other is playing the organ or keyboard: and to prove that this is true, in respect to the first [singing], it is a common axiom among professors that becoming a good composer depends on reaching a sufficient standard in singing, since how can one compose correctly for singing if one has not [learned] to sing well[?] Better still, I would add that progress in the art of counterpoint depends on progress achieved in singing. In regard to the second [playing], it is both indispensable and useful: it is indispensable, self-evidently, because the organist [in Perti's later version: the art (of counterpoint)] is, in a certain way, composing, since every note he plays generates those consonances, in proportion, that the composer, with time and study, has positioned throughout the whole of the composition; it is useful because the composer, after completing the composition, has the possibility to hear it by means of the organ or keyboard, and thereby to check the good progression of the parts and the good modulation of the entire composition.[19]

Around 150 years later, Puccini's musical education continued to involve playing harmony exercises and *partimenti* at the organ or piano and singing counterpoints and *solfeggi,* in addition to mastering "theoretical" or written elements at a desk. The lessons he received in Lucca from his father's "practical" course of counterpoint derived largely from Fenaroli's rules "in playing" (1775), Sala's rules of "practical counterpoint" (1794), and the Bolognese school's teachings as exemplified in Mattei's "practice" of harmony and counterpoint (ca. 1824–25), in which the few exercises that were not intended to be sung were specifically designated "for violin." Mattei's student Luigi Felice Rossi later published realizations of his maestro's instructional bass lines in an edition intended for playing (if not quite performing) on stringed instruments (1850 [1829?]).

In addition to the realization of *partimenti* and *solfeggi,* Puccini and his Italian predecessors would have engaged in a variety of exercises on "bass motions" (*movimenti del basso*) and "settings" (*disposizioni*) in two or more parts, especially as practiced in the Bolognese tradition stemming from Martini, Sabbatini, Sarti, and Mattei and continued by Cherubini and Asioli. As will be explained in more detail below, these involved the application of short sequential melodic figures or designs to the individual parts of model realizations (sung and/or played) of the "bass motion by step," or scale, and to the other bass motions consisting of regular patterns of conjunct and disjunct intervals. In such exercises the stock realizations were not significant in themselves, as prototypical harmonic progressions, but only as guides, or conceptual linear frameworks, for melodic and contrapuntal elaboration through the addition of a short design (*attacco*) together with its repetitions (*ripetizioni*) and contrapuntal imitations (*imitazioni*).

Before exploring this Bolognese tradition in more detail, it may prove helpful to provide an overview of the central Neapolitan system of training in order to show how its rudiments and basic rules provided the material for more advanced exercises in *partimenti,* settings, *solfeggi,* and fugues. Drawing upon a comprehensive survey of the rules left in manuscript by eighteenth-century Neapolitan maestros, Sanguinetti has determined that the harmonic-contrapuntal patterns underlying the *partimento* may be considered, despite differences in the layout and organization of the sources, to fall into five classes, or categories:

Class 1: Basic axioms and procedures [*regole* and *cadenze*]
Class 2: Rule of the octave [*consonanze*]
Class 3: Suspensions [*dissonanze*]
Class 4: Bass motions [*movimenti del basso*]
Class 5: Scale mutations [*terminazioni di tono*][20]

The following brief summary of these rules draws upon the masterful overview by Sanguinetti. In essence, students would learn them in roughly this order, starting with the three main cadence types, the "cadence of natural tones" (see examples 2.1 and 2.2), and associated cadential progressions, before moving on to the rule of the octave, which provided simple models for the conceptualization of a key through harmonizations of major and minor scales in the three (hand) positions (starting either with the first, third, or fifth in the uppermost part), in both ascending and descending directions. Suspensions were introduced initially through the compound and double cadences and featured throughout the course of instruction, (which explains why the discussion of "Class 3" below is integrated into several subsections). In the Neapolitan tradition, only suspensions were considered dissonances (*dissonanze*). All other "dissonances," such as chordal sevenths, were considered part of the basic accompanimental harmonies or "consonances" (*consonanze*), above all those deriving from the rule of the octave. In 1849, the music pedagogue Giuseppe Staffa gave examples of how the *dissonanze* should be integrated into standard bass motions.[21] These bass motions were patterns of regular conjunct or disjunct intervals that gave rise to harmonic-contrapuntal progressions. At various stages within the system of training, students would be introduced to the practice of changing the underlying scale through cues in the bass part called "key endings" (*terminazioni di tono*) and described by Sanguinetti as "scale mutations." By the mid-eighteenth century, particularly in northern Italy, these "mutations" began to be included within a more general category of "modulation" (*modulazione*), corresponding in most important respects to the modern understanding of this term.[22]

Class 1: Basic Axioms and Procedures

These usually involved not only the standard cadence patterns and cadential progressions but also preparatory instructions on intervals, scales, and the voicing of chords. In the early *partimento* tradition, the normative texture consisted of three voices, set out in a manner similar to the Baroque trio sonata as a bass plus two upper parts.[23] By the last quarter of the eighteenth century, however, this had been supplanted almost everywhere by a four-part "choir" texture for exercises in composition. Even the antiquated contrapuntal examples of Martini (1774–75) were interpreted in this way, on the grounds that the "essential parts of the composition, the Soprano and Bass, should be made to stand out from the others," which were regarded merely as "less perceivable middle parts."[24] Asioli similarly acknowledged the predominance of the soprano and bass, which he called the *Manifeste,* over the alto and tenor, or *parti di mezzo,* within a normative four-part texture.[25]

During Puccini's time at the Milan Conservatory, rudiments continued to be taught according to the old Neapolitan rules by Giuseppe Gerli, professor of "armonia e contrappunto complementare" from 1864 until 1885. His textbook (n.d. [1877?]) set out a series of lessons, each occupying a single page and consisting of the same three-stage method. The student was presented with a model harmonization of a scale (or "rule of the octave"), in a different key and soprano position for each lesson, followed by connected examples of the simple, compound, and double cadences. The final stage was a short *partimento,* to be realized at the piano, which helped to consolidate the student's knowledge and practical application of the rules of the given scale and cadences.

Class 2: The Rule of the Octave (Regola dell'Ottava),
Its Divisions, and the Influence of the Basso Fondamentale

The appearance of the rule of the octave in Italy sometime around the year 1700 enabled both theorists and practitioners to frame traditional teachings on the realization of thoroughbass (or *basso continuo*) with a workable concept of tonality. It provided not only a series of closely related models for the harmonization of major and minor scales, ascending and descending, but also a hierarchy of scale degrees that, taken as a whole, served to define the key. Holtmeier thus describes it as "a theory of harmonic functionality."[26] In its simplest, most paradigmatic form—defined by Tartini (1754) as the "common organal scale" (*scala organica comune,* i.e., akin to parallel *organum* or *fauxbourdon*)[27]—the rule of the octave may be conceptualized as a fixed arrangement of chord types upon the notes

4.2. The rule of the octave (first position) according to Fedele Fenaroli, *Regole musicali per i principianti di cembalo* (1775).

of the diatonic scale. Tonic and dominant bass notes, or occasionally tonic and subdominant, were harmonized by perfect consonances—i.e., the chord of the fifth (or triad)—and were considered to embody resting points or cadences. All other scale degrees in the bass were more or less dependent on these triads. They functioned in a similar way to "passing notes" or "preparations" and were assigned imperfect consonances— principally the chord of the sixth (or first-inversion triad) or chords that would now be called dissonant, such as the dominant six-four-two (or third-inversion seventh) on the descending fourth scale degree.[28] According to Sanguinetti, the "Neapolitan masters favored several different versions of this rule, but eventually one version became standard, the one described by Fenaroli [1775]."[29] The "first position" of his standard harmonization of the major scale, with the soprano starting on the tonic, is reproduced in example 4.2. Only the tonic and dominant notes support root position triads.

This rudimentary framework for the articulation of a key through varying degrees of consonance, rest, and motion was accounted for in eighteenth-century Italian theory by the notion of the "dual division of the octave,"[30] which could be traced as far back as the study of authentic and plagal church modes in Heinrich Glarean's *Dodecachordon* (1547) and even to medieval and ancient Greek theory. According to sources such as Tartini (1754) and Martini (1767, 1774–75), the scale, in bass or soprano, could be divided either "harmonically" by the dominant (*divisione armonica*), as in Fenaroli's rule in example 4.2, or "arithmetically" by the subdominant (*divisione aritmetica*). As long as one of these cadential pillars was sufficiently marked, the remaining chords of the scale could be treated relatively freely. Such a notion was quite different from the *Verwandschaft* or "relationship" theories appearing in Germany at roughly the same time (for instance, Riepel [1755]), which attempted more or less arbitrarily to establish fixed connections between the different scale degrees.

Given the profound influence of Rameau's theories in Italy and the consequent weakening of such practical constructs, it is surprising to note that the "divisions of the scale" continued to be taught at the Lucca Conservatory until the late nineteenth century.[31] Michele Puccini's *Corso pratico di contrappunto* (1846), which remained a central resource for the curriculum at Lucca long after his death in 1864, set out the two divisions on its very first page of rules, through two ascending C major scales in the bass annotated respectively with slurs from C to G and from C to F. It is important to note that these divisions could apply equally to bass and soprano lines.

By the early nineteenth century, the rule of the octave and the divisions of the scale were in many places already well on the way to being supplanted in compositional theory by newer, more systematic concepts derived principally from Rameau.[32] The rule of the octave continued to be taught, however, in something approaching its original form by maestros until the late nineteenth century. It was used at the Lucca Conservatory through older books of *regole* such as P. Tomeoni (1795) and Michele Puccini's *Corso practico* (1846), and at the Milan Conservatory through sources such as Rossi (1858) and Gerli (n.d. [1877?]), in conjunction with *partimenti* designed to impart fluency in its application. A footnote appended by Lauro Rossi in 1858 to Fenaroli's rule of the octave underlines the importance placed on mastering the old methods: "N. B. the Maestro will set for the students, as homework, the scales in all the major and minor keys in the three positions."[33] Updated versions of the rule of the octave appeared in Staffa (1849) and Platania (1883), albeit with indications of the influence of Ramellian harmonic theory, such as Staffa's arrangement of his numerous examples beginning with root-position triads and progressing through sevenths, ninths, and so on.[34] Such "modern" harmonic concepts also underlie De Sanctis's treatment of the rule of the octave (n.d. [1887?]), as presented through examples by Sabbatini and Fétis. His interpretation was bound by a notion of "three fundamental chords, tonic, subdominant and dominant, which contain implicitly all the other scale steps that derive from them."[35]

The reception of Ramellian theory in Italy, especially in the nineteenth century, presents a vast and largely uncharted scholarly terrain that would require a separate study. Only a brief survey of the most essential changes that took place within the teaching of the rule of the octave (primarily Fenaroli's version) can be attempted here, in order to demarcate the outlines of the kind of hybrid theory that composers such as Verdi and Puccini would have inherited.

The two most significant new ideas to gain acceptance within the Italian traditions of the mid-eighteenth century were Rameau's concepts of the fundamental bass and of inversional equivalence. They were already circulating in northern Italy by the time that Tartini wrote his *Trattato* (1754), which may be regarded as a starting point for Ramellian theory in Italy, and they feature conspicuously in later sources such as Gervasoni (1800).[36] Such ideas presented a radical alternative to traditional thoroughbass teachings through the rule of the octave and the *partimento*. As Holtmeier observes:

> No music-theoretical theorem of the eighteenth century did more to implement a break with tradition than Rameau's theory of *renversement*— "inversion" sealed the fate of the old intervallic qualities. . . . According to Rameau, a chord of the sixth is no longer an independent sonority in its own right, but becomes a "derivative" chord, an "inversion" of a "fundamental" triad. The old pivotal distinction between fifth and sixth, between a sonority of rest and one of motion, was not only completely leveled, but perfect and imperfect consonances became, in Rameau's thoughts on inversion, "identical." [37]

Wherever Rameau's theories held sway, the fluid linear guidelines of the rule of the octave were reduced to a series of vertical harmonies, derived ultimately from stacks of thirds upon scale degrees that functioned as chord roots. The turning point in the Italian traditions, after which this new way of thinking could be said to have decisively superseded the old *partimento* methods, may be located in the influx of teaching materials from the Paris Conservatory, especially Reicha's treatise on musical composition (1824–26), which replaced the old rules of the *partimento* tradition with more "modern" notions of keys, scale steps, and modulations. Writing at the end of the nineteenth century, De Sanctis acknowledged this historical juncture:

> Reicha, after presenting a table of all the chords that may be applied to the different steps of the scale, says the following of the rule of the octave: this formula does offer some minor resource for practical composition, but it is not worth discussing in this work. It would be truly necessary only in

cases where the bass progressed continually through ascending and descending scales, and where one would need to employ different chords on the same step.[38]

The influence of Reicha's neo-Ramellian theory was much in evidence in Asioli's teachings, which became standard at the Milan Conservatory in the nineteenth century. Asioli's presentation of the rule of the octave in first position—scored for singing rather than playing, as reproduced in example 4.3, with intervals between each voice part and the bass spelled out to help the maestro to direct from the keyboard—appears at first glance to correspond closely to Fenaroli's standard model, with an invented rhythmic setting and with an alternative voicing of the chords in measures 4–6, in which the original soprano, included in black note heads, is shifted to the tenor.[39] But, in keeping with most nineteenth-century versions of the rule of the octave, it required justification through a small additional stave showing a Ramellian fundamental bass. Asioli was by no means the first to suggest such an impractical interpretation of the rule of the octave, nor did he have to draw upon recent Parisian textbooks such as those of Reicha. There was already a long tradition of appending an "analytical" lower stave to the rule of the octave, showing its supposed fundamental chord roots, stemming from the similar example in Tartini (1754).[40] It is clear from Asioli's commentary to example 4.3, as well as his first treatise on harmony (1813), that he no longer subscribed to the old thoroughbass methods, but considered instead that harmonic progression should be determined by root position triads, or the "proper fundamentals":

> This scale, which [during the 1600s] served for the work of various composers, was unanimously adopted by all the Italian schools toward the beginning of the eighteenth century, or at the end of the seventeenth, under the term *Regola dell'ottava*. Although this rule is losing its strength from day to day, owing to the many and varied successions of harmony through which the proper fundamentals can progress, I will nevertheless teach its first stage here so that the student may arrange the parts upon it and may always keep in mind that the best effects will be obtained, without doubt, by the best *cantilena* of the upper part, by harmonic connectedness, by oblique and contrary motions, by the extension and approximation of the parts [standard voicings of chords and their variants], and by the quiet and good order of the same.[41]

4.3. Bonifazio Asioli, *Il Maestro di composizione* (1832), Examples 1: no. 14a, 20: "the rule of the octave."

In agreement with Rameau's theory that all chords were derived from root position triads, by inversion or by the addition of extra thirds, Asioli arranged his harmony examples in a graded series starting with "generators" (*generatori*), or root position triads upon the degrees of the scale, and progressing through the "first addition" (*addizione*) or seventh chord, the "second addition" or ninth chord, the "third addition" or eleventh chord, and the "fourth addition" or thirteenth.[42] Each stage in the series was supplemented with additional examples involving chordal inversions (*rivolti*). Following Rameau, these were regarded as wholly equivalent to their parent examples in root position, even when they diverged significantly from the original model, because Asioli, like Gervasoni and others before him, understood two species of bass: "the *generatore* or fundamental, and the *perceived* [*sensibile*], whether sung or played."[43] In contrast to traditional thoroughbass teachings through the rule of the octave, the actual bass line (*sensibile*) of a composition was regarded as insignificant in terms of harmonic meaning, being dependent on notional stacks of thirds supported by the fundamental (*generatore*).

Such wholehearted acceptance of the doctrine of the fundamental bass led to a number of harmonic oddities that were peculiar to nine-teenth-century Italian (and, through Parisian connections, French) the-

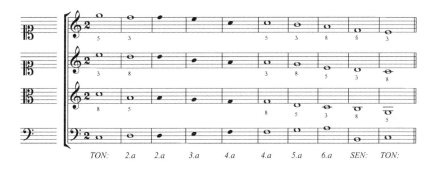

4.4. Asioli, *Il Maestro di composizione* (1832), Examples 1: no. 10a, 15: "ascending scale of fundamental triads."

ory. Since the inversion of a chord was regarded as functionally identical to its parent root position triad, it made no difference whether traditional means of training such as harmonizations of the scale were composed of fundamentals or their inversions. This led to a wholesale leveling of the old Neapolitan distinctions between scales, as rules of the octave or bass motions by step, and the other types of regular bass motion made up of conjunct and disjunct intervals, as may be seen in the two "equivalent" yet entirely different bass lines in example 4.8 below, from Platania (1883).

As Christensen (1993) observes, the theoretical interpretation of the rule of the octave occupied Rameau throughout his life. It was never satisfactorily explained through the doctrine of the fundamental bass. In keeping with several earlier treatises, Asioli's solution to the dichotomy between the practical thoroughbass methods of the *partimento* tradition (Fenaroli) and the more speculative theories of inversion and fundamental bass (Rameau) was to begin his course of harmonic instruction with a "scale of fundamentals" (*scala di genitori*), the ascending version of which is reproduced in example 4.4. It is scored for two sopranos, alto, and bass and replete with interval numbers to assist the maestro in directing the choir of students from the keyboard. Also appended are "theoretical" chord-root symbols, including those for tonic (*Ton.* or *Tonica*) and leading tone (*Sen.* or *Sensibile*). Such an abstract construct, which may also be seen (presumably via Cherubini) in Catel's influential textbook for the Paris Conservatory,[44] would have been inconceivable to the original

authors of the rule of the octave. Even Asioli, who was prepared to accept
the doubled leading tone of the penultimate measure without comment,
felt obliged to censor the most radical of the resulting progressions—II
passing through III to IV—with black note heads.

In seeking to justify this approach, Asioli was compelled to resort
to increasingly desperate and unconvincing pedagogical explanations.
Denying that such a scale was merely a theoretical "example" while at
the same time acknowledging its limited practical use, he made the claim
that it demonstrated how *not* to fashion harmonic connections. Its only
positive aspect was to be found in its avoidance of parallel fifths and
octaves:

> Reason demands that the fundamental diatonic progressions have as
> their basis the Scale made up of so many fundamental triads, not only be-
> cause this must be produced as an example, but also to recognize the bad
> fundamental connections that must be avoided, the small parts of it that
> are of practical use, the total lack of harmonic connection, and the rule that
> needs to be followed to avoid parallel fifths and octaves.[45]

In practice Asioli took a more flexible approach to the integration
of Ramellian theory with traditional teachings through the rule of the
octave. Again, accepting the notion that triads on the scale degrees were
the foundation of all harmony, he dismissed the Fuxian model of species
counterpoint, in which intervals would be added to a given voice in two
or more parts, and advocated instead harmonizations of the scale—which
he (erroneously) considered to be identical to the rule of the octave—
through fundamental triads and their inversions. As he revealed in the
introduction to his book on harmony,

> I find it necessary first of all to make [the student] write out three staves
> on a *cartella* [a reuseable varnished linen board]—not above a short passage
> of cantus firmus, but above the diatonic scale or rule of the octave—and
> to get him to invent as many fundamental triads and inversions as possible
> on it, as many as may make sense. In this way I believe I have arrived at the
> same judgment as our predecessors who, contradicting the contemporary
> practice of starting instruction in two parts, argued with good reason that it
> would have been easier to write in four parts rather than three or two.[46]

Asioli's reputation and influence ensured that this hybrid harmonic
theory continued to be taught at the Milan Conservatory, alongside tra-

ditional *partimento* methods, until the late nineteenth century. The only significant alteration evident in Lauro Rossi's revised 1858 version of the "scale of fundamentals," apart from the obvious scoring for keyboard performance, concerned the acceptance in whole notes of the previously unacceptable chord progression (from II through III to IV) in black note heads.[47] Rossi also incorporated this scale into his models for harmonic progressions (*progressioni*), which, following Asioli, were clearly derived from the old Neapolitan bass motions. One such example harmonized an ascending and descending C major scale in the bass (in its "arithmetic" division) using only root position triads, with the exception of a final cadential phrase. A meaningful shape was imparted to the otherwise bizarre harmonic progression by way of a conventional pattern of melodic designs and their repetitions.[48]

By the time Rossi was instigating his reforms to the curriculum at Milan during the 1860s, these teachings appear to have become commonplace enough to make the transition from textbook examples to *composizione ideale,* or the real practice of opera composition. The opening of the orchestral prelude to act 4 of Arrigo Boito's *Mefistofele* (1868 and 1875), for instance, depicting *La notte del Sabba classico,* appears to reproduce a series of standard exercises on the "scale of fundamentals" (example 4.5). Beginning in mm. 1–5 with an incomplete "arithmetic" division of the B♭ major scale harmonized in *moto contrario* using only root position triads, the second phrase in mm. 6–9 goes on to complete a similar scale, descending. The third phrase in mm. 10–13 comprises a repetition of the first, only this time in "second" rather than "first position," with the soprano part starting on the third scale degree. A closing phrase in mm. 14–17 finishes the "lesson" with an ascending scale of fundamentals, harmonized in contrary motion and ending with both a doubled leading tone and parallel octaves.

From his studies in Lucca, Puccini would have been familiar with both the older thoroughbass teachings on the rule of the octave and the divisions of the scale, and with alternative theories advocating fundamental bass, functional triads on scale degrees, and the equivalence of chordal inversions, of which there was certainly no shortage by the mid-nineteenth century. Examples corresponding to the doctrine of scale divisions and to Fenaroli's rules of the octave may nevertheless be found throughout his early music. The opening of the orchestral prelude to his

4.5. Arrigo Boito, *Mefistofele,* act 4, "La notte del Sabba classico" (Milan: Ricordi, 1875).

first opera, *Le Villi,* for instance, may be understood in these terms. As can be seen in example 4.6 (a), it begins over a dominant pedal with six statements of a thematic figure based on a *quinario-ritmo,* associated later in the opera with Roberto's foresworn oath. A new theme in measure 7, recycled from the early song "Melancolia" (1881?), doubles the duration of the preceding *ritmo* (to which the first violins append a flowing *ende-casillabo* melody in eighth notes) and initiates a bass descent through the scale to a cadence on the tonic. This tonic (C) of m. 9 is reinterpreted, in retrospect, as the dominant of F major by a transposed repetition of the phrase in mm. 9–11.

In this instance, the descending 5–1 bass scales from G to C and from C to F of mm. 7–9 and 9–11, made explicit in the reduction in example

4.6.

a. Puccini, *Le Villi*, orchestral prelude, mm. 1–14 (Milan: Ricordi, 1891).

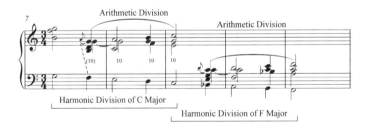

b. Analytical reduction of mm. 7–11.

4.6 (b), may be regarded as outlining the "harmonic" division of their respective scales, since the fourth scale degree is harmonized in both cases
not by a stable triad but by a transient six-four-two chord. In practice,
however, the distinction between the two divisions was not so clear-cut.
Many treatises appeared to divide the octave not only into overlapping

sections bounded by the fifth and the fourth but also into two equal parts, or perfect fourths, as in the ancient Greek tetrachords.[49] It is worth noting also that syntactic considerations, such as the harmonization of the fourth scale degree, habitually took second place to "rhetorical" aspects in the eighteenth-century musical thinking that underpinned the tradition. Given that the descending 4–1 bass scales from F to C and from B♭ to F evident in example 4.6 (b) are made explicit by every musical parameter apart from the harmonic, is it conceivable that they could have been seen as examples of the "arithmetic" division of the scale? One answer may be found in the musical praxis of the tradition. The "arithmetic" progressions in example 4.6 (b) constitute examples of what Gjerdingen (2007a) identified as the most common eighteenth-century formula for ending a musical phrase: the stepwise bass descent from the fourth to the first degree, usually accompanied by parallel tenths, which he named, after an obscure eighteenth-century German theorist, the "Prinner."[50] They also correspond to the most characteristic bass progression associated with the standard formula for the double cadence (*cadenza doppia*).[51] Whether Puccini would have understood this conventional schema in association with the double cadence, with his father's teachings on the "arithmetic division" of the scale, or simply as a common closing formula based on an "equal division" of the scale, is open to conjecture. There does appear, however, to be a connection between this passage and traditional teachings on the rule of the octave.[52]

Class 4: Bass Motions (Movimenti del Basso)

Bass motions, despite their name, were regular patterns of conjunct or disjunct intervals that could, as "basses or *solfeggi*," appear in other voice parts.[53] The motion in the soprano part and its significance to operatic composition will be treated in a separate section below. In their usual position in the lowest voice, bass motions formed a fundamental, yet potentially latent, harmonic and contrapuntal framework for the presentation of musical ideas. In most types of composition they served primarily to generate sequential connecting passages, but they could also form the basis of a principal theme or *motivo*.

There are theoretically twenty regular bass motions—involving only diatonic intervals from the step to the sixth and not counting the ascend-

4.7. Michele Puccini, *Corso pratico di contrappunto* (1846), 3–4: "Movimenti o andamenti regolari del Basso."

ing and descending motion by step (i.e., the scale)—or forty if the same motions are considered to start on their respective second notes, such that the motion of the fourth up and third down becomes the motion of the third down and fourth up. In practice, only around ten appear to have been in common usage at any given time. Following Fenaroli (1775), the bass motions were usually presented in ascending order of interval, progressing through steps, thirds, fourths, fifths, and sixths, as may be seen in Michele Puccini's version of his teachings reproduced in example 4.7, which differ only by way of an additional motion of the step up and the third down and through their cadential progressions. By the nineteenth century, the widespread acceptance of the theory of chord inversion meant that a bass motion harmonized by root position chords could give rise to *derivati,* or derived motions, through the exchange of voices and harmonic inversions.[54] By these means Asioli (1832) required

4.8. Pietro Platania, *Trattato d'armonia: seguito da un corso di contrappunto dal corale al fugato e partimenti analoghi divisi in tre fascicoli* (1883), examples, no. 29, 36.

only eleven bass motions throughout his numerous examples, while Rossi (1858) employed only seven within a series of thirty-six *progressioni*; Platania (1883) went one step further and specified only five basic patterns, from which all others could be derived.[55] Essentially the same chord-based interpretation of bass motions (or progressions) continued to be taught at the Milan Conservatory until the turn of the twentieth century, as set out in the manual of harmony (1898) coauthored by Edgardo Codazzi and Guglielmo Andreoli, professor of complementary harmony and counterpoint from 1891 to 1899.[56]

Example 4.8, taken from Platania (1883), shows the simplest such realization of a bass motion in root position triads. It is not clear whether the *movimento derivato* in the lower system relates to the *movimento principale* in the upper by way of harmonic inversion (each second half note being altered to a first-inversion chord) or by way of voice exchange. The actual bass motion of the "fourth down and step up" has clearly shifted from the bass part to the alto part in the derived progression, to be replaced by its stepwise descent.

In cases such as this, it is important to distinguish between the scale in the bass as a foundation for standard harmonizations representative of a tonality (*regola dell'ottava*) and as a regular pattern of steps that underlies a series of sequential transpositions (*movimento di grado*). The bass motion by step, as presented by Durante and other maestros, most commonly gave rise to a regular pattern of 5–6 intervals over the bass when ascending and 7–6 intervals when descending. The resulting harmonies were not regarded as functional triads and inversions in the modern sense.

Class 5: Scale Mutations (Terminazioni di Tono) and Modulations (Modulazioni)

At a variety of points within the Neapolitan course of instruction, students would be shown how to change the underlying scale through what would now be called a modulation. In the early partimento tradition, such changes of scale were marked by cues known as "key endings" (*terminazioni di tono*), such as the bass progression of a step up and falling fifth.[57] In nineteenth-century treatises, these "scale mutations" were subsumed under a broader concept of "modulation" (*modulazione*), usually premised to a greater or lesser degree upon the Ramellian notion of fundamental scale steps. Roman maestro Giuseppe Pintado was already using concepts such as the "perceived bass," or *basso sensibile,* in 1794, while Staffa (1849) gave several examples of a "modulating scale" (*scala modulata*) taken from Fenaroli and Zingarelli to demonstrate various types of passing modulation or "key endings," and presented several short modulating progressions based on scales and cadences.[58]

Northern Italian traditions developed a more systematic approach, dividing modulation into three species—fixed, secondary, and passing—and assigning five "closely related keys" (*modi analoghi*) to each tonic in accordance with the available major or minor triads on the notes of the scale.[59] Gervasoni classified the *modi analoghi* in major keys in terms of two "ordinary modulations" (*ordinaria*) to V and IV and three "extraordinary modulations" (*straordinaria*) to VI, II, and III. In minor keys, there were three ordinary modulations to III, V, and VII and two extraordinary ones to VI and IV.[60] The half-diminished or "semi-diatonic" (*semidiatonica*) triads on the seventh scale degree in major keys and on the second in minor keys were considered unstable and could not be rationalized as goals of modulation, although the diminished seventh chord had a significant role as a prefix to functional harmonies. A chart showing the "Deceptions or modulations to the five closely related keys" (*Inganni o modulazioni ai 5 modi analoghi*) upon the bass motion of the rising fourth may be found in Asioli (1832).[61] Matters were complicated by the use of the same term, "analogues" (*analoghi*), to describe any triads that could be considered common to two or more keys. Following Reicha (1824–26), Asioli provided a table of such connections at the beginning of his examples of modulations, seemingly oblivious of the confusion this might cause.[62]

"Modulation" encompassed a range of techniques as broad and inclusive as the modern understanding of this term. It related in general to diatonic changes of key, to one of the five *analoghi*. Chromatic and other unconventional changes came under the heading of "deceptions" (*inganni*), although in practice the distinction between the two categories was not carefully maintained. Similar accounts of *modulazioni* and *inganni* may be found as early as Tartini (1754) and also in Mattei (ca. 1824–25).[63] As Asioli made clear in his discussion of the dominant, which, following Rameau, he called the *producente*, both "deceptions" and "modulations" could be "fixed, secondary, or passing. Fixed modulations are those that establish the principal divisions of the composition: the secondary have a place within the fixed ones; and the passing ones are found everywhere."[64]

Asioli's theory of modulation is of particular interest because it formed the basis of countless subsequent treatises and continued to be taught at the Milan Conservatory throughout the nineteenth century. It also encapsulates the early nineteenth-century fusion (or perhaps collision) of Ramellian theory with the old thoroughbass methods of the *partimento* tradition. In deference, as ever, to the doctrine of the fundamental bass, Asioli began by examining "all the fundamental chords of the scale to get to know their natural tendencies and their possible deceptions," and ordered his examples accordingly.[65] For each fundamental triad he identified, in a manner reminiscent of Catel (1802), "natural connections" to their diatonic *modi analoghi* and "deceptions" to a wide variety of chromatic and enharmonic chords. Despite their arrangement according to the fundamental triads of the scale, however, and the identification of every chord root with a Roman numeral equivalent (T.ᵃ, 2.ᵃ, 3.ᵃ, 4.ᵃ, P.ᵉ, 6.ᵃ, and 7.ᵃ), these constitute not so much a theory of modulation as a relatively comprehensive series of exemplars corresponding in part to the old "scale mutations" and demonstrating how to connect one chord with another, in the manner of a thoroughbass manual.

II. MICHELE PUCCINI'S *CORSO PRATICO DI CONTRAPPUNTO* (1846)

Michele Puccini's practical course of counterpoint may be taken as a case study to show how Neapolitan, Bolognese, and more general northern Italian methods were taught to apprentice composers, such as the young Giacomo Puccini, at a provincial conservatory. It is essentially a handwritten compilation of pedagogical materials drawn for the most part from early Neapolitan sources and Sala (1794), Fenaroli (1814), and Mattei (ca. 1824–25, ca. 1827, and 1850 [1829?]).[66] As explained in chapter 2, musical training in Lucca was if anything even more conservative than elsewhere. Because Michele's own father, Domenico Puccini (1772–1815), had died while Michele was still an infant, he received his first instruction in music from his grandfather, Antonio Benedetto Puccini (1747–1832), maestro of the Cappella Palatina in Lucca and organist at the cathedral of San Martino. Antonio had studied initially with Abbé Frediano Matteo Lucchesi before traveling to Bologna in 1768 to complete his training with Giuseppe Carretti, who had also been the maestro of the elder Giacomo Puccini (1712–81). Michele's initial lessons in composition may therefore be traced directly to mid-eighteenth-century sources. They would no doubt have been supplemented by the teachings that his father, Domenico, received from Mattei in Bologna and from Paisiello in Naples. After his grandfather's death, Michele continued his studies in Lucca with Domenico Fanucchi, Marco Santucci (a renowned student of Fenaroli), and Eugenio Galli before proceeding to Bologna to study with maestro Giuseppe Pilotti and, if Domenico Cerù's historical surveys are to be believed, to one of the conservatories of Naples.[67] The curriculum at Lucca thus drew in equal measure upon *partimento* methods as taught at the original Neapolitan conservatories and at the church of San Francesco and Liceo comunale in Bologna.

Although it remained unpublished, Michele's *Corso pratico* was held in high esteem by Lucca's musical establishment. In a survey of every treatise to emerge from the town since the Middle Ages, Luigi Nerici included only two from the nineteenth century: one by "Maestro Cav. Giovanni Pacini, 1834" and another by "Prof. Michele Puccini, 1850 [*sic*]."[68] Santucci's *Dissertazioni* (1828) was brushed aside. Michele's standing may further be gauged through Cerù's list of the thirty-two maestros active in Lucca in 1871, seventeen of whom were students of Michele, including Giacomo Puccini's first teachers, Carlo Angeloni and Fortunato Magi.[69] That Michele's *Corso pratico* continued to form the cornerstone of the curriculum at Lucca well into the 1870s may be confirmed by comments in Pacini's memoirs, which describe the basic teaching materials as a combination of his own counterpoint and harmony treatises (1834 and

1844a) with "a progressive course of *movimenti*, scales, leaps, and *solfeggi* for two voices."[70]

Michele's *Corso pratico* condensed the basic rules of the Neapolitan and Bolognese methods, remarkably, into just three-and-a-half pages. After illustrating the three basic Neapolitan *partimento* cadences using only the figured bass lines in the key of G that appeared in Sala (1794), it presented thirteen scales in the major and minor keys of C, compiled (or rather copied) from Mattei and Fenaroli,[71] followed by twelve "regular bass motions or progressions" (*Movimenti o andamenti regolari del basso*, see example 4.7), all notated on a single stave with no further indications. The bass motions were clearly modeled on those of Fenaroli (1775), in keeping with most nineteenth-century versions of these rules. They correspond closely, for instance, to the four-part realizations published three years later by Staffa in Naples and five years later by Emanuele Guarnaccia in Milan, in his heavily revised edition of Fenaroli's *Partimenti*.[72] These few pages provided the only guidance on how to realize the ensuing exercises in two, three, and finally four parts, which encompass a complete *zibaldone*, or notebook of exemplars, to equip the young composer starting out on a career as a chapel master. Included in the remainder of the manuscript were 12 basses (*bassi*) and 6 soprano-clef *partiti o solfeggi* to be realized in two parts, 12 *disposizioni* to be realized in three parts, 24 "basses for simple realization" (*bassi con semplice disposizione*) and 15 "basses for contrapuntal, imitative, and fugal realization" (*bassi con disposizione ricercata ed imitativa, e fugata,* mostly from Mattei) to be realized in four parts, 12 chorale themes (*corali o canto-fermi*), 9 church chants (*intonazioni*), and finally 237 fugue themes (*temi, o soggetti per le fughe*), missing the last 12, and 165 themes for double fugues (*soggetti doppj*), missing the last 2.

The only written instruction for the student occurred just before the *partimenti* in three parts and again, slightly varied, before the *bassi* in four parts. It was clearly meant to apply also to the initial section of the manuscript. The student was directed to repeat "All the scales in the bass and upper part, [and] all the regular bass motions in the lower and upper parts, as above in the Studies for two voices." By way of a reminder, the exercises for four voices began with a similar directive to work through "all the scales in both the bass and the soprano, ascending and descending in major and minor modes, [and] all the regular bass motions in both the lower and upper parts, as above in the Studies for two voices."[73]

III. THE BOLOGNESE ATTACHMENT, OR
"LITTLE KEYS FOR WINDING CLOCKS"

To understand the full implications of this solitary guideline, it is essential to note that, in many nineteenth-century accounts, the basic scales and bass motions of the Neapolitan and Bolognese traditions were treated equally as bass and soprano lines.[74] Indeed, almost half of the thirteen scales set out in the first part of Michele Puccini's *Corso* are in the soprano clef. This emphasis on the relativity of soprano and bass parts as bearers of fundamental harmonic-contrapuntal schemata, together with the inclusion of so many basses to be "disposed" in four parts with imitative counterpoint and fugal features, suggests a close affinity with the teachings of Martini, Mattei, and the Bolognese school, which underpinned the training in harmony and counterpoint received by Rossini, Donizetti, and Puccini. Because so much of the original Neapolitan method was communicated orally, however, it is difficult to determine whether contrapuntal exercises based on scales and bass motions in both lower and upper parts represented an innovation particular to the Bolognese maestros or, more likely, a continuation of the conspicuously contrapuntal Neapolitan tradition of the *Leisti,* or followers of Leonardo Leo, which, following an assertion by Florimo (1881–83), has usually been understood to have faded out by the 1770s and to have been superseded by the simpler tradition of the *Durantisti,* or followers of Francesco Durante.[75] Staffa, however, was still referring to these two "schools" in 1857.[76]

The origins of the method in the late eighteenth-century school of Martini may be deduced from the teachings of his students Sabbatini, Mattei, and Sarti—the latter primarily through the pedagogical works of his own student, Cherubini, whose obeisance to the Bolognese tradition was complete.[77] To trace the method any earlier would require further archival researches, such as have been initiated by Pasquini (2004) and Gjerdingen (2005 and 2007b). Martini himself hinted at the Neapolitan origins of the method through an unusually specific reference to Pergolesi's *Stabat Mater* (1736) at the beginning of his two-volume *Esemplare* (1774–75). He claimed that in this work, one of the most influential and frequently printed of the eighteenth century, and also in passages from the intermezzo *La serva padrona* (1733), Pergolesi had achieved a mastery of counterpoint comparable to the old masters of the ecclesiastical style of

4.9. Giovanni Pergolesi, *Stabat Mater* (1736), analytical reduction of mm. 1–5.

the sixteenth and seventeenth centuries.[78] Reducing the famous opening theme of the *Stabat Mater* to its two violin parts and simplifying its bass, as in the analysis shown in example 4.9, discloses the outlines of a sequential series of two-note melodic figures, each consisting of nothing more than a descending step, which are attached to the ascending "hexachord" (*scala semplice*) of the F minor scale.[79] The scale-based melodic pattern of attached melodic figures and their responses is accompanied by a standard "Folia" harmonization in five-three chords (root-position triads).

These short contrapuntal figures were called "attachments" (*attacchi*) by Martini, because they were attached sequentially to the notes of a given line of music. They comprised the first of three types of contrapuntal theme, or "fundamentals" (*vocaboli*): namely, the *attacco* of around one measure, the fugal subject or *soggetto* of around three measures, and the extended fugal theme or *andamento* of around seven measures. Martini illustrated the *attacco* by means of the first four notes of the soprano part of example 4.10 and elaborated upon its use as follows:

> The *Attacco* is a species of short subject which is not bound by all the laws prescribed for the Fugue, but which is free in such a way that it is permitted to attach the responses in the answering parts to whichever lines seem convenient, as shown in the ensuing example [4.10], which is nothing but a simple sketch of the specified *Attacco* in three voices.[80]

The freedom of the "attachments" in example 4.10 may be explained through Martini's threefold definition of contrapuntal imitation, which, he stated, was always composed "partly of Figures, partly of Syllables, and partly of Intervals."[81] As long as one or more of these parameters remained constant, the melodic "attachment" could be manipulated to meet the demands of the contrapuntal context. In example 4.10, for instance, the "response" in m. 2 of the lowest (tenor) part clearly differs from the original

4.10. Giovanni Battista Martini, *Esemplare, o sia saggio fondamentale pratico di contrappunto sopra il canto fermo* (1774–75), 2:viii.

attacco in terms of intervals, but it presents a similar stepwise descending "figure" and the same rhythm or number of "syllables."

Such arcane observations on eighteenth-century counterpoint may, to the modern reader, appear distant or even irrelevant to the training of opera composers in nineteenth-century conservatories. Owing to the inherent conservatism of the tradition, however, and despite the apparent scarcity of imitative counterpoint in Italian *melodramme,* similar methods, originally formulated with the contrapuntal styles of the high Baroque in mind, continued to form the cornerstone of training in harmony and counterpoint within the Bolognese school. The technique of "attaching" brief melodic figures and their responses or imitations to a given framework of contrapuntal lines, in both bass and upper parts, remained central to treatises published in Paris as well as northern Italy throughout the nineteenth century, despite a bewildering proliferation of terminology. Lucchese maestro Pellegrino Tomeoni, for instance, called such melodic attachments "little keys," especially of the sort used for winding clocks (*chiavette*), in allusion to the way they were usually collected on a key ring.[82] In simplest form, the method involved the sequential application of a short, usually one- or two-measure *attacco* to the notes of the ascending and descending scale, both major and minor. Once the basic pattern of attachments was in place, imitations of it could be added in counterpoint through a third part, as demonstrated in paradigmatic fashion by the intertwining two-note motifs of Pergolesi's theme (example 4.9). As the exercises became progressively more complicated and elaborate through the application of suspensions, additions (chordal sevenths and ninths), and diminutions to the melodic figures, the underlying scale was gradually transformed into, or replaced by, the similarly sequential conjunct and disjunct bass motions. Eventually, additional parts could be introduced to impart further contrapuntal interest and to complete the implicit harmonies, and the underlying scales and bass motions could migrate to different parts within the texture, giving rise to "inversions" and variants of the same patterns.

In the introduction (*discours préliminaire*) to his 1814 Parisian edition of the second volume of Fenaroli's *Partimenti,* Emanuele Imbimbo recommended a very similar preliminary method of training to his readers:

> If a young man wishes to make progress in the rules of *partimenti* and counterpoint, he will begin by practicing the scale, creating against it melodies of a single voice, first in note-against-note counterpoint, and then with more notes—and of different values—per each note of the scale. He will continue his exercises by placing above the same scale a florid counterpoint of two voices, first with consonances only, and then with dissonances [i.e., suspensions] between them. And he will do the same thing with three and four voices, not only with brief notes but also with long ones. He will retain the same scale as a subject and will modulate the other parts with it, inverting the intervals [i.e., by placing the guiding scale schema in each voice in turn and adjusting the other parts accordingly].[83]

For reasons that will become clearer below, it seems likely that this preliminary course of training owed more to the Parisian influence of Cherubini than to Fenaroli. Whatever its provenance, the parallels with Verdi's teaching methods, as recounted by his student Emanuele Muzio (see chapter 2), appear striking: "I put eight consonances under the individual notes of the scale, first note against note, then two against one, etc."

The main nineteenth-century sources for instruction according to the Bolognese method were publications and copies of manuscripts by Stanislao Mattei, in particular his course of exercises entitled "Practice of Accompaniment upon Figured Basses and Counterpoints in Several Parts upon the Ascending and Descending Major and Minor Scales" (ca. 1824–25). Arranged in order of triads and additions (sevenths, ninths), and premised unequivocally upon the Ramellian theories of fundamental bass and chordal inversion, its first part begins by providing guidelines for stock realizations of scales and bass motions, appearing in both bass and soprano parts, in order to establish frameworks for the later application of contrapuntal *attacchi.* "All leaps [*salti*] of the rising fourth and the falling third," for instance, "call for the accompaniment of the 3rd, 5th, and 8ve.; as do the leaps of the rising fifth and falling fourth."[84] The "Exercises on the Scale" that follow, as reproduced in example 4.11, were clearly the primary source for the first two pages of Michele Puccini's textbook for the Lucca Conservatory. They are a series of ascending and descending C major scales in the bass, without any further instructions, which are subsequently transposed for similar exercises in each key and followed by short related basses. An ensuing series of "preparatory cadences" (*cadenze prepatorie*) and "figured basses" (*bassi numerati*), presumably for realization at the keyboard, served to consolidate the rules and procedures learned initially through the exercises on the scale. The first system of example 4.11 includes figures that correspond to the rule of the octave according to Fenaroli, while the second presents the same scale as a standard bass motion by step, with the figures 5–6 ascending and 7–6 descending. The series of varied chromatic descents introduced in the third system may be explained through the notion of the "moderated" (*moderata*) minor scale, which includes both natural and flattened sixth degrees.[85] The fourth system supplements the bass motion by step with "additions" of the seventh and ninth. The exercises conclude with a realization of a rising chromatic scale and a descending scale with suspensions, which was extended slightly in Puccini (1846).

The second part of the book, entitled "Counterpoint," contains a comprehensive series of examples demonstrating how to realize these exercises on the scale. In doing so, it provides a key to understanding not only Imbimbo's advice to aspiring contrapuntists and Muzio's lessons with Verdi but also the lone instruction for the students of the Lucca Conservatory contained in Michele Puccini's practical course of counterpoint. Mattei arranged his exemplars into separate sections for major and minor modes, subdividing each into ascending and descending scales. As the extract from the first two pages of exercises on the ascending major scale in example 4.12 demonstrates, they are presented in pairs, as two alternative realizations of a scale, first in the bass and then in the soprano. They involve the addition of a single voice (sung by a soprano or bass) to the scale in simple counterpoint, initially note-against-note, then progressing through counterpoints of two, three (i.e., combinations of half and quarter notes), four, and eight notes. Finally, a free rhythmic species of imitative counterpoint was applied to the scale in two to six parts.

4.11. Stanislao Mattei, *Pratica d'accompagnamento sopra bassi numerati e contrappunti a più voci* (ca. 1824–25), 16: "Esercizio sopra le scale: Cesolfaut 3.ª Maggiore."

4.12. Mattei, *Pratica d'accompagnamento sopra bassi numerati e contrappunti a più voci* (ca. 1824–25), 146.

4.12. Continued, 147.

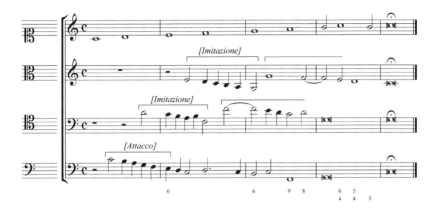

4.13. Mattei, *Pratica d'accompagnamento sopra bassi numerati e contrappunti a più voci* (ca. 1824–25), 154.

Example 4.13 presents one such counterpoint in four parts, in which the *attacco*, presented in the opening measure of the bass part, is imitated freely in the manner of Martini. Although the pattern breaks off after only a single round of imitations, it attaches a six-note descending stepwise *attacco* to an ascending fixed scale in the soprano, as if in diminution and inversion. Once the stock harmonizations of the bass motion by step (example 4.11) had been mastered, together with the practice of "attaching" melodic figures to their separate lines, complicated contrapuntal passages such as this could be generated relatively easily upon the underlying framework of a simple scale. The ways in which these counterpoints were sung will be explored more fully in chapter 6.

Cherubini, from his arrival in Paris in 1785, and especially in his course of harmony and counterpoint at the Paris Conservatory between 1822 and 1835, taught a slightly different version of the Bolognese method founded upon his studies in Milan with Giuseppe Sarti during the 1780s.[86] It was subsequently published in Paris as *Marches d'Harmonie pratiquées dans la composition produisant des Suites Régulières de Consonances et de Dissonances* (n.d. [1835?]) and reissued in 1880 by the firm of Ricordi for the interest of "harmonists" in Milan. Its only substantial written guidance is a closing list of "observations," which, significantly, corresponds to the basic axioms and procedures set out in Fenaroli (1775).[87] The exercises consist of a series of regular bass motions, called *marches d'harmonie* or

4.14. Luigi Cherubini, *Marches d'Harmonie pratiquées dans la composition produisant des Suites Régulières de Consonances et de Dissonances* (n.d. [1835?]), 1.

a.

b. "Different ways to vary the same."

suites régulières in the original French and *andamenti d'armonia* or *successioni regolari* in Italian. They progress from the motion by step to the various types of leap. Each individual bass motion is realized initially (at the keyboard) through the application of a note-against-note counterpoint in three or four parts, to which increasingly complicated and embellished "attachments" and "imitations" are added. Two of the opening exercises upon "a series of notes ascending by step in the bass," otherwise defined as the C major scale, are reproduced in example 4.14. Cherubini provided thirty-two pages of such exercises, demonstrating remarkable inventiveness. Taking the straightforward harmonization involving parallel six-three chords in example 4.14 (a) as a framework for elaboration, example 4.14 (b) introduces suspensions to the melody together with an additional tenor part, filling in the harmony by way of a further regular motion. An "attachment" is added to the soprano part by way of a simple consonant skip of a third that transforms the stepwise melody into a succession of three-note melodic figures, repeated sequentially to form the basis of a *cantilena* (and indicated here by square brackets). By making a similar alteration to the bass part, example 4.14 (b) generates an out-of-phase imitation of the same three-note melodic figure. Already by the first page of instruction the student has learned how to create effective

4.15. Cherubini, *Marches d'Harmonie pratiquées.*

a. Page 36.

b. Page 42.

schemata for the composition of extended melodies and two-part imitative counterpoint, each situated within a full four-part texture. The two
counterpoints of example 4.14 also show how the underlying regular motion by step, or scale, could easily be transformed into one of the leaps or
disjunct bass motions, in this case the motion of the descending third
and ascending fourth.

One final example from Cherubini serves to demonstrate the relationship of his method to the advice offered by Imbimbo (above) in his
edition of Fenaroli's *Partimenti.* Example 4.15 (a) shows one of the first
exercises upon the descending bass motion by step, in which consonant
note-against-note counterpoints are set against each scale degree. The
staggered entries of the parts and their uniform motions make clear that
this is a framework for contrapuntal elaboration, rather than a straightforward harmonization. Cherubini then affixes attachments to these lines
in gradually increasing rhythmic values and complexity until he achieves
the kind of florid two-part counterpoint evident in example 4.15 (b), in
which a two-measure *attacco* is answered by an imitation in the tenor part,
while a sequential progression of "figures" in the alto fills in the harmony
as well as the gaps in the rhythm.[88]

At the Milan Conservatory, Asioli followed Martini's guidelines
in defining this kind of contrapuntal writing as a "first species" within

4.16. Asioli, *Il Maestro di composizione* (1832), Examples 1: no. 13, 17–18.

a. "Fundamental triads of the descending third and ascending fourth."

(a) This progression does not have a plausible or necessary fourth part.

b. "First inversions and fundamental triads of the same progression."

the "genre" of free (*sciolta*), as opposed to strict (*legata*), imitation. "The genre of free imitation gives rise to four species," he claimed, "each less free than the other. The first is the imitation of a theme of a few notes or of around one measure that is also called *Attacco*."[89] The similarity of his examples of this species to those given by Cherubini suggests a common origin.[90] Asioli, however, keen to stress the progressive (Ramellian) harmonic foundations of his method, incorporated this Bolognese contrapuntal method into his course of *harmony* and thereby created a hybrid pedagogical technique that was to prove influential in Milan and other northern Italian musical centers. Although the first volume of *Il Maestro di composizione* (1832) included scores of model realizations of scales and regular bass motions in the Bolognese style, starting with simple note-against-note counterpoints and applying increasingly elaborate attachments and imitations, which were even marked as such in the examples, its written commentary described them almost exclusively in harmonic terms. The note-against-note counterpoint applied to the bass motion of the ascending third and descending fourth in example 4.16 (a) was, for instance, explained as a series of "fundamental triads" upon this pattern. In example 4.16 (b), the obvious transference of the bass motion to the soprano part was not acknowledged as such, but was described instead as a result of chordal inversion. In an unconvincing and, indeed, potentially confusing commentary, Asioli interpreted example 4.16 (b) as a series of "first inversions and fundamental triads" upon the alternate half-note chords of example 4.16 (a), overlooking entirely the obvious swapping of contrapuntal lines. Similar Ramellian interpretations of the Bolognese practice became characteristic of teachings at the Milan Conservatory and featured in many subsequent nineteenth-century treatises.

As mentioned earlier in this chapter, attempting to reinterpret old thoroughbass traditions such as regular bass motions or Bolognese "attachments" in terms of progressive harmonic theory could give rise to musical oddities. Asioli's systematic arrangement of examples in order of fundamental triads and "additions" occasionally resulted in unusual progressions that gave the impression of chains of dissonances or parallel sevenths and ninths. Example 4.17 reproduces the first of Asioli's model realizations of the ascending major scale as a "fundamental motion by step with the first, second, and third additions [i.e., sevenths, ninths, and elevenths]." As his original annotation identifying an *imitazione* suggests, the harmonic interpretation of this example appears to have been applied in retrospect to a series of verticals arising from the application of a three-note stepwise *attacco* and its imitations to the notes of the scale in the bass. In descending motion, the same basic *attacco* was inverted. The "modern" harmonies of example 4.17 are best understood not as chords of the ninth or eleventh, following Asioli's own commentary, but as arising from a coincidence of resolutions and suspensions within an essentially contrapuntal texture.

Evidence of Asioli's influence is not hard to find in later Italian treatises. Even Guarnaccia's heavily revised edition of Fenaroli's *Partimenti* (ca. 1851) appears to have borrowed his hybrid approach to the applica-

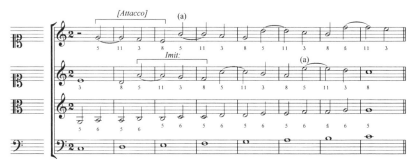

(a) As long as the clash is a minor seventh the ear is not offended, but when it is major, it is rendered tolerable by its short duration and by the symmetrical and directional harmonies that precede and follow it.

(b) The imitations of the two contraltos provide the 5th to every chord of the 11th.

4.17. Asioli, *Il Maestro di composizione* (1832), Examples 1: no. 25, 44.

tion of *attacchi* to scales and bass motions.[91] The continued relevance and authority of the method during the 1880s may be verified through a three-volume treatise published in Milan by Roman maestro De Sanctis (n.d. [1887?]). It defined the "progression" (*progressione*), or realized bass motion, in essentially harmonic terms as "the ascending and descending repetition of two or more chords or of a melodic design. Incidental notes, both harmonic and melodic, and imitations can serve to vary and enrich the progression."[92] According to De Sanctis's five "Norms to Observe" for progressions, "The reproduction of the formula or design must occur at different intervals, both ascending and descending, provided that it is a natural connection: passing notes, including those in the bass, do not alter the progression." Further underlining the Bolognese origins of the practice, moreover, these norms also state that "Each part can contribute

4.18. Cesare De Sanctis, *La polifonia nell'arte moderna* (1887?), no. 316, 141.

to forming a regular progression; one predominant part should neverthe-less contain a melodic progression, leaving the movement of the others free."[93] De Sanctis subsequently clarified this notion of the relativity of voice parts within the texture:

> The tonal progressions shown above are the principal ones and may be varied in numerous ways, not only in the bass but also in the upper parts. They are used often in sacred music and in the strict style. . . . We may ob-serve in conclusion that since a melodic progression may be formed from a harmonic series, so too can a harmonic progression, either in one key or modulating, be obtained from a fragment of melody.[94]

Example 4.18 reproduces the first of De Sanctis's model vocal realiza-tions of the bass motions, exhibiting similar features to those given in Asi-oli (1832). In accordance with the Ramellian theory of the fundamental bass, this initial example purports to demonstrate a series of (more or less parallel) root-position triads. Upon closer inspection, however, a bracket (added by De Sanctis) distinguishes a four-note *disegno*—synonymous with the Bolognese *attacco*—together with a succession of imitations, at-tached to the notes of an ascending scale, which is doubled at the third.

IV. REGULAR MOTIONS AND MELODIC COMPOSITION

Until the very end of the nineteenth century, Italian approaches to har-mony and counterpoint, outside the Florentine circle of progressives, generally presupposed the supremacy of vocal music. Yet rarely was the precise relationship of melodic composition to contrapuntal exercises upon the bass motions made clear—in print, at least. On the contrary, Rossini, who underwent an entire course of counterpoint according to Bolognese methods, was provoked into voicing doubts to his teacher, Mattei, as to its relevance. Verdi, whose lessons appear to have derived from a similar source, was likewise vague in his recommendation of the fugue as an essential prerequisite for operatic composition. Recalling Basevi's criticism of traditional methods in chapter 3, however, in which he railed against composers who "adapt new notes," based on *successione* or "leaps of the ascending fourth, the major sixth, the third, the descending fifth, etc.," to old phrase rhythms, it appears that attachments upon the regular bass motions did form one of the standard techniques for constructing an operatic melody. As will be explored in more depth in chapter 6, sung counterpoints formed the basis of *solfeggio* exercises, which, in turn, according to sources ranging from Sabbatini (1789–90) to De Vecchis (1850), provided standard models for melodic composition. Short melodic phrases drawn from segments of a given bass motion were repeated to form what was called "a regular Melody on the Bass of the lessons":

> The Composer begins by turning his attention to all the notes of the Bass of the lesson and by picking out those with which he wishes to form some little Phrase. He then makes a note of where the same Phrase, made up of these Bass notes, may be repeated as a kind of little melodic *Progression,* with *Repetitions,* etc. Once it has passed this test, it [the Phrase derived from the Bass] will form the Melody, which will always be well made and unified if it is regulated rationally.[95]

Broadly speaking, the adaptation of disjunct regular motions to melodic composition had already begun to fall into decline by the time of Paisiello, together with the high Baroque contrapuntal style from which they derived. Simple patterns of arpeggios and scales became the favored guiding voices for operatic melodies from the late eighteenth century onwards. There were exceptions, of course, such as the ancient *romanesca* pattern of the fourth down and step up that underlies Gernando's andante grazioso "E questi son gli allori" from act 1, no. 4 of Rossini's *Armida* (1817). With the surge in nostalgic nationalism that accompanied the increasingly overwhelming influence of Austro-German music during the 1880s, old-fashioned bass motions made something of a comeback. The

4.19.

a. Puccini, Preludio a orchestra (1876), mm. 1–8 (reduced score).

b. Analytical reduction.

romanesca returned, for instance, in Argelia's *racconto* "La stessa voce eterea i sensi miei colpì" at the beginning of act 1 of Catalani's *Dejanice* (1883) and, more obviously still, in the theme of Roberto's prayer from Puccini's *Le Villi* (1883–85; see example 3.13), which Ashbrook considered "a leitmotif or motto for the opera."[96]

The conservatism of Puccini's Lucchese education and its commitment to outmoded practical counterpoints shows through in one of his earliest surviving student works, a Prelude for Orchestra in E minor, dated August 8, 1876.[97] As may be seen from the reduced score in example 4.19 (a) and its further reduction in (b), the main theme of this instrumental work dovetails two old-fashioned constructs: in the first four measures, a descending scale of suspensions or *dissonanze* is attached to the bass motion of the third down and step up; and in the next four measures an elaborated version of the motion of descending thirds is arranged into four-note designs, doubled at the tenth above, and directed through a

c. De Sanctis, *La polifonia nell'arte moderna* (1887?), no. 326, 150.

sequence of falling sixths. The roving harmonies that result from the extravagant application of accidentals to the basic pattern would presumably have been regarded as adventurous by Puccini's maestros, given Asioli's advice on sticking to the five "closely related keys."

A more typical diatonic version of the same practical counterpoint may be seen in example 4.19 (c), reproduced from De Sanctis's textbook. It is scored conventionally for soprano, alto, tenor, and bass voices and incorporates occasional figured-bass symbols for the benefit of the maestro, who would direct the choir of students from the piano. The connection with Puccini's Prelude is made explicit by the addition of passing notes to a regular motion of descending thirds in the bass part, which is imitated at the octave above by the alto. As a three-note design, rising sequentially by thirds, a similar basic counterpoint underlies the contrasting passage from Anna's *romanza* "Se come voi" from Puccini's *Le Villi* (act 1, R14, mm. 16–23).

Puccini, Edgar *(1889), act 1, R43, mm. 3–10, "D'entrambi nel sangue"*

A brief analysis of a passage from Puccini's *Edgar* (1889) may serve to demonstrate more precisely the way in which the repetitive melodic designs of Bolognese exercises in *attacchi,* in paradigmatic form, could underpin the construction of a *cantilena,* often by integrating with analogous repetitions of the *ritmo* corresponding to the verse meter.

The final set piece of the first act of *Edgar* is a quintet with chorus, a form of *pezzo concertato* in which the characters of the drama express conflicting emotions simultaneously within an ensemble setting.[98] Mo-

ments before this finale, Edgar (tenor) has leapt to the defense of Tigrana, the village seductress (mezzo), to protect her from the wrath of
a crowd of church-going peasants. Having threatened them with his
sword and set fire to his own house, he invites Tigrana to accompany
him in a life devoted to lust and carnal pleasures. The secondary character, Frank (baritone), unable to contain his own love for his stepsister
Tigrana, tries to stop them by starting a duel. At this point their father
Gualtiero (bass) emerges from the church with his daughter Fidelia
(soprano—in love, of course, with Edgar) and manages to quell the
violence, if not the flames. This contrived situation provided the librettist with an opportunity to set out the conflicting emotions required
for a conventional *pezzo concertato*. In response to Gualtiero's pleas for
restraint, Edgar expresses remorse, Fidelia concern, Frank anger, and
Tigrana contempt.

The text for Fidelia's opening melody of the quintet offers a good
example of Ferdinando Fontana's unmistakable style of libretto writing.
The imagery concerns a blind old man soaring like a nimbus to burst a
delirium of rage within the bloodstreams of the two knights:

D'entrambi nel sangue (6)	In the blood of both,
qual nembo veloce (6)	like a soaring lofty cloud
il cieco delirio (6)	the blind old man has burst
dell'ira scoppiò! (6)	the delirium of rage!

The stanza is made up of six-syllable *senari,* with accents on the second and fifth syllables. It ends conventionally with a *tronco* line. Puccini
evidently conceived a standard *senario-ritmo* as a phrase rhythm for the
passage, as set out in example 4.20 (a). Since the verses are entirely regular, four simple repetitions of this *ritmo* suffice to generate the opening
phrase of the ensemble. As mentioned in chapter 3, however, the *ritmo* is
an abstract construct that requires realization through complementary
melodic and harmonic devices. Example 4.20 (b) suggests a reconstruction of this compositional process by "attaching" the bass motion of the
ascending step and descending third, in the manner of a Bolognese practical counterpoint, to the regular flow of the verse rhythm. Only the initial
rising step of the progression coincides with the *ritmo.* Its falling third
occurs within the gap between the phrases. The attached bass motion is

4.20.

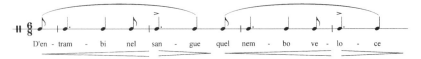

a. *Senario-ritmo*

b. *Ritmo melodico.*

c. Puccini, *Edgar,* act 1, R43, mm. 3–10 (Milan: Ricordi, 1905).

then embellished and varied in order to create a more pleasing *cantilena* that is not so obviously repetitive.[99]

The relevance of this analytical reconstruction to Puccini's actual melody may be gauged from example 4.20 (c). A decorative consonant skip is included within each phrase, passing notes serve to smooth the connections between the individual *ritmi,* and an octave displacement in the first measure provides the melody with an initial rising contour. The final phrase is altered so as to bring about a cadence in the tonic key. In terms of the Bolognese tradition, the supporting harmonies are secondary to, and regulated by, the essential melodic-contrapuntal framework furnished by the regular progression in the soprano part. Indeed, the melody may be considered to be an example of a "bass-less" form, since the soprano is effectively doubled by a tenor part with only a vague outline of a functional bass.[100]

FIVE

Lessons in Dramatic Composition III: Affect, Imitation, and Conduct

The ability to conceive an appropriate *ritmo* for a given dramatic text, to furnish it with a suitable melodic design, and to construct from this a coherent musical phrase was an essential yet mechanical aspect of the craft of composition. Without the more elusive properties of expressiveness or beauty, or a satisfying overall shape to the musical discourse, such formulas mattered little. Audiences took it for granted that operatic music should sound well crafted. They placed considerably greater emphasis on its ability to capture the meaning and emotion of the words and to impart them through song.

Such matters were considered too important to be left to chance or to the creative instincts of individuals. In the Italian traditions, musicians received teachings on ways to represent sentiments and feelings, and guidelines were issued on how to link together different types of phrase and period in order to ensure a serviceable structure over longer spans of music. There were doctrines on the musical "imitation" of feelings, on the choice of standardized "affects" (rationalized emotional states) to suit the meaning of a particular section of verse, and on the "conduct" of a musical discourse.

These prescriptive techniques derived from methods taught during the eighteenth century, when they appear to have been intended to provide students with guaranteed means to generate the maximum musical effectiveness for the minimum effort in the shortest time. Composers trained in this way would have been able to determine, at a glance, not only an appropriate *ritmo* and choice of harmonic-contrapuntal progression for a given verse but also a suitable key, tempo, texture, style, and conduct or form. Busy maestros would have had neither the time nor the inclination to indulge in individual, original interpretations of each text. It was far simpler and more professionally astute to make use of a variety of prefabricated materials and formulas, adapting and refashioning them as their abilities allowed and in response to immediate demands.[1]

While such reliance upon conventional musical devices to convey the meaning of a text reflects the eighteenth-century aesthetics of imitation and affect, it appears profoundly at odds with later Romantic notions of creative genius, spontaneous inspiration, and personal expression. Antiquated methods governing affect, imitation, and conduct nevertheless continued to form one of the cornerstones of Italian training in dramatic composition, contributing to the tension between convention and originality that was to persist throughout the nineteenth century.[2] New concepts associated with the Romantic image of the artist—typically a Byronic or Beethovenian figure, driven by inner compulsion to bestow fresh and provocative acts of creativity upon the world—began to find their way into Italian musical life during the 1820s, especially following the debate between the *romantici* and *classici* instigated by Mme. de Staël's appeal for a revitalization of Italian literature and opera.[3] The cult surrounding Bellini during the 1830s drew heavily on such notions, willfully overlooking his reliance on more or less standard methods and formulas. In those places where the new Romantic aesthetic took hold, high value began to be placed on originality, innovation, and individual genius, but only, it appears, when it was underpinned by familiar and recognizable conventions. Anything too overtly original was ignored, unless it had the excuse of being foreign. Composers and public were complicit in this: amid the hullabaloo that accompanied each new work or newly discovered talent, everyone knew that (commercial) success depended ultimately upon a sense of familiarity with established musical conventions. This was provided, in part, by a vague adherence to the outmoded doctrines of affect, imitation, and conduct that continued to be taught in the conservatories until at least the time of Puccini's studies. Indeed, his early operas offer evidence of the continuity of these "Enlightenment" traditions. In accordance with the doctrine of "dominant affect" and its associated "movements," for instance, almost every cantabile moment from *Le Villi* to *Tosca* is an andante of some sort, ranging from *lento* and *calmo*, through *amoroso*, *religioso*, and *doloroso*, to *mosso* and *animato*.[4]

I. DOMINANT AFFECTS AND THEIR MOVEMENTS

The notion of musical expression, as it pertains to Italian *melodramma*, is rooted in the eighteenth-century tendency to regard the affects of music as more or less direct representations or descriptions of human passions.[5] According to this aesthetic, the composer did not offer up his or her own inner experience as a testament in sound to feelings and insights that would be shared by listeners, as the Romantics later came to believe. Rather, he sought to identify the emotions inherent in a given text and to convey them through conventional means, which would be understood and felt by others through the agency of an appropriately executed performance.[6] The feelings aroused by music were regarded as *objective* entities: a particular musical device would give rise to similar responses or "affects" regardless of differences between composers and audiences. Some composers were simply better than others at manipulating the devices, just as some listeners were more susceptible to their results. Although the doctrine of affects emphasized that music should resemble an outpouring of emotions, this referred more to the practice of musical *performance* than to composition. C. P. E. Bach's insistence that "a musician cannot move others unless he himself is moved" should not be taken to imply that the emotional content of musical material was regarded as arising from some original, individual feeling on the part of the composer or performer. Understanding of, and empathy with, the given affect served only to ensure that "the expression *of the piece* will be more clearly perceived by the audience."[7] Similar attitudes continued to inform the theory and practice of composition in nineteenth-century Italy, even in the writings of progressives such as Basevi, whose discussion of "musical language" in 1856 remained focused on the notion of affects and their expression.[8]

Friedrich Marpurg, a student of J. S. Bach whose treatise on fugue (1753–54) proved highly influential in Italy, epitomized this Enlightenment way of thinking in his advice to composers on how to set text to music. The most important part of the process, he maintained, was the accurate identification of what were considered to be fixed and objective feelings embodied in a given passage of words. Only after these feelings had been adequately defined, in order, as is implicit in his instructions, that they could be aligned with appropriate and corresponding musical devices, was the composer regarded as free to apply a degree of individual initiative:

> In pieces for singing let us seek first to study and determine exactly which affection resides in the words; how high a degree of the affection; from what sort of feelings it is composed. . . . Then let us be concerned to inspect closely the essence of this affection and what sort of motions the soul may be exposed to; how the body may even suffer from it; what sort of motions may be caused in the body. . . . Only then, after having considered, tested, measured, and settled all this exactly, thoroughly, and carefully, may we entrust ourselves to our genius, our power of imagination and invention.[9]

The affects available to the composer were generally reduced to lists of what would now, somewhat misleadingly, be regarded as terms for the indication of tempo. As Clive Brown explains: "[Theorists], particularly in the eighteenth century, regarded many of these terms as primarily regarding expression, or signifying a particular mode of execution, rather than tempo; some grouped them in more or less broad categories; some explicitly recognized divergent usages; others simply contented themselves with prescribing a hierarchy of tempo terms without comment."[10] In nineteenth-century Italy such lists of affects were usually given in two parts: first, the "movements" (*movimenti*) or "degrees of movement" (*gradi di movimento*) that indicated the motion corresponding most closely to the character of the affect; and second, the terms that signified the "dominant affect" itself (*affetto dominante*). Together, they formed the paired terms that are understood today largely as tempo designations, such as *Andante affettuoso* or *Allegro agitato*.[11] It was not until the mid-1840s that these terms started to lose their broader significance in Italy, primarily in response to the application of the metronome to performance.[12] The publication of Barbirolli's *Principii di metodica musicale coll'applicazione del metronomo* (Principles of Musical Method with the Application of the Metronome) in 1857, and its promotion by Filippo Filippi in the pages of the *Gazzetta musicale di Milano,* served to accelerate this shift in terminological meaning from affects to tempo. In response, Giuseppe Staffa even proposed a new simplified system of terms for tempo and character, together with their modification, which failed to take root.[13]

It was nevertheless generally agreed by nineteenth-century Italian writers on the subject that any significant span of music should be governed by a single, most appropriate "dominant affect," which should regulate the overall "movement" and expressive character regardless of any local variations that might arise in response to the immediate demands of the text. In practice, this meant that operatic pieces were normally controlled by a single "movement." Should the text require it, however, a piece could also make use of several dominant affects, giving rise to what would be regarded as a "multi-movement" composition. It follows that an understanding of the theory of affect and its associated movements is a significant factor in any historically informed study of form, structure, and genre in Italian opera, as is discussed further below.

The most widely read list of musical movements and affects in nineteenth-century Italy appears to have been Asioli's, especially as set out in his frequently reprinted textbook of elementary principles for the students at the Milan Conservatory (1824 [1809]):

> *Movimenti* or *gradi di movimento* are the signs at the beginning of a composition that give the character of the affect: Largo, Grave, Larghetto, Adagio, Andantino, Tempo giusto, Tempo di minuetto, Andante, Allegretto, Allegro, Presto, and Prestissimo.
> Terms indicating the dominant affect of the composition [are]: Sostenuto, Maestoso, Affettuoso, Amoroso, Grazioso, Cantabile, Espressivo, Moderato, Agitato, Brio, Vivace, etc.[14]

Similar lists appeared in later publications, such as De Macchi's *Grammatica musicale* (ca. 1830)[15] and Pacini's *Trattato di contrappunto* (1834),[16] in which *movimenti* were designated by the more familiar modern term "*tempi.*" Ritorni's *Ammaestramenti* (1841) reduced Asioli's twelve *movimenti* to three basic *muovimenti* [*sic*]: "First: the majestic [*il maestoso*] in largo, grave, larghetto, adagio; second: the medium [*il medio*] in andantino, tempo giusto, tempo di minuetto, andante; [third:] the quick [*il celere*] in allegretto, allegro, presto, prestissimo."[17] De Vecchis provided detailed descriptions of the same list of *tempi* or *affetti,* which he regarded as "terms to indicate the Character of the composition."[18] These standard affects remained largely unchanged in the Italian traditions until the end of the nineteenth century, as is evident from the account given in Giusto Dacci's *Trattato teorico-pratico* (1886), which supplemented Asioli's standard *movimenti* with contemporary additions such as "*Tempo di Mazurka, Tempo di Valzer, Tempo di Galop, Tempo di Bolero,* etc."[19]

Asioli went into more detail on the application of these affects to different types of aria in *Il Maestro di composizione* (1832). He emphasized above all the importance of remaining true to the dominant affect of an individual piece (or movement), regardless of its position within a larger grouping of pieces and regardless of the variety of expression required by individual moments. In considering the affect as a property of the verses, to be expressed primarily through the vocal part and secondarily, and separately, by what he called the "movements" of the orchestra, Asioli demonstrated his conformity with much older traditions:

> [The aria] can be formed of a smooth thread of embellished phrases, called *di bel canto;* it can be of a single cast [*un getto solo*], when a single phrase in a single tempo dominates from beginning to end; and it can be made up of various pieces, various genres, and of a varied vocal range. In each of these compositions, the young student must seek the true expression of the dominant affect of the verses in the voice, and in the *movimenti* of the orchestra, and not just the expressions of the moment, which, if done for expression, must nevertheless not overshadow and distract from the dominant *movimento,* since from this alone must derive the value, often the entire sum, of the unity of thought that genius and good taste alone can inspire.[20]

In terms of the methods employed to imitate or express the dominant affect within a single tempo or movement, Niccolò Cattaneo's textbook, *Grammatica della musica* (1828)—written early in his career for the music students of Bergomanero before he became known as a writer for the *Gazzetta musicale di Milano*—also confirmed the centrality of the inflection of the vocal part. His answers to the following rhetorical questions appear to concentrate exclusively on the accents and characterization of the voice, offering no mention of the *movimenti* of the orchestra:

> Question: What is understood by the *dominant affect of the composition*?
> Answer: Just as in speech the accents are louder and more vibrant when expressing strong and noble sentiments than when expressing sweet, moderate, and peaceful sentiments, so too, in music, must the accents be more marked and vigorous in phrases or entire pieces expressing vigorous, lively, and strong concepts than in those expressing calm, sweet, and tender concepts. Therefore, the *dominant affect of the composition* is to be understood as the character, or one could say the style, that should be practiced in the execution of one or other types of piece.
> Question: What are the most usual means to represent these diverse styles in musical phrases?
> Answer: There are greater or lesser levels of loud and soft, appoggiaturas and suspensions of greater or lesser force, more or less staccato, more or less

vigorous crescendos and decrescendos, more or less quick and vibrant rendi-
tions of the *gruppetto,* mordent or trill, more or less marked strong beats of
the measure, greater or lesser accuracy of the value of the note: in short, all
that which serves to convey the true expression intended and indicated by
the composer.[21]

Over the course of the nineteenth century the musical means to express the dominant affect expanded considerably beyond such traditional
limitations, especially in terms of the importance of the orchestra. But the
vocal part remained the primary expressive agent. Cattaneo's definition
testifies also to the flexibility of the rhythmic pulse in performance. In
spite of the fixed "movement," observance of the strict note values was
evidently open to considerable expressive license. The *movimento* of the
dominant affect appears to have been regarded as an overall unifying
device, rather than a continuous regulator of the rhythmic pulse. As an article in *L'Italia musicale* of 1853 made clear: "The nature of the affects that
come to be determined by the rhythm depend very much upon the diverse
progress of the *movimento.* . . . The rhythm of the pulse is not the same in
joy as it is in sadness, in raging anger as it is in peaceful tenderness."[22] Cattaneo's definition of the dominant affect also testifies to the broad meaning of the terms *crescendo* and *decrescendo.* In the Italian traditions they
were by no means confined merely to dynamics. They concerned fluid
adjustments to all of the means employed to express the dominant affect. A leading article on melody that appeared in the Neapolitan journal
La Musica in 1883 categorized the crescendo and decrescendo into three
species, relating to the number and type of sources of sound, the intensity
of the harmony, and the movement of the rhythm: "The Crescendo is the
progressive gradation of an Affect. . . . For clarity I distinguish three types:
the crescendo of sounds, of tonality, and of *ritmo.*"[23]

II. PHYSICAL AND SENTIMENTAL IMITATION

In the Italian *Ottocento* traditions, the process by which the affects, or
objectified sentiments encapsulated in a dramatic text, were transferred
to music continued to be known as "imitation" (*imitazione*). This term
was often used synonymously with "expression" (*espressione*), although
it should not be confused with the later German Romantic notion of
emotive or "personal expression" (*Ausdruck*). The Romantic belief in the

metaphysical status of art rejected the ancient theory of truth as correspondence and replaced it with a theory of truth as creation or production.[24] Espousing the subjective worldview of Kant's *Critique of Pure Reason* (1781), A. W. Schlegel and Schelling, for instance, did not believe that
nature provided the rule for artists, but rather that the artist provided the
rule for nature.[25] Frederick Beiser makes the case, however, that the Romantics never completely rejected the ancient theory of imitation: "What
is indeed most striking about early Romantic aesthetics is its *synthesis* of
the doctrines of imitation and expression [i.e., personal expression, or
Ausdruck]. It holds that in expressing his feelings and desires, in fathom-
ing his own personal depths, the artist also reveals the creative powers of
nature that work through him."[26]

Within the opera traditions of nineteenth-century Italy these new
ideas, while impacting significantly upon the image of the artist and the
status of the artwork, never quite reached the same degree of synthesis.
The established doctrine of imitation continued to hold sway, if not always in the minds of audiences and critics, then at least in the teaching
of dramatic composition at the conservatories. Alberto Mazzucato, for
instance, who taught singing and composition at the Milan Conservatory
from 1839 until his appointment as director in 1872, wrote of the "faculty"
of imitation through which emotions and indeterminate concepts were
conveyed through music.[27]

Such attitudes derived directly from eighteenth-century doctrines.
According to Galeazzi (1796), who echoed the writings of countless other
maestros, in order to "speak to the heart," a melody must imitate human feelings.[28] But these feelings were not understood to emanate from
any subjective interpretation on the part of the composer, from some
individual reaction to a text. The notion of imitation was always tied inextricably to objective properties of the music. It concerned matters of
compositional technique, grounded in counterpoint. Galeazzi's definition of musical expression, which referred also to the practice of imitation,
made no mention of individual feelings but engaged rather with practical
instructions on how to achieve certain expressive effects. Even taking into
account the limitations of the late eighteenth-century style that Galeazzi
presumably had in mind, his guidelines on musical expression may appear
surprisingly limited to modern musicians familiar with later Romantic
concepts:

> Expression consists principally of three things: 1, in the knowledge of how to select appropriate diminutions and to attach them to the proper places; 2, in the selection of the arch-like melodic shapes most adapted to *cantilena*; and 3, above all in the gradation of the volume of the instruments, or, as practitioners say, knowing how to achieve a good distribution of loud and soft, otherwise known as *chiaroscuro*.[29]

Similar lists of practical techniques, encompassing various aspects of ornamentation, instrumentation, and performance, etc., continued to define what was understood in the Italian traditions as musical "expression" or the "imitation of feelings." Gervasoni's guidance on vocal music, for instance, appears to equate "the true expression of the feeling that is to be rendered" with a correct application of the most basic principles of text setting: "the composer must depict all the author's thoughts and express his words truly in the vocal part of the aria, and for this reason the long syllables always fall on the strong beats and the short on the weak."[30]

Gervasoni also laid the foundations for later accounts of *imitazione* by dividing melody into two broad types: first, as a "simple succession of tones" that was limited merely to "flattering the ear with beautiful *cantilena*," and second and more significantly, as "an art of imitation."[31] On the basis of this division he postulated a qualitative difference between vocal and instrumental music. While instrumental melody was viewed in essentially formalist terms, as a pleasing yet abstract series of tones, vocal melody was regarded as the highest musical achievement, which required the composer to know how to employ the most effective means to express (or imitate) the "true" sentiment contained in the text. It seems never to have occurred to Gervasoni to consider that instruments might also participate in this art of imitation, by playing, for instance, melodies from operas.

The theory of *imitazione* was taken up and developed by Giuseppe Carpani in his recollections of Haydn (1823 [1812]), especially in response to the conspicuous descriptive elements in his late friend's oratorios, *Die Schöpfung* (The Creation, 1798) and *Die Jahreszeiten* (The Seasons, 1801). In attempting to explain why Haydn's musical depictions of nature and natural events went beyond discredited notions of "word-painting," Carpani put forward a theory that was to prove influential enough to resurface in Asioli's later writings. With the benefit of hindsight, it also suggests some rudimentary parallels with the modern theory of the musical *topos* established in Leonard Ratner's *Classic Music* (1980) and could thus make a contribution to the debate surrounding the historical legitimacy of "topic theory."[32]

Carpani defined two categories of imitation: "physical or direct" (*imitazione fisica o diretta*) and "sentimental or indirect" (*imitazione sentimentale o indiretta*).[33] Direct musical imitations of physical objects, such as the barking dogs, rustling leaves, or babbling brooks of earlier eighteenth-century "pictorial" music, were denigrated by him as tokens of an inferior style of composition. Applying C. S. Peirce's later terminology, Carpani was critical of musical "icons": sounds which, although culturally conditioned and dependent on received conventions, appear to resemble their objects.[34] For his second category of "indirect or sentimental imitation," on the other hand, he reserved the highest praise. With reference to *Die Schöpfung,* Carpani claimed that Haydn had managed to create the impression of natural sounds and events without recourse to any crude "physical or direct" imitation. He posited the idea that Haydn had somehow established a set of musical means as "analogous" to the concepts or feelings they were intended to represent:

> Sentimental imitation is that which, by incorporating sounds and movements analogous to those of the designated object, imparts to us an idea of diverse affects that move the hearts of men and the thoughts of the soul.[35]

The term "simulated imitation" (*imitazione simulata*) was coined to describe this correlation between the musical techniques employed by the composer and the meanings inherent in a text. Again, applying Peirce's terminology in retrospect, Carpani appears to suggest the operation of musical "indexes" and "symbols" in Haydn's music: sounding elements that act as signs to convey, metonymically, the meaning of the given text and that signify through inference, causality, and learned cultural codes.[36] Carpani's vague theory of "indirect" or "simulated" imitation, which drew upon older Italian teachings on the regulation of musical expression by fixed affects, suggests not only a theoretical basis for investigating conventional musical portrayals in Italian opera but also testifies to a profound split between Italian and German (Romantic) concepts of musical expression. The assumption of an accepted set of correlations between particular musical techniques and particular affects is one of the defining features of the Italian traditions. It accounts for the continued reliance on standardized effects and clichés throughout the nineteenth century, even in Puccini. Difficulties arise, however, in attempting to define precisely which musical means were applied, when and how, and to which affects. Practice was far too complicated to be reduced to some kind of historically informed lexicon. Authors were content for the most part to allude only to generalized techniques—orchestration, melodic contour, phrase rhythm, etc.—and even in these vague terms they occasionally disagreed.

The most concrete examples of musical *imitazione* are perhaps to be found in the examples to chapters 5 and 6 of the third volume of Asioli's *Il Maestro di composizione,* which drew upon Carpani's ideas and examples to formulate a generalized theory. Asioli retained Carpani's division of *imitazione* into two categories of "physical" and "sentimental," as well as his Haydn-inspired acknowledgment of the importance of orchestration in supporting the chief means of expression, the vocal part. Maintaining the centrality of the aesthetic of affect, Asioli claimed that the principal purpose of the dramatic orchestra was to "adapt sounds and rhythmic movements to the quality of the passions that it imitates or expresses."[37] Although it is not clear whether by *i movimenti ritmici* he meant to refer to the underlying meter of the accompanimental rhythm (*ritmo armonico*) or to the overall tempo designations of musical units (also called *movimenti*), Asioli evidently subscribed to the basic idea of musical analogues for objectified passions or affects. In his outline of *imitazione sentimentale* he also betrayed his reliance upon long-established principles, including the fixed nature of the feelings and passions to be imitated or expressed and a bias toward the vocal part as the ultimate conveyor of feelings, notwithstanding an increased emphasis on the supporting function of the orchestra. He stated that music had no "prototypes" for the affects, even though he mentioned a variety of techniques—involving rhythm, orchestration, and dynamics—through which the composer should translate the feelings into music using his own intuition:

> Sentimental imitation, or the expression of the affects of the soul, is that which bestows greater honor upon the composer. Since the music has no prototypes to guide it, [the composer] must give rise to everything by the dominant affects expressed through the words, by his own way of feeling the passions, by his fervid imagination, good taste, and good musical sense. The vocal part, the primary concern of the dramatic composer, must suffice to

express any affect, whether pathetic, amorous, angry, jolly, agitated, etc. But
if the voice is accompanied by faster or slower movements of the orchestra,
by higher or lower sounds, by immense effects resulting from the variety of
instruments, by greater or lesser louds and softs—provided that all of this is
in accordance with and confirms the dominance of the affect, then the voice
will be enhanced in itself and the harmony that encircles it will produce an
inexpressible delight.[38]

Whether through a misunderstanding or an attempt to improve upon
the original theory, Asioli went on to subdivide Carpani's category of
"physical imitation" into two types. One of these followed Carpani and
described the practice of crude musical mimesis, or "direct imitation,"
while the other should more logically have been classified as a subcat-
egory of "sentimental imitation," since it added further meaning to the
concept of *imitazione simulata* by speculating upon the analogous musical
means required to depict noiseless, visible phenomena:

> Physical imitation is divided into two types: that which expresses ob-
> jects that are visible but devoid of sound, and that which is concerned with
> an approximation of indeterminate sounds. The first is created through the
> imagination of the composer, since it is not possible to represent through
> approximation the rising and setting of the sun, the unexpected appearance
> of light, the horror of darkness, etc., unless by accelerating and decelerating
> the movement, or by higher or lower, or softer or louder, tones. The second
> species is actually demeaning since it compels the composer to imitate, with
> particular musical tones in the orchestra or on specific instruments, the in-
> determinate rumble of *thunder,* the mooing of *cows,* the singing of *birds,* the
> murmuring of *brooks,* etc.[39]

In attempting to account for the seemingly implausible musical representation of visual or abstract concepts, Asioli hinted at the importance of
relative pitch, dynamics, and especially rhythm in the practice of "simulated imitation," in particular when the feelings to be expressed were
brought on by reactions to natural events. This emphasis upon general
musical parameters rather than specific "figures" is borne out in his supporting examples, drawn from works by Haydn, Paisiello, and Cimarosa.
For instance, the famous depiction of a sunrise in part 1 of *Die Schöpfung*
("In vollem Glanze steiget jetzt die Sonne") is explained in vague formalist terms, as if the imitative correlations exploited by the music were
self-evident:

5.1. Bonifazio Asioli, *Il Maestro di composizione* (1832), Examples 3: no. 16, 78, (Paisiello, *Nina* [1789]).

The rising scale in the first violins and flutes, the harmony that grows slowly within the softer tones in the middle, the increase of the high and low instruments, and the contrary motion between the ascending scale and the descending parts, which little by little strengthens, expands, and intensifies the harmony—[these] produce an effect that signifies the gradual steps of a sunrise, through the regular increase from pianissimo to *sforzato*. And with the fortissimo the fullness of the heavens is bathed in light.[40]

Of significance here is not so much the omission of what would now be called "topical" features but rather the firmness of the Enlightenment belief in music as an imitative art. Asioli did, however, offer slightly more specific guidelines in explaining the depiction of sleep from Paisiello's opera *Nina, o sia La pazza per amore* (1789), as reproduced in example 5.1:

Andante sostenuto

5.2. Asioli, *Il Maestro di composizione* (1832), Examples 3: no. 16, 86
(Cimarosa, *Il matrimonio segreto* [1799]).

> The *affettuoso* key of E♭ major, the placid motion of the melody, the gentle
> sweetness of the instruments, and the ineffable pleasure of the chord of the
> triad inspired by nature are the correct means to make the spirit tranquil
> and to induce sleep.[41]

Apart from the association of a key signature with a particular affect
(even though the passage cited comprises a plagal cadence in B♭ major),
Asioli mentioned few of the features that would, in modern musicology,
mark this passage out as a typical pastoral "romance" of late eighteenth-
century French *opéra comique*: its $\frac{2}{4}$ time signature, gentle andante, and
dialogue between clarinets and bassoons playing in parallel thirds.

In example 5.2, presenting the opening of "The Horse's Gallop" from
Cimarosa's *Il matrimonio segreto* (1799), Asioli did specify a conventional

musical representation of the gallop—in this case, a strong dactylic rhythm—only to expand the range of acceptable tokens of the type by citing a contrasting variant in eighth-note triplets:

> A horse's gallop should be heard by means of three strokes, the first loud and of double length and the other two weak and of half duration. Although in this example the gallop does not strictly follow the aforementioned principle, being of three equal strokes, it succeeds nevertheless in a grand effect because the first stroke is marked by a strong accent.[42]

Asioli's theory of imitation, together with his teachings on harmony and counterpoint, remained central to northern Italian traditions throughout the nineteenth century. Its presentation was occasionally updated, as when Raimondo Boucheron, who was at that time *maestro di cappella* at the cathedral of Vigevano and later took up the same position at the Duomo in Milan, applied the more philosophical-sounding labels of "subjective" (*subbiettiva*) and "objective" (*obbiettiva*) to the categories of "sentimental" and "physical" imitation. Despite its progressive Germanic title, Boucheron's *Filosofia della musica o estetica applicata a quest'arte* (Philosophy of Music, or Aesthetics Applied to That Art, 1842) continued to uphold all the basic tenets of the conservative, pre-Romantic theory of expression and affect. It still regarded composition as a means for the artistic representation of fixed affects, not as an individual act of creativity:

> This genre of [subjective] imitation is the most noble and worthy of the artist, in that all the means available to the composer must be used to represent wherever necessary the expression of the affect and to supplement the words and accents of the melody if they are not in themselves sufficient to represent it.[43]

There was, however, a progressive aspect to this statement, in its implicit acknowledgment of the importance of instrumental and orchestral features. It suggested that the "words and accents of the melody" were occasionally inadequate and in need of support from "all means available." In the older traditions, the musical imitation of a given affect was considered almost exclusively a function of the vocal part, in particular through its capacity for embellishment and expressive deviations from the *ritmo*. Lucchese maestro Marco Santucci, for instance, who echoed Carpani's theory through his use of the compound term *espressione imitativa*, placed the usual emphasis on the importance of capturing the quality of the overall affect of a given text: "Expressive melody is that which corresponds to the feeling contained within the words as a whole, adapted to music. This feeling is taken up, made pleasing, illuminated, and ennobled by the musical setting."[44] But, like Cattaneo, he seemed incapable of contemplating this in anything other than vocal terms. His guidance to students on how best to achieve this concerns almost entirely the rhythm of the text setting:

1. The sentiments of sweetness, tranquility, and so on demand a short, light, easy *ritmo* in order to be realized and continued.
2. If it is necessary to express varied sentiments that increase or decrease [in intensity], a more varied *ritmo* should be chosen, made up of long and short durations, which should vary between fast and slow in accordance with the sentiment.
3. Regularity can be abandoned when there are contradictory elements in the sentiment. It is not difficult to understand how one can express irresolution, uncertainty, embarrassment, and so on through variations of the *ritmo*.
4. In extraordinary cases, when one wants to make use of a particular energy, this can be done by changing the movement [i.e., overall tempo] and also by altering the *ritmo* in an expressive manner.
5. Another specific use of *ritmo* that frequently has a most pleasing effect involves the introduction of a measure during which the voice may remain silent while an instrument repeats or imitates the last passage of the vocal part.[45]

III. FORM AND CONDUCT

Large-Scale Genres, Movements, and Affects

In its attempt to explain the processes through which music captured the affect of a given passage of text, the theory of musical imitation succeeded primarily, and inadvertently, in demonstrating the richness, variety, and general unruliness of Italian compositional practice. While the affects may have been regarded as fixed, their corresponding musical features were evidently anything but. They were subject to changing tastes, evolving traditions, individual styles, and the many parameters that together afforded music its inherent flexibility of expression.

A similar complexity surrounds the relationship of the dominant affects (in whatever ways they may have been "imitated") to the forms or structures of dramatic music, to the layout of individual pieces or movements and larger genres. Their involvement rested on fluid interactions between the three main "systems" of opera, as defined by Petrobelli: "dramatic action, verbal organization, and music."[46] On the one hand, the dominant affect of a passage of text, once identified, would presumably govern not only the choice of *movimento,* such as andante or allegro, but also its rate of change. The pattern of movements would in this respect have been determined by perceived shifts in the affect controlling the dramatic situation at any given moment. On the other hand, the distribution of affects was regulated by established musical-dramatic conventions, the so-called *convenienze teatrali,* such as the division of the libretto into blank verse (*verso sciolto*) and lyric verse (*verso lirico*), or the connection between the number and placement of arias and the relative qualities of the singers, or the pattern of movements of the mid-nineteenth-century central finale (*scena, tempo d'attacco, largo concertato, tempo di mezzo,* and *stretta*), or the aria form, as described by Ritorni (*scena, primo tempo / cantabile, tempo di mezzo,* and *cabaletta*), or the four parts of the "usual form of duets" (*la solita forma de' duetti*) as outlined by Basevi: "the *tempo d'attacco,* the *adagio,* the *tempo di mezzo,* and the *cabaletta.*"[47]

This apparent antithesis of form and affect arises only at the level of larger genres or, as Boito wrote in 1863, to the *formula* of Italian opera, which included categories such as "aria, rondò, cabaletta, stretta, ritornello, pezzo concertato," etc.[48] Ritorni's 1841 overview of the standard "sung pieces" (*pezzi cantabili*) of his age,[49] together with the insights scattered throughout Basevi's *Studio sulle opere di G. Verdi* (1859), has provided scholars with a plentiful source of historical information on the musical conventions of nineteenth-century Italian opera.[50] Such standardized genres, which were occasionally referred to also as "lyric forms," could contain a number of predetermined changes of *movimento* or affect. A substantial body of research has shown that the norms or expectations of the genre, whether aria, duet, finale, *introduzione,* or any other kind of set piece, decisively took precedence in the construction of the libretto and its musical setting.[51] A precise and comprehensive account of the ways in which the distribution of pieces (*pezzi*) related to the dramatic flow of the libretto remains more open to debate, much as it did in the nineteenth century, owing to the different requirements of the subject matter or *argomento* for each opera.[52]

Quadratura, Fraseologia, *and* Periodologia

At the level of the single-movement piece (*pezzo*), however, which could comprise as few as one or two periods,[53] the doctrine of dominant affect exerted far greater influence. Together with the relation of the phrase to the different poetic meters (*fraseologia*) and their arrangement into symmetrical units (*quadratura*), the affect was an essential factor in what was commonly called *periodologia,* or the construction and arrangement of different types of musical period.[54] Operatic genres, however grand and extended, were made up of a series of shorter or longer members, phrases, periods, parts, and movements, each determined by considerations of verse and *ritmo,* and grouped into a variety of more or less conventional *pezzi.* As Reicha maintained, in his advice on constructing melodies of two periods: "Since music, like poetry and oratory, can only proceed from period to period, there are first two important operations required, not only by melody, but by any piece of music: the first is to create interesting periods, and the second is to blend and connect them clearly."[55] Even the amateur critic Ritorni, the source for much modern scholarship on the historical "forms" of Italian opera, spoke of larger genres in terms of their component periods. The rondò, for example, he described as "an aggregate of various grave and allegro periods, if desired with a reprise [and] other subordinate periods," while the cabaletta was characterized as "a resolute period of tight-knit phrases."[56] Later nineteenth-century accounts were relatively consistent in this respect. An analysis of melodic form designed to assist aspiring singers, for instance, published in the Neapolitan journal *La Musica* in 1884, emphasized the importance of self-contained periods as the basic building blocks of composition: "Melody is informed by a concept, like a speech, and made up of periods. The periods are divided into phrases, and the phrases in turn are divided into designs, members, or incises. A period expressing one complete musical meaning is defined by means of a cadence."[57]

This last observation is crucial to an understanding of the musical period as it was defined throughout the Italian traditions. Like a written sentence, the musical period could be as short as a few measures or as long as an entire composition, depending on the "sense" to be expressed. Although made up of various arrangements of *ritmi,* members, and phrases, its only syntactic requirement was a concluding cadence, usually of the "perfect authentic" variety, which could be in a variety of keys but had to sound sufficiently final. Similar dominant-to-tonic cadences, even those including the first scale degree in the soprano part, could occur as part of the period without necessarily signifying its end. The perfect cadence that served to close a period was generally proclaimed by a variety of conventional signs, such as a melodic descent or an ensuing pause. Confusion arises, however, in the casual use of the term by a number of contemporary writers, who occasionally described units at various levels of form, from short phrases to extended parts, similarly as "periods." Asioli, moreover, included a category of "unfinished periods" in his description of the standard layout of a melodic composition:

> A few phrases suffice to form an unfinished period that has its inflection on the chord of the dominant, or on the tonic with a half-cadence, in this way leaving the musical, and poetical, discourse interrupted. An entire period comprises a greater number of phrases and finishes on the tonic with a full stop, with a final or semifinal cadence.[58]

During the 1850s, Neapolitan composer and pedagogue Staffa continued to employ the term *periodo* according to this traditional definition. He analyzed the opening forty-four measures of the cabaletta "So anch'io la virtù magica" from Donizetti's *Don Pasquale,* for instance, as a single period made up of "phrases" (*frasi*) of between eight and sixteen measures and defined through "incomplete," "central," and "final" cadences (*sospensiva, media, finale*).[59] Staffa (1856) provided numerous similar analyses of passages from *Nabucco, Il trovatore,* and *Ernani*—among the earliest such accounts of Verdi's music—to substantiate this notion of melodic conduct (or musical form) in terms of long phrases and even longer periods. Like most theorists of the Italian traditions, he defined a *periodo* on the basis of both its overall "sense" and the placement of its final perfect cadence, which had to indicate closure both syntactically *and* rhetorically. One of Staffa's analyses of a passage from Verdi's *Ernani* (1843) features in example 5.4 and is discussed more fully toward the end of this chapter.

The "Lyric Prototype"

The most common arrangement of musical phrases within a period, through which were generated many of the melodies that made up the single-movement (i.e., single-dominant affect) *pezzi* and principal genres of Italian opera during the first half of the nineteenth century, has become known in modern musicology as the "lyric prototype." It was first identified as such in Friedrich Lippmann's 1966 study of the melodies of Bellini and the young Verdi, where it was represented by the symbols $a^1 a^2 b a^2$, with each letter standing for a four-measure phrase in a prototypical sixteen-measure melody (generally of one period, although each subsection could, in theory, constitute its own separate period). Joseph Kerman and Scott Balthazar later elaborated on this theory, formulating more precise alphanumeric systems of symbols—such as $A_4 A'_4 B_4 C_4$, where the subscript figures indicate the number of measures in each phrase—and articulating the varied functions of the different units within the form.[60]

Several extracts from nineteenth-century writings have been put forward in support of the historical legitimacy of the modern theory of the "normative" sixteen-measure lyric prototype. Parker (1997) cited Basevi's 1859 description of Pagano's andante, "Sciagurata! hai tu creduto," from act 1 of Verdi's *I lombardi*: "This *andante* has one of the most common and simplest forms, that is: a first period of eight measures in two phrases, a second of four measures, the reprise of the second phrase of the first period, which is followed by another period as an *appendix,* and then the *cadenza*."[61] Fabbri (2007) took this notion further, ascribing such regular periodic structures to the melodies of nineteenth-century Italian opera as a whole. He claimed that composers worked primarily with two-measure units, arranged not only in the form of the lyric prototype as $a_4 a'_4 b_{2+2} a''_4$, or $a_4 a'_4 b_{2+2} c_4$, but also in the form of $a_2 a_2 b_4$.[62] In support of his assertion that "the melodic design [*disegno melodico*] was always conducted with periodicity and symmetrical structure," he put forward the following two historical sources.[63] The first is a quotation from Pietro Lichtenthal's "Aesthetics" (1831):

> The *square* period [*periodo quadrato*] contains four members [*membri*] ... those that are called *square* [*quadratura*] have a similar number of members [i.e., four], whether of three, four, five, etc., measures; the most agreeable are those with four [measures].[64]

It is worth noting that whereas Lichtenthal clearly alluded to a melody of one period, subdivided into four members, Basevi described a

similar melody of three or four periods. Fabbri's second quotation is taken
from a little-known publication by Emanuele Bidera (1853), a librettist of
Sicilian origin based in Naples:

> The most agreeable, or most perfect, period is that which has four mem-
> bers [*membri*] or similar phrases. . . . Each member of the *typical square
> period* [*periodo quadrato tipico*] should consist of four measures, and each
> perfect period should comprise four good, well-composed such units, that is,
> [it should be] sixteen measures.[65]

Such descriptions may serve to underpin the theory of the lyric prototype with historical foundations, but they lack the degree of detail offered
by modern musicological approaches. Through observations and analyses
of a representative range of examples, Balthazar identifies the following
principal features of "an archetypal mid-century melody":

> 1) it includes three kinds of thematic material—an opening 'thematic
> block' (A A' or one of the variants), a contrasting idea (B), and a closing
> phrase or phrases (some version of A or C); 2) it comprises a regular hierar-
> chy of two-measure subphrases, four-measure phrases, and eight-measure
> periods; 3) units from the two- and four-measure levels combine to create
> large-scale rhythmic closure across the entire form; and 4) each phrase of
> music sets two lines of text, with no text other than individual words or short
> phrases being repeated until its coda reuses entire lines.[66]

Balthazar's identification of regular phrase patterns based on two-
measure units corresponds closely to the description of Verdi's "*cadenza
regolare*" in Moreen (1975) and to the practice of applying "melodic
rhythms" (*ritmi melodici*), as set out in chapter 3, while the assumption
of large-scale rhythmic closure, as a kind of hypermeter, recalls Reicha's
theory of melody. In terms of the formal function of component units,
Balthazar put forward a tripartite classification in which musical devices
signifying thematic exposition, contrast, and closure may be seen to conform to the Aristotelian categories of beginning, middle, and end.

Although this definition proved flexible enough to deal with the majority of Italian opera melodies of the mid-nineteenth century, Huebner
(1992) pointed out that its system of "letter analysis" was not designed to
communicate important additional melodic criteria such as tonality and
types of cadence. He set out accordingly to add further specificity to the
understanding of formal functions within the lyric prototype. The eight-

measure antecedent-consequent period was, for instance, identified as the most common arrangement for the opening thematic block, whether as a pair of "balanced phrases" with equally weighted cadences at the end of each four-measure unit, or in the usual form, characterized by relatively weaker and stronger cadences in these positions. A modulation of some sort to the mediant or submediant typically took place in the "medial phrase" or B section, together with varying degrees of fragmentation (of the phrase structure) or development. Depending on whether or not the fourth or closing phrase began with a firm tonic, it could be classified as either an "integrated return," which exhibited tonal but not necessarily melodic reprise, or as an "additive return," which regained the main key only gradually. The separation of the functions of return and closure in the fourth phrase gave rise to a "binary design (first part / period; second part / development / closure)," whereas their concurrence generated a "ternary shape (first part / period; middle / development; return / closure)."[67] In both cases, a sixteen-measure melody remained the "normative" model. Unconventional or exceptional melodies were derived from "Techniques of internal 'expansion,' 'extension,' and 'compression' rooted in the 16-bar type."[68]

Huebner's research into issues of function within the lyric prototype not only provides a convincing account of the most common forms of operatic melody in mid-nineteenth-century Italy but also offers a set of analytical tools for the compilation of a thorough and sophisticated taxonomy of possible "variants." Were his approach to be applied to every melody in Verdi, let alone to a broad range of melodies drawn from the work of a variety of nineteenth-century operatic composers, the resulting chart of lyric forms would undoubtedly be as extensive and full of intricate detail as Webster's analogous chart of "principal formal types in Mozart's arias of the 1780s," which lists no fewer than nineteen separate formal templates.[69]

The compilation of such a comprehensive system of classification for melodies in nineteenth-century opera, while undoubtedly of considerable benefit to an understanding of compositional practice, would nevertheless present a daunting scholarly challenge—owing partly to the conspicuous lack of detail and specificity in the relevant historical sources. A definitive theory of lyric forms was evidently not a priority for those actively involved in the business of creating and promoting nineteenth-century Italian opera. On the contrary, the evidence left by maestros is frustratingly vague in regard to the *precise* definition of forms and genres. Only in the writings of professional critics (such as Basevi or Marselli), self-proclaimed pedagogues (such as Asioli and guitar virtuoso Picchianti), and especially in the writings of amateurs (such as aristocrat, theater critic, and town mayor Ritorni) is there any degree of detail, and even this falls far short of the clarity sought by modern musicology. Given the varying exigencies of dramatic situation, character, and cast, it is understandable that librettists and composers should have treated conventional large-scale genres—such as the central finale or the multi-movement aria—with a degree of looseness. There is, however, as Wedell (1995) demonstrates, a body of historical evidence that documents in detail the normal "forms"—or, more accurately, rules for the correct conduct (*esatta condotta*)[70] of musical periods—for the single-movement *pezzi* that made up these larger genres. It may account for the sixteen-measure lyric prototype operating at various levels of meter and form as well as its many possible variants, including those encountered as late as Puccini's operas.

The survey of historical concepts that follows, and its application to case studies from Verdi, Boito, and Puccini at the end of this chapter, is intended to demonstrate not only the continuity of the theory of what is now described as "form" in the Italian traditions of the nineteenth century but also the inherent flexibility of compositional practice. Modern notions of fixed abstract formal templates (such as *AABA* or *AAB*) did not apply. As Zingarelli's student De Vecchis confirmed, there were no strict guidelines for the structure of arias and duets, because "the conduct of such pieces of music is regulated more by poetry than by musical rules."[71]

Types of Phrase and Period and Rules for Their Conduct

Central to nineteenth-century descriptions of individual operatic movements was a particular type of phrase or period known as the *motivo* (or *motivo principale, tema,* or *soggetto*), which may be regarded as the Italian equivalent of Heinrich Koch's more familiar *Thema* and which corresponds in all important respects to Balthazar's and Huebner's formal category of the "thematic block."[72] It bore no relation to the modern concept of a fragmentary musical "motive" or "cell," signifying rather a self-contained theme of typically eight measures. The overall "conduct" of an individual melody or piece was determined in response to this guiding concept or *motivo*. Just as a speech was understood to require a clearly defined theme in order to guarantee a sense of unity to its many episodes and digressions, so too was the meaning and coherence of a musical composition understood to depend on a cognitive thread emanating from its principal subject. The subsidiary phrases or periods that made up the remainder of the melody or piece had somehow to relate to the character, implications, and affect of the *motivo,* although the success or failure of this overall interrelatedness remained largely a matter of taste. As Galeazzi commented, "This is an art whose principles reside in the human heart and in the sentiment; and yet which is impossible to reduce to fixed rules."[73] Lichtenthal defined conduct in these terms as "the art of adapting a principal idea to subsidiary ideas, of bringing back the main theme to this end without abusing it, and of connecting its modulations within the key in a way that is neither too wide-ranging nor [too limited]."[74] He distinguished two types of conduct: "simple" (*semplice*), in which the dominant affect was maintained throughout, and "artificial" (*artificiale*), which presented the main idea in various aspects and guises and through contrasting material.

Later Italian definitions continued to rely on an analogy with rhetoric to account for the overall shape of a musical form, its disposition of phrases or periods. There was, however, a tension between the assumed immediacy of inspiration through the poetic text and the apparent uniformity of the resulting musical structures. Boucheron praised the effects of a well-disposed conduct but lamented the reliance of his fellow maestros on standard patterns:

> Good conduct gives the artwork a spontaneous character which is vulgarly called "a cast," making it seem in fact as if the work emanated from the mind of the artist with the same facility as a statue emerging complete in all its parts from a prepared form. The Italians have an admirable attitude in this respect; and if they would take more care to vary the forms, they would easily surpass the foreigners.[75]

There were reasonably well formulated guidelines for the arrangement of musical periods (*periodologia*). In keeping with standard eighteenth-century concepts of musical form as analogous to the art of speech or discourse,[76] they relied primarily on the identifiable rhetorical function of each unit—specifically, whether or not it was characterized as a main subject, a deduction based on this subject, a transition, contrasting element, closing passage, or appendix—as well as a range of other factors such as the positioning of "fixed, secondary, or passing" modulations (explained in chapter 4) and types of cadence. Composers retained a considerable degree of freedom in terms of which periods to include within the piece, their relative lengths, the choice of secondary cadences and modulations, and the number of "parts" (usually one, two, or three for an operatic *pezzo*, or more for genres such as the instrumental rondo or set of variations).

The Principal Theme (Motivo Principale)

As a starting point for a survey of the relevant historical sources, Galeazzi provided one of the clearest accounts of the various types of phrase and period in his chapter on the "parts, members [*membri*], and Rules" pertaining to the conduct of an entire piece.[77] He was, after all, a professional violinist and composer writing primarily for an amateur readership that demanded simple and comprehensive definitions of key concepts. Although firmly rooted in late eighteenth-century practice, clear echoes of Galeazzi's terms and concepts resound throughout Italian musical writings of the nineteenth century. Indeed, his unusually thorough definitions occasionally provide a key to the interpretation of ambiguous passing references and vague allusions in later works, suggesting that subsequent authors assumed their readers possessed some prior knowledge of the concepts he described.

Although Galeazzi explained the *motivo* exclusively as a period, operating as the principal theme of an extended composition and defined by a firm closing cadence, later authors allowed it more flexibility. It could, for instance, be used to describe the principal phrase of a short melody consisting of a single period. Galeazzi gave the following generalized account:

> The *Motivo* is, I maintain, none other than the principal idea of the piece [*Melodia*], the Subject [*Soggetto*], the Theme [*Tema*] of the musical discourse around which the entire composition must be based. It is permissible for the *Preludio* to begin on any chord, even one outside of the main key, but

the *Motivo* must infallibly begin with the chord that constitutes the key, the chord with its first, third, and fifth notes. It must also be sufficiently distinctive and noticeable since, as the theme of the discourse, if it is not well understood, then the subsequent discourse will likewise be incomprehensible. The *Motivo* always finishes with a cadence either on the principal key or on its dominant or subdominant. In vocal as well as instrumental duets, trios and quartets, this period is often repeated twice in different parts. . . .

    The *Motivo* is thus an essential component [*membro*] in every piece [*Melodìa*]. It is characteristic of beginners to rack their brains for a good *Motivo* for their compositions, without reflecting that every good composition must always increase in effect from the beginning to the end. If one selects a striking *Motivo*, it will be very difficult to get the composition to intensify; on the contrary, it will dwindle considerably and this will utterly discredit the composition in spite of a most beautiful *Motivo*. If, on the other hand, a mediocre *Motivo* is used, well arranged [*condotto*] according to the precepts given here, the composition will always increase its effect. This will render every moment more interesting and pleasing to the audience and will receive more than the usual applause. We see precisely this practiced by the most classic authors: so much so that an excellent *Motivo* is normally regarded as a sign of a bad composition, which is judged, as has already been said, by its conduct and not by the *Motivo* of which this conduct consists.[78]

Galeazzi's preference for well-structured "conduct" over melodic invention stems from what was regarded as the most important property of the *motivo:* its role as the guiding "motive" or concept of the musical discourse. The origins of the term are to be found in an analogy with the underlying "motivation" that gave shape to a drama or poem. It was essential that listeners should be left in no doubt as to the identity of the principal theme, since every other phrase, period, and connecting passage depended on it for meaning and coherence. Just as a well-constructed speech or poem was unified by a single subject, so too were the many parts of a composition heard in relation to the expressive character, or affect, of the *motivo*. Its suitability as a recognizable (musical-rhetorical) theme was of considerably greater import to the composition than any immediate qualities, such as beauty, originality, or momentary effect. Asioli recognized this property of the *motivo* at the beginning of his description of "the entire composition":

    The melodic composition is an entity made up of phrases, unfinished periods, whole periods, and of the main divisions called *parts*. The composer must first of all take the utmost care in the selection of phrases that make

up the *motivo*; since this, in order to fix its shape [in the mind], is usually
repeated to ensure that it best exhibits a significant character that is easy to
remember.[79]

Ritorni had this broad interpretation of *motivo* in mind when he
claimed that the composer drew inspiration from the poetic text for the
invention (or principal theme) as well as for the basic overall form of an
aria:

> The maestro reads an aria in order to receive inspiration for an idea of the
> motive [simultaneously poetic and musical]; and when he has thus dealt
> with the invention, nothing concerns him more than the subordinate forms
> that together make up what he has obtained more easily as a whole. Thus a
> stock pattern is extracted from the form of the poetic strophe and then su-
> perimposed anew, lacking individual parts, but, in an abstract sense, outlin-
> ing the whole physiognomy.[80]

Galeazzi's emphasis upon the internal dynamic of the piece, its dramatic (kinetic) flow, was common to many nineteenth-century accounts.
Milanese organist Boucheron's first law of good conduct, for instance,
was expressed by the Latin maxim "Cave ne decrescat oratio" (Be careful
that the speech does not wane). His three-stage advice on how to avoid
dullness of overall form concerned a graded increase of complexity, ex-
pressivity, and thwarted desire:

> (1) To present the ideas at the beginning with maximum simplicity, re-
> serving elaborations, which can give them greater prominence, for their suc-
> cessive repetitions. (2) To dispose the melodies and contrasting passages in
> such a way that the more expressive ones succeed the less, passing from one
> idea to another without difficulty. (3) To avoid long-windedness, reflecting
> that it is much better to generate desire than satisfaction.[81]

A further account of the origins of the term *motivo* in the poetic or
dramatic "motivation" behind a musical work, dating from 1883, serves to
underscore the continued relevance of Galeazzi's definition throughout
the nineteenth century:

> Each melody is a consequence of a thematic period which, through its
> unfolding, forms a piece of music. This theme is called *motivo*; this is be-
> cause its origin, its impulse, is the *motivation* that brings about or gives rise
> to the melody. The *motivo* determines the overall tempo and gives *motion*
> to the components of the thematic rhythm that should regulate the general

rhythmic coherence of the piece. . . . The component phrase of the *motivo* is that which, through the unfolding of sounds in time, gives *motion* and life to the diverse phrases, periods, and parts of the musical composition, and through its progress weaves the cloth of the melody and therefore of the piece.[82]

Syntactical considerations, which tend to receive greater attention in modern musicology, were treated more flexibly. While the establishment of the tonic key was regarded as crucial, for instance, the *motivo,* in its guise as a complete period, could finish upon any one of Rameau's three fundamental chords—I, IV, or V (the subdominant, though rarely used in practice, was usually included in such accounts for the sake of theoretical completeness)—or occasionally upon the other "closely related keys" (*modi analoghi*). Although the "square" pattern was favored, there were no standard templates for the form of the *motivo.*

Its internal construction, as Galeazzi explained in a later passage, was generated by the number of required component phrases (or rhythms) and by their types of melodic cadence, which were compared to the punctuation marks of speech.[83] As a type of period, the *motivo* was made up of a series of phrases that he called "clauses" (*clausole*), each possessing a melodic cadence of greater or lesser finality. The strongest such cadences, which occurred only at the end of a period, were compared to the linguistic period or full stop as *termini musicali.*[84] The others were ranked in order of relative strength. The weakest was the "hidden cadence" (*cadenza occulta*), which was in practice an indeterminate term applied to almost any phrase ending that could not be classified as a recognizable cadence, such as a fall from the fourth to the third tone of a key without firm harmonic support.[85] The remaining cadence types included what is now known as the "imperfect authentic cadence" (*cadenza minore*), similar to the "perfect authentic cadence" but lacking the melodic movement to the tonic note, the "half cadence" (*cadenza maggiore*), ending on the dominant, and, of course, the "perfect authentic cadence" (*cadenza finale*).[86] Galeazzi's reduction of the *motivo* into phrases and diverse melodic cadences accords well with the theory of *ritmo* (as set out in chapter 3 above), which applied in particular to vocal music. The inherent flexibility of his guidelines—stipulating only that the *motivo* should establish the tonic and, as a period, finish with a perfect authentic cadence on chord I, IV, or V—allowed for the setting of a variety of verse types. Vocal phrases within the *motivo* were governed by the *ritmi* and their associated melodic designs and subject to expressive adjustment through the *accento musicale*. Their individual endings, comprising the main inflection of the verse (*desinenza* or *accento comune*), were regarded, as much by Verdi as by Galeazzi, as various types of "cadence." This way of understanding the structure of the main period of a piece as analogous to the punctuation of a written sentence remained central to the Italian traditions throughout the nineteenth century.[87]

In practice, as Balthazar, Huebner, and others have demonstrated, owing largely to the regularity of lyric verse, the eight-measure period, arranged either as a complete period of four-measure antecedent and consequent units or as an unfinished pair of "balanced phrases," may be regarded as the normative form for the *motivo* or "thematic block" for much of the nineteenth century. The advice of Galeazzi and others indicates, however, that unconventional forms were not so much the result of alterations to a common template as they were generated in response to the text at the level of the individual phrase.

The Secondary Theme or Secondary Thought (Secondo Motivo *or* Secondo Pensiero)

The "second principal theme" or, in vocal music, "second thought" may be understood as a set of subsidiary, supporting ideas that expand upon the character and implications of the *motivo* and that often, but not always, effect a transition to a new key. It belongs to the broader category of "subsidiary ideas" that serve to enact the consequences of the main theme or motivation of the piece. As Neapolitan maestro Michele Ruta explained: "Within the diverse fragments that make up a piece of music, there is a principal subject, called a theme, through which it unfolds. All the other parts are only varied divisions, deductions, or unfoldings of this."[88]

Modern musicology lacks a clear equivalent, although similar concepts are common in eighteenth-century German descriptions of form.[89] Darcy and Hepokoski (2006) touch upon similar issues in their discussion of the "transition" section in classical first-movement sonata form. Acknowledging that the term is "problematic, at times misleading," they identify the most common transition strategies as independent, developmental, or dissolving.[90] In each case, the transition is defined in terms of its relation to the principal theme. Moving beyond "analytical contexts that assume as a first principle that tonal considerations trump all others, thus suggesting that the term means a transition or bridge from one *key* to another," they point out that "some transitions do not modulate at all."[91] They characterize the transition as a group of "continuation modules" that act as a commentary on, or addition to, the principal theme and that do not necessarily modulate but rather prepare the arrival of the ensuing period. This corresponds very closely to the concept of the *secondo motivo* in Italian traditions.[92]

Galeazzi's definition is predictably vague, since it is intended to apply to all manner of compositional genres. His stipulation that this second theme should be "entirely ideal, but well connected to the first" encompasses a number of possible strategies, ranging from independence through development to dissolution:

> What we call the *secondo motivo* is called the countersubject in fugue, in that it is a thought, or a deduction from the first [*dedotto dal primo*], to be sure entirely ideal, but well connected to the first and following directly after the period of the *motivo*. Sometimes, it serves also to move away from the main key in order to arrive at the dominant or, in minor keys, the mediant. What is more, if the *motivo* finishes its period on the dominant, then the *secondo motivo* will begin in this same key; but if the *motivo* has a cadence in the principal key, then the *secondo motivo* will begin in the key that leads, as written above, to the dominant or subdominant etc. This period does not appear exclusively in very long pieces, but it is left out of short pieces, so it is not essential.[93]

In operatic *pezzi* the category of the "secondary thought," following on from the first, provides a useful analytical tool to account for a number of unconventional melodies.

The Departure from the Key (Uscita di Tono)

While rhetorical function was regarded as the most significant feature of the *secondo motivo,* the *uscita di tono* was defined primarily by its syntactic (harmonic) function. For this reason the *uscita* was in general shorter and less characteristic than any new musical idea inferred or deduced from the first. It may be regarded as similar to the short conventional modulating passages or "bridges" that were common in eighteenth-century music, such as the rising sequence usually articulating chords IV and V, which Riepel called the *monte*.[94] Nevertheless, it is not always clear how the musical phrase or period labeled as the "departure from the key" differs from a modulating secondary theme. In cases where the final cadence of the principal theme ends on the dominant or mediant, the departure may also be understood to have taken place within the *motivo* itself.

Galeazzi's definition concentrates almost exclusively upon the modulating function of this "departure," as a type of period within an extended composition:

> The departure from the key [*uscita di tono*] follows the *secondo motivo* directly, or, if there is no *secondo motivo,* then it takes place immediately after the true *motivo.* In pieces of some length it is not a good idea to leave the key too quickly, since there will be insufficient time for the principal key to become fully established in the ear. If it is left too soon, then the key of the composition will not be known. The first modulation thus goes to the most closely related keys: to the dominant or subdominant in major keys and to the mediant in minor keys, as already stated. This period is not drawn out for long but finishes on the dominant, as a consequence of which the following period is highlighted and actually made more distinctive.[95]

The Characteristic Passage or Intermediate Passage
(Passo Caratteristico *or* Passo di Mezzo)

A phrase or period that functioned primarily as a contrasting element within a melody or piece, as if to cast the main ideas into higher relief, was called the "characteristic passage" in nineteenth-century Italian writings. In terms of the opera tradition, it corresponds very closely to the *B* section or "medial phrase" of the lyric prototype. Huebner (1992) defines this as typically a four-measure phrase that "is heard as medial because it articulates, however modestly, another key," and that may also include developmental aspects such as fragmentation of the phrase structure. "Other very common strategies for developmental middle phrases," he continues, "include tonicization of the mediant or submediant (or at least a suggestion of those key areas with their dominants) and stepwise sequence of a two-bar unit. The introduction of new melodic motives or even a change of texture may also occur in the middle section."[96] These observations supplement Galeazzi's otherwise straightforward summary, which, once again, avoids additional details in order to accommodate a range of different genres within his universal "two-part" layout (explained below):

> The Characteristic Passage or Intermediate Passage is a new idea introduced, for the sake of greater diversion [*vaghezza*], somewhere near the middle of the first part; it should be gentle, expressive, and tender in almost every genre of composition, and should be in the same key as that of the transition. Often, such a period is repeated, but only in greatly extended compositions. In short compositions it is often left out altogether.[97]

Asioli's similarly generalized account of the *passo di carattere* began with a description of what would now be regarded as the "second subject" in an instrumental rounded binary or sonata form, and continued by outlining the possibilities for leaving the period unfinished. Notably absent was any mention of the contrasting character of the passage, whether gentle and expressive or otherwise:

> Receiving no less care is the *passo di carattere,* which will be placed towards the end of the first part in the dominant and towards the end of the second and final part in the tonic, but only in instrumental [pieces].[98]

The Cadential Period (Periodo di Cadenza)

In the theory of the lyric prototype, closure, or preparation for closure, is not considered the only function of the fourth and final phrase (or period). Considerations of tonal and thematic return also feature prominently, giving rise to a choice of *A* or *C* as symbols (within the representative formulas *AA'BA'* or *AA'BC*) and to a variety of subcategories. As Huebner observes, "Melodic reprise of material from the first two phrases may or may not occur in the fourth phrase. That is, the function of integrated return in this repertory is best understood in a tonal sense, with two subcategories: one consisting of melodies with melodic return, the other of those without."[99] This combination of functions guarantees considerable flexibility to the closing phrase. It may begin with the return of the tonic key, as part of an "integrated return," or it may not, in which case it constitutes part of an "additive return" that will regain the tonic at a later stage. It may or may not reprise melodic material from earlier periods.

In the Italian traditions, the cadential period had only one main function: to prepare the melody (and consequently the listener) for its final cadence. This could be achieved in a variety of ways, depending on the genre. Coloratura and *passaggi* were common strategies in faster movements, for instance. In terms of its thematic content, the cadential period was subject to the requirements of the *condotta*. It had to make sense in relation to the overall musical discourse guided by a principal *motivo*, but this did not necessarily entail the return of earlier themes. As Galeazzi explained, "Although this is a new idea, it is always dependent on the preceding [material], especially the *motivo* or *secondo motivo*."[100] In other words, the typical cadential period possessed its own theme, albeit one recognizably connected in one way or another to the principal themes of the melody or piece. The degree of similarity was left to the discretion of the composer. Thematic and tonal recapitulations remained incidental to the primary function of this period, as Galeazzi's additional observations make clear:

> In it the piece [*Melodia*] is prepared and made ready for the cadence. If the voice or instrument exhibits its gentleness and expression in the *passo caratteristico*, then in this period it is given to dazzling display [*pompa di brio*] and to bravura with the voice or the hand. Consequently, in this period are placed especially the ornaments and trills of vocal music and the most difficult passages of instrumental music, closing with a final cadence.[101]

The Coda

"After the final cadence that closes the last *periodo di cadenza*," Galeazzi continued, "instead of finishing the first part [of the composition] it is not uncommon to append, elegantly, a new period called the *coda*. This is an addition to, or prolongation of, the cadence and is thus not a necessary period. It does, however, serve very well to connect the ideas that end the first part to those that began it, or to connect them to those ideas that begin the second part, as we shall go on to describe. This is its principal purpose."[102]

Although Galeazzi's description could be taken to relate most convincingly to the "codetta" section of an extended instrumental form, such additional periods, serving to round off a movement and, occasionally, to effect a transition to the ensuing piece, were reasonably common in the *primo Ottocento*. Huebner gives a comprehensive survey of the typical features of such codas:

> If there is more music, the usual strategy followed after the fourth phrase . . . is reinforcement of a final perfect authentic cadence in the tonic key with a "coda" that is characterized by several of the following features: an accompanimental role for the orchestra, confinement to dominant and tonic harmonies or reiterated cadential progressions, repeated melodic articulation of the first scale degree, literal repetition of two- or four-bar units, and a greater amount of coloratura.[103]

Later in the nineteenth century there were also "codas" or "additional periods" that followed on from the final cadence but no longer served to consolidate its main key. In some cases these may be regarded as corresponding approximately to the third and final phase of the "normative structural unit" evident in Verdi's *Otello*, as identified by Hepokoski: "(rhymed) *scena* / *pezzo* / (rhymed) *scena*, or, in terms perhaps more directly relatable to dramatic and emotional effect, entrance (transition-in) / set piece / exit (transition-out)."[104] In other cases, such as, arguably, the final section of "In quelle trine morbide" from act 2 of Puccini's *Manon Lescaut* (see example 6.7), such "codas" appear to provide a satisfactory conclusion to a piece without the need either for reprise of the theme or closure of the initial key.

Principal and Subsidiary Periods

Much of the terminology used by Galeazzi continued to inform Italian writings on music throughout the nineteenth century. A similar inventory of basic phrase or period types remained integral to traditional accounts of compositional practice, even when their labels were replaced by alternatives. The "Compendium of Counterpoint of the Ancient and Modern Neapolitan School of Music" (1850) by De Vecchis, for instance, explained "good conduct" in general terms as "that which sets out all the components [of a work of art] regularly and arranges them well into a single whole," and divided the standard piece into two parts, each consisting of short periods (*periodi*) that functioned as principal theme (*canto principale*), modulating subsidiary theme (*canto accessorio*), contrasting theme (*canto caratteristico*), and cadential period (*periodo di cadenza*).[105] A tendency to simplify the theory led, however, to a general reduction in the number of categories, often through a distinction between "principal" (*principali*) and "secondary," "subsidiary," or "additional" periods (*secondarii, accessorie, addizioni*). The two basic species outlined in Luigi Picchianti's eleventh lesson on "the art of joining and connecting periods," which are drawn directly from Reicha (1830), are fairly typical in this respect:

> 1. Principal Periods
> 2. Secondary Periods
>
> The Principal Periods are those that constitute, in essence, a piece of music and that contain, consequently, the main themes, or subjects, or ideas that are to be musically expressed. The Secondary Periods contain supplementary ideas and serve in some cases to complement, to extend, or [to function] as a coda to a Principal Period, and on other occasions to join together two of these Principal Periods: thus the little secondary periods can be either additions, complements, or connections.[106]

This passage could be interpreted as suggesting a manner of composition in which standard patterns of primary phrases were varied and extended by a number of secondary devices. In this sense it recalls Huebner's explanation of the processes of expansion, extension, and compression which, according to his account, gave rise to unconventional variants of the sixteen-measure lyric prototype.[107] Against such a reading, however, Picchianti's fifteen "exercises for the composition of short pieces," from which the above extract is taken, placed considerable emphasis on the fundamental role of the individual phrase or *membro* in generating periods of varied lengths. The principal periods were just as likely as the secondary to end up with irregular layouts, owing to the formative function of component phrases in their construction. As Boucheron later made clear in his use of similar terms, both types of period were, at least in theory, subject more to the "natural development of the Affect" than to any predetermined formal template:

> The disposition, in terms of music, is most commonly called *conduct* and consists of the art of disposing the principal and subsidiary ideas in such a way that they prepare one another and appear neither arbitrary nor forced, but rather result from the necessary progression of the natural development of the Affect.[108]

Galeazzi's General Advice on Musical Conduct

Galeazzi offered his readers a standard pattern for the disposition of the various phrases or periods into different types of melody or composition. It was, at the time, neither intended nor understood to establish a normative template or ideal "form," which might be represented by patterns of letters or symbols. Such concepts were to surface only much later, primarily through German musicology.[109] For convenience and practicality, not to mention commercial considerations, Galeazzi concocted a kind of stock recipe that would, he claimed, be perfectly serviceable for "all large pieces of music, whether arias or other pieces of musical theater, church pieces, or instrumental works like symphonies, trios, quartets, concertos, etc." Such inclusivity required a simple basic structure that could accommodate every conceivable genre, which Galeazzi identified in a two-part or binary design: "Every well-conducted melody is divided in two parts, whether joined together, or separated in the middle by a ritornello."[110] Given that Galeazzi himself frequently contradicted this sweeping generalization, for instance, in his discussion of what were clearly three-part compositions, and considering also the more refined theories of several later authors on the subject, the number of parts would not appear to be the most significant aspect of his standard disposition of phrases or periods. On the contrary, its primary purpose was to recommend a versatile and dependable ordering of the types of musical unit in order to create a "part" of a composition, which, according to most later Italian accounts, could either stand on its own as a one-part *pezzo* or be conjoined with others to form larger pieces of two or more parts. Here is Galeazzi's two-part outline of "every well conducted melody":

The first part includes the following components [*membri*]:

1. *Preludio*
2. *Motivo principale*
3. *Secondo motivo*
4. Departure to closely related keys [*uscita a' toni più analoghi*]
5. *Passo caratteristico* or *passo di mezzo*
6. *Periodo di cadenza*
7. *Coda*

The second part contains these components:

1. *Motivo*
2. Modulations
3. Reprise [of either the principal or secondary *motivo*, in I or IV]
4. Repeat of the *passo caratteristico*
5. Repeat of the *periodo di cadenza*
6. Repeat of the *coda*[111]

Aspirant composers were advised by Galeazzi to make a selection from this list appropriate to the conduct of the *motivo* and the norms of intended styles, which he classified as "unaccompanied vocal" (*vocale puro*), "instrumental without voices" (*istromentale puro*), "mixed style" (*Musica di stile misto*), "church style" (*Musica ecclesiastica*), and "theatrical music" (*Musica teatrale*).[112] According to the requirements of the particular style or genre, sections such as the "second thought," the "departure from the key," or even the various reprises could be omitted.

The section that fitted least convincingly into Galeazzi's all-inclusive two-part layout was the beginning of the second part of the composition, which appears to have been misleadingly defined by the term *motivo* in order to conceal its variety of strategies. These were reduced by Galeazzi to four options. Beginning the second part with either a reprise of the *preludio* (if there was one) or the principal *motivo,* both in the dominant key, were considered common but outdated strategies. His more favored options were to start with "some passages taken at will from the first [part] and especially from the coda," or with the surprise of a "new and unknown thought."[113] In practice, such variables meant that Galeazzi's summary of possibilities could be applied to almost any type of composition.

In a later chapter, entitled "On the Conduct of Compositions in Mixed Style," Galeazzi gave a more detailed overview of the conduct of a range of operatic arias. Although his comments relate most directly to late eighteenth-century styles, especially the operas of Paisiello, Cimarosa, and Haydn, they are cited here as a starting point for the discussion of common theoretical threads that run throughout the nineteenth-century Italian traditions.

Galeazzi began by encouraging the composer to seek inspiration in the text of the entire drama and in the sentiments of its individual parts. He went on to describe the structure of an old-fashioned extended opening ritornello, only to advise against its inclusion "because it is truly indecent to keep an actor wandering about dumbly on stage for so long."[114] A "single period of a few bars" was judged sufficient to establish the sentiment of the aria. For ease of understanding, his detailed comments on the remaining patterns of disposition for different types of aria have been extracted and set out in graphic form below, in emulation of a similar table in Wedell (1995).[115]

The Conduct of Arias, according to Francesco Galeazzi (1796, 300–301)

First Part
1. Aria, verses 1–4
   (a) In a *cavatina* or *mezz'aria*:
      Motivo
      Normally, a little instrumental *periodo di cadenza*
      Secondo motivo or departure to closely related keys [*sortita a' toni analoghi*],
         finishing on the dominant with a little *periodo di cadenza* with *passaggi* and
         vocalizzi
   (b) In an *aria eroica:*
      Motivo
      Normally, a little instrumental *periodo di cadenza*
      Secondo motivo or departure to closely related keys [*sortita a' toni analoghi*],
         finishing on the dominant with a little *periodo di cadenza* with *passaggi* and
         vocalizzi
      Instrumental *passo caratteristico* as an introduction
      A sung *periodo di cadenza* (*di bravura*)
      Instrumental *ritornello*, taken from the first *ritornello* or introduction

Second Part (the final 4 [or 3, 5, or 6] verses)
1. If the words have the same character and expression as those of the first part:
      Periodi di melodìe, expressive and in the same tempo, but modulating and circling
      Motivo principale, with the same words as the first part
      Passo caratteristico, in the tonic
      Periodo di cadenza
      Instrumental *ritornello,* similar to the first but with less cadential material
2. If the words have a different character and expression to those of the first part:
   (a) If the aria is *allegro* or *andante:*
      A little cantabile [*cantabilino*] in another tempo
      Motivo in the first tempo with the words and music of the first part
      Passo caratteristico
      Periodo di cadenza
      Instrumental *ritornello*
   (b) If the aria is a *cantabile* or *largo:*
      A new *allegro* tempo until the end, based on "the oft-repeated rules"

"Such is the *condotta* in the serious style; how much it is varied in the *buffa* style depends upon the bizarreness of the words."

Resembling some impractical species of *ars combinatoria,* Galeazzi's description offers a bewildering assortment of strategic choices that may or may not match up.[116] The genres of *cavatina* and *mezz'aria* mentioned in the overview of the first part presumably correlate with the andante, cantabile, or largo of the second, while the *aria eroica* appears to tally with subsequent mentions of an allegro. Most conspicuously absent are any conceivable combinations that would result in a standard early eighteenth-century ternary aria, classified by *The New Grove* (2001) as "five-part *da capo," "da capo al segno,"* or *"dal segno"* (according to the degree of fullness of its reprise). This seeming omission may be explained by the limitations Galeazzi imposed upon the first part of the aria. It must always end in a newly established key, whether the dominant or, in minor keys, the mediant. Each possible aria thus corresponds to the modern category (as defined by *The New Grove*) of the "through-composed, compound ternary, with compound return," roughly equivalent to an A section in the tonic, an A^1 section either in or moving toward the dominant or mediant, and a central B section, followed by a reprise in the tonic. The modern category of the "compound binary," which lacks a central contrasting or developing section, is ruled out by Galeazzi through the inclusion of some sort of central episode for each available option for the second part of the aria. In the final suggestion for the second part, a concluding "new allegro tempo," corresponding to the modern category of the *stretta* or *cabaletta,* appears to follow on directly from the modulation to the new key that ends the first part.

Much of this can be explained by the observation that Galeazzi overlooked, or decided not to mention, the possibility of ending the first part of the aria in the tonic key. He may perhaps have considered operatic ternary forms to be redundant in the year 1796, which seems unlikely, or, more understandably, he may have realized that to include such a contingency would seriously undermine the claims of his universal two-part arrangement. Given these contradictions and uncertainties, Galeazzi's general overview is of significance to later theory and practice primarily for its suggested disposition of phrases and periods within a "part" of a composition (specifically, *motivo, second motivo* or modulation, *passo caratteristico,* and *periodo di cadenza*), and secondarily for the inherent flexibility of its rhetorically inspired concept of musical structure.

Before moving on to the different "dimensions" of the operatic melody or *pezzo*, it may prove useful to address two potential sources of confusion deriving from Galeazzi's unsystematic use of terminology relating to periods, parts, and tempos and from the vagueness of his comments on modulations and tonal structure.

One of Galeazzi's options for the second part of an aria (2a in table 5.1) includes a *cantabilino* in a different tempo, while another ends with a new *allegro* section (2b in table 5.1). Depending on context, these could be treated as "parts" (*parti*) within a single piece or as entirely new "movements" (*movimenti* or *tempi*) within a larger structure. More confusingly still, in shorter pieces a "part" could also be a single "period," and what might today be regarded as a period was often referred to as a "phrase" (*frase*) or "member" (*membro*). These distinctions were not always clearly maintained by Italian authors. Gervasoni avoided such uncertainty in his list of three types of aria by using the term "piece" (*pezzo*) to signify a principal section defined by a single tempo: "Arias are composed of a single piece in either allegro or adagio, and can also be divided into two pieces, the first with a rather slow *grado di movimento* and the second with a more lively *movimento*."[117] Internal subdivisions within these self-contained pieces were designated as "parts."[118] Other authors were not so systematic. Reicha's later theory of the relativity of formal categories through different "proportions," explained more fully below, led to a considerable degree of ambiguity in the terminology connected to musical structure.

Galeazzi's use of the term "related keys" (*analoghi*) to describe the available modulations for the first part of an aria refers to the Ramellian theory outlined above in chapter 4, according to which each tonic key was considered to possess five such analogues upon the available scale degrees. The ways in which they could be mapped onto the usual conduct of an individual *pezzo* were explained by Asioli, in a passage that is significant enough to be cited below in full. It clarifies not only the concept of "fixed modulations," which served to articulate the "principal parts" of a piece, but also the normative status of compositions in two or three parts. From the patterns of modulations specified by Asioli, these appear to correspond to the modern categories of "compound binary" and "*da capo*" arias:

Since there is at present a craving amongst composers to modulate, through a failure to compel composition students to observe strictly the five related keys, I will outline here the conduct of an entire musical piece, or where the proper places for distant modulations and the chief positions of the tessitura are to be found.

The composition is divided into two or three principal parts. Each of these is formed of passages of harmony [in one key] and of modulations. The passages establish their own key, moving around within its harmonies. The modulations may be fixed, secondary, or passing. Fixed modulations are those that establish the principal divisions of the composition; the secondary have a place within the fixed ones; and the passing ones are found everywhere.

In the case of a composition divided into two principal parts, the first fixed modulation will, according to the law of convention, be on the dominant if the mode is major and on the mediant if it is minor; and the second and final fixed modulation will be on the principal key, which, by the law of convention, must have closure. If the composition is divided into three parts, the first and last fixed modulations will invariably be the same, and the central one will be on any key, or analogue, that contrasts with the principal key.[119]

Dimensions of Pieces in One, Two, or Three Parts

The clarity of Asioli's account owed much to the systematic treatment of musical forms in Reicha's *Trattato della melodia* (1830 [1814]), which was to prove extremely influential in later Italian writings. Reicha's theoretical approach served to consolidate and standardize the notion that operatic compositions should normally be constructed in one, two, or three parts.[120] On account of the complementary notion of "dimensions" (*dimensioni*), however, these parts could consist of a variety of musical units ranging from short periods to extended movements,[121] depending on the proportions of the genre. Reicha explained:

Melodies or airs of a single period are the least important and the easiest to create, for they contain almost no development, and consequently do not have time to modulate, and require neither conception nor plan; in general, they are only the sweet outpouring of a momentary inspiration, and usually come about spontaneously. They may be compared to improvised poetry, which results from the fleeting impulses of the mind or of feeling.

There are approximately three kinds of these melodies:

(1) Songs, or *canzonette* [in Italian]....

(2) Various small airs in ballet music with two reprises....

(3) Rather more significant melodies occur when the period is so artfully
elongated that a more developed melody is presented, particularly in a
slow movement. These may be called *Cavatines*.[122]

As an example of the *canzonetta*, Reicha cited a sixteen-measure
melody by Rousseau that, as he suggested, could hardly be seen as more
than a casual ditty. For the more extended *cavatine*, he annotated a reasonably substantial thirty-six-measure aria by Sacchini. The common feature
that served to define both as one-part forms was the avoidance of a firm
perfect authentic cadence until the end. His second category, ballet airs,
consisted of one-part forms that gave the impression of having two parts
through repetition. It was essential that the cadences closing each statement of the air should be completely final; if the first reprise closed with
a weaker cadence, the form would be considered a type of melody in *two*
periods, parts, or movements.

Reicha listed five varieties of these, as follows:

(1) variation themes; (2) romances [*romanze*]; (3) ballet and pantomime
music consisting of two reprises; (4) melodies with only one period as a
base, this being repeated, either in whole (with slight changes) or in part,
which may happen in *cavatines*; (5) religious and military marches.[123]

The most significant of these two-part forms in opera was the *romanza*, which was required to modulate at some point to one of the five
related keys and was marked, primarily, by a clear central cadence in the
key of I, III, or V. Endorsing the significance of rhetorical concepts to notions of musical form, the perfect authentic cadence that closed the first
part of the *romanza*, even if in the tonic key, was still regarded as only a
"three-quarter" cadence, in deference to the true final cadence. The difference between Reicha's third and fourth categories of two-part form
and the one-part ballet air with reprise remained vague, but appeared to
rest once again on the relative strengths of the central and final cadences.
He seemed to suggest, however, that an extended one-part form such as
the *cavatine*, if repeated, could be seen as a two-part form.

Melodies of three principal periods, parts, or movements correspond
to what would now be described as ternary form, in which an initial

section, closing always in the tonic, returns after a central contrasting episode, often in III or V. As Reicha succinctly expressed it:

> We have felt that a well-conceived beginning period, followed by a second period, may be effectively repeated. Consequently, melodies may be constructed in the following way:
> First Period, Second Period,
> Third Period, or Repetition of the first.[124]

In the first French edition, he added: "The Italians call this form a *rondo* [*Rondeau*], if the movement is very slow. It is also often called a *cavatine*. The first period may be called the *theme*." These sentences were omitted from the Italian edition, presumably because they made no sense. Ironically, while Italians such as Asioli adopted Reicha's French version of what he thought was an Italian term, *rondeau,* for the three-part form, French authors, like Choron and De LaFage, employed the same term for the instrumental rondo form, quite separately from the *coupe ternaire*.[125] Reicha also described a type of ternary melody "where the third period is a repetition (in part or in whole) of the second, instead of the first," and mentioned the possibility of increasing the total number of parts through the inclusion of short free periods as "additions" to the principal divisions of the form.[126]

The theory of proportions or dimensions, according to which these compositional species of *cavatine, romanza,* and *rondeau*—representing one, two, or three principal divisions—could be regarded as essentially equivalent at different levels of form would appear to provide a logical, inclusive, and orderly system for classifying a wide variety of pieces. In practice, however, its conflation of smaller units such as periods with large-scale genres such as the adagio-allegro aria occasioned considerable terminological confusion. The passage setting out the theory of the four principal "dimensions" is reproduced below from the Italian edition of 1830, which differs in some respects from the original French edition.

> We will call the various ways to conduct, extend, and link melodic ideas *plans, forms,* or *dimensions* [in French, *cadres, coupes,* or *dimensions;* in Italian, *quadri, divisioni,* or *dimensioni*].
> Thus the dimension of a melody which is composed of only two principal parts (as, in general, the *Romanza*), will be called the *First Dimension of the*

Romanza [*1° Dimensione della Romanza*], or the Small Binary Dimension [*piccola dimensione binaria*].

When the melody is composed of three principal periods, of which the third is only the *da capo* of the first, its dimension will be called the *Second Dimension of the Rondeau* [*2° Dimensione del Rondeau*], or the Small Ternary Dimension [*piccola Dimensione Ternaria*].

The dimensions of melodies separated into two principal parts (any of which may contain various periods) will be called the *Third Grand Binary Dimension* of the piece [*3° Grande Dimensione binaria*].

The dimension of melodies divided into three principal parts (where each may likewise have many periods, and where the third part is only the *da capo* of the first) will be called the *Fourth Grand Ternary Dimension* of the piece [*4° Grande Dimensione ternaria*].

A melody divided into two principal parts is in the large what the *Romanza* is in the small: the latter is divided into two periods, while the former is separated into two parts. A melody divided into three principal parts . . . is also in the large what the Rondeau is in the small, which is to say that the latter is divided into three periods, just as the former divides into three parts.

In these four different forms, the most beautiful, interesting, and striking melodies have been composed. They serve as the basis for all the others.[127]

The influence of Reicha's theory of the dimensions of the *Cavatina, Romanza,* and *Rondeau* is evident in many subsequent Italian writings on musical form, often merged with alternative doctrines. It underpinned the five "cuts" (*tagli*) documented in Picchianti's "Specific Observations on the Varied Conduct of Pieces of Music," for instance, which reserved the category of the "binary or ternary division" for "theatrical arias, duets, terzetts, quartets, and more vocal as well as instrumental pieces, such as sonatas, symphonies, etc."[128] Asioli's account of the conduct of an entire composition was similarly indebted to Reicha, in its description of the aria as "a little self-contained musical piece that increases little by little and extends over various dimensions, to the point where it may serve as the Finale of the *Dramma*."[129] In terms of the internal construction of these dimensions Asioli also relied on the notion, familiar from Galeazzi, of types of period and their disposition into the succession: *motivo, passo di carattere,* and *periodo di cadenza.*

IV. CASE STUDIES FROM VERDI,
BOITO, AND PUCCINI

From the above survey of concepts, a few generalizations may now be put forward regarding nineteenth-century Italian approaches to issues of form and structure, in order to arrive at an array of suggested analytical and interpretative tools.

The basic building block of set pieces in Italian opera was the *period*, expressing one musical, dramatic, and/or poetic "sense" and defined by a rhetorically reinforced final cadence, which was occasionally omitted in the case of an "incomplete" period. The internal structures of periods were determined primarily by the *ritmi* of the verses and, depending on context, were accounted for, at the level of approximately one or two measures, through subdivision into designs, senses, incises, melodic and harmonic *ritmi,* and clauses or cadences and, at the level of approximately four to eight measures, into members or phrases. Periods, either singly or in groups, made up the principal divisions or *parts* of a *piece*. Entire pieces, or occasionally periods and parts, were governed by one dominant affect and its *movimento* (or tempo). A piece could contain as little as one period, in which case it was most often described as a *melody,* but such a melody could also form a period within a larger piece of one, two, or three parts, often as its *motivo*. Parts, pieces, or movements could be grouped together by convention to form larger genres, such as multi-movement arias, ensembles, and finales.

In terms of the semantic or syntactic functions of individual units, there was a profound relativity between different levels of form. Categories such as the principal theme or *motivo,* its related second theme or *secondo motivo,* the departure from the key or *uscita di tono,* the contrasting passage or *passo caratteristico,* and the *cadenza finale* or more extended *periodo di cadenza* could each apply to any length of musical unit from an individual *phrase* of a few measures within a melody of a single period, to an extended *part* within a large-scale composition. To take an example that will be familiar to many readers, the opening twenty-one-measure period (starting in m. 2) of the F major andante from Mozart's Piano Concerto K. 467 may be understood to correspond—according to this generalized method drawn from Italian sources and without implying any intention on the composer's part—to the succession: *motivo* (6 measures), *uscita di tono* or *monte* (4), *passo caratteristico* (5), and *periodo di cadenza* (6). But the same formal-rhetorical categories may also be seen to apply to the movement as a whole, in such a way that this twenty-one-measure period would itself constitute a ritornello (incorporating a *motivo principale*) at a higher level of structure.

The Canzonetta *of One Period: Puccini,* La bohème, *act 1, R1, m. 44, "Nei cieli bigi"*

There are many passages in Puccini's operas that appear significant enough to deserve recognition as some kind of lyrical form, yet are too short to classify as arias. In Reicha's terminology, these would fall under the heading of "songs, or *canzonette*" in one period or part or, as Asioli expressed it, "the Arietta or *Canzone* made up of little periods."[130] One such lyrical moment occurs at the start of *La bohème* (example 5.3, "Nei cieli bigi") to introduce the character Rodolfo and to establish itself as a kind of Leitmotif for him throughout the opera. Although undeniably a significant theme (borrowed, incidentally, from an 1894 sketch for an unfinished project entitled *La lupa*), in modern musicology this fifteen-measure passage would seldom be considered a self-contained period, let alone a piece, owing primarily to its modulation from the tonic to dominant of B♭ major, which leaves it "tonally open." Nineteenth-century Italian treatises were, however, more flexible on the issue of tonal closure. A period could end on any of the fundamental triads (I, IV, or V) or related keys (*modi analoghi*) as long as it included a cadence that sounded sufficiently final. "Nei cieli bigi" thus corresponds to the type of period known as the principal theme or *motivo,* notwithstanding its closure in the dominant.

Considered as a melody (*canzonetta*) of one period it may be understood to contain three reasonably well articulated "members" (cf. Reicha) or "little periods" (cf. Asioli), which, for consistency and clarity, are labeled as "phrases" in example 5.3. They correspond in microcosm (according to the theory of dimensions) to the categories of *motivo, passo caratteristico,* and *cadenza finale.* While the opening melodic descent from the fifth to the first scale degree provides the "motive" for the period in mm. 1–5, by way of its three-note attachments (*attacchi*) or "melodic rhythms" (*ritmi melodici*) and their repetitions, the second phrase, or *passo caratteristico*

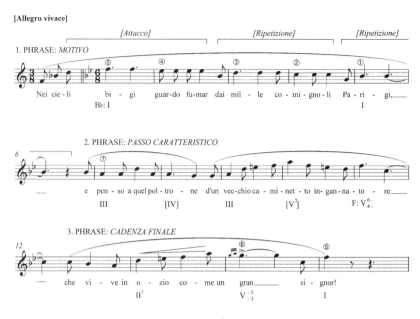

5.3. Puccini, *La bohème,* act 1, R1, mm. 44–58 (Milan: Ricordi, 1896; melody only, with analysis).

in mm. 7–11, not only complements it with a central contrasting element but also touches upon the key of III, in typical fashion, and features a fragmentation of the phrase structure. The third phrase in mm. 12–15 involves neither tonal nor thematic return, but serves rather to prepare for the end of the melody through cadential harmonies and a brief closing flourish upon a high note.

Although these subsections could not be considered periods in their own right, since they lack firm concluding cadences, they correspond nevertheless to the overview of standard melodic "conduct" outlined by Galeazzi, Asioli, and others. As will be discussed in more detail in chapter 6, this melody may also be considered to relate to the genre of the *solfeggio* or *vocalizzo* through its foundation upon an embellished scale descending in "third position," as indicated in example 5.3 by the circled numbers. In this respect, the melody could just as well be described through the similar categories of *canto principale, canto caratteristico,* and *cadenza finale* which, according to De Vecchis, comprised the standard layout of three periods in the first part of a *solfeggio.*[131]

An Extended Canzonetta *or* Cavatina *of One Part:*
Staffa's 1856 Analysis of Verdi, Ernani *(1844),*
act 1, no. 3, "Ernani! Ernani, involami"

In the Neapolitan traditions of the mid-nineteenth century, much longer melodies in a single dominant affect could be described as "periods," their subdivisions reduced to the status of component "phrases" even where they contained conspicuous cadential progressions. Example 5.4 reproduces one of Giuseppe Staffa's analyses of an aria by Verdi, which identified three such self-contained phrases within a single overarching period. This analysis was, however, intended to relate not so much to the overall conduct of the *motivo* as to the layout of melodic material according to the model of the *solfeggio*, paying particular attention to the placement of cadences. It began the section on vocal melody (*Del canto*) in the second volume of Staffa's "Method of Musical Composition of the Neapolitan School" (1856) and would presumably have been supplemented by verbal instruction from the maestro. Apart from the omission of the piano part and the addition of a few annotations and chord symbols in square brackets, example 5.4 remains true to the original. Staffa saw fit to omit the poetic text of the aria as well as the conventional syllabic notation of its rhythm, possibly to draw attention away from aspects of *fraseologia* and to focus instead on the structure of the melody as a quasi-instrumental line or perhaps merely to simplify the type setting. The choice of A♭ major, rather than the more familiar key of B♭, suggests that he made use of a manuscript copy of the score connected with the Neapolitan performances of 1848.[132]

This *cavatina* serves to introduce the leading soprano Elvira, together with her plight. Betrothed against her will to her elderly uncle, Don Ruy Gomez de Silva, and kept within the picturesque but unwanted grandeur of his castle in medieval Aragon, she awaits the arrival of dashing local bandit-chief Ernani to whisk her away to a life of passion and excitement. With a nod to the moral code of the censor, Ernani turns out to be the outlawed nobleman Don Juan in disguise, and with another nod to the nationalist sympathies of the audience, his bandits are actually freedom fighters rebelling against an unjust and illegitimate king. The text of the *cavatina,* reproduced below, consists of two quatrains of seven-syllable verse (*settenari*), scanned conventionally onto a principal theme (*motivo*) and a contrasting passage (*passo caratteristico*), with repetitions of the final lines providing material for a closing section (*periodo di cadenza*).

"First phrase—repetition of the first phrase varied at the end—final cadence of the phrase"
[1. Period, 9 measures: *motivo*]

Ernani! . . . Ernani, in*v*olami (7)	Ernani! Ernani, release me
all'abborrito am*p*lesso. (7)	from an abhorred relationship.
Fuggiamo . . . se teco *v*ivere (7)	Let's flee . . . if love would allow me
mi sia d'amor con*c*esso, (7)	to live with you,

"Second phrase—repetition of the second phrase varied at the end—final cadence of the phrase"
[2. Period, 8 measures: *passo caratteristico*]

per antri e lande in*o*spiti (7)	my footsteps would follow you
ti seguirà il mio *p*iè. (7)	through inhospitable caves and moors.
Un Eden di de*l*izia (7)	Such caves would be
saran quegli antri a *m*e. (7)	an Eden of delights to me.

"Third phrase—final cadence of the period"
[3. Period, 4 [15] measures: *periodo di cadenza*]

[Un Eden di de*l*izia	[Such caves would be
saran quegli antri a *m*e.]	an Eden of delights to me.]

As example 5.4 shows, Staffa interpreted these subsections of the melody not as integrated periods but as four-measure phrases with varied repetitions. The initial eight-measure period with its emphatic modulation to the mediant was, in his analysis, a four-measure "first phrase" followed by a varied repetition. Similarly, he divided the contrasting period in mm. 10–17 into a "second phrase" and its varied repetition, notwithstanding the even more emphatic final cadence that leads back to the tonic key in mm. 16–17. Most tellingly of all, Staffa included only four measures of the closing period (18–21), omitting a further eleven measures by Verdi from his example. According to Budden's standard "groundplan" for this aria, the first eight-measure period corresponds to a conventional a^1 a^2, the second to a contrasting b section (although b^1 b^2 would seem more consistent), and the third phrase to an extended a^3 c a^3.[133] By ignoring the cadential repetitions designated by Budden as c a^3, Staffa's analysis would appear to testify to an acceptance of the normative status of the "typical square period" (*periodo quadrato tipico*) or, as it is known in modern mu-

5.4. Giuseppe Staffa, *Metodo della Scuola Napolitana di composizione musicale* (1856), 9: analysis of Verdi, *Ernani* (1844), act 1, R17, "Ernani! Ernani, involami."

sicology, the "lyric prototype." The closing passage of the aria, together with its flamboyant and captivating coloratura, seems to have been dismissed as an inessential adjunct to a basic formal pattern corresponding to the formula $a^1\ a^2\ b\ a^3$. But, as will be explained more fully in chapter 6, this attests not so much to the significance of some abstract formal template as to *solfeggio* practice in Naples at that time. Staffa's analysis was intended to demonstrate the importance of (improvised) variations upon short phrases, especially those involving different types of cadence, in the construction of a complete vocal melody (*canto*).

The Cavatina *of One Period with Reprise:* *Puccini,* Tosca, *act 3, R11, "E lucevan le stelle"*

Despite his well-known penchant for logical systems, Reicha employed the term *cavatine* (in Italian, *cavatina*) to describe forms of one, two, and three periods, parts, or movements. The term originally signified a short aria without *da capo,* such as might appear within a passage of recitative, but by the beginning of the nineteenth century, Italian composers began to use it also for the principal singer's opening aria, in one or two movements. Disregarding the application of the term *cavatina* to the three-part dimension or, as Asioli later put it, to the small dimension of "the *Cavatina* that has beginning, middle, and end,"[134] Reicha employed it most often to describe a short melody of one period or part, which, like the "ballet air with reprise," could be repeated to give the impression of two periods or parts.

Cavaradossi's famous lament, "E lucevan le stelle," would appear to correspond to this category of the one-part *cavatina* with repeat, notwithstanding its supplementary formal strategy of a transition from declamation and orchestral melody in the first reprise to full-blown *sviolinata* and vocal cantabile in the second. Example 5.5 (a) presents a reduction of its second reprise, in which the singer takes up the main melody. Although perfect cadences in the tonic key are evident in mm. 2, 7, and R13, m. 3, only the last of these is sufficiently pronounced to define the preceding material as a period. The others serve to mark the beginnings of the first and second component phrases, labeled as "1. Period (a)" and "1. Period (b)" in example 5.5 (a). The entire melody may thus be regarded as a single period of fifteen measures.

Of particular interest are the short, single-measure ritornellos which serve to separate the three phrases or members of the period in a manner reminiscent of the initial section of an early eighteenth-century *da capo* aria: ritornello; opening phrase; ritornello; contrasting phrase; final ritornello (and cadence). By the mid-nineteenth century, extended orchestral ritornellos had, of course, long gone out of fashion, as Boucheron recognized in his espousal of the "Ex abrupto" opening as opposed to the "Esordio."[135] But short instrumental passages nevertheless remained a common feature of arias. Placed judiciously at the beginning, middle, and end, as Reicha pointed out, they provided an effective means to allow singers to catch their breath.[136] The ritornello indicated as such in example 5.5 (a) may be interpreted as a kind of commentary upon this tradition: not only is it so short as to resemble more an upbeat "vamp" to a popular song than an orchestral ritornello, especially given its emphasis on the dominant chord, but it is also *sung* in the second reprise.

The first main phrase in mm. 2–5 of the period, corresponding to its *motivo,* encompasses an elaboration of the "harmonic division" of the ascending B minor scale, as the scale-degree numbers added to example 5.5 (a) suggest. In this sense the melody could be seen to acknowledge the ancient convention of deriving the first sung passage from the opening (instrumental) ritornello, since it too outlines a similar division of the scale (with the initial $f_\#^1$ in m. 1 substituting for b^1 over an implied cadential six-four chord on the dominant). The second main phrase in mm. 7–12, identified here as a modulating *passo caratteristico,* begins a balancing descent through the scale from the upper neighboring note g^2. Before closing upon the tonic, however, the ritornello makes a third, seemingly unexpected appearance at R13 in the mediant minor (D), a mixed-mode variant of the key most often associated with central contrasting passages in operatic arias. The short *cadenza finale* in R13, mm. 2–3, hardly counts as a third phrase at all, since it consists of little more than a perfect cadence in the tonic.

In terms of the construction of the period on a more detailed level, "E lucevan le stelle" may be understood to present a particularly fine example of the expressive treatment of a regular melodic *ritmo* through the fluctuations of the "musical (speech) accent" (*accento musicale*), as defined in chapter 3. The text for the aria—created with Puccini's close collaboration—consists of a first strophe mainly in *settenari,* with one out-of-place *decasillabo,* and a second strophe mainly in *endecasillabi,* with the inclusion of a single *quinario,* as set out below:

1. Period, 15 measures: *motivo, passo caratteristico, cadenza finale*

E lucevan le *stel*le (7)	And the stars were shining
e olezzava la *ter*ra, (7)	and the earth was perfumed
stridea l'uscio dell'*or*to (7)	the gate of the garden creaked
e un *pas*so sfiorava la *re*na (10)	and a footstep grazed the sand
entrava ella, fra*gran*te, (7)	she entered, fragrant,
mi cadea fra le *brac*cia. (7)	she fell into my arms.

1. Period [Reprise], 15 measures: *motivo, passo caratteristico, cadenza finale*

Oh! dolci *ba*ci, o languide ca*rez*ze, (5+7)	Oh! sweet kisses, oh languid caresses,
mentr'io fre*men*te (5)	while I, impatient,
le belle *for*me disciogliea dai *ve*li! (5+7)	freed the beautiful form from its veils!
Svanì per *sem*pre il sogno mio d'a*mo*re (5+7)	My dream of love vanished forever,
l'ora è fug*gi*ta e muoio dispe*ra*to! (5+7)	the hour has fled, and I die in despair!
E non ho a*ma*to mai tanto la *vi*ta. (5+7)	And I have never loved life so much!

5.5.

a Puccini, *Tosca*, act 3, R12, mm. 1–15 (Milan. Ricordi, 1900; melody only, with analytical symbols).

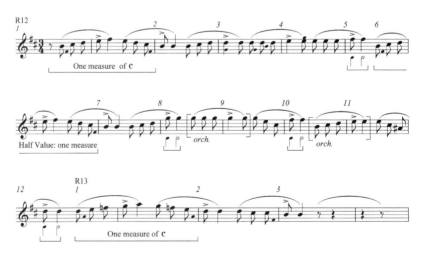

b. Reduced to regular *ritmi melodici* (*quinari*).

In spite of the unevenness of the verses and the seemingly irregular alternation of $\frac{3}{4}$ and $\frac{4}{4}$ time signatures in their musical setting, the melody may be understood as a written-out series of *rubati* upon an essentially regular underlying *ritmo*. The first strophe is fitted onto this *ritmo* freely, as a *parlando* over the orchestral melody. In the second strophe, however, each eleven-syllable verse is consistently divided *a minore* into an initial *quinario* followed by a *settenario* and scanned onto the same basic *ritmo melodico*. Example 5.5 (b) presents a hypothetical restoration of this underlying regular *ritmo* corresponding to each *quinario / settenario* line of verse, together with its characteristic syncopated inflection (*desinenza*) and with an indication of differences in the actual melody by way of small note heads. Lending support to this interpretation are not only the natural accents of the Italian verses, which, if positively observed, subdivide the melody in a manner comparable to the rhythmic reduction in example 5.5 (b), but also Puccini's own performance directions, as recorded by the repetiteur Luigi Ricci.[137] Some of his instructions for breaths, pauses, and *rubando* are indicated in parentheses in measures R12, m. 2, R13, m. 1, and R13, m. 2 of example 5.5 (a) and suggest a similar awareness of the divisions of the *ritmo*.

The One-Part Cavatina: *Verdi*, Macbeth *(1847)*,
act 1, no. 3, "Vieni! t'affretta!"

Example 5.6 (a) presents the melody of one of Verdi's most arresting arias: the *cavatina* from Lady Macbeth's entrance scene. It is reproduced here in a version that conforms closely to the revised 1865 score, from the complete critical edition of Verdi's operas.[138] Its text, given below, maps two quatrains of *settenari* onto a conventional disposition of a modulating principal theme, a contrasting passage that returns to the tonic, and a cadential period, in much the same way as the *cavatina* from *Ernani* discussed above (example 5.4).

1. Period, 10 measures: *motivo*

Vieni! t'affretta! ac*cen*dere (7)	Come! Make haste!
ti vo' quel freddo *core*! (7)	I will fire up your cold heart!
L'audace impresa a *compiere* (7)	I will give you the courage
io ti darò va*lore*; (7)	to carry out the brazen enterprise;

2. Period, 10 measures: *passo caratteristico*

di Scozia a te pro*met*tono (7)	the witches promise you
le profetesse il *trono* . . . (7)	the throne of Scotland . . .
Che tardi? accetta il *dono*, (7)	Why are you waiting? Accept the gift,
ascendivi a re*gnar*! (7)	ascend and reign!

3. Period, 11 measures: *periodo di cadenza*

[Che tardi? accetta il *dono*,	[Why are you waiting? Accept the gift,
ascendivi a re*gnar*!]	ascend and reign!]

The analytical reduction in example 5.6 (b) divests the melody of characteristic features and ornaments in an attempt to reveal its underlying guiding voices and its seven-syllable melodic rhythm. Slurs demarcate each individual *ritmo,* with accents indicating their principal verse inflections (*desinenze*). Beneath the simplified bass line, Asioli's symbols for strong (1. / *primo*) and weak (2. / *secondo*) movements serve to outline the corresponding harmonic rhythm (*ritmo armonico*). Dotted vertical lines highlight shifts in meter.

The principal theme or *motivo* scans the first four lines of verse onto four regular *ritmi* in mm. 2–9, before quickening the pace for the cadence in the dominant key through two compressed repetitions of the final line in mm. 9–11. As indicated by the rhythmic movements beneath the stave of example 5.6 (b), this results in a doubling of the speed of the underlying meter in mm. 9–10. In terms of melodic construction, the *motivo* is underpinned by a three-note descending stepwise attachment (*attacco*), marked with square brackets in example 5.6 (b). The first attachment is sounded an octave above the others in m. 2, which serves to disguise the underlying sequential ascent in mm. 2–5 through three steps of the scale (F–G♭–A♭). The pattern gives way in m. 8 to a cadential formula.

Although the *motivo* modulates firmly to the dominant (A♭) in m. 11, the second period undermines this new key from the start. It begins in mm. 12–15 with two phrases in the tonic key encompassing a descending scale in third position. Upon reaching the third line of verse (m. 16), the characteristic passage embarks upon a remarkable harmonic progression that leads to a strong confirmation of the tonic in m. 21. It is regulated by an ascending first position soprano scale in A major, the last two notes of which (F♯ and G♯) are enharmonically reinterpreted as G♭ and A♭ (mm. 18–19) in preparation for the cadence in D♭ major (mm. 20–21). Rhyth-

5.6.

Andantino (Met: ♪ = 72.)

Vie - ni! t'af - fret - ta! ac - cen - de - re   ti   vo'quel fred - do   co - - re!   L'au-da-ce impre-sa   a

com-pie - re   io   ti   da - rò va - - lo - re,   io ti da-rò va - lo - re, da rò_____ va -

lo - re;   di   Sco-zia a te, a te pro-met - to - no   le pro-fe tes - se un tro - no... Che

tar - di?   ac - cet - ta   il   do - no,   a-scen-di-vi   a reg - nar,_____ a - scen - di-vi a re-

gnar,_____ ac-cet -ta,accet-ta il do - no,   a scen-di-vi   a   re-gnar!   Che tar- di?   che   tar - di?   ac-cet - ta il

do - no, a-scen-di,   a-scen-di,   a-scen-di-vi a re- gnar!   Che tar   di?ac-cet-ta il do - no,   a- scen-di vi a re

gnar! Che tar - di? ac-cet-ta il do - - no, a- scen - di - vi   a re gnar! Che tar - di?   che tar -

di?   Ah! -   -   -   a - scen - di - vi   a   re - gnar!

a. Verdi, *Macbeth,* act 1, no. 3, "Vieni! t'affretta!" (Chicago and Milan: Chicago University Press and Ricordi, 2005; melody only).

b. Analytical reduction.

mically, the final line of the quatrain ("ascendivi a regnar") ushers in a quickening of the underlying *ritmo* in m. 17 that lasts until the end of the period.

Although the melody that begins the final cadential period (mm. 21–31) bears some relation to the initial principal theme by way of its emphasis on the same notes and its slurred eighth-note gestures, it could not be said to constitute a reprise. It is, rather, a new idea that relates to the guiding "motive" in a discursive way. In regard to the requirements of the overall musical discourse or *condotta,* it could be heard to combine elements from the *motivo* with the descending scale of the *passo caratteristico.* In typical fashion, the cadential period features repetitions and fragmentations of the last two lines of verse. Following two regular melodic rhythms in mm. 21–25 (albeit preceded by additional three-syllable phrases), the cadential period breaks into a faster meter in m. 25, retaining it until the final cadenza.

A Small Dimension of the Two-Part Romanza: *Boito,*
Mefistofele *(1875), act 2,* duettino, *"Colma il tuo cor d'un palpito"*

The preference for short, single-movement arias and duets during the second half of the nineteenth century owed much to the reforms of Arrigo Boito, especially in Milan. Example 5.7, taken from the revised 1875 version of his opera *Mefistofele,* presents the kind of melody that student composers at the Conservatory, such as Puccini, would have considered representative of a progressive "young school" (*giovane scuola*).

By the 1860s, if not before, the ubiquitous four-phrase melody of the "lyric prototype" was beginning to sound stale to critics and audiences. Composers sought ways to introduce a greater variety of structure. Some twenty years later, at the time Puccini was writing his first operas, there was a feeling that such increased freedom, while generally a good thing, may have gone too far, especially in response to the growing influence of Wagnerian "musical prose." The journal *La Musica,* like several others, came out in defense of the old-fashioned values of "squareness." Warning in equal measure against excessive reliance upon hackneyed standard forms and against the pursuit of progressive yet "anti-national" musical directions, it praised the new forms of the *giovane scuola.* If, it declared, the disciplines of constructing phrases and periods were not studied correctly and assiduously, then:

> Melody would become mistress of the musical artwork, and the Maestros, liberated from scholastic bonds, would obtain their inspiration from wherever it wandered—from the eternal harmony that rules us. But just as everything overreaches itself, so too would the symmetry of the piece and the melodic thread [*filo*] become slave to a servile conventionality; those of mediocre talent, and a few who are obviously talented, take artistic simplicity too far, and the melody resembles a guitar tune. This explains the reaction of the *giovane scuola*; but this reaction, from which new forms arise, must guard against following the way things are going in certain anti-artistic, anti-national, and anti-logical music.[139]

The *duettino* for Faust and Margerite reproduced in example 5.7 may be seen to occupy a midpoint between these two extremes. While clearly based on the old four-phrase paradigm, it introduces some variety into the structure and, most significantly in terms of its progressive credentials, incorporates irregular verse types in such a way as to disrupt the traditional correspondence between poetic lines and *ritmi melodici*. The piece takes place in the garden scene at the beginning of act 2, in which Faust, in a fairly roundabout way, hints at his love for the first time and cements it with the gift of a narcotic to remedy Margerite's sleeplessness. The beginnings of her response—the only elements to categorize this melody as a duet—are confined to a brief flourish upon the final cadence.

Although the cadence in mm. 6–9 would today be classified as "imperfect authentic," owing to the lack of a first scale degree in the upper part, it appears emphatic enough to define the preceding material as a period rather than as a phrase. Example 5.7 thus labels the passage not only as the *motivo*, made up of phrases underpinned by an eight-syllable *ottonario-ritmo*, but also as the first *part* of the composition. The second part begins in m. 10 with a modulating *passo caratteristico* which, through its two-measure sequential steps (founded upon the bass motion of the rising fourth and falling third, and a different seven-syllable *settenario-ritmo*), possesses some of the characteristics of a "departure from the key" (*uscita di tono*). This second period remains incomplete, however, leading directly in m. 16 into the *periodo di cadenza*, which, in deference

5.7. Boito, *Mefistofele*, act 2, *duettino*, "Colma il tuo cor d'un palpito" (Milan: Ricordi, 1875; melody only, with analytical symbols)

to convention, recalls the first phrase of the *motivo,* but continues in the same way as the second phrase. The form of the piece may therefore be described, following Huebner (1992, 127), as a "binary design (first part / period; second part / development / closure)," or, following Reicha, as a small binary dimension of the *romanza.*

A Larger Dimension of the Two-Part Romanza: *Puccini,* Le Villi, *act 2, R43, "Anima santa della figlia mia"*

An extended "dimension" of the same formal pattern or conduct may be discerned in Anna's "Se come voi," from the second "number" of *Le Villi,* and also in example 5.8 (a), which reproduces the melodic line of

Guglielmo's mild revenge aria, "Anima santa della figlia mia." Its first part is made up of two complete periods, both of which modulate from tonic to dominant. Indeed, the period labeled as *secondo motivo* in mm. 9–14 of example 5.8 (a) may be regarded as little more than a parallel construction of the first period, or its "companion" (*compagnon*) in Reicha's terminology.[140] The second part of the composition begins in m. 15 with a *passo caratteristico,* differentiated from its surroundings by the tempo modification *poco più* and by a traditional modulation to the mediant. As in example 5.7, its final cadence overlaps with the beginning of the *periodo di cadenza* in m. 25, which appears at first to encompass a return of the *motivo* but soon gives way to conventional cadential figurations.

The text of the *romanza,* reproduced from the 1891 Ricordi edition, comprises two quatrains of *endecasillabi,* the first of plain (*piano*) verse, corresponding to the first part of the composition, and the second of alternating *piano* and *tronco* verses, corresponding to the second part. This inconsistency proved to be of little relevance to the musical setting, since Puccini chose to overlook the *piano* inflections on "vera" and "sera" in the first strophe and to set them regardless as *tronco* cadences.

First Part
1. Period, 8 measures: *motivo*
2. Period, 7 measures: *secondo motivo*

Anima *san*ta della *fi*glia *mi*a, (5+7) | Blessed soul of my daughter,
se la *leggen*da delle Villi è *ve*ra, (5+7) | if the legend of the Villi is true,
deh! non esser con *lui,* qual fosti, *pi*a (7+5) | ah! don't be kind to him as you have been,
ma qui l'at*ten*di al cader della *se*ra. (5+7) | but wait for him here as night falls.

Second Part
3. Period (incomplete), 9 measures: *passo caratteristico*
4. Period, 16 measures: *periodo di cadenza*

S'io po*tes*si saperti vendi*ca*ta (5+7) | If I could know that you were avenged
lieto salute*rei* l'ultimo *dì* (7+5) | I would happily greet my final day.
ah, perdona, *Si*gnor, l'idea spie*ta*ta (7+5) | Ah, forgive me, Lord, the cruel idea
che dal mio *cor* che sanguina, *fug*gì. (5+7) | escaped me, from my raging heart.

In a similar way to "E lucevan le stelle" (example 5.5), each *endecasillabo* is "broken" into a flexible mixture of *quinari* and *settenari.* A comparison between example 5.8 (a) and the reduction to *ritmi melodici* in example 5.8 (b) would suggest that the underlying pattern of a paired

5.8.

Andante lento

a. Puccini, *Le Villi,* act 2, R43, "Anima santa della figlia mia" (Milan: Ricordi, 1891; melody only, with analytical symbols).

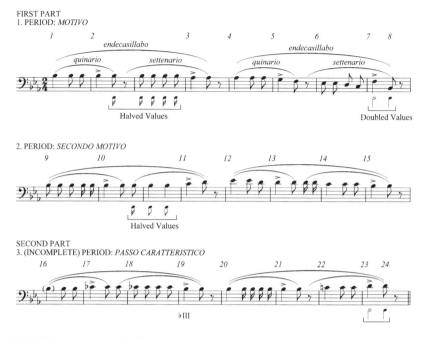

b. Reduction to *ritmi melodici*.

quinario-settenario-ritmo remains relatively stable, in spite of the rhythmic diminutions and augmentations at the surface. In accordance with the demands of the *accento musicale,* the *settenario* of the opening phrase is compressed into sixteenth notes, while the *ritmo* of the first perfect cadence in mm. 7–8 is doubled, as if to balance the phrase and to retain its full eight measures. The reduction in example 5.8 (b) also demonstrates that the *motivo,* through its reliance on the descending scale in third position, relates to the genre of the *vocalizzo* in a similar way to the melodic contour of "Nei cieli bigi" (example 5.3).

A Small Dimension of the Rondeau in Three Periods:
Puccini, Tosca, act 2, R52, "Sempre, con fè sincera"

Luigi Picchianti, whose compilation of teaching materials for his classes at the Scuola musicale in Florence owed a great deal to Reicha and Asioli, singled out the ternary dimension as the most satisfactory arrangement for a short melody:

A little piece of music manages to be most complete when it comprises three periods. The three periods normally contain:

First period: Principal subject.
Second period: Development of the subject, or another subordinate idea.
Third period: Repetition of the subject.[141]

A similar ternary arrangement may be discerned in the main section of Tosca's second act aria, "Sempre, con fè sincera," which follows two statements of an introductory period that begins with the words "Vissi d'arte." As can be seen in example 5.9 (a), the melody opens with an eight-measure *motivo,* framed by a firm perfect authentic cadence in the tonic in mm. 7–8. A central contrasting passage in mm. 9–12, shifting from the mediant to a half-cadence on the dominant, leads back to a reprise of the *motivo,* which is omitted from example 5.9 (a), since it differs significantly from its first appearance only by way of its text, distribution of parts, and more emphatic final cadence.

The text of the aria, reproduced below from the Ricordi edition of 1900, is a mixture of verse types more commonly associated with passages of recitative. The first strophe corresponds to the opening period, the first three lines of the second to the *passo caratteristico,* and the remainder, plus the same three lines of the *Passo* repeated at the end, to the reprise of the *motivo.*

1. Period, 6+2 measures: *motivo* and *cadenza finale*

Sempre con fè sincera, (7)	Always with sincere faith
la mia preghiera (5)	my prayer
ai santi tabernacoli salì. (7+5)	rose at the holy tabernacles.
Sempre con fè sincera, (7)	Always with sincere faith,
diedi fiori agl'altar. (7)	I gave flowers to the altars.

2. Period (unfinished), 4 measures: *passo caratteristico*

Nell'ora del dolore (7)	In my hour of grief
perché, perché Signore, (7)	why, why, Lord,
perché me ne rimuneri così? (7+5)	why do you repay me thus?

3. Period, 6+4 measures: *motivo (ripresa)* and *cadenza finale*

Diedi gioielli (5)	I gave jewels
della Madonna al manto, (7)	to the Madonna's mantle
e diedi il canto (5)	and I gave my song
agli astri, al ciel, (5)	to the stars, to heaven,
che ne ridean più belli. (7)	which rejoiced, more beautiful, in them.

5.9.

Andante lento appassionato

1. PERIOD (a): *MOTIVO*

1. PERIOD (b): *CADENZA FINALE*

2. (INCOMPLETE) PERIOD: *PASSO DI MEZZO*

a. Puccini, *Tosca*, act 2, R52, mm. 1–12 (Milan: Ricordi, 1900; melody only, with analytical symbols).

Since the diversity of the verse types all but precluded a regular correspondence of poetry and melodic rhythm, Puccini resorted to a strategy similar to that used in "E lucevan le stelle" later in the same opera. The principal melody appeared for the most part in the orchestra while the vocal part scanned onto it freely through a *parlando* setting. As the reduction to *ritmi melodici* in example 5.9 (b) demonstrates, however, both orchestral and vocal melodies follow a regular pattern, giving rise to what might be termed a counterpoint of rhythms. While the cello melody progresses through a "slippery" or *sdrucciolo* six-syllable *ritmo* (which helps to explain such notational oddities as the tied quarter notes in the flute and cello parts of the sixth measure), the vocal part attaches a shorter five-syllable *ritmo* to coincide with its main inflections.

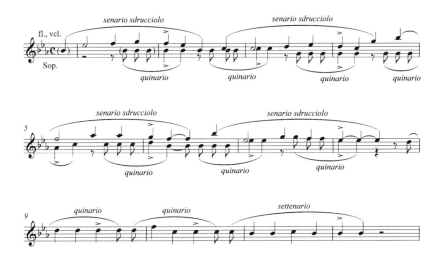

b. Reduction to *ritmi melodici*.

A Larger Dimension of the Rondeau *in Three Parts: Puccini,* Edgar, *act 1, R21, "Questo amor, vergogna mia"*

Example 5.10 demonstrates the overall ternary conduct of the character Frank's opening aria in act 1 of *Edgar*. Even though the melody is constructed from three periods, each rounded off by a well defined cadence, they are also extended enough to be considered parts. The opening part (mm. 1–16) consists of three phrases, labeled as "1. Period (a), (b), and (c)" in example 5.10 and corresponding in microcosm to a standard pattern of conduct consisting of a *motivo, passo caratteristico,* and *cadenza finale.* Its regular correspondence of verse meter and *ritmi melodici* has already been discussed in chapter 3. The central contrasting period (mm. 17–27) also consists of two phrases, whose respective emphases on mediant and dominant harmonies serve to underline their functions as *passo di mezzo* and *cadenza finale* within the same period. As is typical in such ternary forms, the reprise starting in m. 28 differs from its first statement primarily by way of minor melodic alterations, reinforced orchestration, and a more emphatic cadence.

Andante Lento

FIRST PART
1. PERIOD (a): *MOTIVO*

Que - sto a - mor, ver-go-gna mi - a, io__ spez - zar, scor - dar__ vor - re - i; ma d'un'

F: I

or - ri - da__   ma - lì - a   so - no   schia - vi i sen - si

1. PERIOD (b): *PASSO CARATTERISTICO*

miei__   Mil - le vol - te alciel giu - ra - i di fug - gir - la! e a lei tor - na - i!__

I   Am: IV   II⁷   V₄⁶·   ⁻⁵   I
                                                                    ⁻₃

1. PERIOD (c): *CADENZA FINALE*

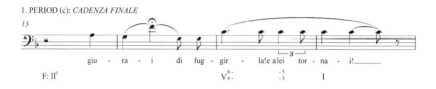

giu - ra - i di fug - gir - la! e a lei tor - na - i!__

F: II⁷   V₄⁶·   ⁻⁵   I
                                                      ⁻³

SECOND PART
2. PERIOD (a): *PASSO DI MEZZO*

El - la ri - de del mio pian - to, ed io,

Am: I   II⁷   I

2. PERIOD (b): *CADENZA FINALE*

vil, col cuo-re in-fran - to, ai suoi pie-di mi pro - ster - no   ai suoi pie-di mi pro - ster - no.
C: II₅⁶   V₂⁴ I⁶   II⁷   V₄⁶·   ⁻⁵   I   F: V⁷
                                                               ⁻♮

5.10. Puccini, *Edgar*, act 1, R21, mm. 2–27 (Milan: Ricordi, 1905; melody only, with analytical symbols).

THIRD PART
3. PERIOD (a): *RIPRESA: MOTIVO*

3. PERIOD (b): *PASSO CARATTERISTICO*

3. PERIOD (c): *CADENZA FINALE*

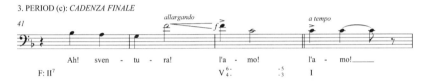

5.10. Continued, mm. 28–44.

SIX

Vocalizzi, Solfeggi, and Real (or Ideal) Composition

I. LESSONS IN SINGING AND COUNTERPOINT

Before the demise of the great tradition, the practice of counterpoint (and, less often, harmony) was commonly taught in Italy by masters of singing. The disciplines were not regarded as separate, as they are today. On the contrary, a glance at the faculty lists of the conservatories shows that expertise in vocal training appears to have been considered a prerequisite for the teaching of counterpoint, just as proficiency at the keyboard was an essential foundation for the teaching of harmony or accompaniment. The founding faculty of 1838 at the Istituto musicale in Lucca included, for instance, Eugenio Galli as professor of "*solfeggio* and counterpoint" and Massimiliano Quilici as professor of "*bel canto* and accompaniment." At the Conservatorio di Santa Maria della Pietà dei Turchini in Naples, the teaching of counterpoint by the *primo maestro di canto* was enshrined in the "Rules and Statutes" of 1746[1] and reaffirmed in Perrino's reformist open letter of 1814.[2] At the Milan Conservatory Nicola Vaccai, having made his name as a singing teacher, composer, and author of a popular method for training the voice (1832), went on to teach courses in harmony and counterpoint from 1835 to 1837 before serving as director and professor of composition until 1844. His colleague Pietro Ray, a student of Sala, delivered lessons in singing for thirty years (1808–38) before taking over the counterpoint class (1837–50). He published courses of instruction in both disciplines, including a progressive series of *solfeggi* for sopranos (1832) and a practical-theoretical treatise on counterpoint (1846). Alberto Mazzucato succeeded Ray as professor of singing from 1839 to 1851 and, like him, went on to teach counterpoint and composition, until his appointment as director of the Conservatory in 1872. Lauro Rossi, his predecessor as director, contributed not only a detailed course book for lessons in harmony (1858) but also vocal exercises for sopranos (1864, 1866).[3] At the time of Puccini's studies in Milan, Alberto Giovannini, who was primarily responsible for lessons in singing from 1877 to 1903, also taught classes in "theory and *solfeggio*" from 1881 to 1886. Similarly, at the Liceo musicale in Bologna, Alessandro Busi delivered the main class in "Counterpoint (composition)" from 1871–95 as well as taking up the position of *professore di canto* in 1884.

This pedagogical overlap between counterpoint and singing, which would appear almost inconceivable nowadays, rested upon the continued influence of eighteenth-century methods of training that regarded performance and composition as inextricably linked. For composers, a practical knowledge of singing was considered fundamental to the creation of effective melodies. By the same token, acquainting singers with the basics of counterpoint through sung exercises allowed them to improvise and embellish with a sound understanding of compositional craft, as well as to learn new scores more quickly. This much was acknowledged as far back as the seminal treatise on singing by retired castrato Pier Francesco Tosi (1723): "I would go so far as to say that any effort to sing would be infallibly vain if not accompanied by some little knowledge of counterpoint. He who knows how to compose knows how to account for what he does, and he who has not the same light, works in the dark, not knowing how to sing without committing errors."[4] Similar observations continued to feature in later singing treatises that took Tosi as their foundation, by authors such as Agricola (1757), Mancini (1777), and Hiller (1779). The pedagogical fusion of counterpoint, vocal training, and real or "ideal" composition (*composizione ideale*) also helps to explain why so many professional singers and singing teachers tried their hands at writing operas (with varying degrees of success), from Pistocchi, Porpora, and Farinelli to the legions of singers-turned-composers (the *benedetti* or "blessed," as Puccini sarcastically called them) who managed to secure a handful of performances at one or another of the Italian theaters during the nineteenth century.

As outlined above in chapter 4, the connections between performance and compositional craft were reflected in the designations *pratico* and *teorico*, which featured in the titles of most Italian harmony and counterpoint treatises. They referred to "practical" methods of learning counterpoint through *singing* and harmony through *playing,* or occasionally vice versa, and to "theoretical" or *written* elements that supported the study of both.[5] Examples of what sung "practical counterpoint" actually involved can be found in countless student exercises, from the *Lezioni* of Martini (ca. 1740–76) to publications by Sabbatini, Sala, Mattei, Asioli, Cherubini, and De Sanctis (ca. 1887). In most cases they are identifiable by their vocal settings, employing various combinations of soprano, alto, tenor, and bass clefs in open score (occasionally with a treble clef indicating a violin) as opposed to the keyboard layout of exercises intended for playing. They normally progressed from formulaic realizations of cadences, scales, and bass motions, in two to eight parts, to more fluent "settings" (*disposizioni*), *divertimenti, solfeggi,* fugues, canons, and short liturgical pieces. They could be sung to a vowel (usually an Italian *a*), as vocalizations (*vocalizzi*), or to sol-fa, as *solfeggi.*[6] Sabbatini's exercises employed a mixture of didactic rhymes, sol-fa according to both ancient and modern systems, and vocalization, as in the following typical text from one of his *solfeggi:* "The Scale you shall do ascending, and you shall descend in the opposite direction, in a moderate tempo; but in tune; thus it will go well: now vocalize. A . . ."[7] Exercises without text presumed the application of sol-fa, at least until the appearance of the instruction "let's voca . . . lize" (*vocalizza . . . mo*). In more advanced settings, such as antiphons (*antifone*) for liturgical use, Latin texts occasionally featured.[8]

Example 6.1 reproduces two typical lessons of sung practical counterpoint from Mattei's "scales with diverse counterpoints, suspensions, imitations, and canons." The first (a) attaches two additional (alto and bass) voices to a fixed part or *canto fermo,* in this instance a descending C minor scale sung by the soprano. The archaic "dorian" key signature of two flats instead of the more conventional three suggests that, as a *scala di Cesolfaut terza minore,* it was intended to be sung to the syllables of the "ancient system" (*sistema antico*) devised by eleventh-century theorist Guido d'Arezzo, as *la-sol-fa-la-sol-fa-mi-re.* According to the "modern system" that emerged during the eighteenth century (*sistema moderno*), which was based on the octave (*scala composta*) rather than the hexachord (*scala semplice*) and which indicated the seventh note of each scale with the syllable *sì,* the C minor scale of example 6.1 (a) would have been sung either to the syllables *do-sì-la-sol-fa-mi-re-do* or, as a vocalization (*vocal-*

6.1. Stanislao Mattei, *Pratica d'accompagnamento e contrappunto del Padre Maestro Stanislao Mattei. Parte seconda: Contrappunti da due a otto parti sopra la scala ascendente e discendente in ambo i modi coll'aggiunta di parecchi contrappunti a 4 parti finora inediti,* ed. Luigi Felice Rossi (ca. 1827).

a. Page 60: "The same scale with diverse counterpoints, suspensions, imitations, and canons. For three voices." (*La stessa scala con diversi contrappunti, dissonanze, imitazioni e canoni. A tre.*)

izzo), to a simple vowel *a*.[9] The figured bass symbols served only to assist the maestro in accompanying the students at the keyboard. In basic exercises, the fixed voice usually took the form of an ascending or descending scale or one of the related regular progressions, although some schools also made use of short simple themes, in the manner of Fux. It could appear in bass, soprano, or occasionally an inner voice and functioned as a guide for the other singers to keep in mind as they attached various counterpoints and imitations to each of its steps.[10] These added voices were not free or arbitrary but were regulated by a designated attachment (*attacco*) or standard progression (*movimento*). Most exercises in practical counterpoint made use of a single device, framed by a more or less conventional opening schema and closing cadence. Underlying example 6.1 (a) is a standard realization of the bass motion of the step up and the third down. After a simple opening gambit in the initial measure, based upon the addition of tonic and dominant bass notes (elaborated by passing motions) to the first two steps of the soprano scale, the alto voice doubles the soprano in syncopated thirds, forming a chain of suspensions (*dissonanze* or *scala sincopata*), while the bass attaches the given *movimento regolare* to the fixed scale through repetitions of the intervallic pattern 6–5. Both added voices prepare the final cadence with conventional figures.

Although the precise ways in which this essentially practical and oral tradition was applied in lessons have gone largely unrecorded, the

b. Pages 65–66: "Counterpoint for seven voices on the descending minor scale." (*Contrappunto a sette sopra la scala discendente di terza minore.*)

earlier parts of treatises, such as those by Sabbatini (1789–90), Mattei (ca. 1827), Asioli (1832), and Cherubini (ca. 1835), indicate that students were introduced initially to a given contrapuntal device in its simplest, most rudimentary form, before embellishing and varying its repetitive outlines together, in class, to arrive at something akin to the more polished

c. Underlying schema of *attacchi* and *imitazioni* of example 6.1 (b).

versions to be found at the end of a course of instruction.[11] The practical counterpoint reproduced in example 6.1 (a) was in this sense not so much an exercise to be performed from the page as it was an idealized version or end-product of a particular learning process, designed to provide the maestro with an exemplar to work toward with his students. The first steps in this process, in the case of example 6.1 (a), would presumably have been the bass singer's application of the intervals of the sixth and fifth below each note of the soprano's descending scale, followed by the alto's syncopated line in parallel motion. Once this basic pattern had been learned and "sung in," conventional framing devices could be added and the whole could be embellished and elaborated in any number of ways through improvised alterations. By these means the pedagogical method served to integrate vocal training with counterpoint and improvisation and, in consequence, to merge the process of composition with the act of musical performance.

Another, more complicated example from Mattei's course of practical counterpoint, also based on a fixed descending C minor scale, is presented in 6.1 (b). This time six voices are added to the guiding soprano to create a brief but well-rounded passage of seven-part counterpoint for two sopranos, two altos, two tenors, and a bass. Despite its forbidding appearance, it too is built upon one simple device, reducible to imitations of the five-note attachment (*attacco*) sung by the bass in the opening measure. Again, the exercise should be understood to suggest an end to one particular learning process rather than a beginning. It recommended to the maestro or student one possible exemplary outcome to be sought through the progressive working-out of a schema that applied a string of "little keys" to a descending scale. The basic underlying pattern is represented by example 6.1 (c), in which the five-note descending stepwise *attacco,* sung here initially by the bass, is attached on each downbeat to the first three steps of the guiding scale: C–B♭–A♭. Another voice (here a tenor) sings imitations of this *attacco* starting one half note later to form a canon at the octave (or unison). On the third half note of the measure another voice (here an alto), entering at the fourth above (F), begins a similar series of descending stepwise attachments, to which a soprano voice adds a further canon at the octave (or unison) through imitations starting on the final half note of each measure. Taken together, the four voices of example 6.1 (c) may be taken to comprise a decorated version of the *movimento regolare* of the fourth up and fifth down (C–F–B♭–E♭ etc.).[12] Although the relation of 6.1 (c) to (b) is not immediately evident, owing to the distribution of the *attacchi* among the voices, which serves to create the appearance of a seven-part imitative texture, and to the passages of simple free counterpoint, which obscure its formulaic origins, the connection is, upon closer inspection, unmistakable. In the fourth measure of 6.1 (b) the voices embark upon an inverted variant of this schema or, in Italian contrapuntal terminology, upon a second "reflection" (*ripercussione*) on the subject.[13] As 6.1 (c) demonstrates, in simplified form it is based on a series of inverted *attacchi*, sung here on each downbeat by the bass and ascending through the scale of E♭ major. The imitations that follow invert the intervals of the preceding *movimento* to generate an underlying progression of a fifth up and fourth down (E♭–B♭–F–C etc.). In the seventh measure of 6.1 (b), a brief return of the original aspect of the *attacco* serves to mark the arrival of an extended final cadence over a dominant pedal note, which would have provided opportunities for the students to try out a variety of cadential figures.

It is not difficult to imagine how years of such training, especially from an early age, would have equipped Italian musicians with a deeply ingrained knowledge of counterpoint, a natural facility in sol-fa and vocal melody, and an ability to improvise effortlessly upon an extensive range of opening, progressing, and closing schemata. Indeed, it seems more than likely that varied and embellished melodies arising from exercises in practical counterpoint, as well as *solfeggi* (discussed more fully below), contributed significantly to the creative vocal performance style, and hence also melodic style, that was inherited from the great *castrati* and known during the early nineteenth century as *bel canto* (fine singing, as in *le belle arti* or "the fine arts"), *canto spianato* (smooth, rolled-out singing), or simply as *cantabile*.[14] Manuscript evidence in Rossini's, Donizetti's, and even Verdi's hands demonstrates unequivocally that there could be an enormous gulf between what was written in a score and what was actually expected in performance.[15] In a profound sense, the music of opera was a product of collaboration between singer and composer, even when the singer's contribution began to be subsumed into the work of the composer and incorporated into scores, for instance those by Rossini, Bellini, and their successors. The notated melodies of later nineteenth-century Italian opera nevertheless owe a great debt to the practices of vocal improvisation that continued to be instilled through lessons in practical counterpoint and *solfeggio*. Melodic composition was, in fact, taught by means of the sung *solfeggio*.

II. LESSONS IN SINGING AND *SOLFEGGIO*

More specialized training was required for singers to acquire such highly valued attributes as fine vocal quality, an expressive "accent" (*accento musicale*), or techniques including the slide (*portamento*), the swell (*messa di voce*), and the trill. This much is clear, but the evidence suggests a common origin for nineteenth-century treatises in both practical counterpoint and vocal method.[16] Lessons in singing began with vocal settings of the standard (Neapolitan) scales and bass motions accompanied by a basso continuo or, later, by chords at the piano. Gervasoni's rudimentary lessons for aspiring amateur singers provide a clear example of this basic method at the end of the eighteenth century, in which the traditional scales and bass motions or "leaps" were placed in whichever voice part was required and sung as *vocalizzi* or *solfeggi*.[17] Together with the accompanying parts they could then be varied in progressively more elaborate ways, involving melodic attachments (*attacchi*), suspensions (*dissonanze*), and embellishments. The principle underlying this method was similar to that of the *partimento,* although sung rather than played and with the emphasis transferred from bass to melody. Standard exercises built upon scales, cadences, and bass motions laid the foundations for more advanced formulas, which were consolidated in practice through *solfeggi:* instructional yet aesthetically satisfactory short melodic compositions with basso continuo or piano accompaniment. In the eighteenth century these were tailored individually to suit the needs of a developing singer. The great Neapolitan maestro Leonardo Leo, for instance, would "write a new *solfeggio* for each of his students every three days, reflecting upon the strengths and ability of each and adapting them accordingly."[18] Many such *solfeggi* were set as duets, in recognition of the practice of adding *imitazioni* in a second voice to the sequential melodic attachments of the first.[19]

With the institutionalization of learning encouraged by the new conservatories and the concomitant growth in student numbers, *solfeggi* were less frequently composed to order and more often gathered into collections according to difficulty and voice type and published within general textbooks for vocal training. The most extensive and influential such textbooks were those compiled for use at the Paris Conservatory, which drew upon the lessons of the founding professors as well as publications by the most prestigious singing teachers established in the city, such as the "Theory of Vocal Music, or Rules That One Should Know and Observe to Sing Well" (1799) by Lucca-born, Naples-educated Florido Tomeoni, or the "Method of Singing for the Conservatory" (1803) by Florentine castrato Bernardo Mengozzi, both of which borrowed heavily from eighteenth-century Italian sources.[20] The first major textbook was compiled by Gossec and published as "Elementary Principles of Music Set Down by the Members of the Conservatory to Serve as Studies at That Institution; Followed by *Solfèges* by Agus, Catel, Cherubini, Gossec, Langlé, Lesueur, Méhul, and Riegel" (1800). Although regularly augmented with additional material, it remained essentially unchanged throughout the nineteenth century, as is evident from Batiste's revised edition of 1867, which boasted of its foundation in the practices of "eighteenth-century masters."[21] In keeping with the teachings of the Neapolitan school it began, like most vocal methods, with countless versions of the scale or *exercice de gamme,* outlining an ascending and descending twelfth (as in Porpora's studies) from c^1 to g^2. This was followed by the leaps or *sauts,* arranged in ascending order of interval from thirds to ninths. After these basic exercises the student progressed to page after page of scales incorporating melodic attachments of two to eight notes, mostly stepwise, which introduced appoggiaturas, suspensions, and embellishments. The studies were finished by way of a large number of *solfeggi,* generally accompanied by plodding chords at the piano and arranged in chronological order, beginning with classic Neapolitan authors such as Scarlatti, Leo, and Vinci.

The similarities between this standard layout for a nineteenth-century vocal treatise and the pedagogical methods of the eighteenth-century Neapolitan and Bolognese schools suggest a common origin, one that also underpinned Parisian treatises on harmony (improvisation) for pianists, such as Kalkbrenner (1849), with its division into scales, bass motions, and *préludes.* Already by the end of the eighteenth century, however, Italian approaches to singing, accompaniment, and composition had begun to diverge, reflecting a more general split between the disciplines of performance and composition. This fragmentation of the tradition was exacerbated by the specialization encouraged by conservatories and, from the 1840s onwards, by the gradual ascendancy of "scientific" or text-based studies of harmony and counterpoint. Methods and treatises intended to assist in the training of singers became increasingly focused on specific issues of vocal technique, marginalizing and eventually overlooking their origins in more wide-ranging approaches to musical education that had at one time merged singing, composition, and improvisation into an inseparable whole.[22] Countless editions of vocal exercises (*esercizi,* *vocalizzi,* and *solfeggi* published during the nineteenth century continued nevertheless to remain dependent upon a progressive division into scales, leaps, suspensions, and embellishments, rounded off with short didactic compositions. While in Paris in 1827, Rossini, for instance, published a short collection of *gorgheggi* (rapid, scale-based exercises upon a single vowel) and *solfeggi,* which together were designed to improve vocal agility and to prepare the singer for the art of *bel canto.* In keeping with the Bolognese method of practical counterpoint, the *gorgheggi* were a series of progressively more elaborate sequential melodic attachments to a scale, increasing in number of notes and ascending and descending, again like Porpora's exercises, from c^1 to g^2. Nicola Vaccai's more extended vocal method, published in Milan in 1832, followed essentially the same layout.[23] It began with scales and leaps of the third to the octave, not including the seventh, and finished with exercises involving a progressive series of embellishments such as suspensions, *passaggi,* appoggiaturas, and *portamenti.* In place of the usual *solfeggi* were exercises in recitative and aria styles. Later vocal treatises continued to retain this basic division. Even the theoretical-practical method of Mathilde Marchesi (1888), which remains in circulation today through a Dover reprint (1970), followed a course through scales, melodic attachments of two to eight notes, embellishments, and vocalizes.[24]

Traditional *solfeggi*—composed by a maestro, using standard contrapuntal formulas and other schemata, for an individual student to sing and embellish—continued to be used throughout the nineteenth century in Italy not only for vocal training but also as *models for melodic composition.*[25] Numerous such singing exercises, as well as old-fashioned *partimenti* by Durante, formed the basis of Bellini's studies with Niccolò Zingarelli at the Reale Collegio di Musica di San Sebastiano in Naples from 1819 to 1825.[26] Like the *partimento* for keyboard realization, the *solfeggio* taught performance and composition simultaneously through an artistically conceived compilation of simple schemata. It provided a fundamental guide to actual composition (*composizione ideale*), as described by Neapolitan maestro Giovanni De Vecchis in the second part of his "Compendium of Counterpoint of the Ancient and Modern Neapolitan Schools" (1850). *Solfeggi,* he maintained, "lead very quickly to the acquisition of good expressive vocal melody; to a greater degree than in similar compositions, the composer is free to use the most agreeable such melody, to embellish it as much as he pleases, and to express whatever affect he wishes."[27]

Among the many published *solfeggi* that became standard during the nineteenth century was a set of twelve composed during the 1730s by Hamburg-born, Naples-based maestro Johann Adolph Hasse for his wife, the renowned mezzo soprano Faustina Bordoni. Example 6.2 (a) presents one of their opening phrases, together with lavish editorial markings and pulsing chordal accompaniment typical of late nineteenth-century compilations; in this case, from the second installment of Vittorio Ricci's *Old Italian School of Singing* (1912).[28] This simple melody may serve as

6.2.

a. Johann Adolph Hasse, *Solfeggio* (1730s), mm. 1–8, as arranged by Vittorio Ricci in *The Old Italian School of Singing. Second Series: 20 Solfeggios for Contralto or Bass* (1912), no. 17, 32.

an example not only of the continuity of the tradition over almost two hundred years but also of the essential relationship between vocal performance and counterpoint in the Neapolitan school. Although it may appear to modern musicians as little more than a "composed" melody with accompaniment, it would have been perceived instantly by those familiar with the tradition as a *cantabile* realization of one of the simplest exercises of practical counterpoint, documented in sources ranging from the early 1700s to Platania (1883) and probably intended as a lesson in the application of appoggiaturas. It is represented in 6.2 (b) by an example from Mattei. Beginning with a fifth rising to a sixth above a *canto fermo* in the bass voice, the exercise involves the attachment of a chain of straightforward 7–6 suspensions to a descending scale. Its relevance to Hasse's *solfeggio* is indicated in example 6.2 (a) by means of scale-degree numbers placed above the relevant notes. The relationship between the two melodies could be described more fully through a process of (modern) reductive analysis, identifying and dismissing as "inessential," for

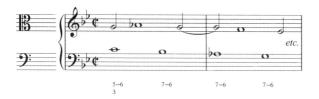

b. "Exercise on the scale," from Mattei, *Pratica d'accompagnamento sopra bassi numerati e contrappunti a più voci* (ca. 1824–25), 26, 193.

instance, the consonant appoggiatura (c^2) with associated *portamento* at the beginning of the first measure, or the dissonant appoggiatura ($b\flat^1$) decorated by a turn figure at the beginning of the second; but a more effective way to realize what this *solfeggio* represented in historical terms would be to *sing* its underlying schema (6.2 [b]), mentally if preferable, together with its bass line. Freed from the visual limitations imposed by the score, each individual voice could then be expanded and varied through attachments, in the manner of an exercise in practical counterpoint, or, as in 6.2 (a), the upper voice could be embellished and transformed into an expressive *cantabile,* in the manner of a *solfeggio.* Just as the *partimento* was a compilation of basic schemata designed to inculcate both an understanding of harmony *and* an ability to perform effectively and expressively at the keyboard, so too was the *solfeggio,* in its original form, designed to teach skills in practical counterpoint, melodic composition, *and* vocal performance.

III. FROM *SOLFEGGIO* TO IDEAL COMPOSITION IN PUCCINI (AND BELLINI)

Puccini, La bohème, *act 4, R21, mm. 4–12, "Sono andati?"*

Puccini, whose studies at Lucca included several years of singing lessons as well as practical counterpoint according to the Neapolitan and Bolognese methods, would have learned the art of melodic composition through *solfeggi.* He made reference to this old tradition in some of his most famous melodies. The dying Mimì's declaration of love to Rodolfo in the final act of *La bohème,* "Sono andati" (example 6.3 [a]), for instance, owes the touching simplicity of its measured descent to a standard practical counterpoint on the *scala nell'acuto* or soprano scale, as well as borrowing the style of its chordal accompaniment from late nineteenth-century *solfeggio* exercises. Comparing the passage with its reduction to a four-voice practical counterpoint in 6.3 (b), which is in all important respects the same as Mattei's exercise reproduced in example 6.1 (a), it is clear that Puccini departs from this standard pattern only twice: at the arrival on a C minor chord in the eighth measure (of R21) at the word *restare,* and through the omission of the A♭ in the tenth measure at *dire.* While the unadorned orchestral voices proceed smoothly, the fixed soprano scale is varied and embellished in the free and expressive manner of a *solfeggio* exercise, albeit with a relatively regular *endecasillabo-ritmo* to match the text (the first phrase of which is divided and compressed into four-plus-seven syllables), and with verse inflections (*desinenze*) highlighted by accented notes on the harp.

Much has been made of the doubling of the underlying vocal scale at the octave below in the cello part, as an example of either "the same line functioning both as a melody and as a bass" or as a "bass-less" melody.[29] But the resulting parallel line does not belong to the fundamental voice leading of this passage.[30] It is a remnant of *solfeggio* practice. It serves to reinforce the guiding scale—which would presumably have been played at the keyboard in more easily audible octaves—that the singer followed when improvising such melodic variations. The remaining three orchestral lines distribute the four parts of example 6.3 (b) freely and smoothly among themselves, in an arrangement that strongly suggests the influence of hand positions at the piano. To contemporary musicians, accustomed from childhood to employing the scale interchangeably in melody and bass as a guide to practical counterpoint and vocal variation, the effect must have been reminiscent of a particularly inspired improvisation on a standard scale exercise during a *solfeggio* lesson.

While working on the fourth act of *La bohème* in late November 1895, Puccini mentioned this "little duet" in a letter to his publisher, Giulio Ricordi:

> The act is composed almost entirely of logical *repetitions,* apart from the *duettino* "Sono andati?" and Colline's overcoat ["Vecchia zimarra"] and a few other things. I think I have found a good beginning for the *duettino* and the culminating phrase is effective although not that new; but then, there's no need to split hairs, is there?[31]

6.3.

a. Puccini, *La bohème*, act 4, R21, mm. 4–12 (Milan: Ricordi, 1896).

b. Reduction to a four-voice practical counterpoint, similar to example 6.1 (a).

With characteristic irony, Puccini described the relatively nondescript, repeated four-measure culminating phrase as "not that new," having just passed over, without comment, a blatant appropriation of an ancient schema that he must have known would be obvious to the trained eye of Ricordi. This would explain the tongue-in-cheek invitation to overlook such borrowings in the final sentence. "Sono andati" was, moreover, by no means the first or last successful melody by Puccini to evoke the sounds of a commonplace *solfeggio* lesson. The main theme or *motivo* of "Un bel dì" from *Madama Butterfly* (act 2, R12) may be regarded as just such a vocal variation upon the scale, with the guiding line doubled at the octave below and the remaining parts outlining a slightly modified version of the most hackneyed contrapuntal schema imaginable: the attachment of the *movimento* of the fourth down and step up to the descending soprano scale (familiar to modern listeners as "Pachelbel's Canon").

Puccini, Edgar, *act 1, R29, "Sia per voi, l'orazion"*

Puccini's second completed opera concerns the alternating affections of medieval Flemish knight Edgar (tenor) for the pure and chaste Fidelia (soprano) and the wild and promiscuous Tigrana (mezzo). At the beginning of the first act, having established Fidelia's credentials as the only village girl worthy of his love (and, according to a tested formula, its ultimate sacrificial victim), Tigrana enters in a thigh-slapping display of vulgarity with a Moorish lute slung across her shoulder. As she attempts to enflame Edgar's passion anew by mocking his almond twig (a gift from Fidelia), to the accusing strains of music from a religious service conveniently underway in the background, a chorus of church-going peasants takes the opportunity to denounce the "vile courtesan." Her response is to strum her lute all the more and to celebrate her sensuality through singing: "The sermon is for you, the song is for me! I want to sing, I want to trill. Whoever does not want to hear should go back to the church and pray!" How fitting that Puccini should have set these words to a standard *vocalizzo* exercise, lifted more or less straight out of the pages of a *bel canto* method (example 6.4). In the first eight measures Tigrana undertakes a series of "leaps" of the fourth, attached to a descending scale of E♭ major that is divided "arithmetically." Exulting in her vocal prowess, for the next eight-measure phrase she raises the scale to its "second position," beginning on the third note of the tonic triad, and increases the size of the leaps to sixths. To accommodate this formulaic progression the text comprises a regular stanza of "double" four-syllable verse (*quaternario doppio*), mostly lacking its final syllable (*tronco*) and readily identifiable by the conventional eighth-note caesura applied to the end of each four-measure *ritmo*.[32] In the cadential passage, from the sixteenth measure, the note values of the *ritmo* are halved. Together with the augmented triads and chromatic scale so typical of the (Liszt-inspired) *giovane scuola* of

6.4. Puccini, *Edgar,* act 1, R29, mm. 1–24 (Milan: Ricordi, 1905).

Boito and Faccio, this provides the overall twenty-four-measure period with a degree of variety.

The orchestral accompaniment evokes the kind of crass support that a singing maestro might typically have provided for such vocal exercises at the keyboard,[33] reinforcing each melodic note with a rolled chord and anchoring the intonation (as well as the truncated fourth syllable of each verse) with a drone fifth in the bass. In terms of form or conduct, the three phrases of example 6.4, which together form the initial period of a larger ternary dimension, could be described as *motivo, secondo motivo,* and *periodo di cadenza,* but such labels are of questionable relevance in this instance. The "motivation" for the conduct derives from a portrayal of a standard *vocalizzo* exercise, which Puccini presumably intended his audience—at least the musicians and singers among them—to recognize and appreciate.

Puccini, Edgar, *act 2, R9, "O soave vision"*

Tigrana's singing lessons appear to have paid off, since the seductive magic of her *vocalizzo* entices Edgar not only to join her in a life devoted to lustful pleasures but also to commit arson upon his own house, thereby destroying all hope of return to the village. By the beginning of the second act, however, he has grown tired of the playboy lifestyle and, in an old-fashioned *scena ed aria,* expresses his yearning for the pure, innocent, and (by implication) morally superior love of Fidelia, who represents, in keeping with a long-held operatic convention, more suitable wife material. The text of the aria, from the final revised edition of 1905,[34] is given below, together with indications of the main subdivisions of its musical setting into what Reicha would have called "a small dimension of the *rondeau,*" or ternary form with three periods.

First Part
First Period, 8 measures: *motivo principale*

O soave visïon—di quell'*al*ba d'*a*pril, (7+7)	O sweet vision of that April dawn,
o visïon gen*til*—d'a*mo*re e di splen*dor*! (7+7)	o kind vision of love and splendor!

Second Part
Second (unfinished) Period, 10 measures: *passo caratteristico*

Nell'a*bis*so fa*tal,*—dove caduto io *son,* (7+7)	In the fatal abyss where I have fallen,
rim*pian*ta visïon, (6/7)	longed-for vision,
te il *mio* pen*sie*ro e*vó*ca sempre an*cor*! (6/7+7)	my thoughts still evoke you always!

Third Part: reprise
Third Period, 8 measures: *motivo principale* with *cadenza finale*

Sovra un sereno *cie*lo—si di*se*gna il pro*fil,* (7+7)	Above in the serene sky is outlined the profile,
dol*cis*simo[, infan*til*]—dell'*an*giol che m'a*mò*! (7+7)	so sweet [childlike], of the angel who loved me!

Although there is no suggestion that the main theme of the aria elicits any direct comparison with a conventional *vocalizzo, solfeggio,* or practical counterpoint, it is like many melodies in Italian opera, based on an expressive variation of the *scala nell'acuto* or soprano scale. From the section

6.5.

a. Puccini, *Edgar,* act 2, R9, mm. 1–13 (Milan: Ricordi, 1905).

of vocal score reproduced in example 6.5 (a) and its analytical reduction in (b), the melody may be seen to descend through the outlines of the tonic scale in "third position," starting with a♭². The first three steps are clearly picked out by the upper part of the accompanying string chords; the remainder is somewhat obscured by the complexity of the melodic figures. This guiding *canto fermo* is hypothetically restored in 6.5 (b) to the five rhythmic phrases (*ritmi*) that make up the opening eight-measure period. Given the centrality of the scale to Italian traditions of counterpoint,

1. PERIOD:
MOTIVO

2. PERIOD:
PASSO CARATTERISTICO

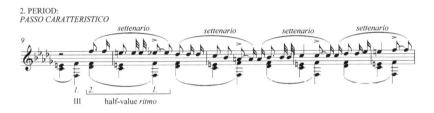

b. Reduction of the melody of example 6.5 (a) to *ritmi* attached to a descending scale in third position.

singing, and melodic composition, there is little need to resort to Schenkerian analysis to demonstrate its significance to example 6.5 (a). Even where the guiding scale is omitted (as in mm. 6–7, which appear to lack the step from C♭ to B♭), its relevance as an overall contour or framework remains. As centuries of Italian theory and practice testify, the scale was a standard compositional tool, far removed from the notion of a profound, composed-out chord of nature or "primeval line" (*Urlinie*). It provided a serviceable formula for many thousands of tunes.[35] What conventional Schenkerian theory would consider the "foreground" or "surface" of this melody was in the Italian traditions regarded as its *essence*. The skill and effectiveness of the realization, by composer as imagined performer, was everything.

The four apocopated or shortened seven-syllable verses within the *settenari doppi* of the *motivo principale* would suggest, in conventional terms, a musical period made up of four regular phrase rhythms (*ritmi*). As example 6.5 (b) shows, however, after two initial phrases, in which the main inflections of each component *settenario* fall on the downbeats of their respective second measures, the established *ritmo* is halved in value (or doubled in speed) to accommodate a repetition of the words "o visïon." The analysis borrows Asioli's symbols for "strong" (*1.*) and "weak" (*2.*) rhythmic movements beneath the stave, as well as slurs and accents above to identify the melodic rhythms and their main inflections. This quickening of the *ritmo* and the resulting shift of inflection to the upbeats may best be perceived by reciting the melodic text and observing the natural accents of the poetic meter (as italicized above). In mm. 7–8 the final phrase of the period restores the *ritmo* to its full value.

With the onset of the contrasting *passo caratteristico* the audience learns that Edgar cannot actually see this enchanting *visïon* (or, less poetically, *visione*) of an April dawn that reminds him of Fidelia's profile, since he has metaphorically fallen into a fatal abyss of despair. The music responds with a switch to a suitably lugubrious affect brought about by a funereal ostinato figure in the mediant—the most common key for characteristic passages. Although this ostinato appears to feature a strong offbeat accent, the *ritmi* of the melody suggest an alternative reading at odds with the notation. As the simplified reduction in example 6.5 (b) demonstrates, this central period is based on regular repetitions of the original individual *settenario-ritmo* reduced to half its value, with the main inflection displaced onto the second quarter note of each measure. In effect, the rhythmic ostinato is notated one quarter note too late. The passage could have been rendered more conventionally by redrawing the bar lines one quarter note to the left, but Puccini evidently wished to underline the sense of disquiet and unease with a cross-rhythm operating between the conductor's beat (the notated measures) and the *ritmo* of the vocal line.

Puccini, Edgar, act 3, *R*2, Preludio

Edgar's unsatisfactory sojourn in the abyss of Tigrana's charms is short-lived. He joins a roving platoon of soldiers and makes a triumphant return, albeit as a corpse, in the third act. (The funeral is later revealed as an elaborate hoax designed to test yet further the relative strengths of the two women's love for Edgar, who witnesses their reactions to the scene

6.6.

a. Puccini, *Edgar,* act 3, *preludio,* R2, mm. 1–8 (Milan: Ricordi, 1905).

b. Ascending scale in third position counterpointed by a bass motion of the third down and fifth up.

while disguised as a friar). In the absence of any indication of the events that led to his death, the opening orchestral prelude serves to remind the audience of his earlier despair and to hint at a glorious apotheosis (or reunion with Fidelia) to come. It alternates between two themes: the first, a version of the lugubrious ostinato from the central section of "O soave visïon," and the second (example 6.6 [a]), a stirring, heroic portrayal of the not-so-pious warrior.

Although played initially by the first violins, this heroic melody is unmistakably vocal in nature. Indeed it returns later in the act (R10, m. 4) set to *settenario* verses as Fidelia bids Edgar what she believes to be a final farewell. In terms of construction it presents a clear example of a guiding *canto fermo* of an ascending soprano scale, here in third position and counterpointed by a regular bass motion of the third down and the fifth up, as represented by example 6.6 (b). The first three steps of the overall progression are repeated and the conventional harmonization is altered slightly so as to intensify the sense of direction, but its outlines remain readily identifiable. Again, the underlying formula provides little more than a framework for the resulting melody, a fixed voice upon which to attach the varied, embellished, and above all expressive phrases inspired by the affect of the (missing) text.

Puccini, Manon Lescaut, *act 2, R6, m. 6, "In quelle trine morbide"*

The first main set piece of the second act, "In quelle trine morbide" (example 6.7 [a]), introduces Manon to the audience in her new role as pampered yet melancholy mistress of the aged Geronte by way of a basic *solfeggio* pattern upon the descending scale in first position, underscored by pulsing "piano" chords that double the guiding melodic line. The effect was presumably intended to call to mind a typical exercise on the scale performed during a singing lesson and accompanied supportively by a maestro at the keyboard, so as to conjure up a suitably evocative image of the cosseted and conventional bourgeois world in which Manon, having abandoned love for money, has now found herself. The relevance of this connection with domestic music making is enhanced by the overall conduct of the aria, which consists of three progressively varied statements of the same descending scale formula, the first two relatively unadorned and the third elaborated with suspensions, as if drawn from a later "lesson." As the reduction in 6.7 (b) illustrates, the first statement of the *solfeggio* scale in the tonic key may be considered as the main theme or *motivo* of the piece. It is followed by a four-measure ascending and balancing answering phrase—simultaneously a "response" (*riposta*) and a "departure from the key" (*uscita di tono*)—that ceases to double the guiding *canto fermo* and restores a more conventionally functioning bass line, leading to an imperfect authentic cadence that is too weak to be considered as the end of a period. In a gesture reminiscent of the practice of raising the pitch of a *vocalizzo* exercise by increments, and suggestive also of a typical key for a central, contrasting "characteristic passage" (*passo caratteristico*), the *motivo* returns in similar form (R6, m. 14), transposed to the flattened mediant (G♭ major). The responding phrase functions also as a final cadence (*cadenza finale*), complete with rising *passaggio* and high note. Taken together, these eight-measure statements of the *motivo*

6.7

a. Puccini, *Manon Lescaut,* act 2, R6, m. 6 to R7, m. 17, "In quelle trine morbide" (Milan: Ricordi, 1893).

a. (*continued*)

comprise the opening period of the piece. Even though both answering phrases (*riposte*) conclude in the dominant key, B♭ major, they appear to stand in relation to one another, in terms of modern (German) theory, as antecedent (*Vordersatz*, ending with a weak cadence) and consequent (*Nachsatz*, ending with a perfect authentic cadence).

The second and final period of the piece (from R7) takes up the descending G♭ major scale of the consequent phrase of the *motivo* and, as if turning to the next "lesson," adapts it to a standard chain of 7–6 sus-

[ANTECEDENT]

1. PERIOD (a):
MOTIVO

1. PERIOD (b):
RIPOSTA (USCITA DI TONO)

[CONSEQUENT]

1. PERIOD (c):
MOTIVO (SECONDO)

1. PERIOD (d):
RIPOSTA (CADENZA FINALE)

2. PERIOD:
PASSO CARATTERISTICO (APPENDICE)

b. Analytical reduction.

pensions. As the accompaniment embellishes each descending step with repetitive melodic attachments, Manon, too distracted by memories of her penniless but passion-filled former lifestyle to sing along, intones an inner voice before taking the soprano line up an octave in preparation for the final cadence. In terms of formal function this second period may be regarded as both a more advanced variant of the descending soprano scale and as some kind of *passo caratteristico,* a contrasting supplement to the first period that confirms the key anticipated by its consequent phrase. In example 6.7 (b) it is described also as an "appendix" (*appendice*), from a term mentioned in passing by Basevi in connection with Pagano's andante, "Sciagurata! Hai tu creduto," from act 1 of Verdi's *I lombardi.*[36]

It is notable that the revised text for "In quelle trine morbide" (reproduced below, from the final version)[37] ended up as a free mixture of five-, seven-, and eleven-syllable lines, more commonly associated with connecting passages or accompanied recitative. Lyrical settings of blank verse (*verso sciolto*) were, however, more common in Italian *melodramma* than is generally supposed, even before Arrigo Boito's loosening of accepted norms in the first version of *Mefistofele* (1868). As the reduction in 6.7 (b) indicates, Puccini set these lines to a regular underlying "harmonic rhythm" (*ritmo armonico*) in which the main verse inflection or *desinenza* occurred on the downbeat of every second measure. This conventional scheme applied equally to the second period or "appendix," even though it was notated in the score in $\frac{2}{4}$ time. The representation of the periodic structure by means of a *quinario-ritmo* in 6.7 (b) serves merely to illustrate the correspondence of the underlying melodic contour (especially the descending scale) with the main verse inflections; in practice, i.e., in 6.7 (a), the beginnings of the *ritmi* are treated flexibly, incorporating a variety of syllables and subsidiary accents.

First Period, antecedent, 8 measures: *motivo* and *riposta* (*uscita di tono*)

In quelle trine *mor*bide (7)	In these soft furnishings,
nell'alcova do*ra*ta (7)	in the gilded alcove,
v'è un si*len*zio, un gelido mor*tal* (5+7)	there is a silence, a mortal freeze,
v'è un si*len*zio, un freddo che m'ag*ghiac*cia! (5+7)	there is a silence, a coldness that chills me!

First Period, consequent, 8 measures: *motivo* (*secondo*) and *piposta* (*cadenza finale*)

Ed io che m'ero av*vez*za (7)	And I, who was used to
a una ca*rez*za voluttu*o*sa (5+5)	a voluptuous caress
di labbra ar*den*ti e d'infuocate *brac*cia (5+7)	from ardent lips and enflamed arms,
or ho tutt'altra *co*sa! (7)	I now have something quite different!

Second Period, 9 measures: *passo caratteristico* (*appendice*)

O mia dimora u*mi*le, (7)	O my humble little dwelling,
tu mi ritorni in*nan*zi (7)	how you appear before me
gaia, isolata, *bian*ca (7)	cheerful, secluded, and white
come un sogno gen*ti*le (7)	like a sweet dream
e di pace e d'a*mor*! (7)	of peace and love!

Puccini, La bohème, *act 1, R30, m. 3,"Che gelida manina"*

The first act of *La bohème* is divided into two parts, the second of which, beginning with Mimì's timid knock at Rodolfo's door (R25, m. 11), is an extended love duet built along traditional lines. Girardi has described how Puccini managed to combine cyclic formal logic with a sense of evolving narrative in this familiar layout of set pieces. His overview of the entire structure, reproduced below, identifies formal units with letter symbols in the left-hand column and the outlines of a traditional nineteenth-century duet scene in the right-hand column.[38] Although it is difficult to generalize, a duet usually began with a fast opening movement or *tempo d'attacco,* characterized by dialogue, recitative, and perhaps a few aria-like moments, leading to two or three lyric set pieces, the last of which was usually, until ca. 1860, a cabaletta. Each song would normally unfold through a statement by one singer (*proposta*) followed by a confirming or contrasting response (*riposta*) by the other, before both sang together (*a due*). The individual movements, each of which observed the doctrine of the dominant affect, could be separated by a fast transitional passage known as a *tempo di mezzo.*

K	"Non sono in vena" (R25)	*tempo d'attacco*
L	"Scusi" (R25, m. 11)	
M	"Sventata" (R27)	
N	"Che gelida manina" (R30, m. 3)	*Rodolfo's cantabile*
O	"Chi son?" (R31)	
B	"In povertà mia lieta" (R32)	
P	"Talor dal mio forziere" (R32, m. 9)	
L¹	"Sì mi chiamano Mimì" (R35)	*Mimì's cantabile*
Q	"Mi piaccon quelle cose" (R36)	
L¹	"Mi chiamano Mimì" (R36, m. 11)	
R	"Sola, mi fo" (R37)	
S	"Ma quando vien lo sgelo" (R38)	
Q	"Germoglia in un vaso una rosa" (R38, m. 11)	
A	"Ehi! Rodolfo" (R39)	*tempo di mezzo*
P	"O soave fanciulla" (R41)	*a due*
L-N	"Che? Mimì!" (R43)	*coda*

Rodolfo's cantabile section, corresponding to a vastly extended *proposta,* contains two distinct arias (labeled N and P in the chart above), separated by a central episode consisting of a short passage of recitative (O) and a reminiscence of the "Nei cieli bigi" theme from earlier in the act (B), which functions here as a type of introduction to the closing set piece. Overall, the section responds musically to the dramatic theme of awakening love, from the tender yet still polite and reserved contours of "Che gelida manina" (example 6.8 (a)) to the passionate and rather fresh outpouring of "Talor dal mio forziere" (example 6.9 [a]).

An interpretation of the conduct of the initial lyric piece as a binary form or "small dimension of the *romanza*" appears within the outline of its text below and as part of the analytical reduction in example 6.8 (b).[39] Alternatively, it could be conceived as a one-part *canzonetta*, subdivided into the usual three-phrase succession of *motivo, passo caratteristico,* and *cadenza finale,* but the component periods seem too well defined to merge together in this way, notwithstanding their lack of firm closing cadences. The first part of the *romanza* comprises one period (mm. 3–11), which is brought to a close by a repetition of its last four measures as a kind of orchestral ritornello, recalling a typical feature of street songs. This main theme or *motivo* makes use of several devices to convey the naturalness and touching simplicity of the lovers' first meeting. Harmonically, it is built upon a four-measure vamp of the sort found in popular songs or café music. Melodically, it is confined to an octave species, like a basic *solfeggio,* from $a\flat^1$ to $a\flat^2$, and follows the simple formula of a rising scale in third position. Example 6.8 (b) highlights this underlying guiding voice by occasionally incorporating both vocal and orchestral lines and by conflating them into a single melody. While the *motivo* reaches only as far as the seventh step ($g\flat^2$) in m. 9, the second period (mm. 16–23) touches upon the upper octave in m. 21 before descending stepwise through the scale. The third and final period (mm. 24–36) also completes the ascent through the octave, reserving the words "who I am" in mm. 28–29 for the *corona* or high point of the phrase in what was presumably intended as a droll commentary on the poet's narcissistic personality. The second part of the *romanza* begins in m. 16 with a "characteristic passage" or *passo caratteristico* that emphasizes, in typical fashion, chords III and VI within its overall dominant tonality and flows without cadence into the similarly unfinished *periodo di cadenza.* Rhythmically, the piece maintains an even distribution of weak and strong *movimenti ritmici* throughout, with the *desinenza* falling every second measure. Considering the ad hoc way in which the irregular numbers of syllables of each line are fitted into this regular meter, the overall effect would appear to strengthen the impression of a dominant affect based on an evocative transfiguration of the

First Part

First Period, 12 measures: *motivo* and *ritornello*

Che *ge*lida ma*ni*na, (7)	What an icy little hand,
se la *la*sci riscal*dar.* (7/8)	let it be warmed.

Cer*car* che *gio*va?—Al *bui*o non
    si *tro*va. (5+7)
	What good is searching? We can't find it in
	    the dark.

Second Part

Second (unfinished) Period, 8 measures: *passo caratteristico*

Ma per for*tu*na—è una notte di *lu*na, (5+7)	But luckily it's a moonlit night,
e qui la *lu*na l'abbiamo vi*ci*na. (5+7)	and here we have the moon near.

Third (Unfinished) Period, 13 measures: *periodo di cadenza*

A*spet*ti signo*ri*na, (7)	Wait, miss,
le di*rò* con due pa*ro*le (7/8)	I'll tell you in two words

chi son, chi *son* e—che *fac*cio, come
    *vi*vo. (5+7)
	who I am, who I am and what I do, how I
	    live.

kind of popular ditty with which Puccini manages to capture the musical "color" or *tinta* of Bohemian life in Paris throughout the opera.

Puccini, La bohème, *act 1*, R*32, m. 9, "Talor dal mio forziere"*

As the extrovert companion to the restrained and inhibited opening piece of Rodolfo's *cantabile*, it is perhaps fitting that this closing *romanza* (6.9 [a]) makes use of a similar guiding scale, descending, however, in first position from a♭^{2} and failing on this occasion to reach closure through the lower octave. The analytical reduction in example 6.9 (b) and the outline of the text below[40] both illustrate the division of the conduct into two periods, each consisting of two distinct phrases. The *motivo* occupies the initial four measures of the first period. It comprises an embellished and varied descent through seven steps of the scale, like a simple *solfeggio*, supported by a progression through the primary triads from tonic to dominant. In terms of rhythm, the opening line (mm. 9–11) establishes a clear *settenario-ritmo* with the main inflection falling on the downbeat of the second measure. Its outlines remain intact despite the compression of two lines of text within the following phrase (mm. 11–13). The remainder of the period (mm. 14 to R33) conforms to a *passo caratteristico*, harmonized almost entirely in parallel tenths and modulating in typical fashion to the mediant, C minor.

First Period, 9 measures: *motivo* and *passo caratteristico*

Ta*lor* dal mio for*zie*re (7)	At times from my coffer
ru*ban* tutti i gio*iel*li (7)	two thieves steal all my gems:
due *la*dri: gli occhi *bel*li. (7)	two beautiful eyes.
V'*en*trar con voi pur *o*ra, (7)	They entered with you just now,
ed i miei sogni u*sa*ti (7)	and my familiar dreams
e i bei sogni *mie*i (7)	and my beautiful dreams
tosto si dile*guar*! (7)	quickly disappeared!

Linking dominant harmony

Ma il *fur*to non m'ac*co*ra (7)	But the theft doesn't grieve me

Second Period, 9 measures: *motivo* (*ripresa*) and *periodo di cadenza* (*passo caratteristico*)

poichè v'ha preso *stan*za (7)	because sweet hope
la [dolce] spe*ran*za! (6)	has taken their place!
Or che mi cono*sce*te (7)	Now that you know me,
parlate *voi,* (5)	you speak,
deh! parlate. Chi *sie*te? (7)	ah! speak. Who are you?
Vi piaccia *dir*! (5)	Please tell!

Although a single dominant affect maintains control throughout the period, a degree of contrast is achieved by doubling the speed (or halving the value) of the established *settenario-ritmo* for the *passo caratteristico*. This is not immediately obvious in the score (6.9 [a]) since the original common time signature is retained, meaning that the inflection, instantly perceivable as such in performance, falls within the middle of the measure. The reduction in 6.9 (b) re-notates this passage in a $\frac{2}{4}$ time signature, while specifying the original measure numbers, to demonstrate the continuity of the underlying *settenario-ritmo*. It is significant to note that where Puccini is compelled to include a measure in $\frac{2}{4}$ time, owing to the uneven number of half-value *ritmi* within the phrase, he places it on both occasions just before the final cadence of the period (see m. 17 and R33, m. 9).

After a short linking *ritmo* (or *inciso*) over a dominant harmony (at R33, m. 1), the second and final period of this *romanza* begins with a reprise of the *motivo*, sounded initially, in Wagnerian fashion, by the orchestra alone. The *passo caratteristico* also returns, but in the guise of a cadential period (R33, mm. 6–10) in which the insistence of Rodolfo's questioning, and its motivation, is reflected in the repetitiveness of the melody and the salacious chromatic swells of the woodwind.

6.8.

a. Puccini, *La bohème*, act 1, R30, mm. 3–36, "Che gelida manina" (Milan: Ricordi, 1896).

a. (*continued*).

Puccini, La bohème, *act 1,* R36, *"Mi piaccion quelle cose"*

Mimì plays down Rodolfo's ardent pleas by responding with a disarmingly simple statement of her refrain, thereby postponing the inevitable until the reprise *a due*. After this brief introductory passage, her answering *cantabile* section comprises an extended three-part form or, in Reicha's terms, "a ternary dimension of the *rondeau*," framed by the eleven-measure *motivo principale* reproduced in example 6.10 (a). By a happy coincidence, especially for Rodolfo, this *andante calmo* reveals her delight in all things to do with poetry. Its conduct progresses through a conventional succession of (1) principal theme, based in this instance on a rising scale in third position from a¹ to a² that fails to reach its upper octave, (2) "characteristic passage" in the mediant key, and (3) a final

b. Analytical reduction.

cadence replete with *corona* (a melodic highpoint with fermata, in m. 9). Adopting a familiar style of orchestral accompaniment, the violins and violas outline the guiding *canto fermo* in octaves within a series of pulsing offbeat chords, omitting the bass in a manner reminiscent of a helpful right hand at the piano. Since the rising scale in the soprano part of mm. 1–6 is the main compositional determinant, the bass line is not so much missing as partially overlooked. Indeed, as the reduction in example 6.10 (b) demonstrates, the harmonic support rests upon little more than the addition of triads to the notes that coincide with each main verse inflection or *desinenza*. This results in what appears to be a rising interval cycle of diatonic thirds, but it is in fact based on a standard counterpoint of the

a. (*above and facing*) Puccini, *La bohème,* act 1, R32, m. 9 to R33, m. 10, "Talor dal mio forziere" (Milan: Ricordi, 1896).

interval of a fifth followed by a sixth added to the notes of the soprano scale or *scala nell'acuto.*

Within the six measures of the *motivo* there are four phrases or "rhythms" (*ritmi*), each incorporating a regular *settenario* meter. The first establishes a pattern of weak and strong rhythmic movements (*movimenti ritmici*) that scans one *ritmo* over two measures, but as Mimì

becomes slightly flustered in alluding to love, the next two phrases halve the value (or double the speed) so that the main inflection falls upon each notated downbeat. In the fourth and final phrase of the *motivo* (mm. 4–6), the original two-measure *ritmo* is restored, but in a way

b. Analytical reduction.

that highlights the incompleteness of the rising scale formula and, some might argue, Mimì's underlying sadness at the mention of springtime, which she knows she is unlikely to survive. Unable to complete the final phrase through emotion or breathlessness, the orchestra does it for her, leading to an inflection on the sinister B minor chord marked out by the triangle with full orchestra in m. 6. The minor-key mood, together with the full-value *ritmo*, continues through the *passo caratteristico*, in reflection of "dreams and chimeras," before relenting in a short cadential passage.

First Part

Period, 11 measures (*andante calmo*): *motivo, passo caratteristico, cadenza finale*

Mi piaccon quelle cose (7)	I like those things
che han sì dolce malìa, (7)	that have such sweet magic,
che parlano d'amor, di primavere, (7+5)	which speak of love, of springtimes,
che parlano di sogni e di chimere, (7+5)	which speak of dreams and of chimeras,
quelle cose che han nome poesia. (7+5)	those things that are called poetry.
Lei m'intende? [Sì]	Do you understand me? [Yes]

Ritornello, 5 measures (*lentamente*)

Mi chiamano Mimì, (7)	They call me Mimì,
[ed] il perchè non so. (7)	I don't know the reason.

Second Part

Central Episode I (*passo di mezzo*), 18 measures (*allegretto moderato*)

Sola, mi fo il pranzo da me stessa. (5+7)	Alone, I prepare dinner by myself.
Non vado sempre a messa (7)	I don't always go to Mass,
ma prego assai il Signor. (7)	but I pray much to the Lord.
Vivo sola, soletta, (7)	I live alone, all alone,
là in una bianca cameretta: (5+4)	there in a little white room.
guardo sui tetti e in cielo, (5+4)	I look out on roofs and into the heavens,

Central Episode II (*passo di mezzo*), 11 measures (*andante molto sostenuto*)

ma quando vien lo sgelo (7)	but when the thaw comes
il primo sole è mio, (7)	the first sun is mine,
il primo bacio dell'aprile è mio! (5+7)	the first kiss of April is mine!
Il primo sole è mio! (8)	The first sun is mine!

Third Part

Reprise (*ripresa*), 12 measures (*tempo primo andante*): *motivo, passo caratteristico, cadenza finale*

Germoglia in un vaso una rosa … (11)	A rose buds in a pot …
Foglia a foglia la spio! (7)	Leaf by leaf I observe it!
Così gentil [è] il profumo d'un fior! (5+7)	A flower's perfume is so delicate!
Ma i fior ch'io faccio, ahimè, (7)	But the flowers that I make, alas,
i fior ch'io faccio, ahimè, non hanno odore! (5+7)	the flowers I make, alas, have no odor!
Altro di me non le saprei narrare:	I wouldn't know what else to tell you about me:
sono la sua vicina	I'm your neighbor
che la vien fuori d'ora a importunare.	who comes at the wrong hour to bother you.

6.10.

a. Puccini, *La bohème*, act 1, R36, mm. 1–11 (Milan: Ricordi, 1896).

The central part of Mimì's *cantabile* is divided into two separate movements, in response to the contrasting dominant affects required by the text.[41] The first central episode or *passo di mezzo* is a cheerful *allegretto* in which she recounts the daily routine of her simple lifestyle (letter R in the formal overview above). The mood changes, along with the tempo and affect, for the second episode (example 6.11 [a]) as she enthuses over the first sunshine of April. This memorable moment owes its effect to a progression of five-note melodic attachments (*attacchi*), commonly found in practical counterpoints (such as example 6.1 [b] or 6.13 [a]), rising by three

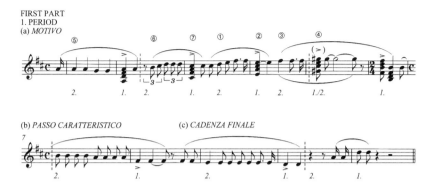

b. Analytical reduction.

steps of a third. The first two statements (mm. 1–4), to regular *settenario-ritmo,* are simple, but the third (mm. 5–8) is elongated and expanded over the course of two *ritmi.* Accompanying this expansion is the basic practical counterpoint of the descending 7–6 scale, as indicated by the figured bass symbols in the reduction of 6.11 (b). The *a minore* division of the eleven-syllable line, into five-plus-seven syllables, allows for each step of the descending chain of suspensions to scan onto the existing pattern of *ritmi.* A reprise of the initial *motivo* (as in example 6.10) closes Mimì's *cantabile* "response" with the same sense of calmness and simplicity as its beginning.

Puccini, La bohème, *act 1, R41, "O soave fanciulla"*

After an interlude in which the other Bohemians finally bid Rodolfo farewell and depart for the Latin Quarter, leaving him alone with Mimì and prey to a beam of romantic moonlight streaming through the open window, the theme from his earlier declaration of love, "Talor dal mio forziere," returns in hushed tones on horns, flute, and shimmering violin arpeggios to initiate the culmination of the love duet (example 6.12 [a]). At first little more than a faint echo in the orchestral part, over which Rodolfo reveals his feelings in Wagnerian fashion through declamatory phrases (two *endecasillabi a maiore* superimposed onto a regular *settenario* melody, in this case), the theme gradually increases in intensity until both singers join in a full-blown cantabile rendition, *a due,* as he admits

6.11.

a. Puccini, *La bohème*, act 1, R38, mm. 1–11 (Milan: Ricordi, 1896).

his pleasurable physical twinges ("Extreme sweetnesses already stir in the soul") and she offers her submissive response ("Ah! Love, only you command"). As the reduction in example 6.12 (b) demonstrates, this preparatory crescendo is built upon a series of melodic attachments (*attacchi*) articulating a regular motion (*movimento regolare*) of the step down and

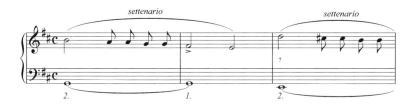

b. Analytical reduction.

the fourth up. It is counterpointed in the bass with a complementary motion of the fourth down and the sixth up.

Although the melodic attachment derives unmistakably from the theme of Rodolfo's earlier aria (6.9 [a]), it was also commonly encountered as a standard component of sung practical counterpoints on this particular progression. Example 6.13 reproduces an "inverted" version of the exercise from De Sanctis (n.d. [1887?]), in which the regular motion of the fourth up and step down, evident in the melody of "O soave fanciulla," is relegated to an unsounded Ramellian "fundamental bass" of chord roots (*basso fondamentale*) while the "perceived bass" (*basso sensibile*) replaces it with a rising scale. The melodic attachment in the soprano voice of 6.13 resembles the contours of Puccini's theme. This suggests not so much a direct borrowing as a general connection with the tradition of sung practical counterpoint.

6.12.

a. Puccini, *La bohème*, act 1, R41, mm. 1–8 (Milan: Ricordi, 1896).

Puccini, Tosca, act 2, R47, m. 6, "Già mi struggea"

One final example from Puccini (6.14) sets out to demonstrate that the basic *solfeggio* schema of a descending scale with attached phrase rhythms continued to underpin even some of the more overtly progressive lyrical moments in *Tosca*, such as Scarpia's second act *andante appassion-*

b. Reduction of 6.12 (a) to a *movimento* of a step down and fourth up, set to a regular *settenario-ritmo*.

16.13.   Cesare De Sanctis, *La polifonia nell'arte moderna* (1887?), no. 322, 146.

ato, "Già mi struggea," in which he gives free rein to erotic imaginings while contemplating the service Tosca must perform for him to secure Cavaradossi's release. This reflective *cantabile* occupies the central section of an extended monologue, "Già, mi dicon venal," which begins at R46 with a "transition-in" (to borrow Hepokoski's term) involving vocal declamation over obsessive repetitions of Scarpia's so-called Lust motive and ends with a short, related "transition-out." The commencement of the set piece is marked by an array of conventional signs, including a recitative-like cadence and throbbing orchestral chords that quickly subside from forte to piano (see 6.14 [a]). The overall conduct of the aria, outlined below,[42] suggests parallels with two earlier monologues by evil baritones—Barnaba's "O monumento!" from act 1 of Ponchielli's *La gioconda* and, especially, Iago's "Credo" from Verdi's *Otello*—through its arrangement into three related sections, the last of which dissolves into the ensuing material. The initial two periods have been designated as "antecedent" and "consequent" below, owing to their similarity and to the relative strengths of their final cadences. The third takes on the function of a *passo di carattere*, providing a degree of contrast for four measures before a new "movement," *sostenuto* (at "Ah! in quell'istante"), marks the point where the final cadential passage and the "transition-out" coincide.

1. Period, antecedent, 9 measures: *motivo*

Già mi strug*gea* (5)	The love of the diva
l'amor della *diva*! (6)	was already consuming me!
Ma poc'anzi ti mir*ai* (8)	But a little while ago I looked upon you
qual non ti vidi *mai*! (7)	as I had never seen you!

2. Period, consequent, 9 measures: *motivo*

Quel tuo pianto era *lava* (7)	That weeping of yours was lava
ai sensi *miei* (5)	to my senses,
e il tuo sguardo che odio in me dardeg*giava*, (11)	and your gaze, which darted hatred at me,
mie brame infero*civa*! (7)	made my desires fierce!

3. Period (dissolving): *passo caratteristico* and *cadenza finale* (incomplete)

Agil qual leo*pardo* (7)	Agile as a leopard
t'avvinghiasti all'*amante*. (7)	you clung to your lover.
Ah! in quell'is*tante* (6)	Ah! At that moment
t'ho giurata *mia*! (6)	I swore you were mine!

From the reduction in 6.14 (b) it is clear that the principal theme follows a stepwise descent through the notes of the tonic scale. Its most distinguishing feature is a melodic substitution of the initial "guiding" tonic note $(g_\flat^1)$ by a rising scale figure at "Già mi struggea" in m. 8, which results in a characteristic leap to a dissonant seventh f^1 in the following measure. The four different meters of the first four lines of verse are accommodated through the simple device of mapping each main inflection onto the strong "movements" of a regular "harmonic rhythm" (*ritmo armonico*), compressing or extending the other syllables as required.

6.14.

a. Puccini, *Tosca,* act 2, R47, mm. 6–15 (Milan: Ricordi, 1900).

b. Analytical reduction.

Bellini, La sonnambula, *act 2, no. 14, "Ah! non credea mirarti"*

To anchor these Puccinian melodies from the 1880s and 1890s within a broader historical context, as well as to show just what could be achieved with a couple of scales, example 6.15 (a) reproduces the melody of the final *cantabile* from Bellini's "The Sleepwalker" (1831). This brief *romanza* has often been taken to represent the quintessence of *bel canto.* Indeed, it has acquired the status of one of the great melodies of the nineteenth century. Opera audiences would dissolve in euphoric transports at its seemingly endless unfolding, their senses heightened by its unworldly delivery from above by the sleepwalking maiden Amina, teetering precariously along a high mill bridge while expressing her grief over the loss of Elvino's love. (He had called off their engagement earlier in the opera after catching her in Count Rodolfo's bed, unaware that she had innocently clambered through the window and nestled under the covers while still fast asleep.)

In a well-known analysis, Carl Dahlhaus attempted to locate the effectiveness of this melody in its irregular meter, which, according to Riemannian norms, appears to shift from downbeat to upbeat, and in its continual allusions to conventional cadence formulas, which remain unfulfilled over long stretches.[43] The seeming complexity of the melody may, alternatively, be understood to result from its origins in *solfeggio* practice. Bellini would have conceived the process of melodic composition as inextricably bound up with the act of expression through singing, in much the same way as his Italian predecessors, including the great eighteenth-century *castrati.* While earlier composers such as Paisiello were often content to leave the vocal parts of their scores incomplete, as mere guides to performance, encompassing little more than simple formulas for singers to vary and embellish through the expressive nuances of the vocal "speech accent" or *accento musicale,* Bellini, following Rossini's lead, notated a finished melody more or less in full. Example 6.15 (b) attempts to remove this essential expressive layer from "Ah! non credea mirarti" and to uncover its underlying framework of guiding scales and cadences and its pattern of "melodic" and "harmonic" rhythms. Given the exceptional beauty of the melody, such an analysis could be regarded as an act of vandalism, destroying everything of value through a reducing-out of what might misleadingly be called "surface" features. But the suggested framework of scales in 6.15 (b) is not intended to represent a deeper level of form or structure for the melody, let alone its "essence." It is an attempt to capture something of the guiding formulas, distilled from many years of *solfeggio* practice, which would have been at the back of the minds of composers/singers when creating melodies such as this. Conventional scales, progressions, and cadences were little more than common foundations for musical creativity. They represented, so to speak, sturdy and dependable tables on which each individual feast was to be laid.

The conduct of the melody is outlined in the table below, with text drawn from the original Ricordi vocal score of ca. 1832. Its two quatrains of *settenari* correspond to the two parts of what Reicha termed a *romanza*, with each part divided in turn into two component periods or phrases. The first part, in A minor, opens with a period functioning as a principal theme (*motivo*, mm. 5–15) and closes with an independent and well-defined cadential period (mm. 15–23), founded upon repetitions of the final lines of the first quatrain and interjections (*pertichini*) from an instantly enlightened and repentant Elvino. After a short modulating link in the orchestra (mm. 23–24)—bland and formulaic enough to elicit special pleading from Dahlhaus as to its hidden motivic connections to the overall "form"—the second part begins in m. 25 in the mediant or relative major key, commonly encountered in such contrasting "characteristic passages" and responding here to Amina's forlorn hope. The *romanza* remains in this closely related key (*modo analogo*) through its highly ornamented cadential phrase (mm. 32–40) to the end. This would in no way have signified incompleteness or a lack of finality. As discussed above in chapter 5, in the Italian traditions musical coherence was considered to reside more in the perceived "rhetorical" integrity of the discourse than in (modern) syntactical concepts such as "tonal closure" and "thematic return."

First Part
First Period, 11 measures: *motivo*

Ah! non credea mirarti	Ah, I didn't believe I would see you
sì presto estinto, o *fiore*;	withered so soon, o flowers.
passasti al par d'*amore*,	you have faded away like love
che un giorno sol durò.	that lasted only a single day.

Second Period, 8 measures: *periodo di cadenza*

(Elvino: Io più non *reggo*.)	(Elvino: I can't bear any more.)
Passasti al par d'amore.	
(Elvino: Più non reggo a tanto *duo*lo.)	(Elvino: I can't bear so much heartache any more.)
Che un giorno sol durò.	

Bridge (*Ponte*), 1 measure

Second Part
Third Period, 16 measures: *passo caratteristico* and *periodo di cadenza*

Potria novel vigore	Perhaps my tears
il pianto mio re*carti* [do*nar*ti (1834 edition)]	will bring you new life,
ma ravvivar l'*amore*	but my tears cannot
il pianto mio non *può*.	revive love.

In accordance with the doctrine of dominant affect, the principal theme (*motivo*) establishes an overall mood and tempo of regret and sadness through an eleven-measure period. Its initial two phrases (or rhythms) in mm. 5–8 encompass the conventional *solfeggio* formula of an ascending scale in third position over a tonic pedal note, adorned in the resulting melody with poignant swooping appoggiaturas upon the words "withered so soon" and with turn figures to emphasize each main verse inflection. Example 6.15 (b) removes these expressive embellishments to reveal the underlying scale, while identifying the melodic rhythms (*ritmi*) with slurs and accents and the harmonic rhythms, following Asioli, with symbols for weak (2.) and strong (1.) rhythmic movements (*movimenti ritmici*).

After these four opening measures, the regularity of the melodic and periodic structure begins to give way to an increasing sense of freedom, resulting in an eleven-measure period that appears to resist interpretation according to modern notions of phrasing and meter derived from German instrumental traditions. Although the third phrase in mm. 8–10 ("Passasti al par d'amore") continues to maintain the established seven-syllable phrase rhythm (*settenario-ritmo*) and thus prolongs the broader "harmonic" meter of one "strong movement" every second measure, the melodic stress placed on "pass*a*sti" in m. 9 of example 6.15 (b) and the repetition of this stress in m. 10 hints strongly at a quickening of the underlying pulse, to a "strong movement" or main verse inflection on every downbeat or bar line. A shorter, five-syllable rhythm does indeed follow in mm. 10–11, as highlighted by the dotted line in example 6.15 (b), but it quickly returns to the initial seven-syllable rhythm in mm. 11–13 for a complete statement of the fourth and final line of verse, before reverting once again in mm. 13–15 to the faster five-syllable rhythm to end the period. Overall, these last five measures of the *motivo* comprise a fluid, extended, *sung* variation upon a latent fourth regular phrase, such as might have been left intact in an exercise, or by a lesser composer, with or without a fermata symbol to indicate the expected embellishment. Upon reaching the poetic crux of the stanza in m. 11 ("love that lasted only a single day"), the melody breaks down into an expressive cascade of fragmentary phrases that supplant an implicit, unsounded, and conventional two-measure closing phrase, which, as conceived, would have conjoined the words "che un giorno sol durò" with a stepwise cadential

6.15.

a. Bellini, *La sonnambula,* act 2, no. 14, "Ah! non credea mirarti" (Milan: Ricordi, 1831; melody only, chord symbols added).

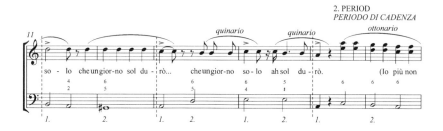

b. (*above and facing*) Analytical reduction.

descent from the high e² of the period to the tonic a¹. In this respect
the opening period of the *romanza* evokes the sound of an improvised
elaboration upon a simple *solfeggio* formula, ascending through a third-
position scale and descending back to the tonic over four regular seven-
syllable phrase-rhythms.

Elvino's response to the unexpected revelation of his former fian-
cée's innocence, in her nightdress in front of the entire village, calls for
a separate period (mm. 15–23). It takes the form of an additional closing
section appended to the principal theme (*motivo*). Its new melody, with
which the oboe captures the moment as Amina's somnolent tears fall

onto the dehydrated bouquet, could perhaps be regarded as a subsidiary idea, or *secondo motivo,* deduced from the principal theme, but its guiding schema, consisting of two scarcely varied statements of the descending tonic scale in first position, is so obviously cadential in function that it is labeled as a *periodo di cadenza* in 6.15 (b). Bellini supported this scale with the simplest possible harmonization: a descending succession of first-inversion triads, otherwise known as the "common organal scale" (see chapter 4). In rhythmic terms, the second period (mm. 15–23) introduces an alternative eight-syllable phrase rhythm (*ottonario-ritmo*), which scans unobtrusively onto the basic "harmonic rhythm" of the original seven-syllable phrase rhythm, as may be seen from Amina's continuations of its descending contour in mm. 17–19 and 21–23. The two rhythmic systems are nevertheless in conflict in this passage, owing to the placement of Amina's main verse inflections ("d'*amore*" and, in theory at least, "*durò*") upon weak beats of the measure that do not coincide with the "strong movement" (*primo movimento*) in the orchestral part (6.15 [b], m. 18 and m. 22). Additional syllables serve to mitigate this discrepancy in the case of the second phrase (m. 22), but it is thrown into relief in the first (m. 18) presumably to underscore the poignancy of the word "love."

The third and final period (mm. 25–40) occupies the second part of the *romanza* and consists of a contrasting "characteristic passage" (*passo caratteristico*, mm. 25–32) and a "cadential period" (*periodo di cadenza*, mm. 32–40), both in the relative key of C major. The cadence that marks the end of the second quatrain (m. 32) seems too understated to be seen as the close of a period, especially in comparison with the emphatic closing descent of the analogous passage in the first part (m. 15). The second part of the *romanza* is therefore divided into two component phrases in example 6.15 (b) rather than two periods.

Melodically, it circles around a simple schema of just three notes, the so-called *do-re-mi*,[44] with an occasional *fa* to assist at cadential points. Like the principal theme, it is based on a straightforward series of four regular, seven-syllable phrases, which establish a "harmonic rhythm" over two measures. Already by the third phrase in mm. 29–30 ("Ma ravvivar l'amore"), however, a sudden increase in harmonic movement prefigures an impending shift to a faster *ritmo,* which is realized in the fragmentary *quinari* of the fourth phrase in mm. 30–32 ("il pianto mio non può"). The ensuing cadential period (mm. 32–40) shifts into an even higher gear as it brings the main inflections forward, in effect syncopating them over a bass motion of the fourth up and fifth down. The final passage comprises repetitions of the "cadence of natural tones," recalling the pages of similar lessons to be repeated over and over by students recorded in Staffa's "Method of the Neapolitan School" (1849) and De Vecchis's "Compendium of Counterpoint of the Ancient and Modern Neapolitan School of Music" (1850, vol. 1). The main inflection is restored to its downbeat position in mm. 35–37, before the final flourish stretches this *ritmo* to its furthest extent.

The most effective way to grasp the process of composition in historical context is to sing or recite (again, to oneself, if preferable) the basic schema in 6.15 (b), feeling the ebb and flow of the melodic *ritmi* and the impassioned, almost obsessive repetitions of the basic cadential pattern, and then to sing or recite the finished melody in 6.15 (a), noting Bellini's masterful expressive fluctuations and embellishments through the musical speech accent (*accento musicale*). It is, however, scarcely feasible for us today to understand and appreciate fully the kind of musical imagination, accustomed since childhood to singing and improvising upon a range of counterpoints and formulas, that was required to create melodies such as this. Tonic scales in third and first positions, the *do-re-mi* schema, conventional cadences—these are merely children's exercises, ultimately meaningless without an understanding of their inseparable relation to practice. The great traditions of Italian opera rested on the art of expressive singing and its ability to move and entertain an audience, in terms of both performance *and composition*. Although this *filosofia,* as it was called, gradually declined over the course of the nineteenth century, to be replaced by an Austro-German Romantic mainstream that shifted the emphasis decisively away from voice to instrument, and from performance toward reverence for the composer and the work, its influence may still be heard as late as the turn of the twentieth century, especially in the melodies of Puccini.

*   *   *

In bringing together and synthesizing the many and varied concepts surveyed in earlier chapters, these final case studies are intended to offer a guide to the informed interpretation—and appreciation—of the music of nineteenth-century Italian opera, in terms that would have been understood by contemporary composers and performers. They set out to demonstrate the significance to the repertory of once commonplace compositional theories and practices, not merely for their historical "authenticity," but also for their effectiveness in elucidating important properties of the music and its relation to poetry and drama. Many of these archaic methods formed part of a European musical mainstream in the eighteenth century, and remained fundamental to Italian and French opera during the nineteenth, yet they have featured fleetingly, if at all, in modern musicological discourse. The Italian theory of dual rhythmic systems, for instance, as outlined by maestros from Gervasoni and Asioli to Staffa and De Sanctis, and as documented in chapter 3, provides a valuable tool for the interpretation of melodies that appear to resist analysis according to modern notions of phrase structure, which, following Hauptmann and Riemann, tend to subsume both the expressive fluctuations of the melodic rhythm and the supporting movements of its harmonic rhythm under an abstract concept of a strict and all-encompassing metrical hierarchy. Bound by such limits, modern approaches leave little scope for an understanding or appreciation of the central place that performance and improvisation occupied in the Italian traditions of composition. As recounted in chapter 4, musical training was, from the earliest lessons, grounded on playing and singing. This radically influenced attitudes and procedures. As Neapolitan maestro De Vecchis observed, "A talented young student should begin, as soon as possible, to shape his Melodies [sung, played, or written] into Phrases and Periods, as required by the nature of the instructional Bass [i.e., regular interval pattern], if he wants to benefit from the study of Counterpoint."[45] From the start, accordingly, units of rhythm, or phrases, were inextricably bound up with practical considerations of harmony and melody. Even if the resulting pattern of *ritmi* was uniform, it would generally be subject to creative distortions and variations through the application of an appropriate "musical accent," in performance both real and imagined. More advanced techniques of harmony and counterpoint were similarly reliant upon expressive departures from underlying formulas, whether played at the keyboard in the form of *partimenti,* sung as *solfeggi,* or written down as *disposizioni.* Italian approaches to expression (or imitation) and conduct, as documented in chapter 5, were also at odds with conventional modern interpretative strategies. They rested on long-established rhetorical metaphors, which were accessible and fully comprehensible only through vague intuitions of coherence drawn from performance as a "thread" of meaning (*il filo*). Modern approaches to musical form, by contrast, generally presuppose the operation of more or less fixed abstract templates and rigid systems of tonal and thematic classification.

An image emerges of a tradition that appears to have more in common with what would now be described as a "popular," rather than a "classical," musical culture—one that was directed toward commercial success, fundamentally reactionary in spite of modish changes of style, and founded upon simple formulas that enabled a close rapport between performers and listeners. But this should in no way be taken to indicate a lack of sophistication and artistic worth. On the contrary, nineteenth-century Italian opera, like the music of the Viennese classics, managed that rare feat of bridging the gap between "high" and "low" art. Its continued appeal to large numbers of musically uneducated listeners, as well as to an élite, serves to remind us of the achievement of the great tradition.

PREFACE & ACKNOWLEDGMENTS

1. Kiesewetter (1834, 96).

2. Ibid., 97. So dominant was opera in the Italian traditions that the cultural clash with Germany was sometimes conceived in terms of *Meyerbeer,* rather than Beethoven, versus Rossini or Bellini. See, for example, the important series of twelve articles in Rovani (1856). Although this book concentrates exclusively on the Italian traditions of the nineteenth century, incidentally, there were, of course, others in addition to the Austro-German, perhaps most notably the French and the Russian. A contemporary account of the three schools (Italian, German, and French) may be found in Anon. [G. N.] (1857a).

3. Wagner (1898, 7:95–96). See also p. 101: "it is more possible for the German, than for anyone else, on foreign soil to bring a national artistic epoch to its highest pitch and universal acceptance." In a later article, written (significantly) during negotiations for the Bayreuth Theater project and entitled *Über die Bestimmung der Oper* (usually translated as On the Destiny of Opera, 1871), he warned against allowing any letup in the struggle for universal German dominance (1896, 5:129–30): "the ruling theatrical element of our day, with all its outward and inward attributes, entirely inartistic,

un-German, both morally and mentally pernicious, invariably gathers again like a choking mist over any spot where the most arduous exertions may have given one for once an outlook on the sunlight." On January 17, 1873, Wagner outlined a ten-point manifesto for the future of "drama" to an invited Berlin audience, which included the following requirements for the composer, as cited in Deathridge (2008, 232–33): "regard German music as victorious over all its rivals" and "create a new kind of drama that appeals not to opera-lovers, but to truly educated persons concerned with the cultivation of a genuine Culture of the German spirit" (*eine originale Kultur des deutschen Geistes*).

4. Josef Danhauser, *Liszt am Flügel* (1840). The image may have been inspired by Nikolaus Lenau's poem *Beethovens Büste* (1838). The identity of the figures was provided in an article entitled "Danhausers neueste Bild," published in the *Wiener Zeitung* of May 13, 1840. A reproduction appears on the front cover of Taruskin (2009b).

5. Brendel (1852, 542–46; 1867, 593–95). In keeping with this interpretation, Brendel automatically dismissed post-Rossinian Italian opera as inferior to contemporary German works (1867, 467). Contrary to a common modern

misconception stemming from Dahlhaus
(1989, 250–52), Liszt featured as a *leading*
member of the latest "Epoch" only from
the third edition (1860) onwards.

6. Hauptmann (1873 [1853], 296).
Hasty (1997, 34–35) summarizes this aspect of Hauptmann's theory. The opposing
Italian point of view was clearly expressed
in an article by Milan-trained composer
and critic Gerolamo Biaggi (1847, 1,
no. 17), which contrasted the regular
meter integral to Haydn's "scientific"
instrumental music with the free melodic
rhythm of Rossini's "artistic" operas.

7. Italian attempts to resist this universalizing tendency of the German tradition were largely ineffectual. Representative examples may be found in Biaggi's
rallying call for young composers (1848),
in Neapolitan maestro Michele Ruta's
"pedagogical notes" (1855, 1856a, 1856b,
1856c, 1876, 1877a, 1877b), in articles by his
colleague Pietro Trisolini (1855a, 1855b),
Anon. (1858b), and in Florentine maestro
Riccardo Gandolfi's polemic against
what he perceived as the leveling effect of
the German tradition on characteristic
national styles (1884, 5, no. 12). Some last
glimmers of resistance may be perceived
in Benzo (1883a, 1883b), Persico (1883a,
1883b, 1883c), and Bovio (1885).

8. As explained more fully in
chapter 1, the new orthodoxy spread
gradually through Italy from north to
south. A sense of crisis and the need to
reform was already evident in Milanese
musical circles by the mid-1840s; see
Perotti (1844), Mayr (1844–45), and
Anon. (1848). This led to a review of the
curriculum at the Conservatory intended
to bring it into line with competing
foreign institutions, such as Leipzig and
Brussels, and in the 1860s to the launch
of the "Futurists" (*Avveniristi*) by Arrigo
Boito and Franco Faccio. A group of
progressives in Florence, led by Abramo
Basevi, established the journal *L'Armonia*

as an "Organ for the Reform of Music in
Italy" in 1856. The last to give way were
the maestros of the Naples Conservatory,
whose increasingly futile arguments,
following the attempted modernization of
the curriculum in 1876, may be sampled in
the journal *La Musica*; see, for instance,
Anon. (1876), Rossi (1877), and Caputo
(1877). Marino (1999) offers an overview
of the reforms.

9. Gossett (2004, 77). For more on
the "continuity draft," see Gossett (2006,
50–52).

1. Santucci (1828, 61), corresponding
in part to Picchianti (1834, 41).

2. Santucci (1828, 61, 72).

3. De Vecchis (1850, 2:43).
De Macchi (ca. 1830, 12).

4. Galli (1902, 444).

1. MUSICAL TRADITIONS IN
NINETEENTH-CENTURY ITALY

1. Martini (1774–75, 2:294).
Martini's student Stanislao Mattei,
teacher of Rossini and Donizetti, traced
the Bolognese tradition specifically to
"Gaffurio" (Franchinus Gaffurius, 1451–
1522) in his manuscript textbook for the
newly founded conservatory in Bologna
(1804, 1).

2. Lichtenthal (1826, 1:364–66).

3. Florimo (1881–83, 1:26–35, 65).

4. A variety of dates have been appended to Furlanetto's name; those given
here derive from Florimo (1881–83, 1:121).

5. Masutto (1882–84, 109). An idea
of what was taught at the "Franciscan"
school of Padre Martini from the mid-
eighteenth century onwards may be
obtained from the numerous volumes of
Lezioni (Lessons), or *Studi di contrappunto
fatti alla scuola del padre Martini* (Studies
in Counterpoint as Carried Out at the
School of Padre Martini), compiled

in the late 1850s by Gaetano Gaspari, professor of *solfeggio* (*vocalizzo*) at the Liceo musicale from 1840 until 1856. They are currently held at the Museo internazionale e Biblioteca della Musica di Bologna (see Pasquini [2007, 151–52]). The pedagogical method was kept alive, practically unaltered, for 150 years. The student exercises of the young Luigi Sabbatini (ms. KK. 1), for instance, dated 1759–61 in the *Lezioni* but most likely completed before 1747, his fifteenth year, correspond very closely to the course of instruction published by Stanislao Mattei (ca. 1824–25) and especially to Michele Puccini's course of practical counterpoint (1846), which formed the cornerstone of training at the Istituto musicale in Lucca until at least the 1870s. Michele Puccini's grandfather, Antonio, studied with Martini in Bologna during the 1760s, and his father, Domenico, studied with Mattei.

6. In this book, "tradition" is used in the conventional sense, as opposed to the "invented tradition" described by Hobsbawm and Ranger (1983, 1–14), which served to legitimize and reinforce a present institution and to maintain the supremacy of its beliefs and value systems.

7. Bianconi and Pestelli (1998, 2002, 2003) offer the best overview of the Italian opera tradition currently available.

8. The attempt, in chapters 3–6 of this book, to reconstruct the teachings that young composers would have received in nineteenth-century Italy builds upon the foundations of previous research on text-setting, the "lyric prototype," and the musical-dramatic conventions (*convenienze teatrali*) that underpinned Italian opera. A representative list of scholars would include the following: Bianca Maria Antolini, William Ashbrook, Scott Balthazar, Julian Budden, Martin Chusid, Marcello Conati, Fabrizio Della Seta, Gabriele Dotto, Andreas Giger, Philip Gossett, Arthur Groos, James

Hepokoski, Steven Huebner, Francesco Izzo, Joseph Kerman, David Kimbell, Jürgen Maehder, Marina Marino, Roberta Montemorra Marvin, Jay Nicolaisen, Giorgio Pagannone, Roger Parker, Giorgio Pestelli, Perluigi Petrobelli, Harold Powers, David Rosen, Peter Ross, Guido Salvetti, Emanuele Senici, Gary Tomlinson, and William Weaver.

9. At the music school in Bologna, these were more specifically designated as *cartellette di contrappunto*. See Lichtenthal (1826, 1:145–46).

10. For information on the Puccini family library, see Burton (1996, 173–86) and Guidotti (1990, 38). Whether or not Puccini had read all of these books, he was certainly aware of their value. During his lean student years he sold off several of the most important volumes and donated the entire collection to the Lucca Conservatory in 1891.

11. On the curriculum of the Neapolitan conservatories at the turn of the eighteenth century, see Di Giacomo (1924, 87–90) and Florimo (1881–83, vol. 1). Valuable insights may also be found in Burney (1773, 311f.).

12. See, for instance, the summary in Ledbetter (2009, 87–91) of bass motions that were standard at the time of J. S. Bach. Dirksen (1997, 328f) offers a useful survey of the main traditions of musical improvisation in Italy and northern Europe during the sixteenth and seventeenth centuries.

13. Gjerdingen (2007b, 88, 126–30).

14. Tomeoni's brother Florido, likewise educated in Naples, became a well-known professor of *bel canto* in Paris during the 1780s, publishing a theory of singing in 1799 that offers a wealth of information on Italian methods of vocal training. As well as informing the discussion of *solfeggi* in chapter 6, Tomeoni (1799) provides early evidence of the Italian origins of some of the teachings that

were later established within the curriculum of the Paris Conservatory.

15. Carpani (1817, 171–77).

16. Gennaro Grossi (1820, 1:8) echoed this assessment of Durante as "the first to succeed in perfecting the grammar of music" (il primo che riuscì perfezionare la grammatica della musica).

17. According to Stella (2007, 182). Sanguinetti (1997, 161) pointed out that the last publication to contain *partimenti* by Fenaroli was De Nardis (1942).

18. Stella (2007) describes some of the innovations of Raimondi and Platania.

19. Manuscripts in the Museo internazionale e biblioteca della musica in Bologna (UU.10 [Olim NN. 251] and NN. 256) show that the teachings published and attributed to Mattei during the 1820s were written down by him in 1788; see Mattei (1788a–b).

20. De Vecchis (1850, 2:31): "I primi Componimenti musicali, che da tutti i Maestri si fanno fare ai Principianti, sono i Solfeggi."

21. Vitali (1850a, 1).

22. Sartori (1959, 69).

23. Biographical information on Asioli is taken from Coli (1834).

24. Vitali (1850a, 5): "Osservando le opere de' compositori, si vede infatti che niuna unità d'intento servi loro di guida. Come fu già altrove osservato, ora la melodia primeggia sull'armonia, ora l'armonia sulla melodia; ora si studia d'esprimere gli affetti, ora non si cerca che il diletto de' sensi; ora il canto governa l'accompagnamento, ora l'accompagnamento inceppa ed abbatte il canto; ora il recitativo compone quasi tutta un' opera, ora è quasi un fuori-d'-opera che cede tutto il campo al cantabile; ora le immagini son grette, ora son prolisse in guisa che non si può fuggire da un senso di noja."

Vitali's invective against Asioli was the product of a long and unsuccessful campaign to market a new system for designating rhythmic tempos. According to one of his articles in the *Gazzetta musicale di Milano* (1844a), the system was endorsed by no less a figure than Verdi. This claim was, however, completely false, as may be seen from a letter of May 20, 1844, by Verdi's student Emanuele Muzio, recounting the incident (Garibaldi 1931, 159).

25. According to Wedell (1995, 57).

26. Anon. (1835, 115). Further biographical information on Choron can be found in Simms (1971).

27. According to Montemorra Marvin (1997, 395).

28. Lichtenthal began his new career in music with an extraordinary book entitled *Der musikalische Arzt* (The Musical Doctor, 1807), which prefigured many of the concerns of modern research into music and/or health. It not only provided case studies (often offensively personal) to support the claim that music could help to cure a number of ailments, including "stupidity" and "nymphomania" (pp. 142–44), but also investigated the effects of music on various animal species (pp. 105f).

29. See De LaFage (1845).

30. Berlioz (1990 [1865], 138).

31. The following survey of musical periodicals owes a great deal to the thorough introductions provided online for the *Retrospective Index to Music Periodicals* (www.ripm.org) by Marco Capra, Marcello Conati, Luke Jensen, and Marina Marino.

32. In *L'Italia musicale*, see Anon. (1848), "On Music in Germany," Anon. (1851a), "Polemic," Anon. (1851b), "On Lyric Drama," Anon. (1851c), "Is Art Dead?" Anon. (1853a), "A Question and a Wish," and Anon. (1853c), a series of eleven articles "On Music in Germany."

33. The Florentine progressives included Melchiorre Balbi, descendent of a noble Venetian family who abandoned studies in mathematics to take up music, becoming in 1854 *maestro di cappella* (and noted composer of sacred music) at the Basilica

di San Antonio in Padua; Abramo Basevi, "doctor of medicine in Florence; philosophical writer and amateur of music, he is the author of two operas, which premiered . . . without success" (Fétis 1866–75, 1:261–62); Luigi Ferdinando Casamorata, a Bolognese "lawyer, composer, and distinguished writer on music" (Fétis 1866–75, 2:200); Carlo Andrea Gambini, composer and professor of piano at the school of music; Baldassare Gamucci, a scholar of literature and philosophy who turned to composition and music criticism following a course of lessons with Picchianti; Olimpio Mariotti, professor of singing at the school of music and composer of *operette* (Masutto 1882–84, 107); Ermanno Picchi, director of the school of music; and Luigi Picchianti, a guitar virtuoso who toured Europe from 1821 to 1825 before taking up the chair in harmony and counterpoint at the school of music, later accepting the chair in history and aesthetics of art (*Gazzetta musicale di Firenze*, 11 October 1855; Masutto 1882–84, 141). By 1855 Basevi had effectively taken over as leader of the group, founding and editing its journal, *L'Armonia*.

34. According to Basevi himself (1862, 8). Sanguinetti (1997, 163–69) points out that Fétis also provided the basis for the harmonic teaching of Alberto Mazzucato and his student Amintore Galli.

35. Basevi (1862, 62–74).

36. Sessa (2003, 420).

37. Wilson (2007, 2).

38. Ibid., 7. In fairness, it should be noted that Wilson's study succeeds admirably in its aims without the need for any additional notes on the prehistory of Puccini's musical language. The observation relates to a *general* avoidance of detail on the Italian tradition in recent Puccini scholarship.

39. It is interesting to note, however, that Puccini, contrary to the modernist aesthetic, always placed great importance

on the audience's reaction to avant-garde works. On Stravinsky's *Le Sacre du Printemps,* for instance, which he saw in Paris in 1913, he had the following to say (Adami 1982 [1928], 153): "I was at the *Sacré de Printemps* [*sic*]: ridiculous choreography. The music a cacophony in the extreme. Curious, however, and done with a certain talent. But altogether sheer madness. The public booed, laughed, and . . . applauded."

40. Although born and raised in Bavaria, Mayr spent his entire working life as a composer and pedagogue in northern Italy. He represented the end of a long line of German composers who traveled to study with Italian maestros. Following formal education in Ingolstadt, the twenty-six-year-old Mayr began lessons with Carlo Lenzi in Bergamo before moving to Venice to study with Ferdinando Bertoni, *maestro di cappella* at San Marco. In 1794 he produced *Saffo,* the first in a series of successful operas. His main interest lay, however, in establishing a charitable school of music for the benefit of young musicians in his adopted town of Bergamo. In his notebook he claimed to have written operas only for money (Mayr 1977 [1840s], 10). From 1805, as director and principal professor, he compiled a large body of teaching materials for the school, and he appears to have taken a keen interest in musical developments beyond the Alps. Donizetti studied under Mayr from 1806 to 1815 and again, after a time in Bologna with Padre Mattei, from 1819 to 1821.

41. Sanguinetti (1997, 169) describes the Accademia dell'Istituto musicale di Firenze as "the most important *forum* for music theory in Italy" from 1865 to around 1883.

42. Antolini (ed., 1999) offers a comprehensive overview of musical life in Milan 1861–97. A justification and summary of the reforms, citing the importance of the German tradition from Beethoven to

Wagner and the need to bring the Conservatory into line with foreign competitors, was published by lawyer and music critic Filippo Filippi in the *Gazzetta musicale di Milano* (1860). In the next issue, Basevi published a very similar article on the need to reform the school of music in Florence. The Naples Conservatory gave in to the pressure to restructure the curriculum only in 1876: see Anon. (1876), Rossi (1877), and Caputo (1877).

43. See Crotti and Ricorda (1997 [1910], 1534–39). The operas were Faccio's *I profughi fiamminghi* (1863, to a libretto by Emilio Praga) and *Amleto* (1865, to a libretto by Boito), and Boito's *Mefistofele* (1868, to his own libretto). Praga and Boito together founded *Il Figaro* in January 1864.

44. From a review of Verdi's *I vespri siciliani* published in *Il Figaro*, February 11, 1864 (Boito [1942, 1119]). For more on Boito's reforms, see Ashbrook (1988). Conati and Medici (1994, xiii–lv) provide a useful chronological overview of the activities of the Avveniristi.

45. Although Girardi accepts this marginal sketch at face value as evidence of Puccini's Wagnerian sympathies and tendencies, this is not the only plausible interpretation. The sketch, which features in no known work by either Puccini or Wagner, presents a crude parallel progression ineffectively disguised by, or simplistically revealed as, a chromatic passing note. In this context, could "alla Wagner" suggest mockery rather than respect and emulation? Could Puccini not have sketched something more sophisticated or meaningful as worthy of the Meister's name?

46. See, for instance, Nicolaisen (1977) or Budden (1992 [1981], 263–92).

47. Basevi (1859a, 109).

48. "Giacomo Puccini: Questo grande musicista nacque a Lucca l'anno . . . e puossi ben dire il vero successore del cele-

bre Boccherini. Di bella persona e di intelletto vastissimo portò in campo dell'arte italiana il soffio di una potenza quasi eco dell'oltralpica Wagneriana."

49. Lamperti (1891, 24).

50. Reported in the *Neue Zeitschrift für Musik* 79 (1912): 241; as cited in Deathridge (2008, 234).

2. STUDIES IN LUCCA AND MILAN

1. Rosselli (1984) and (1998) provide comprehensive overviews of the opera industry.

2. Surian (1983) was among the first to raise this point. See also Della Seta (1998).

3. Hegel (1998 [1806], 2:1236).

4. Elias (2000, 6).

5. Berlioz (1990 [1865], 158–60). For an earlier discussion (and defense) of similar Italian attitudes toward music, see the extract from Giuseppe Baretti's *An Account of the Customs and Manners of Italy* (1768) in Fubini (1994, 214–16)

6. S. Puccini (1994, 3–38) provides a detailed overview of the musical dynasty.

7. According to the biographical notice of Albina Puccini (née Magi) written, at Puccini's request, by his sister Ramelde for the magazine *La Scena Illustrata* in 1906; see S. Puccini (1994, 9–11).

8. De Napoli (1936, 11).

9. Zurletti (1982, 13).

10. Surian (1998, 303–304).

11. Little is known of Puccini's life in Lucca prior to his move to Milan. Schickling (1989) gives the most carefully researched account, drawing upon sources such as Baggiani (1982), Bonaccorsi (1950 and 1967), Damerini (1942), Del Fiorentino (1952), Giovannetti (1958), and Landucci (1905).

12. According to Del Fiorentino (1952, 9–10), one of Puccini's teachers at the Seminario scribbled the following marginal note on his educational record:

"He comes to school only to wear out the seat of his pants. He pays no attention to anything and keeps tapping on his desk as though it were a keyboard. He never reads a book."

13. Carlo Giorgi was an outstanding student at the Istituto during the early 1860s, winning first prizes for counterpoint, practical harmony, and cello; see Pacini (1875, 177).

14. Verdi to Francesco Florimo, letter of January 4, 1871; translation from Osborne (1971, 168). Verdi's esteem for the Neapolitan tradition is documented in letters of January and February 1871 to Cesare De Sanctis, Francesco Florimo, and Cesare Correnti. He described Durante and Leo as the founders of the tradition, included Martini in Bologna and Cherubini in Paris as members, and made special mention of the teachings of Fenaroli, "who left his *partimenti* now adapted by everyone." See Luzio (1935–47, 3:66–70).

15. As reported by Fétis and quoted in Gjerdingen (2007a, 370).

16. Garibaldi (1931, 160–61); letter of May 29, 1844: "Ho terminato i libri d'armonia del Fenaroli. Adesso faccio la ripetizione generale.... Egli non vuole che vi siano due quinte od ottave implicite di seguito (bene intesi che le scoperte sono scomunicate), che tutte le parti siano come una scala senza mai un salto; che non ascendano mai tutte assieme per moto retto; e che tutte le stesse parti, in qualunque chiave siano non passino questa nota: ... le condizioni sono poche, ma il difficile stava nel metterle in esecuzione. ... Adesso sono ad un altro studio avendo finito anche le melodie sulla scala; ed invece metto otto parti tutte consonanti sotto una sola nota della scala; e poi una nota contro una, due contro una, ecc.; questo è propriamente Contrappunto."

17. Garibaldi (1931, 168); letter of 24 June 1844: "Sono già arrivato alla famosa opera Quinta del Corelli, la più bella, diffi-

cile e lunga. Questa mattina ho cominciato le imitazioni; il signor Maestro adopera gli stessi ch'Egli fece sotto la direzione di Lavigna, migliorati però da Lui."

18. See Holtmeier (2007, 9–10).

19. Schickling (2003, 406).

20. See Cerù (1871, 31). Additional historical information on musical life in Lucca may be found in "Avvocato A. G." (1844); Nerici (1879); Landucci (1905); Damerini (1942), one of a series commissioned by the Mussolini government to celebrate the Italian conservatories; Bonaccorsi (1950) and (1967); and Battelli (1990). In 1818, incidentally, the Royal Luisa Carlotta Conservatory in Lucca also drew up new regulations for the education of orphans in fields other than music.

21. Antonio Puccini's "Repertorio di musica del Puccini" of 1818 is currently held in the Biblioteca dell'Istituto Musicale Luigi Boccherini, Fondo Puccini O.IV.14. It is discussed in Guidotti (1990, 38) and Burton (1996).

22. See Burton (1996, 175).

23. According to Cerù (1871, 32) and Nerici (1879, 64–66).

24. For instance, by Colombani (1900, 155–60) and Sessa (2003, 350–51).

25. Pacini (1865, 82); (1875, 69): "Principiai a conoscere ch'io doveva ritirarmi dalla palestra.—Bellini, il divino Bellini, e Donizetti mi avevano sorpassato."

26. See Pacini (1864). Michele Puccini is often mentioned in exceptionally glowing terms in Pacini's memoirs.

27. Pacini (1834, 18–19): "P. Maestro Mattei allievo del celebre P. Maestro Martini, un Furlanetto allievo del gran Valotti, un Minoja, Asioli, Basili, Santucci, Raimondi, Quilici, i quale come custodi del sacro fuoco transmetterano ai posteri le vere traccie da seguirsi della Musica ecclesiastica."

28. The following summary is taken from Pacini (1834, 17–20).

29. Lichtenthal (1826, 1:363).

30. Biographical notes on the most important musicians in Lucca up to 1870 may be found in Cerù (1871, 39f.). The note on Santucci appears on pp. 76–78.

31. Quoted in Cafiero (2007, 142).

32. Santucci (1828, 76).

33. Ibid., 5.

34. This list is taken from Nerici (1879, 67). Pacini's faulty recollection of the founding faculty in his 1875 memoirs (75) names an Alessandro (not Giuseppe) Rustici and includes Michele Puccini and an unidentifiable Rodolfi. Eugenio Galli was at that time *maestro di camera e cappella* for Prince Carlo Lodovico, Duke of Lucca.

35. Nerici (1879, 69).

36. As quoted in Nerici (1879, 70–71): "Il professore di composizione dà il suo corso in un anno, e tratta dell'accento musicale, della frase a confronto dei diversi metri poetici, della periodologia, della natura della voca umana, del modo di comporre le arie, i duetti, i terzetti ed altri pezzi concertati, e dell'uso dei cori "

37. Cerù (1871, 32–34): "meglio si è riescito a scrivere dai nostril Maestri in questi ultimi tempi."

38. Nerici (1872, 41): "E qui finisco sperando di aver dimonstrato colla storia alla mano, che l'arte musica bellissima tra le arti, è nata in Italia insiem colla Chiesa, cresciuta ed allevata dalla Chiesa, finchè divenuta adulta, ha fato il giro del mondo portando il canto ed il nome Italiano alle straniere genti."

39. Holtmeier (2007, 16).

40. Sanguinetti (2007, 56).

41. In the section entitled "General study of practical and theoretical counterpoint," Sala (1794, 2v–3r) began "the Practice" (*la Pratica*), i.e., sung or at the keyboard, with the G major cadences that were to resurface in M. Puccini (1846, 1).

42. Sanguinetti (2007, 57).

43. Tartini (1754, 118). As will be explained more fully in chapter 4, the perfect and plagal cadences in the bass were known respectively as *cadenza armonica* and *cadenza aritmetica*.

44. Staffa (1849, 4, 24–35).

45. As recorded by Zingarelli's student De Vecchis (1850, 1: 24–26, 53): "The Bass that should be used for the first lesson of Counterpoint should be that given to us by nature. This Bass is included in the Mixed Cadence." (Il Basso che deve adoprarsi nella prima lezione di Contrappunto, deve essere quello che ci dà la natura; questo Basso è compreso nella Cadenza Mista.) Zingarelli's method began with a variety of counterpoints over what would now be described as a IV–V–I bass, in two, three, and four parts, before progressing to similar counterpoints over scales and "leaps" (*salti*).

46. Fenaroli (1775, 16): "Si nota, che la quarta si può anche preparare dalla settima minore, e dalla quinta falsa. Per preparare la quarta dalla settima minore, il Partimento deve salir di quarta; cioè dalla quinta del tono alla prima di esso." According to Staffa (1849, 24), the suspended seventh was explicitly associated with Fenaroli.

47. Ibid., 19: "La nona si può preparare dalla terza, e dalla quinta. . . . Per prepararla dalla quinta, il Partimento deve salir di quarta, o scendere di quinta."

48. Antolini (ed., 1999) offers a detailed overview of musical life in the city at that time.

49. Historical information on the Milan Conservatory is taken primarily from Melzi (1878), Corio (1908), Mompellio (1941), and Salvetti (2003a).

50. See Mompellio (1941, 42–43).

51. In 1898 the new director, Giuseppe Gallignani, shortened the composition course to six years, within which were three separate three-year modules in harmony, counterpoint and fugue, and composition (see Mompellio 1941, 52). According to Gallarani (1999), five or six

students graduated each year in composition from the Milan Conservatory during the 1880s.

52. As evidence, see Puccini's mother's anxious correspondence with his professors: Bazzini, quoted in Budden (2002, 24–25), and Ponchielli, in Marchetti (1968, plates 24–25).

53. Schickling (2003, 107). The fugue subject appears in M. Puccini (1846, 74).

3. LESSONS IN DRAMATIC COMPOSITION I: RHYTHM

1. Hasty (1997, 3–21) theorizes the essential opposition of rhythm, in its various guises, and regular meter.

2. Anon. (1852–53, 5, no. 2: 7): "Il ritmo è il legame che unisce così strettamente la musica alla poesia, giacchè l'armonia de' versi, dipende dal ritmo, che in ultima analisi non differisce dal ritmo musicale. . . . La *misura* segna le relazioni del ritmo col tempo, il quale la racchiude essenzialmente; non sempre però secondo l'assoluto rigore della regola a cui la sottomette il nostro sistema musicale." This article was appended to a series of nine; its author was probably Alberto Mazzucato, professor at the Milan Conservatory.

3. Anon. (1854a, 261): "La melodia e il ritmo sono dunque strettamente uniti. Quella è il senso sviluppato da una successione di suoni; questo è la forma e le proporzioni di quella successione. La melodia è il principio vitale, è l'anima della musica; il ritmo ne è la respirazione. . . . Alcuni [trattati musicali] lo confusero colla *battuta,* e giunsero persino a dire, che la battuta ha generato il ritmo;—non riflettendo che il ritmo è un elemento essenziale, primordiale, anteriore a tutti i sistemi. La battuta non è che un principio materiale, il quale risulta da certe divisioni metriche e razionali del tempo, che si modificano a norma dei gradi di lentezza o di rapidità; essa non è che un elemento

convenzionale, e sta alla musica, come le leggi della versificazione stanno alla poesia. È però a dirsi, che la battuta oggi è così inerente col nostro sistema musicale che vi appare appunto coll'importanza di un elemento essenziale. La melodia sgorga della fantasia del compositore, informata nella battuta, adagiata nelle sue forme, assoggettata alla successione alterna dei tempi forti e deboli. Ma ciò non vuol dire che la melodia non possa momentaneamente sottrarsi a questo gioco."

4. Anon. [Michele Ruta?] (1883, 4, no. 10: 2): "Il *ritmo,* battuto nell'accompagnamento in passato con uniforme insistenza, arrecava meno danno all'opera d'arte di quello che arreca il confuso abuso di complicazioni inconsulte. Quello, quantunque monotono e triviale, rendeva libera la melodia, la quale sorvolava leggiera e dominava su tutto, incatenandola solamente alle naturali leggi della *tonalità,* dell'*armonia* e del *ritmo.*"

5. Maehder (1988) deals with some of these issues in regard to the setting of prose-like texts in what he calls Italian *Literaturopern* at the turn of the twentieth century. Contemporary analytical demonstrations of the two rhythmic systems of Italian opera occur in Asioli (1832), Mampieri (1840, 57–60 and *Tavola XV*), De Vecchis (1850, 2:2–6), and Staffa (1856, 7–9).

6. See, for instance, Martini (1757), Sacchi (1770, 59–113, 120), Venini (1798, 68–140), Bonesi (1806), or Baini (1820, 2–3). Anon. [Michele Ruta?] (1883, 4, no. 4: 2) provides an overview of the debate as it was perceived in late nineteenth-century Naples, while Houle (2000, 62–77) offers a clear summary of theoretical writings. The best account of the importance of supposed ancient models to Italian opera may be found in the opening chapter of Maguire (1989).

7. Lichtenthal (1826, 1:311): "Ne' tempi antichi, allorchè la musica era ancora semplicissima e destinata solo al Canto, il ritmo musicale regolavasi esattamente dietro il ritmo de' versi cantati. Tutte le sillabe erano o lunghe o brevi. Una sillaba lunga durava il doppio di una breve; dall'unione di più sillabe lunghe o brevi formavansi i piedi musicali, e dall'unione di questi il ritmo."

Earlier eighteenth-century German theorists commonly defined meter in terms of successions of poetic feet; see Mattheson (1739, chap. 6), Marpurg (1759, 166–88), and Hiller (2001, 67). Koch (1983 [1787], 66–78) gave a full account of verse feet and their relation to settings of German poetry.

8. Fabbri (2003, 153).

9. Choron (1808, 6:4).

10. See Arteaga (1783, 1785, 1788) and Manfredini (1788).

11. Sacchi (1770, 114–25).

12. Although some of his ideas resurfaced in the *Ammaestramenti* (1841) of aristocratic amateur, theater critic, and town mayor Carlo Ritorni, Baini (1820) effectively marked the end of theoretical attempts to define contemporary Italian rhythmic practice through ancient Greek notions of *ritmopoeia*. Many antiquated ideas continued nevertheless to influence writers on music. Asioli and others, for instance, persisted in assigning exactly twice the rhythmic value to accented syllables as to unaccented, in a manner reminiscent of the theories of Jean-Antoine de Baïf and the group of poets known as the Pléiade during the 1580s, who sought to apply the quantitative meters of Greek and Latin poetry to the French language and to generate from this *musique mesurée à l'antique*. Similar notions could potentially be traced as far back as the "modal rhythm" and *ordo* of the thirteenth-century Notre Dame school.

13. The assumed correspondence of regular pulse with repetitions of poetic feet was nevertheless maintained. According to the definition of meter in Pietro Lichtenthal's dictionary (1826, 2:37), "the verse-feet correspond in a certain way to the musical beat, and for this reason a measure is often described by a musical foot" (il piede del verso corrisponde in certo modo alla Battuta musicale, ed è perciò che sovente si dà il nome di piede musicale ad una Battuta).

14. Galli (1902, 385) on *ritmo*: "un ordine estetico nella successione dei valori (figure) musicali, il quale si riproduce identicamente, o similmente, una o più volte. Vi ha l'accento ritmico, che si riproduce isocronamente, e vi ha il disegno ritmico, che è quello di cui parliamo." Galli (1900, 109f.) expanded upon this definition in a discussion of meter and musical rhythm.

15. Galli (1902, 294) on *misura*: "La respirazione è il prototipo della misura musicale e la generatrice del ritmo, constando di due istanti fisiologici: l'inspirazione e la espirazione, la *thesis* (accento forte) e l'*arsis* (accento debole), il *battere* e il *levare* della misura musicale."

16. Hiller (2001, 46–47).

17. Even in cases where composers drafted melodies prior to the text, as for instance in the sketches for act 1 of Verdi's *La Traviata,* there is ample evidence to suggest that they were still conceived in terms of words and verses. See Della Seta (2000) and Gossett (2006, 371–74). The drafting and versification of the text for an opera was to a greater or lesser extent a process of collaboration between librettist and composer, because minute details of the wording and the selection of verse types would have a significant impact on numerous aspects of the musical setting.

18. Galli (1902, 10): "preferenza che si dà a certe note della melodia; inflessione della voce; modo di eseguire un pezzo di musica secondo il quale esso acquista o

perde di effetto. È, in tal caso, sinonimo di espressione." Lichtenthal (1826, 1:6) distinguished three types of accent in music, none of which related to rhythmic emphasis: "the *grammatical,* the *oratorical,* and the *pathetic*" (nella musica l'accento è di tre sorte: *grammatico, oratorio, e patetico*). The same teachings were reproduced in De Vecchis (1850, 2:37).

19. De Macchi (ca. 1830, 24): "D: Che intendesi per *Accento musicale?*

R: S'intende il *Ritmo* che regola l'intiera frase o periodo; le *diverse parti* di un periodo regulate dai tempi forti o deboli della misura; l'*accrescare* e *diminuire* di forza; il *legare* o *scogliere;* il rallentare ed accelerare; il forte e piano, in fine tutto ciò che può dar colore alla *frase.*" The passage was paraphrased from Asioli (1824, 52).

20. Pacini (1834, 28): "*L'Accento* secondo il comune sentimento, e per dir meglio in natura, non è altro che una modificazione della voce nel tempo in cui deve tenersi nel tuono conveniente, nell'avvertanza alle sillabe, alle parole, al sentimento, con il quale è composto un periodo, un discorso, perciò considerar si devono tre cose. Primo, qual suono convenga alla sillaba, se grave, se acuto, se breve, o lungo. Secondo, qual relazione ha la parola con quelle che la seguono per legarne o staccarne il senso. Terzo, quale espressione convenga a qual sentimento, che dal periodo unito è spiegato, se è patetico, se è grave, se è allegro, se è d'ira, se è di timore, od altro." Lo Basso (1855) offers further details on *accento.*

21. See Maehder (1988) and Fabbri (2003, 204–14). Giger's 2008 account of the influence of French prosody on Verdi's style is exemplary. Budden (1987) makes the case that Puccini was "Wagner's best Italian pupil."

22. Galeazzi (1791, 91).

23. See Moreen (1975, 38–46).

24. Anon. (1854a, 262): "Le modificazioni e le anomalie introdotte nella battuta dal ritmo non sono rare. Le pause, le sospensioni, i riposi, gli *accelerando* ed i *ritardando,* a cui ricorrono tante frequentemente e compositori ed esecutori, ne sono prove incontrovvertibili. Le esperienze hanno dimostrato che l'esecuzione d'un pezzo musicale a rigore di metronomo è impossibile. E ciò avviene perché il ritmo ha la sua ragione nella melodia, della quale manifesta il movimento.

Il ritmo appartiene a tutte le arti che hanno per principio il movimento. V'ha ritmo tanto nella prosa come nel verso; tanto nella musica misurata, come nel canto-fermo; v'ha ritmo nella voce, nel gesto, nel periodo dell'oratore e dell'attore, come nella strofa del poeta, come ne' passi della danzatrice."

25. Maguire (1989) argues convincingly that the art of singing was largely understood as an expressive mode of poetic recitation in the Italian traditions of the *primo Ottocento,* with significant consequences for the composition of vocal melody. On p. 57 he notes that the verb "to speak" (*dire*) was commonly substituted for the verb "to sing" (*cantare*).

26. Giuseppe Giacosa, "Verdi e il *Falstaff,*" *Vita Moderna* 2, February 12, 1893, 50–52; quoted in Conati (1984, 161).

27. Puccini would have been well aware of this. The professor of poetic and dramatic literature at Milan from 1877 to 1911, Lodovico Corio, was working on his seminal study of Metastasio (1882) at the very time that Puccini was attending his classes.

28. See Algarotti (1763), Sacchi (1770, 161), and Planelli (1981 [1772], 75–77).

29. Fabbri (2003, 201).

30. See, for instance, Ruta (1884, 1): "The art of writing and arranging phrases is called *fraseologica* [sic; more often *fraseologia*] or the art of phrasing; for this reason a well-phrased piece is called that which unfolds according to the art of *fraseologica.*" (L'arte di scrivere e disporre

le frasi si chiama arte fraseologica o arte del fraseggiare, perciò si dice un pezzo ben fraseggiato quello che si svolge secondo l'arte fraseologica.)

31. Petrobelli (1994, ix), translated by Roger Parker. A more detailed account may be found in Beltrami (1996). A contemporary overview of the main verse types, similar to Petrobelli's but including a two-syllable line (*dissillabo*), occurs in De Vecchis (1850, 2:43–47). See also Venini (1798, 140–56).

32. Throughout this book, *italics* are used to identify accented syllables.

33. Moreen (1975, 9–26) gives more thorough explanations of these details of versification.

34. Asioli (1832, 3:39). Similar guidelines can be found in Tartini (1754, 138–41) and Arteaga (1785, 31).

35. Lippmann (1973–75) and Moreen (1975) agree on this point. Webster (1991, 137) arrives at a similar conclusion with regard to Mozart's operas.

36. De Vecchis (1850, 2:54–56) describes this method for assigning words to *ritmi* or *frasi melodiche*.

37. Cattaneo (1844b). Responses were printed by Boucheron (1844) and Balbi (1845b).

38. Ruta (1884, 1): "Sotto l'aspetto melodico la frase fa l'ufficio del verso nella poesia, essa quindi non ha una durata determinata, può essere di un inciso il quale si può prolungare per una battuta, per due o più; ma le più comuni sono quelle che si svolgono in una prima battuta per riposarsi nella seconda.

Si considera sotto l'aspetto armonico nelle cadenze o semi-cadenze che servono, di moto e riposo alla frase medesima. Sotto l'aspetto estetico la frase è l'espressione di quel bello ideale il quale nello svolgersi e riprodursi dipinge i sentimenti informatori di una data melodia."

39. Many studies of Italian opera have built upon the rhythmic theories set out in the pioneering work of Lippmann (1969c and 1973–75) and Moreen (1975); too many to acknowledge here. With the notable exception of Giger (2008), which offers an excellent outline of conventional Italian versification in its discussion of the influence of French prosody upon Verdi's melodic style, most have not been occupied with placing these theories in the context of a broader range of primary sources.

40. The caesura (*cesura*) as applied to the operatic phrase was not an arbitrary "rest," but was intricately bound up with issues of poetic meter. For summaries, see Lichtenthal (1826, 1:156) and De Vecchis (1850, 2:3–5).

41. Instances where the main accent of a *ritmo* falls on the middle of a measure, as opposed to its first "downbeat," may be found later in this book in Examples 3.18, 5.5, 5.9, 6.5, 6.9, and 6.15.

42. Lippmann (1986 [1973–75], 276f.).

43. Moreen (1975, 38–46).

44. R = Rehearsal Number.

45. From a letter to Verdi of January 14, 1881, quoted in Busch (1988, 62–63). Boito presumably hadn't heard "Casta Diva" from Bellini's *Norma* for a while (see Example 3.17).

46. Lippmann (1986 [1973–75], 188, 231) discusses variants of this rhythmic-musical type.

47. Picchianti (1834, 145).

48. The clearest explanation of the terms *progressio harmonica* and *progressio arithmetica*, as they relate to Italian music theory of the eighteenth and nineteenth centuries, may be found in Martini (1767, 3–9).

49. Huebner (1992, 127). The "lyric prototype" is discussed in detail in chapter 5.

50. Koch (1983, 110). Although Koch uses the term "phrase" to indicate longer units, usually of four or more measures, as opposed to the shorter melodic units he calls "incises," the essence of the argument stands. Riepel (1752–68, 2:44)

makes it a cardinal rule that there cannot be two consecutive phrases ending with the same harmony.

51. Moreen (1975, 54) also concludes that tonal closure is not a major factor in defining rhetorically unified passages in Verdi's operas.

52. Puccini applied the same principle conspicuously to the melodic exercise he was required to complete in the entrance exam for the Milan Conservatory. See his letter to his mother of November 1880 in Gara (1958, 1).

53. Basevi (1859a, 108–109), translation adapted from Parker (1997, 48): "Ed a questo proposito vuolsi avvertire, che il ritmo costituisce sì gran parte della melodia, che non è secondo la giustizia, il dare il nome di scrittore *originale* a colui che, sopra ritmi vecchissimi, cangiando le note, formi *motivi* nuovi. La tanto vantata *facilità* di molte *arie* italiane deriva in gran parte dalla vecchiezza dei ritmi."

54. Basevi (1859a, 109): "Volete voi la ricetta per comporre *melodie* facilissime ed orecchiabili? Prendete un ritmo vecchio, tra i più chiari. Per adattarvi le nuove note non fa bisogno di troppa fatica; imperciocchè, quanto a trovare una grata successione, vi sono delle regole quasi fisse, come quella che raccomanda i salti di 4° salendo, di 6ª maggiore, di 3ª, di 5ª scendendo ec. ec; quanto alla condotta o alla *forma* del pezzo, seguite pure, come su d'una falsariga, quella già in voga, senza darvi briga d'introdurvi veruna modificazione; quanto poi alle armonie, avete quelle del *tuono* in cui è il pezzo, ed ove vogliate fare altre modulazioni grate, vi sono le opportune regole. È in questa guisa che vengon creati molti pezzi di musica i quali usurpano il nome di *nuovi*."

55. Lippmann (1986 [1973–75], 121–25).

56. Kirnberger (1982 [1771–79], 375). Hasty (1997, 22–33) provides overviews of the rhythmic theories of Kirnberger and Koch.

57. Kirnberger (1982 [1771–79], 403–13).

58. Ibid., 404.

59. Ibid., 408.

60. Ibid., 413.

61. Koch (1793, 13n.).

62. Galeazzi (1791, 32).

63. Gervasoni (1800, 430–32). Recounted in Lichtenthal (1826, 1:283) and explained more fully in De Vecchis (1850, 2:3).

64. See Moreen (1975, 38–46).

65. Choron (1808, 6:2).

66. Ibid., 6:4: "L'intonation et le Rhythme combinés donnent naissance à la phrase, à la période, au discours musicale."

67. Ibid., 6:4: "Chacun de ces sons est, ainsi que je viens de le dire, est une vraie syllabe musicale."

68. Ibid., 6:12–13.

69. Ibid., 6:13: "La seule règle qu'il y ait à donner sur cette matière est, que le repos de la phrase musicale correspondent à ceux de la phrase oratoire; que le sens de la première soit suspendu, lorsque celui de la seconde est suspendu. Et qu'il se termine, quand celui de l'autre est terminé."

70. Ibid., 6:5.

71. Ibid.: "J'observerai cependant que la période musicale a des rapports marqués avec la strophe poëtique qui se compose de vers de différentes mésures, mais disposés semblablement: que cette symétrie, cette ordonnance régulière, sans être des conditions nécessaires de sa structure, sont de nouveaux agréments, et de nouveaux moyens d'effet. Les divers membres de la période sont composés de repos plus ou moins parfait. Ces repos se font toujours au temps fort."

72. See Caplin (1998, 9–58).

73. Momigny (1823, 87).

74. Ibid., 50, 75.

75. Baini (1820, 5): "Si rassomigliano nel numero, nella proporzione, nella simmetria, nella continuazione indefinita dei

ritorni eguali degli accenti musicali e poetici, nella ripetizione uniforme dei piedi
somiglievoli proporzionati alla ripetizione
uniforme delle musicali battute."

76. Santucci (1828, 63): "Può la misura
esser ben anche considerata rapporto alla
natura della lingua, cui si adatta la musica,
e segnatamente rapporto a quella proprietà comune a tutte, che chiamasi prosodia.
È necessario pertanto che la misura rilevi
con esattezza la quantità delle sillabe brevi
e lunghe, onde la pronunzia delle parole
sia tale, qual debb'essere; nè si senta quello sconcio, non sì raro a' di nostri, per cui
le sillabe lunghe si fanno brevi, e brevi le
lunghe."

77. Ibid.: "Consideriamo adunque la
misura sotto l'aspetto del ritmo. Il ritmo
nella musica altro egli non è che un certo
ordine nella succession de' suoni. L'idea
pertanto che può darsi del ritmo ella è
questa: ei fa in essa quello che la misura
de' versi nella poesia."

78. Reicha's reputation as an authority
on music theory rested on his studies with
Salieri and Albrechtsberger in Vienna,
prior to his arrival in Paris in 1808. From
1818 he was professor of counterpoint and
fugue at the Paris Conservatory.

79. As claimed by Wedell (1995, 115–17).

80. His former pupil Berlioz (1990
[1865], 40–41) described him as having
a "taste for abstract permutations and
elaborate musical jokes. He loved solving
problems; but this kind of thing can be the
enemy of art, by diverting it from the main
purpose which it should always be striving
to achieve."

81. Reicha (2000, 28).

82. Before Reicha, the word *disegno*
was used in Italy to signify the initial stage
of an ancient threefold rhetorical division
of the artwork into invention, layout or
disposition, and embellishment or presentation. Lichtenthal (1826, 1:228), for
instance, described "a three-part scheme
of works of art, which consists of the *in-*

vention, the *conduct,* and the *finishing*" (un
triplice maneggio de' lavori d'arte, che
consiste nel *disegno,* nella *condotta,* e nel
perfezionamento). A detailed description
of what these categories meant in practice
appears in De Vecchis (1850, 2:26–31). For
an account of similar rhetorical schemes
in relation to Bach, see Dreyfus (2004,
1–32).

83. Reicha (2000, 13–16) and (1830,
12–14).

84. See, for instance, Reicha's comments on Example O3 (2000, 137).

85. See, for instance, the summary of
Reicha's theory, using similar terminology, in Picchianti (1834, 142–43).

86. Wedell (1995, 85) suggests, as additional direct sources for Asioli's theory,
Momigny (1803–1806) and (1823).

87. On the contrary, they often paraphrased his teachings. The account of
verse types and rhythm in Ritorni (1841,
103–109) is, for instance, a scarcely altered
summary of the relevant passages in Asioli
(1832, vol. 3), as acknowledged by the cita-
tion on p. 108.

88. Asioli (1832, 3:40): "Dopo questo
confronto tra il metro e la frase, confronto
che, a parer mio, non può essere più vero,
più dimostrativo e più identico, credo di
poter smentir alcune tacce che mal a proposito si danno alla Musica."

89. Ibid., 3:41: "Non è colpa della
Musica se un inesperto cantore si ferma
inutilmente a gorgheggiare sulle vocali *i,
o, u,* ed il buon Maestro scrivendo eviterà
quest'errore."

90. Ibid., 1:15–16: "Il Ritmo, che ha tan-
ta forza sul senso sino al punto di offende-
re il più zotico orecchio qualora ne venga
transgredito l'ordine, si distingue con due
movimenti, dei quali il primo è qualifi-
cato *forte* dal senso, ed il secondo *debole.*
Questi due movimenti ritmici sono divisi
ora in due, ora in una, ed ora in una mezza
battuta, secondo la qualità dei tempi o
pari, o dispari, e secondo le voci *Allegro,*

Andante, Adagio, ec., poste a fronte della composizione.

Il primo o forte movimento è quello su cui comincia e termina la frase, o il ritmo armonico; ed il 2.° o debole è quello che fa presentire nel suo fine una semicostituzione, o costituzione del Modo, che tende a riprodurre il 1.° e forte movimento; così che si può affermare che questa riproduzione, salve poche eccezioni, decide fra i movimenti ritmici qual sia il forte, e quale il debole."

91. Ibid., 3:37: "Il ritmo Melodico, ossia la frase, è una particella del discorso musicale retta costantemente dal ritmo Armonico già dichiarato nel primo Libro. Questo, co' suoi due movimenti, de' quali il primo è forte e l'altro debole, regge colle cadenze il ritmo Melodico, che ha forzatamente la desinenza sul primo od ultimo movimento; giacchè, quasi per istinto naturale, cade sopra di questi il piede e la mano della persona più ignara in musica; desinenza colla quale va perfettamente d'accordo la penultima sillaba del verso piano, l'antepenultima del verso sdrucciolo, e l'ultima del verso tronco."

92. Ibid., 3:37: "Sebbene il ritmo melodico riconosca la sua origine nelle armonie sottostanti, e vada soggetto ai movimenti cadenzati del ritmo armonico, nondimeno è, e sarà sempre, il padrone, la vita e l'anima del discorso musicale. Questo infatti attrae la principale attenzione, a motivo della sua piacevolezza; e quasi, sdegnando l'uniformità di quello che lo regge, cerca incessantemente la varietà, ora incominciando la frase sul 2.° o 1.° movimento armonico, ora sui varj tempi della misura pari o dispari, ed ora sulle più minute suddivisioni di essa."

93. Ibid., 3:37: "La frase talvolta arbitrariamente formasi di tre ritmici movimenti armonici, il 1.° de' quali è forte, il 2.° debole, e l'ultimo forte; ma non potendosi prendere quest'arbitrio ne' tempi marcati e veloci, senza non ferire il senso, converrà

farne uso soltanto nei tempi medj e lenti, dove il disgusto sarà minore, e pressochè insensibile, in ragione della lentezza del tempo, e dove da frase a frase i movimenti armonici passeranno indifferentemente dal 1.° al 1.°, o dal 2.° al 2.°."

94. Although the passage is without words and intended for instruments, Asioli employed it to demonstrate aspects of poetically determined rhythm. Italian writers generally assumed a fundamental identity of melody with poetry, regardless of whether it was vocal or instrumental.

95. Asioli (1832, 3:38): "Non a tutti è dato l'esser Poeta, e forse nessun autore di Musica è mai uscito dai limiti della mediocrità in questo genere. È necessario però che il giovine Compositore sia sufficientemente istruito nelle regole della versificazione, per intendere e profittare del seguente Confronto. Il Metro e la Frase musicale sono due cose identiche in quanto al numero delle sillabe, e ai tempi musicali, e in quanto agli accenti o sillabe lunghe, e ai tempi ritmici; cosicchè, in forza di questa identità, si può dire che le Frasi musicali sono Decasillabe, Novenarie, Ottonarie, Settenarie, ec. La Sillaba lunga, seguendo le leggi della prosodia, è considerata del doppio valore della breve. Ma nella Frase musicale non è valutata a rigore, poichè questa, avendo sempre di mira la varietà di concento, le accresce, o le diminuisce la durata, coll'unica avvertenza di collocarla impreteribilmente sul tempo ritmico. La sillaba breve, che invariabilmente trovasi sui tempi deboli della misura, è talvolta del valore della lunga ne' tempi veloce e pari, conserva il proprio valore, ossia la sua metà, nelle Triple, Sestuple e Dodecuple, e cade spessissimo nelle frazioni più minute dei tempi deboli, le quali, precipitandosi, quasi direi, sulla sillaba lunga, e sul tempo ritmico, ne rendono l'accento assai più vivo e più rimarcato. Stabilito così in quali tempi mu-

sicali cadono le lunghe e le brevi, diamo principio dal verso Endecasillabo."

96. Ibid., 3:38–39): "L'Endecasillabo, siccome suona il suo nome, è composto di undici sillabe, e perciò di undici tempi musicali. Ma i suoi accenti, sulla 6.ᵃ e 10.ᵃ, o sulla 4.ᵃ, 8.ᵃ e 10.ᵃ, o sulla 4.ᵃ, 6.ᵃ, 8.ᵃ e 10.ᵃ sillaba, non essendo in ogni verso uniformi, e non potendo identificarsi colla regolarità dei ritmi armonici che hanno sempre un' egual distanza, fanno nascere tali e tante discrepanze diametralmente opposte alla buona costruzione, e collegamento delle frasi ritmiche, che constringono il Musico ed il Poeta ad usarli nel solo canto non misurato, cioè nel Recitativo del Dramma. È vero che, nullostante le difficoltà accennate, non pochi Scrittori di Musica hanno composti e compongono Sonetti, Stanze, ec., ma è altresì incontrastabile, che un orecchio delicato sente gli sforzi loro per ottenere frasi uniformi, e le stiracchiature, irregolarità, e sconnessioni di queste frasi."

97. Moreen (1975, 133f.) surveys the lyric settings of *endecasillabi* in Verdi's early operas.

98. Paradigmatic instances of this type of *endecasillabo-ritmo* may be found in Bellini's cavatina for contralto and piano, "Dolente immagine" (ca. 1824), or in the cantabile theme of the first movement of Chopin's Piano Concerto in E minor, op. 11, mm. 61–90 (1830).

99. See Lippmann (1986 [1973–75], 256) and Fabbri (2003, 154). Ritorni (1841, 118) discussed this division of the *endecasillabo* in terms of two "versicoli." It formed the basis of Hepokoski's category of the "rhymed scena" in late Verdi (1987, 160f.).

100. Asioli (1832, 3:39): "La misura del Recitativo è quella che appare, non sensibilmente, ma visibilmente dalla divisione de' quattro quarti del tempo Ordinario, tempo adottato per convenzione, a preferenza delle Triple, Sestuple e Dodocuple, le quali sembrerebbero più adattate alle

regole di prosodia, che assegnano il valor doppio alla lunga, e la metà alla breve. La durata delle figure musicali dipende assolutamente dall'arbitrio del Cantante che declama: giacchè egli deve accelerare il moto del recitativo nelle passioni incalzanti, colleriche, e veementi; dare un moto posato e grave agli affetti imperiosi e forti; e rallentarlo nelle passioni amorose, meste e patetiche. Nel primo di questi tre diversi generi di passioni il Compositore porterà le voci verso l'acuto; nel 2.° non uscirà dal centro e dalle corde di petto; e nel 3.° si fermerà nei gravi o nei bassi. Dovrà inoltre far cadere l'accento o la sillaba lunga sul 1.° e 3.° quarto, e talvolta sulla prima metà del 2.° e del 4.°; scandagliar bene il verso onde elidere all'uopo le due, le tre, ed anche le quattro vocali in un sol tempo musicale; esaminare il luogo in cui può usarsi, a vantaggio della declamazione, la cesura, che aggiugnerà al verso una sillaba, e un tempo musicale. Finalmente prenderà norma dagli esempj seguenti intorno all'espressione dei punti esclamativi, ammirativi, e interrogativi; perché una tal maniera di canto, e di modulazioni ha preso forza dal tempo, e per convenzione se ne è fatta una legge."

101. See Lippmann (1986 [1973–75], 232–34).

102. Asioli (1832, 3:39): "Qui comincia il confronto tra il metro e la frase misurata, poichè dal Decasillabo al Ternario gli accenti prescritti dalla prosodia ad ogni metro vanno perfettamente d'accordo coi movimenti del ritmo armonico. Qui il compositore acquista un'illimitata facoltà di variare, accrescere e diminuire le note, e la durata delle sillabe; come pure d'immaginare sullo stesso metro e parole, tante e diverse frasi quante ne possono scaturire dalla sua fervida fantasia, ciò che produrrà sempre nuovo e crescente allettamento nell'uditore.

L'Ordine con cui son disposte le dieci sillabe brevi e lunghe del Decasillabo è lo stesso che quello dei dieci tempi o note che formano la frase Decasillaba, poichè questa incomincia colle due brevi nell'ultimo tempo della misura per cadere coll'accento della 3.ª sillaba sul movimento ritmico in battere, colle due brevi nel secondo tempo debole della misura per cadere coll'accenta della 6.ª sillaba sul secondo movimento ritmico in levare, e colle due brevi nell'ultimo tempo debole della misura per cadere di nuovo coll'accento comune o della 9.ª sillaba in battere; regola impreteribile per qualunque accento comune, sia piano, sia tronco, sia sdrucciolo il verso. La frase potrà cominciare ancora sul movimento ritmico in battere, allorchè un Bisillabo, di una lunga ed una breve, sarà a capo del verso; come pure un solo potrà comprendere due versi musicali o due frasi, rallentando il canto, o facendo uso della cesura, o delle pause."

103. Ibid., 3:37: "Le frasi de' tempi pari potranno essere diminuite di una metà, togliendola dal valore delle note; come pure si raddoppieranno aumentando il valore, senza alterare il tempo, e senza turbare i ritmici movimenti armonici."

104. Ibid., 1:32–33, examples 19 and 20.

105. Ibid., 3:39: "Non si saprebbe dire perché il Novenario sia quasi escluso dal Dramma, mentre i ritmi melodico ed armonico si adattano a questo verso non meno che agli altri. Gli accenti o sillabe lunghe del Novenario si trovano sulla 3.ª, 5.ª e 8.ª; così che il Compositore comincia la frase in levare colle due brevi, per cadere nel movimento forte sulla 3.ª sillaba, nel debole sulla 5.ª, e nel forte della seconda misura sull'8.ª."

106. Ibid., 3:39–40: "Gli accenti necessarj dell'Ottonario cadono sulla 3.ª e 7.ª, per cui il Compositore deve cominciare la frase due note prima del battere, affinchè il primo accento si trovi sul tempo forte, e le tre brevi seguenti abbiano luogo nel rimanente della misura per cadere coll'accento della 7.ª sul primo movimento dell'altra

misura. L'Ottonario però sarà alquanto più armonioso e musicale, quando avrà l'accento anche sulla 5.ª, perché questo allora combina col secondo movimento ritmico."

107. Ibid., 3:40: "I versi settenarj hanno gli accenti ora sulla 4.ª e 6.ª, ora sulla 2.ª e 6.ª, ed ora sulla 2.ª, 4.ª e 6.ª. Quest' ultima costruzione, che è la più comune, è anche la più armoniosa, perché gli accenti poetici si trovano perfettamente d'accordo coi tempi ritmici, mentre nelle surriferite maniere le brevi s'incontrano su questi tempi con maggior o minor ripugnanza dell'udito, in proporzione della lentezza del tempo. Ciò peraltro poco importa, allorchè il Settenario è frammischiato coll'endecasillabo nel Recitativo, per la ragione accennata."

108. Ibid., 3:40: "Il Senario ha due accenti, l'uno sulla 2.ª, e l'altro sulla 5.ª. La frase perciò dovrà cominciare colla breve in levare, per cadere sulla 2.ª nel movimento ritmico in battere, e sulla 5.ª nello stesso movimento della seguente misura, il quale, trovandosi sotto l'accento comune, sarà sempre, in qualsivoglia metro, il forte, ed il primo."

109. Ibid., 3:40: "Il Quinario non ha altr' obbligo di accento che sulla 4.ª; ma se l'avrà ancor sulla 1.ª, o sulla 2.ª, diverrà molto più armonioso, giacchè la frase, invece di cominciare con tre sillabe brevi in levare, comincerà sulla 1.ª, o sulla 2.ª sopra il movimento debole, per avere la sua desinenza sull'accento comune nel forte."

110. For a detailed background to the work and its performance, see Elphinstone (1992); a facsimile of the score has been made available by the Centro Studi Giacomo Puccini at www.puccini.it.

111. Girardi (2000, 14–16).

112. See Gjerdingen's survey of cadence types (2007a, 139–76).

113. Asioli (1832, 3:40): "Si avverta che due Quinarj formano un decasillabo in quanto al numero, e non in quanto alla

posizione degli accenti, e della cesura. Il decasillabo infatti ha gli accenti sulla 3.ª, 6.ª e 9.ª, e i due Quinarj che lo compongono gli hanno sulla 2.ª, 4.ª, 7.ª e 9.ª, il che altera talmente l'armonia di questi due metri, che l'orecchio il più insensibile agli accenti ed ai ritmi non può non accorgersi della somma diversità che passa fra l'uno e l'altro."

114. Puccini (2002, 10).

115. A similar arrangement of *quinari doppi* features in Tigrana and Edgar's love duet, "Dal labbro mio," from Puccini's *Edgar*, act 2, R14.

116. Asioli (1832, 3:40): "I Quaternarj ed i Ternarj di rado si trovano soli, ma spesso fra gli Ottonarj, e i Senarj, perché li dividono in due eguali emistichj, o sezioni di frasi, e perché gli accenti comuni dei primi collimano perfettamente coi ritmi e gli accenti della 3.ª e 7.ª dell'Ottonario, come quelli dei secondi s'incontrano cogli accenti e ritmi della 2.ª e 5.ª del Senario. Perciò nei seguenti esempj le frasi degli uni si vedranno frammischiate con quelle degli altri."

117. Ibid., 3:41: "Il verso e la frase possono prendere diversi aspetti, se si acceleri il loro corso, se si comprendano due frasi in un verso o al contrario, se si faccia perdere persino il senso del movimento e del ritmo colla lentezza. Tutto questo però dev'esser diretto all'espressione della parola."

118. Ibid., 3:40: "Il cangiamento istantaneo proveniente dalla riunione di varj metri, o di due ineguali emistichj formanti un endecasillabo, costringe il ritmo melodico, o la frase, a cambiar indole, mentre il ritmo armonico segue i proprj passi, per non recar offessa all'udito."

119. Ritorni (1841, 105–109) began his detailed discussion of versification by paraphrasing directly from the chapter on poetic meters in Asioli (1832, 3:37–41).

120. Bernardoni (1990, 53).

121. Vitali (1847, 4): "E s'intende per ritmo: una parte di melodia, la costante regolarità delle battute, l'omogenea quadratura delle frasi, e l'intero sviluppo dell'immagine. . . . Dissi simmetrico perché le parti tutte che formano un concetto musicale hanno tra loro una certa simmetria di estensione e qualità che le rende l'una all'altra conformi, e costituisce la cosiddetta quadratura, uno dei primi elementi della bella melodia." In his later polemic (1850a, 5), Vitali pointed out that not all contemporary operatic music appeared to make use of a regular phrase rhythm: "Sometimes the *ritmo* advances without number and symmetry, at other times the words, empty of every dramatic accent, serve the symmetry and the number" (ora il ritmo procede senza numero e simmetria, ora spoglia d'ogni accento drammatico la parola per servire alla simmetria ed al numero).

122. Masutto (1882–84, 62).

123. De Sanctis (n.d. [1887?], 1:65): "Ora quantunque il ritmo trovisi incarnato colla melodia, non è meno necessario all'armonia. . . . Per *frase* o *periodo musicale* s'intende una successione di suoni regolata simmetricamente dagli accenti o dai riposi sui tempi forti o deboli."

124. Ibid., 1:66: "Le prime due battute costituiscono il *disegno* o *motivo ritmico*; per formare un periodo musicale regolare sono necessarie le frasi e le contro-frasi, che hanno origine dalla ripetizione del disegno ritmico e della sua riposta. Le frasi poi si possono anche suddividere in sezioni o cesure, che alla loro volta servono a formare gli *incisi*."

125. Ibid., 1:66, 69: "I periodi possono essere composti di più disegni ritmici." "I ritmi sono *misti* o *alternati* quando ad una frase ne succede un'altra formata da un gruppo diverso di accenti; se ne fa molto uso nella musica moderna."

126. This standard form or "conduct" for a mid-nineteenth-century Italian melody corresponds closely to one of the most common Baroque ritornello for-

mulas, as described in Ledbetter (2009, 83): "1) character opening; 2) sequential continuation; 3) a closing motif, often with a pedal or chromatic tinge; and 4) a cadence."

127. In Bellini's original key of G major, this high note would have been an even more *sfogata* top C. Circumstantial evidence suggests that the *cavatina* was transposed down to F major at the request of Giuditta Pasta, the soprano who created the role.

128. Fabbri (2003, 209).

129. This text corresponds to the libretto for the premiere of 1884; see Puccini (2002, 8).

4. LESSONS IN DRAMATIC COMPOSITION II: HARMONY AND COUNTERPOINT

1. Strictly speaking, these consisted of one discipline, not two, since in the Italian traditions, "to *study counterpoint* and to *study harmony* signify the same thing" (*studiar il Contrappunto, e studiar l'Armonia* significa la stessa cosa; Lichtenthal [1826, 1:197]).

2. Pacini (1834, 23, n. 16) stated that his treatise on counterpoint was drawn from his studies with Bolognese maestros Tommaso Marchesi and Stanslao Mattei and especially with Bonaventura Furlanetto in Venice. According to Masutto (1882–84, 81), Pacini's teaching was based on an unpublished *Trattato di contrappunto* (1789 or 1811?) by Furlanetto.

3. The best introductions to the *partimento* tradition are Gjerdingen's monumental study of *Music in the Galant Style* (2007a), the special issue of the *Journal of Music Theory* 51 (2007), edited by Gjerdingen and containing articles by Holtmeier, Sanguinetti, Gjerdingen, Cafiero, and Stella, and the 2009 issue of *Rivista di Analisi e Teoria Musicale* 15, no. 1 (Lucca: Libreria musicale italiana), edited by Stella, entitled "Composizione e

improvvisazione nella scuola napoletana del Settecento," and containing articles by Cafiero, Gjerdingen, Paraschivescu, Sanguinetti, Stella, and Sullo. A concise historical survey of the tradition may be found in Gjerdingen (2007b, 126–30). A comprehensive and authoritative study by Sanguinetti is expected to be published soon.

4. A further written-out component, at least during the eighteenth century, was the *intavolatura:* a short, simple piece for keyboard that occasionally came close in style to the sonatas of Domenico Scarlatti or Giovanni Platti. Michele Ruta (1876, 2) outlined this division of learning at the Naples Conservatory: applied skills acquired through the realization of *partimenti* at the keyboard were described as studies in *armonia,* while sung and written elements, such as "le modulazioni, le progressioni, i solfeggi, i canoni, le fughe, e le altre formole" were seen as studies in *contrappunto.*

5. Gjerdingen (2007b, 126).

6. Gjerdingen (2007a, 470–80) and (2007b, 102–109).

7. Sanguinetti (2007, 68, 77).

8. Staffa (1849, 21). A similar *partimento,* entitled "Examples of the way to practice suspensions in modulations," may be found on p. 39.

9. Cafiero (2007, 142); quoted from Francesco Maria Avellino, *Elogio di Fedele Fenaroli letto nell'Accademia delle Belle Arti della Società Reale Borbonica* (Naples: Trani, 1818), 17.

10. Sanguinetti (2007, 51).

11. Holtmeier (2007, 8).

12. See Cafiero (2007, 140).

13. Cafiero (2007, 154–55); see also Stella (2007, 161–62).

14. For an overview of this tradition, see Woodring Goertzen (1996).

15. Kalkbrenner (1849, 12–17, 30).

16. Martini (1774–75, 1:92).

17. See Sanguinetti (1997, 160–61).

18. While modern clefs serve primarily to accommodate the notes of a given part neatly within a stave, the seven clefs adopted by the Italian schools specified and determined the actual voice or instrument to be used. According to Sabbatini (1789–90, 1:18–20): "There are seven Clefs in music, which are the *Bass, Baritone, Tenor, Contralto, Mezzo-Soprano, Soprano,* and *Violin.* . . . The gradations of the human voice are thus divided into seven parts." (Le Chiavi nella musica sono sette, cioè di *Basso—Baritono—Tenore— Contralto—Mezzo-Soprano—Soprano—*e *Violino.* . . . In sette parti adunque fu divisa la gradazione dell'umana voce.)

19. Giacomo Antonio Perti, "Esemplare di contrappunto" (Biblioteca del Civico Museo Bibliografico Musicale, Bologna, Ms. P.123, 106r–121r); as quoted in Pasquini (2004, 324–26): "L'arte del contrapunto, per quello [quanto] s'aspetta alla prattica della musica, è la più nobile rispetto alle altre parti, che sono o di canto o di suono: perché questa partorisce e dà in luce quelle composizioni che dipoi o il cantore [musico] canta o il sonatore suona. Non è però per questo che qualcheduna di queste parti non sia non dico [dirò] solamente utile, ma [precisamente] necessaria al contrapuntista, essendo certo che dipende da queste il progresso in quella. [Presuposta la cognizione de' principii primi della musica,] Due però sono principalmente necessarie, l'una è l'essercizio del canto, e l'altra è il suono del organo o cembalo: e vaglia il vero, in quanto alla prima, è comune [assioma] tra' professori che dipende dall'aver cantato il giungere ad esser buon compositore, perché come potrà far le [sue] composizioni proprie da cantarsi quando egli non ha ben cantato; anzi, io soggiongo [di più] che tale sarà il profitto [progresso] nell'arte del contrapunto quale sarà stato il profitto [progresso] nel canto. Q[u]anto [poi] alla seconda, ella è necessaria ed

utile: necessaria, si conosce evidentemente perché l'organista [l'arte] non fa altro, in un certo modo, che comporre, stanteché ad ogni nota che egli suona [egli] dà quelle consonanze, proporzionatamente, che il compositore, con tempo e studio, ha poste nel complesso della composizione; utile, perché il compositore, doppo fatta la composizione, ha il comodo per mezzo dell'organo o cembalo di sentirla, coll'esaminare e l'andamento [buono] delle parti e la [bu[o]na] modulazione di tutta la composizione."

Despite his public disagreements with Martini, Rome-based Spanish theorist Antonio Eximeno wrote at length on the prosodic and poetic foundations of music, remarking (1774, 312) that "before the student begins to tackle the study of counterpoint, he should get practice in singing . . . with the sole aim of acquiring good taste" (prima che lo Scolare intraprenda lo studio del contrappunto si eserciterà nel canto . . . solo per formare il gusto); quoted in Maguire (1989, 116).

20. Sanguinetti (2007, 55–67).

21. Staffa (1849, 22–25, 36–38).

22. See, for instance, the chapter "On Intervals and the Particular Modulations of Modern Music" in Tartini (1754, 156–70).

23. Holtmeier (2007, 10).

24. Martini (1774–75, 1: xx, 16, 250).

25. Asioli (1832, 1:11).

26. Holtmeier (2007, 11).

27. Tartini (1754, 106); see also Handel's composition exercises of ca. 1724–35 in Ledbetter (1990, 10).

28. Gjerdingen (2007a, 467–69) provides a concise overview of this basic form of the rule of the octave.

29. Sanguinetti (2007, 59).

30. This formulation is taken from Gervasoni (1800, 110). See also Mattei (1804, 9).

31. Similar teachings featured in other nineteenth-century Italian treatises, such

as Gervasoni (1800, 110), Staffa (1849, 7–9), and De Vecchis (1850, 1:5).

32. Even Fenaroli (1814, 50) included a scale in the soprano harmonized by the three Ramellian fundamental triads (I, IV, and V).

33. Rossi (1858, 51); teachings on the rule of the octave appear on pp. 47–55 and 90.

34. Staffa (1849, 52f.); Platania (1883, 5, Example 9). Platania's interpretation of the Neapolitan rules is discussed more fully in Stella (2007).

35. De Sanctis (n.d. [1887?], 1: 118, Example 249).

36. In order to evaluate an essay submitted by Rameau in 1760 to the Accademia delle scienze in Bologna, Martini had all of his major works shipped from Paris and translated into Italian. See Damschroder and Williams (1990, 186). Martini (1774–75, 1: 92) later acknowledged the importance of Tartini (1754) in introducing Rameau's theories to Italy.

37. Holtmeier (2007, 22–23).

38. De Sanctis (n.d. [1887?], 1:119): "Reicha, dopo avere esposto un quadro di tutti gli accordi che si possono fare ai differenti gradi della scala, parlando in seguito della regola dell'ottava, così si esprime: 'Questa formula offre sì poca risorsa nella composizione pratica, che non merita la pena di venir discussa in quest'opera. Essa sarebbe indispensabile solo qualora il basso dovesse progredire continuamente per scale ascendenti e discendenti, e dove non vi fosse modo d'impiegare diversi accordi sullo stesso grado.'"

39. It is interesting to note that Staffa (1849, 1), purporting to represent the authentic methods of the Neapolitan School, gives this same variant of Fenaroli's rule.

40. Tartini (1754, 104–106) constitutes, as far as I know, the first Italian published source to interpret the rule of the octave or "common organal scale" through an appended *basso fondamentale*. A similar presentation of Fenaroli's rule of the octave occurs in Gervasoni (1800, examples: 87).

41. Asioli (1832, 1:15): "Questa scala, che fu l'opera del tempo e di varj compositori, venne poi unanimemente adottata da tutte le scuole italiane verso il principio del secolo decimottavo, o sul fine dell'antecedente, colla denominazione di *Regola dell'ottava*. Sebbene questa regola vada perdendo di giorno in giorno della sua forza, in ragione delle tante e varie successioni d'armonia con cui può far progredire i proprj fondamentali, qui nulladimeno le assegnerò il primo posto, acciocchè lo studioso le sovrapponga le parti, ed abbia sempre in vista che, dalla miglior cantilena della parte superiore, dalla concatenazione armonica, dai moti obbliquo e contrario, dall'estensione ed approssimazione delle parti, e dalla quiete e dal buon ordine delle medesime, ei ritrarrà indubitamente il miglior effetto."

42. Asioli (ca. 1829, 62–69).

43. Asioli (ca. 1829, 4). The two basses were explained in Lichtenthal (1826, 1:92). Gervasoni (1800, 441) and De Vecchis (1850, 1:7) described a similar distinction between the *basso fondamentale* and the *basso continuo*.

44. Catel (ca. 1825 [1802], 24).

45. Asioli (1832, 1:14): "Ragion vuole che i movimenti fondamentali diatonici abbiano il loro principio dalla Scala composta di tanti generatori, non già perch'essa debba prodursi in esempio, ma solo per far conoscere i cattivi collegamenti fondamentali che devonsi evitare, le poche di lei porzioni che rendonsi praticabili, la mancanza totale di concatenazione armonica, e la regola che bisogna seguire per evitare le quinte, e le ottave di moto retto."

46. Asioli (1832, 1:11): "Trovo necessario primieramente che egli scriva sulla *Cartella* tre parti, non sopra un versetto di Canto fermo, ma sopra la scala diatonica o regola dell'ottava, inventando di più sulla

medesima tanti fondamentali i rivolti, quanti potranno meglio collegarsi fra loro. In tal guisa credo di conformarmi al giudizio de' medesimi nostri predecessori, i quali, non avvedendosi della loro contradizione, nel cominciare ad istruire a due parti, opinavano, e ben giustamente, che fosse più facile lo scrivere a quattro, che a tre, e a due."

47. Rossi (1858, 25).

48. Rossi (1858, 105): *Progressione* no. 1: "succession of the third and fifth upon the scale."

49. See, for instance, Staffa (1849, 7–8, Examples 33 and 35).

50. Gjerdingen (2007a, 45–60). One of the most common schemata of all, the variation upon the descending bass scale described by Gjerdingen (2007a, 33–40, 46–50) as a combination of the "Galant Romanesca" and "Prinner," offers a clear example of the arithmetic division, since the fifth scale degree receives a weak six-three chord leading to a perfect triad on the fourth degree.

51. According to Holtmeier (2007, 16–17).

52. Statements of the rudimentary rule of the octave arise elsewhere in Puccini, as if to exploit its connotations of simplicity. At the very opening of *La Bohème* (act 1, mm. 25–37), for instance, the light and carefree mood of the young Bohemians is captured by a straightforward harmonization of the C major scale—known as "first inversions of the scale of fundamentals" (primi rivolti di scala di genitori) in Asioli (1832, Examples 1:15)—ascending through parallel six-three chords and descending through a version of its "arithmetic" division. The narrow-minded Sacristan in *Tosca* is portrayed through a similar parallel six-three-chord harmonization of a descending scale, firstly in C major and then, in a manner strongly reminiscent of a conservatory exercise, in C minor (act 1, R6–R7).

53. See, for instance, the guidance given to students by Lucchese maestro P. Tomeoni (1795, 5). Sanguinetti (2007, 59–67) gives a clear overview of the bass motions in the original Neapolitan tradition. Some sources, such as Tomeoni (1795, 23) or Staffa (1849, 117), used the term "leaps" (*salti*).

54. The term *derivati* is taken from Platania (1883, Examples: 33).

55. Asioli (1832, Examples 1:15–70); Rossi (1858, 105–15); and Platania (1883, Examples: 33–36).

56. Andreoli and Codazzi (1898, 42).

57. Sanguinetti (2007, 67).

58. Pintado (1794); Staffa (1849, 17–21). De Vecchis (1850, 1:29–31) clarified the distinction between a *modulazione* involving notional chord roots and a *transizione di tuono* or "the change of key, vulgarly called endings" (il Passaggio di Tuono, dette volgarmente Terminazioni) arising from the motion of the actual bass, or *basso continuo*.

59. See, for instance, the "Tavola per la Modulazione" illustrating correspondences between scales upon the five principal notes of a key in Martini (1774–75, 2:xxx-vii), or Reicha (2000 [1814], 39).

60. Gervasoni (1800, 419–21, 466–67).

61. Asioli (1832, Examples 1:75, no. 37).

62. Asioli (1832, Examples 1:70, no. 36).

63. The examples given in Tartini (1754, 167–70) correspond closely to those in Asioli (1832, Examples 1:70–104). Mattei (ca. 1824–25, 125–29) provided numerous short basses as examples of modulation and discussed chromaticisms under the heading of "false cadences, elisions, and deception" (Cadenze False, Sospese, ed Inganno).

64. Asioli (1832, 1:22): "Le modulazioni sono stabili, secondarie, e di sfuggita. Le stabili sono quelle che fissano le divisioni cardinali della composizione: le secondarie hanno luogo fra le stabili; e quelle di sfuggita lo trovano dappertutto."

65. Asioli (1832, 1:20): "Vedute le alterazioni che sono prodotte dai modi analoghi, ora prendo ad esaminare tutti gli accordi fondamentali della Scala, onde far conoscere le loro naturali tendenze, e i loro possibili inganni."

66. A full account of Puccini's manuscript, currently held at the Museo Puccini in Celle (Pescaglia), may be found in Burton (1996). It was bequeathed in 1864 to Carlo Angeloni, Michele's student, who presumably made use of it when teaching the young Giacomo Puccini. It remained in the Angeloni family until 1979, when it was acquired by the Associazione Lucchesi nel Mondo. I am very grateful to Deborah Burton for providing me with a photocopy of the manuscript.

67. Cerù (1871, 89).

68. Nerici (1879, 108–11).

69. Cerù (1871, 113).

70. Pacini (1875, 73).

71. Mattei (ca. 1824–25, 16) and Fenaroli (1814, 55).

72. Staffa (1849, 14–16) and Guarnaccia (ca. 1851, 73–88).

73. Puccini (1846, 15, 27): "Tutte le scale nel grave, e nell'acuto, tutti i moti regolare del Basso / nel grave e nell'acuto come nello Studio a 2." "Tutte le scale sì nel grave come nell'acuto / a salire e scendere in modo maggiore, e minore / Tutti i movimenti regolare del Basso sì nel grave / come nell'acuto, come addietro nello Studio a 2."

74. Milanese maestro Gervasoni (1800, 455), for instance, wrote of "Changes of Harmony" (*Cambiamenti d'Armonia*) in which the "true bass" would shift to other voice parts, giving rise to a type of textural inversion. He also set out a series of lessons, or *solfeggi,* for aspiring singers that consisted of traditional scales and bass motions placed in whichever voice part was required (1800, Examples: 9). Mattei's student Luigi Felice Rossi supplemented his edition of his master's "Counterpoints

from Two to Eight Parts" (ca. 1827, 68–78) with a series of unpublished "counterpoints in four parts," which demonstrated how a bass line could be shifted to the soprano or alto.

75. See Florimo (1881–83, 2:81) and Cafiero (1993). The obvious parallels between Mattei's methods and the progressive course of counterpoints on the scale in Sala (1794), from note-against-note to eight-notes-against-note, suggest a strong Neapolitan connection.

76. In response to an article by Casamorata that appeared in the *Gazzetta musicale di Milano,* Staffa (1857f, 1, no. 13: 97) outlined a brief history of "musical systems," starting with Guido d'Arezzo and concluding with the Neapolitan "system of the octave," which "shows itself in definitive form in the works of Fenaroli and Tritto, since they are the principal foundations, who speak and transmit all the rules and the facts they have learned, the latter [Tritto] to the school of *Leonardo Leo,* and the former [Fenaroli] to that of *Francesco Durante.*" (Come il Monteverde stette nel mezzo del tempo in cui il sistema esacordale depose le sue glorie ai piedi di quello di ottave, che fu l'ultimo sistema, che si mostrò sotto una determinata forma nelle opere del Fenaroli e del Tritto, i quali ne furono i primi sostegni, perchè dichiararono e ne trasmisero scritte tutte le regole, ed i fatti che appresero, il secondo alla scuola di *Leonardo Leo,* ed il primo a quella di *Francesco Durante*). On the continued relevance of the *leisti* and *durantisti* in the early nineteenth century, see Rosenberg (1999).

77. According to Berlioz (1990 [1865], 40), who portrayed Cherubini in general as a pedant, stubbornly bound to the "old masters."

78. The appropriateness of this comparison was questioned at the time by Antonio Eximeno; see Pasquini (2004, 123–27). Pergolesi's relevance to contem-

porary composition continued to feature in Italian publications until Mariscotti (1858).

79. A similar arrangement of two-note melodic attachments upon the scale, with octave displacements, underpins the canon at the second in the sixth of the *Goldberg Variations* (BWV 988). During the 1740s J. S. Bach reworked Pergolesi's *Stabat Mater* into a setting of the psalm *Tilge, Höchster, meine Sünden* (BWV 1083).

80. Martini (1774–75, 2:viii): "L'*Attacco* è una specie di Soggetto breve, il quale non è legato a tutte le leggi prescritte alla Fuga, ma è libero in maniera tale, che alle parti che rispondano vien permesso di attaccar le Risposte in qualunque Corda loro si presenti, e loro sia comodo, come si rileva dal seguente Esempio, che non è, che una semplice abbozzo a tre voci dell'accennato *Attacco.*" See also Mattei (1804, "Della Fuga"). After acknowledging Martini's concept of the *attacco*, Ruta (1877b) defined an additional Neapolitan use of the term to signify a passage that served to connect "diverse thoughts" within a single piece.

81. Martini (1774–75, 1:18): "in parte di *Figure,* in parte di *Sillabe,* e in parte d'*Intervalli.*" There are obvious similarities between Martini's teachings on contrapuntal imitation and the account of the "free fugue" (*fuga sciolta*) in Zarlino (1573 [1558]). De Vecchis (1850, 1: 20–21) continued to divide contrapuntal imitation into "Strict" (*Legata, o Rigorosa*) and "Free" (*Sciolta, o Libera*).

82. P. Tomeoni (1795, 5, 39). Martini's concept of the *attacco* was later signified by a wide range of terms, each chosen to emphasize one or more of its attributes. In Asioli (1832), for instance, it was described variously as a "theme" (*tema*), "attachment" (*Attacco*), "figure" (*figura*), "melodic phrase rhythm" (*ritmo melodico*), "rhythmic phrase" (*frase ritmica*), "repetition" (*ripetizione*), or "imitation" (*imitazi-*

one). De Sanctis (n.d. [1887?], 1:140–56) characterized it as a "design" (*disegno*), adapting the term from Reicha (1830). See also Lichtenthal (1826, 1:34, 73).

83. Quoted in Cafiero (2007, 147).

84. Mattei (ca. 1824–25, 13).

85. Mattei (ca. 1824–25, 144).

86. A rudimentary form of the same method appeared in the ninth chapter of Catel (ca. 1825 [1802]), entitled "On the different progressions of the bass through the diatonic scale."

87. Cherubini (n.d. [1835?], 138–39).

88. The resemblance of this standard Bolognese exercise to the second of Bach's *Goldberg Variations* is presumably coincidental.

89. Asioli (1832, 2:27): "Il genere d'imitazione sciolta produce quattro specie, una meno sciolta dell'altra. La 1.ª è l'imitazione di un tema di poche note, o di una misura incirca che dicesi anche *Attacco.*" The second species involved the imitation of a slightly longer *soggetto* within what was known as a *Fuga d'imitazione sciolta.* This genre formed a central part of advanced contrapuntal training in the Italian traditions. An example given by Martini (1774–75, 2: xxxiii) and analyzed by Asioli (1832, Examples 2:13), for instance, demonstrated how the regular bass motions, incorporated into themes (by way of a technique described by De Vecchis [1850, 1:27, 44–45]), could form the basis of fugal imitation. The third and fourth species of "free imitation" comprised the tonal and the real fugue. Strict imitation applied only to canonic procedures. In his *Harmonologia musica* of 1702, incidentally, Andreas Werckmeister, a close friend of Dietrich Buxtehude, claimed to have discovered the significance of sequential imitative subjects to contrapuntal composition and improvisation, seemingly unaware of the existence of the Italian doctrine of "bass motions"; see Dodds (2006).

90. Compare Asioli (1832, Examples 2) with Cherubini (n.d. [1835?]: 67–69).

91. Guarnaccia (ca. 1851, 73–89). Staffa's survey of the Neapolitan traditions appears, by contrast, free from any Asiolian influence. It incorporated the technique of adding *attacchi* and *imitazioni* into its realizations of *disposizioni* in two, three, and four parts (1856, 16–34).

92. De Sanctis (n.d. [1887?], 1:140): "Essa è infatti la riproduzione ascendente o discendente di due o più accordi, o di un disegno melodico. Le note accidentali, armoniche e melodiche, e le imitazioni possono servire a variare e ad arricchire la progressione."

93. Ibid., 1:141: "La riproduzione della *formula* o del *disegno* si può fare a differenti intervalli, sia ascendendo che discendendo, purchè vi sia naturale concatenazione: le note di passaggio, anche introdotte nel basso, non alterano la progressione. . . . Ciascuna parte può concorrere a formare una progressione regolare; tuttavia una parte predominante può contenere una progressione melodica, lasciando libero il movimento delle altre."

94. Ibid., 1:151, 156: "Le progressioni tonali che abbiamo esposto sono le principali, e si possono variare in molte maniere, sì nel basso, che nelle parti superiori. Sono molto usate nella musica sacra e nello stile rigoroso. . . . Infine facciamo osservare che siccome da una successione armonica si può formare una progressione melodica, così da un brano melodico si possono ricavare delle progressioni armoniche tonali o modulanti."

95. De Vecchis (1850, 1:44–45): "il Compositore incominci a far attenzione a tutte le note del Basso della lezione, e puntare quelle in cui si vuol formare qualche piccola Frase, e segnare ancora quelle note di Basso, dove si potrà ripetere l'istessa Frase, come ancora qualche piccolo *Andamento* di canto, *Riprese* etc.; dopo tale esame si passerà a formare la Melodia, la

quale sarà sempre Benfatta, ed Unita, se questa è ragionatamente regolata." See also p. 27.

96. Ashbrook (1995, 30); the theme appears most conspicuously at R1, m. 8, R24, m. 21, and R50, m. 15.

97. An edition of the work, edited by Michele Girardi, is available online at www.puccini.it.

98. Marselli (1859, 138–40) provides a description of the *pezzo concertato* in relation to midcentury Verdi.

99. The embellishment of standard schemata formed a crucial part of the Italian methods of composition. It was discussed under the headings of "*rifioritura*" in Asioli (1832, 1:23) and "*melodia variata*" in Rossi (1858, 64–68). Gjerdingen (2007b, 92–106) provides an important series of examples showing the "diminution" of a bass motion from Ugolino (ca. 1400), through Durante, to Martini.

100. A discussion of the "*baßlose Satztyp*" may be found in Christen (1978, 99–102). Alternative harmonizations of a similar regular motion in the soprano are not difficult to find in earlier Italian music: see, for instance, the famous *allegro non molto* theme from the first movement of "L'inverno" (mm. 22f.) from Vivaldi's *Le quattro stagioni* (1723).

5. LESSONS IN DRAMATIC COMPOSITION III: AFFECT, IMITATION, AND CONDUCT

1. This argument is explored in depth in Gjerdingen (2007a).

2. Although it is generally accepted in modern music historiography that the metaphor of rhetoric as a model for music died out in the late eighteenth century, to be replaced by an aesthetic of personal, subjective expression (*Ausdruck*), this does not hold true for the Italian traditions. The assumption rests almost exclusively on primary sources in German, especially those that relate to

instrumental traditions. See Bonds (1991, 4, 132–34, 162–64); Bartel (1997, 156–64); and Patrick McCreless, "Music and Rhetoric," in Christensen (ed., 2002, 872–79). Bonds (p. 138) points out that Carpani (1823 [1812], 43–44) was among the first to apply the metaphor of the oration to an instrumental movement by Haydn.

3. Anna Luisa Staël-Holstein, "Sulla maniera e la utilità delle traduzioni," *Biblioteca italiana,* January 1816, pp. 9–18; quoted and discussed in Tomlinson (1986). Lord Byron contributed significantly to the image of the "Romantic artist" in Italy through his scandalous affair with the married Countess Teresa Guiccioli in Ravenna and his association, in 1820, with the revolutionary Carbonari movement against Austrian rule.

4. According to Zingarelli's teachings, as recorded in De Vecchis (1850, 2: 15–17), the andante was a general tempo for use "in all compositions of agreeable Character" (in tutte quelle composizioni di Carattere aggradevole). De Vecchis provided detailed descriptions of each type of andante, which correspond closely to those found in Puccini's operas.

5. The term "doctrine of the affections," or *Affektenlehre,* was coined by German musicologists in the early twentieth century to describe one of the central concerns of Baroque aesthetics: the definition and artistic representation of feelings and passions that were regarded as fixed and objective. It was closely associated with the "doctrine of figures," or *Figurenlehre,* which sought to identify the operation of rhetorical devices in music. The original aesthetic was perhaps most influentially formulated by Batteux (1773 [1746]). Important writers on musical affects include Mersenne, Kircher, Werckmeister, Prinz, Mattheson, Marpurg, Scheibe, and Quantz. The basic precept of relevant

eighteenth-century writings—that an entire piece or extended passage should be unified by a single dominant affect—continued to be taught in Italian conservatories until the end of the nineteenth century.

Lichtenthal (1826, 1:24–25) gave the following definition of *affetto:* "Three different meanings are usually given to the word *affect.* 1) Passion of the soul arising from a wish for good things or a hatred of bad (*affectus*); 2) desire, longing (*lust*); and 3) affection, benevolence. The word *passion* is defined together with suffering, affect of the soul, compassion, commotion of the soul. . . . The affects and the passions are divided 1) into the *agreeable,* e.g., cheerfulness, joy, hope, love, glory, honor, pride, friendship, etc., and 2) into the *disagreeable,* e.g., sadness, fear, worry, terror, anger, nostalgia, hatred, jealousy, etc." (Ordinariamente si danno alla parola affetto tre varj significati. 1) Passione d'animo nata dal desiderio del bene, o dall'odio del male [*affectus*]; 2) desiderio, bramosia [*cupiditas*]; 3) affezione, benevolenza. La parola passione viene definita con patimento, affetto d'animo, compassione, commozione d'animo. . . . Gli affetti e le passioni si dividono 1) in *aggradevoli,* come p. e. l'allegrìa, la gioia, la speranza, l'amore, la gloria, l'onore, l'orgoglio, l'amicizia ec., 2) in *disaggradevoli,* p. e. la tristezza, la paura, l'affanno, lo spavento, l'ira, la nostalgia, l'odio, la gelosia ec.). A similar account appeared in De Vecchis (1850, 2:7–10).

6. Under the heading of "pragmatic and expressive orientations," Bonds (1991, 54–57, 181–83) discusses the transition from eighteenth-century listener-centered approaches to music to later Romantic notions of "self-expression" and "the work itself."

7. Italics added; Bach (1949 [1753], 152). Although C. P. E. Bach's practice of noting down solo keyboard

improvisations in the "empfindsamer" or "fantasia" style may be taken as a starting point for Romantic notions of subjective expression through composition (see Taruskin [2010, 409–18]), his account of performers' "feelings" in the *Versuch* still rested on the notion that they arose in response to objective "affects," such as those embodied in "languishing, sad passages" or "lively, joyous passages."

8. Basevi (1856d, 45–46). In this connection it is interesting to note the similarities between C. P. E. Bach's attitudes toward composition and those evident in Lichtenthal's dictionary (1826, 1:260): "The expression of music will be perfect only when it is given assistance by poetry. In sharpening, through music, the arrows that the poet shoots at the heart, the two arts unite to form a divine language. If the composer wants to obtain such a felicitous agreement of words and music, he must read the libretto with the utmost attention and transfer it to the moments of the action with the full force of his fantasy; you live in the characters of the poem; you are yourself the tyrant, the hero, the lover."

9. Marpurg (1754–62, 1778, vol. 5), as quoted in Dahlhaus (1982, 20). Johann Heinichen provided a detailed list of such corresponding musical devices by demonstrating how to set the same text according to different affects; see Buelow (1992, 331–62).

10. Brown (1999, 337).

11. Studies of tempo designation in Verdi have tended to interpret the historical evidence through ideologies particular to modern musicology. *Movimenti* are habitually understood only as tempos, while the indications concerning character (*carattere*) or the affects (*affetti*) are reduced to what were called "modifiers" of the basic tempo terms; see, e.g., Montemorra Marvin (1997, 394–95).

12. See, e.g., Casamorata (1846).

13. Staffa (1857–58, 1, no. 20: 158–59).

14. Asioli (1824 [1809]: 56–59). Galeazzi (1791, 36) provided a similar chart of twenty-four "Progressions or Movements" (*Andamenti o Movimenti*), ranging from *larghissimo* to *prestissimo*, which appended additional descriptors of affects only to its nine forms of allegro. Asioli's list also corresponds closely to that given in Gervasoni (1800, 174–77).

15. De Macchi (ca. 1830, 34).

16. Pacini (1834, 26).

17. Ritorni (1841, 136).

18. De Vecchis (1850, 2: 6–17): "Termini per indicare il Carattere delle composizioni" (p. 16). Alessandro Mampieri (1840: 34), "maestro di contrapunto [*sic*] e di canto" at the Naples Conservatory, listed five *andamenti*—adagio, andante, largo, allegro, and presto—together with five to twelve different affects for each.

19. Dacci (1886, 69).

20. Asioli (1832, 3:43): "Questa . . . può esser formata di frasi filate adorne, e dette *di bel canto*; può essere di un getto solo, allorchè una sola frase, e un sol tempo dominano da principio a fine; e può essere di varj *pezzi*, di varj *generi*, e di varia *tessitura*. In ognuna di queste composizioni, il Giovine studioso dovrà ricercare nel canto, e nei movimenti d'Orchestra, la vera espressione dell'affetto dominante nei versi, e non già le espressioni d'incidenza, le quali, se gli verrà fatto di esprimere, non dovranno però distruggere e far obbliare il movimento dominante, giacchè da questo solo può derivare il pregio, non men raro che sommo, dell'unità di pensiero: unità che il genio e il buon gusto soltanto possono ispirare."

21. Cattaneo (1828, 53): "D. Che cosa s'intende per *affetto dominante della composizione*?

R. Come nel discorso gli accenti sono più vibrati e forti nell'esprimere sentimenti forti e nobili, che nell'esprimere sentimenti dolci, moderati e placidi, così nella Musica gli accenti devono essere più marcati e vigorosi nelle frasi, o intieri pezzi esprimenti immagini vigorose, vivace e forti, che in quelli esprimenti immagini di calma, dolcezza e tenerezza, e quindi per *affetto dominante della composizione* s'intende il carattere, o dirò altrimenti, lo stile che si deve praticare nell'esecuzione di tale, o di tal altro pezzo.

D. Quali sono i mezzi più ordinarj per far rilevare questa diversità di stile nelle frasi musicali?

R. Sono il grado maggiore o minore nel forte e piano, la maggiore o minor forza nelle appoggiature e note legate, il più o meno staccato, il crescere o diminuire con maggiore o minor vigore, il rendere più o meno accelerati e vibrati il gruppetto, il mordente, od il trillo, il marcare più o meno i tempi forti della battuta, la maggiore o minor esattezza nel dar il valore alle note: in fine tutto ciò che serve a dare la vera espressione voluta ed indicata dal compositore."

22. Anon. (1852–53, 5, no. 2: 7): "La natura degli affetti che vengono ad esser determinati dal ritmo, dipende moltissimo dal diverso andamento del *movimento*. . . . Il ritmo del polso non è lo stesso nella gioia come nella tristezza, nella collera impetuosa, come in una tenerezza tranquilla."

23. Anon. [Michele Ruta?] (1883, 4, no. 9: 1): "Il Crescendo è la gradazione progressiva di un affetto. . . . Per essere più chiaro io lo distinguo in tre specie, cioè in crescendo di suoni, di tonalità, di ritmo." In performance, the notated terms *cresc.* and *descresc.* concerned primarily the volume of sound.

24. See Frank (1989, 9–14).

25. Beiser (2003, 74).

26. Ibid., 75.

27. Mazzucato (1851). His ideas and formulations suggest a connection with Blasis (1844).

28. Galeazzi (1796, 185): "Dell'imitazione."

29. Galeazzi (1791, 197): "Consiste principalmente l'espressione in tre cose: 1. nel saper far buona scelta delle opportune diminuzioni, e saperle annicchiare a' proprj luoghi; 2. nella scelta delle arcate più addatte alla cantilena; 3. e principalmente nella gradazione del volume della voce dell'istromento, o come dicono i pratici saper ben distribuire il *piano*, e *forte,* o sia il *chiaroscuro*." Celentano (1867, 12) understood *chiaroscuro* primarily in terms of vocal, rather than instrumental, coloring.

30. Gervasoni (1800, 439): "Deve qui il Compositore dipingere tutti i pensieri dell'Autore, e nel canto dell'aria esprimere veramente le parole della medesima, e così che le sillabe lunghe cadano mai sempre sopra i tempi forti, e le brevi sopra i deboli."

31. Gervasoni (1800, 85): "Considerar si deve inoltre la Melodia sotto due diversi aspetti, cioè come una semplice successione di suoni, e come un'arte d'imitazione. Nel primo caso tutta la sua forza è limitata a lusingare l'orecchio con suoni piacevoli: nel secondo opera maravigliosamente effetti morali che superanno l'immediato potere de' sensi, e nello spirito s'insinuano e lo accendono mirabilmente." See also p. 438: "un pezzo solamente istrumentale d'ordinario non è destinato a rappresentare al vivo una data immagine, ma piuttosto a lusingare l'orecchio con belle cantilene. Non è così della Musica vocale: questa più precisamente richiede la vera espressione di quel dato sentimento che si ha a rendere."

32. Monelle (2000, 24, 33) claimed that "Ratner's mistake was to announce a basis in the writings of contemporaries, that is, a *historical* basis for his ideas," and concluded that "contemporary writers are not good as buttresses of topic theory. Each topic needs a full cultural study."

33. Carpani (1823 [1812], 166).

34. For an account of Peirce's semiotics in relation to musical signification, see Tarasti (1994, 54–58).

35. Carpani (1823 [1812], 171): "L'imitazione sentimentale è quella, che con suoni e movimenti analoghi a questi stessi suoni assegnati, desta in noi l'idea dei diversi affetti, che muovono il cuore degli uomini e dei pensieri che li animano."

36. See Monelle's discussion of the indexical properties of icons (2000, 17–18).

37. Asioli (1832, 3:41): "i buoni effetti musicale non devono esser lo scopo principale dell'Orchestra drammatica, ma bensì l'adattare i suoni e i movimenti ritmici alla qualità delle passioni che imita od esprime."

38. Asioli (1832, 3:41): "L'imitazione sentimentale, ossia l'espressione degli affetti dell'animo, è quella che più onora il Compositore, poichè, non avendo la Musica prototipo alcuno da prefiggersi, egli deve far nascere il tutto dagli affetti dominanti espressi delle parole, dal suo modo proprio di sentir le passioni, dalla sua fervida immaginazione, dal buon gusto, e dal buon senso musicale. Il canto, primo pensiero del Compositore drammatico, dovrebbe bastare ad esprimere qualunque affetto, o patetico, o amoroso, o collerico, o gajo, o concitato, ec.: ma se al canto si aggiungeranno i movimenti d'Orchestra più o men veloci, i suoni più o meno acuti, gl'immensi effetti risultanti dalla varietà degl'istromenti, il piano e il forte maggiore o minore, purchè tutto ciò assecondi e avvalori il dominio dell'affetto, allora il canto diverrà superiore a sè stesso, e l'armonia che lo circonda produrrà un diletto inesprimibile."

39. Asioli (1832, 3:42): "L'imitazione fisica si divide in due specie: quella cioè che esprime gli oggetti soltanto visibili e privi di suono, e quella che ha per oggetto di approssimarsi ai suoni indeterminati. La prima è creata dall'immaginazione del Compositore, giacchè il nascere tramontare del Sole, l'improvvisa comparsa della luce, l'orror delle tenebre, ec., non possono esser rappresentati approssi-

mativamente se non dai movimenti più o meno accelerati, dai suoni più o meno acuti, più o men sommessi, più o men forti. La seconda specie è affatto servile, poichè constringe il Compositore ad imitare coi suoni determinati e musicali dell'Orchestra, o di qualche istromento, il rombo indeterminato del *tuono*, il mugito dei *bruti*, il canto degli *augelli*, il rumore dell'*acque*, ec."

40. Asioli (1832, Examples 3:77): "La scala ascendente nei primi Violini e nei Flauti, l'armonia che cresce lentamente fra i suoni medj e meno forti, l'aumento degl'istromenti gravi ed acuti e il moto contrario fra la scala ascendente e le parti discendenti che a poco a poco rinforzano, estendono e aggravano l'armonia, producono un effetto che dal pianissimo regolarmente crescendo sino allo sforzato, indica a gradi a gradi il sorger del Sole, e col fortissimo l'immersa luce che innonda l'ampiezza dei Cieli."

41. Asioli (1832, Examples 3:78): "Il Modo affettuoso di Mi maggiore, il moto placido della melodia, la soave dolcezza degl'istromenti che la compongono e l'ineffabile piacere dell'accordo di Triade ispirato dalla natura, sono mezzi proprj a tranquillar l'animo e a conciliar il sonno."

42. Asioli (1832, Examples 3:86): "Il galoppo del Cavallo si dovrebbe far sentire con tre tocchi, il primo forte e di doppio valore, e gli altri due deboli e di metà durata. Sebbene in questo esempio il galoppo non segua a rigore il menzionato principio, essendo di tre tocchi uguali, nondimeno riesce di un grandioso effetto perché il primo tocco è distinto da una forza maggiore."

43. Boucheron (1842, 91): "Egli è in questo genere d'imitazione il più nobile e degno d'artista, che tutti i mezzi posti in opera dal compositore debbono assumere di rappresentare quanto è necessario all'espressione dell'affetto, supplendo a quanto la parola e gli accenti della

melodia non bastano a significare." See also his list of correspondences between melodic types and affects on p. 56. In addition to the influence of Asioli, many of Boucheron's insights match those in Ritorni (1841).

44. Santucci (1828, 71): "Si è visto che la melodia debb' essere espressiva e ben modulata. Espressiva: che dee corrispondere al sentimento intero racchiuso nelle parole, cui si adatta la musica; che co' suoi tratti dee rilevar questo sentimento, farlo gustare, lumeggiarlo, ingrandirlo."

45. Ibid., 70–71):

1. I sentimenti dolci, tranquilli e continui vogliono un ritmo leggiero corto facile ad apprendersi e continuato.
2. Se debbonsi esprimere sentimenti variati, crescenti o decrescenti, bisogna scegliere un ritmo più variato, composto or di membri grandi, ora di piccoli, e cambiamenti debbono esser pronti o lenti a tenore del sentimento.
3. Si può abbandonare la regolarità, quando il sentimento ha qualche cosa di contradittorio. Non è difficile comprendere come si possa esprimere la irresoluzione, l'incertezza, e l'imbarazzo ec. colle variazioni del ritmo.
4. Ne' casi straordinarj, quando si vuol far uso d'una particolare energìa, si può, cambiando il movimento, cambiare anche il ritmo in una maniera espressiva.
5. Un'altra particolarità del ritmo fa sovente un effetto piacevolissimo, e consiste nell'introdurre una misura durante la quale, per esempio, la voce tace, e fra tanto uno strumento ripete o imita l'ultimo tratto del canto della voce.

46. Petrobelli (1994, 13).

47. Basevi (1859a, 191). Balthazar (2004) provides a clear description of these set piece forms. The Italian terms

(*scena, tempo d'attacco,* etc.) are derived principally from Ritorni (1841) and Basevi (1859a). Marselli (1859) offers an alternative, largely uncharted source of similar contemporary terms for standard genres.

48. Boito (1942 [1863], 1080).

49. Ritorni (1841, 1:40–50).

50. See, e.g., Balthazar (1988–89), (1990), and (1991a). The introduction—in Powers (1987)—of Basevi's "usual form" (*solita forma*) as a catchword for a range of conventional practices and expectations has given rise to a rich seam of debate and scholarship. The concept was first applied extensively to Puccini's music in Ashbrook and Powers (1991) and, more recently, in Rosen (2004) and Davis (2010). Parker (1997) raised questions concerning the authority of Basevi's categories, to which Powers (2000) responded.

Basevi's "usual form" recalls Gervasoni's comparison of the flexible "movements" of the aria with those of the instrumental sonata (1800, 512–13), and corresponds closely to a number of contemporary descriptions of the Rossinian set piece, such as the definition of the "modern" aria in Lichtenthal (1826, 1:53), or the outline in Asioli (1832, 3:44) of the "grand aria," which is "preceded by a recitative and formed into a whole by one, two, or three little compositions," or the detailed account of the "modern aria" consisting of largo and cabaletta in De Vecchis (1850, 2: 59–60).

51. The literature on the forms of set pieces (or genres) in Italian opera, not to mention associated structures of verse and libretto, is far too voluminous to summarize here. Balthazar (2004) gives a useful overview.

52. See, e.g., Giovanni Mazzini's comments on what he perceived as the haphazard, "mosaic" layout of set pieces in opera (1836, 128), or the anonymous advice offered to librettists in the Florentine journal *L'Armonia* (1856b, 1, no. 36: 141–42),

or Marselli's description of the "general form" of a mid-nineteenth-century opera (1859, 145–54). Kimbell (1981, 75) offers a concise overview of a standard Rossinian layout.

53. According, e.g., to Reicha (2000, 37). Picchianti (1834, 155–56), who followed Reicha closely in most respects, disagreed: "A single period is too small to form an entire piece of music. The smaller species of composition need at least two distinct periods: the first to present the original idea, commonly called *motivo,* or *soggetto,* and the second as either a continuation or a development of the same *motivo.*" (Un solo periodo è troppo piccola cosa per formare un intero pezzo di musica. La più piccola specie di composizione abbisogna almeno di due distinti periodi: il primo per esporre l'idea primitiva, comunemente detta *motivo,* o *soggetto:* il secondo, o per una continuazione, o per uno sviluppo del *motivo* medesimo.)

54. According to an article in *La Musica* (1883, 4, no. 4: 3) probably authored by Michele Ruta, founder of the journal and professor at the Naples Conservatory from 1879, the study of what would now be called musical form was divided into "la *quadratura,* la *fraseologia,* and la *periodologia.*"

55. Reicha (2000 [1814], 38).

56. Ritorni (1841, 42): "Il rondò è un aggregamento di varj periodi gravi ed allegri, se piace con riprese, altri periodi subalterni, ed il più delle volte con interlocuzione ed accompagnamento di cori. . . . Dirò la cabaletta: un periodo deciso di frasi unite con estrema vivacità, il quale colpisce dilettevolmente l'orecchie, e facilmente si imprime nella memoria."

57. Ruta (1884, 1): "Analizzando la musica dal lato della esecuzione, noi troviamo che la melodia informatrice d'un concetto, come il discorso, è formata di periodi. I periodi si dividono in frasi, e le frasi alla loro volta si dividono in disegni, membri o incisi. Il periodo esprimendo un senso musicale compiuto, si determina per mezzo della cadenza." A similar description of the *periodo musicale,* emphasizing its identity with verses and strophes, may be found in De Vecchis (1850, 2:4–5).

58. Asioli (1832, 3:43): "Poche frasi bastano per formare un periodo non finito, che abbia la sua desinenza sull' accordo della 5.ª, o sulla Tonica con una semicadenza, lasciando in tal guisa interrotto il discorso musicale, e poetico. Il periodo intero si compone di un maggior numero di frasi, e finisce sulla Tonica, e sul punto affermativo, con una cadenza finale o semifinale."

59. Staffa (1856, 6).

60. This summary draws upon the more detailed overview of the literature given in Huebner (1992, 123–24). The works cited are Lippmann (1969c), Kerman (1982), and Balthazar (1988).

61. Basevi (1859a, 24); as cited in Parker (1997, 50). Although the units identified by Basevi consist of only a few measures, their closing cadences match the definition of the period given above.

62. Fabbri (2007, 131). The discussion of the "barform" *aab* appears to derive from Pagannone (1997).

63. Fabbri (2007, 127–28). The quotations from Lichtenthal and Bidera are drawn from Pagannone (2004a, 232).

64. Lichtenthal (1831, 232–33). A further quotation in support of the normative status of the eight-measure period may be found in De Vecchis (1850, 2: 6): "Periods comprised of even numbers of measures, and particularly those with eight measures, are called *Square Periods,* and these are the most effective and make the greatest impression on the soul." (I Periodi quando sono composti di battute pari, e particolarmente quelli d'otto battute, si dicono *Periodi Quadrati,* e questi sono i più sensibili, e che fanno più impressione nell'animo.)

65. Bidera (1853, 83, 85). For an assessment of Bidera's work, see Miragoli (1924, 156–57).

66. Balthazar (1988, 107).

67. Huebner (1992, 127).

68. Ibid., 131.

69. Webster (1991, 115–16). Webster's approach is premised on a concept of "multivalent analysis," in which formal function constitutes only one of many analytical parameters.

70. The term was commonly used in nineteenth-century Italy. See, e.g., Galeazzi (1796, 253): "The art of the perfect composer does not consist of finding galant themes [*galanti motivi*] or pleasing passages, but rather in the correct conduct [*esatta condotta*] of an entire piece of music." Bonds (1991: 92–100) provides a survey of writings on music as a type of discourse based on a principal "motive," beginning with Rousseau's definition (1792, 20:313–14) of "dessin" (*sic*; not "dessein") or overall layout as "the invention and conduct of the subject, the disposition of each part, and the general order of the whole" (l'invention et la conduite du sujet, la disposition de chaque partie et l'ordonnance générale du tout). Wedell (1995, 203–89) was the first to investigate these theories in relation to nineteenth-century opera, providing analytical commentaries to arias by Bellini, Donizetti, and the young Verdi.

71. De Vecchis (1850, 2:54): "la condotta di simili pezzi di musica viene regolata più dalla poesia, che dalle regole musicali."

72. See also the entries for *motivo* and *tema* in Vissian (1846, 138, 186).

73. Galeazzi (1796, 236). He also declared that "the fundamental rule of Conduct consists in the *Unity of the ideas*" (1796, 254). Gjerdingen (2007a, 369) gives an account of this notion of "conduct" from an eighteenth-century perspective. In particular, he interprets Leopold Mo-

zart's emphasis on the importance of "the thread," in a letter to Wolfgang of August 13, 1778, as a reference to the "cognitive thread (*il filo*) that, like Ariadne's thread which led Theseus through the labyrinth, guides the listener through a musical work." See also De Vecchis (1850, 1:72) and Anon. (1856a, 8, no. 42) on *condotta* in fugue.

74. Lichtenthal (1826, 1:186): "L'arte di conformare un'idea principale alle idee accessorie; ricondurre il *Motivo* a proposito senza abusarne, e di concatenare le sue modulazioni in modo, che sieno nè troppo, nè poco estese." According to Lucchese maestro Eugenio Galli (1840, 8), "The musical composition cannot be just a heap of *melodies*, it should resemble rather a well constructed speech." (E di fatto la musicale composizione non può essere un ammasso di *cantilene*, ma nella condotta vuolsi assomigliare ad un ben regolato discorso.)

75. Boucheron (1842, 113): "La buona condotta dà ai lavori d'arte quel carattere di spontaneità per cui volgarmente li diciamo di *getto*, parendo infatti essere quel lavoro uscito dalla mente dell'artista colla medesima facilità con cui una statua esce in ogni sua parte compiuta da una forma precedentemente preparata. Gl'italiani hanno in ciò un' attitudine mirabile; e se ponessero maggior cura di variare le forme, vincerebbero agevolmente gli stranieri."

76. The touchstone for approaches of this sort was Johann Mattheson's explanation of the "disposition" of a musical work through the six parts of an oration: namely, the introduction, the narration, the discourse, the corroboration, the confutation, and the conclusion (1739, 235).

77. Galeazzi (1796, 253–63). A parallel-text translation of most of the relevant passage may be found in Churgin (1968). Churgin's title and commentary are misleading, however, since Galeazzi explicitly

described *general* guidelines that may be
adapted to more specific genres (260). He
neither mentioned nor alluded to the later
concept of "sonata form."

78. Ibid., 254–55.

79. Asioli (1832, 3:42–43): "La composizione melodica è in tutto formato
di frasi, di periodi non finiti, di periodi
interi, e di divisioni cardinali chiamate
parti. Il Compositore primieramente
deve avere somma cura nella scelta delle
frasi che costituiscono il motivo; poichè
questo, oltre al fissar l'indole delle medesime, è solito riprodursi, primeggiare e
vestire un carattere significante e facile a
rammentarsi."

80. Ritorni (1841, 111): "il maestro legge un' aria, onde gli suggerisca l'idea del
motivo; e quando poi n' ha tratta l'invenzione, nulla si cura più che le forme subal-
terne rendano insieme ciocchè ottiene in
più facile modo complessivamente. Così
dalla forma della poetica strofa ricavasi
una maschera, che le si sovrappone poi
nuovamente, la quale non ne ha le singole
parti, sibbene, astrattamente, ingigantita
la fisonomia."

81. Boucheron (1842, 116): "Primo,
Esporre le idee da principio colla massima
semplicità riservando alle successive ripetizioni quegli artifizii che possono dare
alle medesime maggior risalto. Secondo,
Disporre le melodie e i passi caratteristici
in modo che i più espressivi succedano
ai meno, e si passi senza stento dall'una
all'altra idea. Terzo, Evitare le lunghezze,
ritenendo essere assai meglio il generar
desiderio che sazietà." Boucheron's advice
recalls Robert Hatten's category of "pleni-
tude" in relation to the music of Mozart,
Beethoven, and Schubert, which "may be
understood as a desired goal achieved by
processes that lead to the ultimate satura-
tion of texture and fulfillment" (2004, 43).
In the *primo Ottocento*, a sense of *telos* was
often achieved through rhythmic means,
as Asioli made clear (1832, 3:43): "The

second part, which closes the composition, increases in strength and movement
toward the end, approaching the final or
semi-final cadence at first broadly, then
with notes twice as fast, then even more
quickly [*più strette*], since this determines
the ultimate end of the composition."

82. Anon. (1883, 4, no. 8: 1): "Ogni
melodia è conseguenza di un periodo
tematico che svolgendosi forma il pezzo
di musica. Questo tema chiamasi *motivo;*
cioè che *motiva*, occasiona, cagiona la
melodia, dandole origine, impulso. Col
motivo si mette in *movimento*, si dà *moto*
alle frazioni del ritmo tematico che deve
regolare l'euritmia generale del pezzo....
l'inciso del *motivo* è quello che dà *moto* e
vita coi suoni svolti nel tempo alle diverse
frasi, periodi, parti del componimento
musicale, e succedendosi tesse la tela della
melodia e quindi del pezzo."

83. Bonds (1991, 68–79) offers an excellent survey of primary sources on the
metaphor of musical "grammar," extending as far back as Saint-Lambert (1702).
An analytical demonstration of a normative eight-measure period, suggesting the
influence of Reicha, occurs in Mampieri
(1840, 57). Beneath an example of a "first
half of a period," in common time and divided by two verse inflections (*desinenze*),
he wrote: "The period is completed with
another four measures, which, depending
on inspiration, may be extended in a thousand different ways involving a single meter of even-numbered beats." (Con altra
quattro battute ha compimento il periodo,
che a seconda del genio potrà stendersi in
mille fogge, una in un sol metro di battute
pari.)

84. Galeazzi (1796, 260).

85. Ibid., 261.

86. To avoid confusion I have translated Galeazzi's terms according to modern norms, as set out in Caplin (1998, 43).
The Italian traditions employed a very
wide variety of terms for cadence types.

To provide a comprehensive taxonomy would require a separate study.

87. See, e.g., the obvious parallels between Reicha (2000, 13–19) and this quotation from Ruta (1884, 1): "The phrase has a less marked resting point that can be called a semi-cadence, and, moreover, the incise, design, or members have an even less perceivable resting point, which can be called a quarter-cadence. . . . The cadences, semi-cadences, and quarter-cadences of music can be compared to the punctuation of normal written language." (La frase ha un riposo meno determinato che potrebbe chiamarsi semi-cadenza, ed infine l'inciso, il disegno e membri hanno un riposo anche meno sensibile il che potrebbe appellarsi quarto di cadenza. . . . Le cadenze, le semi-cadenze ed i quarti di cadenza della musica possono paragonarsi alla punteggiatura dell'ordinaria scrittura di una lingua.)

88. Ruta (1884, 2): "Tra i diversi frammenti che compongono un pezzo di musica, havvi un soggetto principale chiamato tema che è il tipo col quale il medesimo si svolge, tutte le altre parti non sono che smembramenti, deduzioni, o svolgimenti vari del medesimo."

89. To cite one representative example, Johann Forkel's conventional application (1788, 1:66–68), as quoted in Bonds (1991, 121–23), of the divisions of an oration to musical form begins with "(1) a main sentiment, (2) similar subsidiary sentiments, [etc.]." His category of Nebensätze or "subsidiary themes" corresponds in all important respects to the Italian secondo motivo.

90. Darcy and Hepokoski (2006, 93–116).

91. Ibid., 2006, 93.

92. In this regard, see also Boucheron (1842, 114).

93. Galeazzi (1796, 255–56).

94. Riepel (1996, 1: chap. 3, 1). A representative example of the monte operating as a modulating bridge passage between

the motivo and the passo caratteristico of an operatic melody may be found in measures 9–12 ("quando suonar per l'aere . . .") of Leonora's "Tacea la notte," from act 1 of Verdi's Il Trovatore.

95. Galeazzi (1796, 256).

96. Huebner (1992, 125).

97. Galeazzi (1796, 256).

98. Asioli (1832, 3:43): "Non minor cura richiede il Passo di carattere, che verrà collocato verso il fine della 1.ª parte alla 5.ª del Modo, e verso il fine della 2.ª ed ultima al Modo primo, ma soltanto nell'istromentale."

99. Huebner (1992, 125).

100. Galeazzi (1796, 257).

101. Galeazzi (1796, 256–57).

102. Ibid., 257.

103. Huebner (1992, 126).

104. Hepokoski (1989, 139).

105. De Vecchis (1850, 2: 25–31): "In un lavoro d'arte, la buona condotta è quella che dispone regolarmente tutti i suoi membri, e che gli medesima in un solo tutto ben composto, ed in ciò consiste la sua primaria bellezza" (p. 25). See also Sullo (2009, 99–103).

106. Picchianti (1834, 155): "I periodi principali sono quelli che costituiscono essenzialmente un pezzo di musica e che contengono per conseguenza i motivi, o soggetti, o le idee, che musicalmente prendesi ad esprimere. I periodi secondarii contengono idee accessorie, e alcune volte servono di complemento, di aggiunta, o di coda ad un periodo principale, ed alcune altre volte servono a congiungere due di questi principali periodi: così i piccoli periodi secondarii possono essere, o addizionali, o complementarii, o congiunzionali." This corresponds closely with Reicha (2000, 43–46) and with Lichtenthal's definition of "idea" (1826, 1:324): "Ideas are also defined as principal or secondary; the first really provide the basis or essence of a composition, while the others are intended to develop the principal idea."

(Si distinguono anche le *idee* in *principali* e *secondarie;* le prime sono proprie a far la base o il fondo di una composizione, le altre sono destinate allo sviluppamento dell'idea principale.)

107. See Huebner 1992, 127.

108. Boucheron (1842, 112–13): "La disposizione, parlando di musica, dicesi più comunemente *condotta,* e consiste nell'arte di disporre le idee principali e le accessorie in modo che le une preparino le altre, ed appariscano non già capricciosamente o a stento, ma pel naturale sviluppo dell'affetto necessariamente succedersi."

109. Bonds (2010) demonstrates that Antoine Reicha was the first to represent musical form in graphic or spatial terms, in his *Traité de haute composition musicale* (1824 26). The concept gained acceptance only gradually, and it was not until the last quarter of the nineteenth century that "letter-symbol" analyses became commonplace.

110. Galeazzi (1796, 254).

101. Ibid., 253.

112. Ibid., 276–80.

113. Ibid., 258.

114. Ibid., 300.

115. Wedell (1995, 51–53).

116. Such versatility is common in descriptions of aria forms in the Italian traditions. As Gervasoni (1800, 515) commented: "Then let it be observed that the form of the aria is subject to quite a few variations, according to the sentiment of the poetry."

117. Gervasoni (1800, 512–13): "Si compongono *Arie* d'un sol pezzo in allegro o in adagio, e se ne fanno ancora in due pezzi divise, il primo con un grado di movimento piuttosto lento, ed il secondo con un movimento più vivo." Wedell (1995, 63–64) misleadingly translates Galeazzi's *pezzo* into German as *Teil,* or part.

118. For instance, Gervasoni (1800, 518).

119. Asioli (1832, 1:22): "Siccome al presente domina nei Compositori la smania di modulare, per non costringere il Giovine alla stretta osservanza dei cinque analoghi, traccerò qui la condotta dell' intero pezzo musicale, ove vedrà il luogo proprio alle modulazioni estranee, e i cardini immobili della tessitura.

La Composizione è divisa o in due o tre parti cardinali. Ognuna di queste è formata di passaggi d' armonia e di modulazioni. I passaggi stabiliscono i Modi su cui si trovano, percorrendo le loro armonie. Le modulazioni sono stabili, secondarie, e di sfuggita. Le stabili sono quelle che fissano le divisioni cardinali della composizione: le secondarie hanno luogo fra le stabili; e quelle di sfuggita lo travano dappertutto.

Data adunque una composizione divisa in due parti cardinali, la prima modulazione stabile per legge di convenzione sarà alla 5.ª se il Modo è maggiore, o alla 3.ª se è minore; e la seconda ed ultima modulazione stabile sarà sul Modo principale, ove pure, per legge di convenzione dovrà avere il suo fine. Se poi la composizione è divisa in tre parti, la prima, ed ultima modulazione stabile sarà invariabilmente la stessa, e la media sarà su qualsivoglia Modo, o analogo, o estraneo al principale."

120. Evidence for this assertion may be found in Vitali (1850b).

121. Reicha (2000, 59). Bonds (1991, 149–52) provides a concise overview of Reicha's theory in terms of its significance to the development of "organic and mechanistic concepts of form throughout the nineteenth century and into the twentieth." He discusses the relativity of formal units on pages 27, 79–80, 84–85, and 119–20.

122. Reicha (2000, 37–38), (1830, 29).

123. Reicha (2000, 38), (1830, 30). Ruta (1855, 66–67) offers a Neapolitan definition of *la romanza.*

124. Reicha (2000, 44).

125. Choron and De LaFage (1836–39, 2: 272).

126. Reicha (2000, 46).

127. Reicha (1830, 31). Owing to the relativity of the various dimensions and the flexibility inherent in the guidelines for tonal structures, Reicha's formal types do not lend themselves well to graphic representation through letter symbols or Roman numerals.

128. Picchianti (1834, 155–57).

129. Asioli (1832, 3:44): "L'Aria, pezzo musicale piccolo in sè stesso, cresce a poco a poco e si estende sopra varie dimensioni, a segno da poter servire come Finale nel Dramma."

130. Asioli (1832, 3:44): "Chiamasi Arietta la *Canzone* di pochi periodi."

131. De Vecchis (1850, 2:31).

132. In Verdi's autograph score, held at the archives of Casa Ricordi in Milan, Elvira's *cavatina* was originally notated in A major and subsequently transposed up a semitone to B♭. Also, the tempo modifier "*piuttosto vivo*" was added to the original marking of "*andantino*." See the facsimile of f.40v. reproduced as plate 1 in Verdi (1985a) and the accompanying critical commentary (1985b, 36). Staffa presumably used the manuscript dating from 1848, currently held in the Library of the Conservatorio di Musica San Pietro a Maiella in Naples (Fondo Verdi, 285–89).

133. Budden (1992, 1:151).

134. Asioli (1832, 3:44): "dicesi Aria la *Cavatina* che ha principio, mezzo e fine."

135. Boucheron (1842, 112).

136. Reicha (2000, 41).

137. L. Ricci (1954, 127), translated in Dunstan (1989, 159).

138. Verdi (2005a); see also (2005b, 73–84).

139. Anon. (1883, 4, no. 4: 3): "La *Melodia* divenne signora dell'opera d'arte musicale, ed i Maestri, liberati dai lacci scolastici, attinsero le loro ispirazioni là dove svolgesi—l'eterna armonia che ci governa—Ma siccome in tutto si eccede, anche la quadratura del pezzo ed il filo melodico divennero schiavi di un servile

convenzionalismo; i mediocri ingegni, ed anche qualche ingegno distinto, oltrepassarono i limiti di una artistica semplicità, e la melodia resero cantilena *chitarristica*. E quindi la reazione della giovane scuola; ma questa reazione, dalla quale nasceranno le nuove forme, deve guardarsi dal seguire l'andazzo di certa musica antiartistica, antinazionale ed antilogica."

140. See Landey's glossary of terms in Reicha (2000, xiii).

141. Picchianti (1834, 156). In the next sentence, he inadvertently contradicted himself by paraphrasing a passage that occurred slightly later in Reicha (1830): "A musical composition can therefore be divided into two, three, or more sections."

6. VOCALIZZI, SOLFEGGI, AND REAL (OR IDEAL) COMPOSITION

1. Florimo (1881–83, 3: 18).

2. See Cafiero (2009, 14–16). Marcello Perrino, who became rector of the newly amalgamated Reale collegio di musica di San Sebastiano in 1806, sought to preserve the ancient school of singing in his *Metodo di Canto,* which also confirmed the fundamental division of counterpoint into theory and practice; see Florimo (1881–83, 2:41).

3. On Rossi's earlier *solfeggi,* see Corghi (1847).

4. Tosi (1723, 54): "Stò quasi per dire, che sia infallibilmente vana qualunque applicazione al Canto se non è accompagnata da qualche poca cognizione di Contrappunto. Chi sa comporre sa render conto di quello, che fà, e chi non ha l'istesso lume opera allo scuro, ne può cantar molto tempo senza errare." See also Agricola (2006 [1757], 185).

5. Eighteenth-century accounts of the daily training regimes of *castrati* offer further evidence of this division of counterpoint into "practice" and "theory." Caffarelli's studies under Neapolitan

maestro Nicola Porpora included vocal exercises in front of the mirror, designed to improve agility, a half hour each of "theoretical work" and "counterpoint on a *canto fermo* (in other words, practice in improvisation)," followed by an hour of written counterpoint with the *cartella;* see Heriot (1980 [1956], 48), who drew upon primary source material from Haböck (1927) without reference. Florimo (1881–83, 2: 30), in his account of instruction at the Neapolitan conservatories, continued to refer to harmony as either played or written (*armonia sonata e scritta*).

6. In the Italian schools of the eighteenth century, singers were required to spend an entire year doing nothing but solmization on the medieval hexachords. See Agricola (2006 [1757], 8) and Hiller (2001 [1779], 47). This was largely replaced by the simpler seven-note sol-fa system around the year 1800, although Stanislao Mattei (ca. 1824–25) continued to refer to exercises using the ancient methods. As confirmed by Fausto Fritelli (1743, 12), *maestro di cappella nella metropolitana di Siena*, the seven-note system arrived in Italy from France during the 1730s. Sabbatini (1789–90, 1:40–43) recommended and described in detail both the *sistema antico* of Guido Arentino [*sic*] and the easier *sistema moderno,* otherwise known as the "system of sì." For example, a rising major scale would be rendered *do-re-mi-fa-sol-re-mi-fa* according to the ancient system and *do-re-mi-fa-sol-la-sì-do* according to the modern. A radical proposal for a simplified system was contemplated by Picchi (1853c). Musical lexicons often included the Guidonian Hand as a frontispiece, even as late as Galli (1902).

7. Sabbatini (1789–90, 3:5): "La Scala nell'ascendere farete, ed in contrario voi discenderete, in tempo moderato; ma intuonate; così và bene: or vocalizzate. A . . ."

8. See, e.g., Sala (1794, Milan Conservatory Library, Ms. TM40: 40r–47v).

9. See Sabbatini (1789–90, 1:22–39).

10. That this method of training was in use in Naples at least as early as the late seventeenth century, and that it served to unite counterpoint and sol-fa (singing), may be observed in the three-voice *solfeggiamenti* of Cristoforo Caresana (director of the Conservatorio di Sant'Onofrio a Porta Capuana from 1667 to 1690), one of which was reproduced as an example of a fugue *a tre* by Martini (1774–75, 2:31–33); the relevant passage is translated in Mann (1986, 272–74). Scored for two sopranos and tenor, it places an ascending and descending scale of C major in each voice in turn, to which the others add imitative counterpoints. As Martini explained, *solfeggiamenti* were "works based on subjects made up of scale progressions using all intervals from the second to the octave . . . written with the greatest skill yet with the characteristic ease of *solfeggio* exercises."

11. The reliance upon simple scales and bass motions, never exceeding the range of an octave plus a fifth, as guiding voices for improvisation (i.e., counterpoint), would also explain how Nicola Porpora, teacher of the great *castrati* Farinelli and Cafarrelli, managed to confine five or six years' worth of singing exercises to a single page. According to an editorial note in Porpora (1858, 1): "Porpora wrote all his vocal exercises on *one sheet of paper* and considered *practical examples* of teachers as essential to all vocal students." Saverio Mattei confirmed in 1791 that the art of singing should begin with studies on a *canto fermo;* see Florimo (1881–83, 2:58).

12. A similar pattern may be found in a variety of sources, from the psalm Glorias of Monteverdi's *Vespers* (1610), through Corelli's op. 1, no. 2 (vivace, mm. 2–4) and the chorus "Was betrübst du dich"

from Bach's Cantata BWV 21, to Handel's composition exercises for Princess Anne (1724–35, Cambridge, Fitzwilliam Museum, MU MS 260, 57) and the Amen chorus that closes his *Messiah* (1741). The device appears as a three-part *canone all'unissono da potersi fare all'improviso* in Berardi (1687, 109), as a vocal canon by Gottfried Heinrich Stölzel in Marpurg (1763, 171), and as a *fuga tonale a tre voce* in De Vecchis (1850, Examples 1:64).

13. For definitions of the fugal *ripercussione*, see Lichtenthal (1826, 1:284) and Asioli, "On the Order of the Parts of a Fugue" (1832, 2:30 and Examples 2:28–34).

14. This suggested connection between the practice of sung exercises in counterpoint, *solfeggi*, operatic melodies, and Italian vocal performance style before ca. 1840 has received very little scholarly attention, partly because modern studies of *bel canto* (Celletti, Manén, Stark, etc.) concentrate almost exclusively on vocal issues. While an emphasis on vocal technique and interpretation accords well with modern (actually, late nineteenth-century) ideologies of training in musical performance—discipline-specific, highly specialized, insular—it would have made little sense to the original practitioners of the art, for whom singing, composition, and improvisation were essentially inseparable (much as they are today in the work of some popular singer-songwriters).

On the use of the term *bel canto*, it is wrong to suggest that it was applied only in retrospect as an expression of a lost golden age, for instance by Rossini in 1858 or in conversation with Wagner in 1860. This unfounded claim originated in Duey (1951, 4–12) and has been repeated in many later publications, such as Owen Jander's entry on *bel canto* in *The New Grove* (1980 and 2001), Stark (1999, xviii), and Taruskin (2009b, 37–40). The term is commonly encountered in early nineteenth-century Italian sources. The

vocal department at the Liceo musicale in Bologna was renamed, for instance, the year after Rossini's departure from it, as the Scuola di bel canto (from 1811–39). After that, it was called the Scuola di canto perfezionato and, from 1866, the Scuola di canto solfeggio.

Gervasoni (1800, 350) used the terms *canto spianato* and *bel canto* interchangeably, as did Santucci (1828, 113) in his composite formulation *bel canto spianato*, to signify the embellished vocal style of the late eighteenth century. Perrino (1810, 38) used the alternative term *canto spianato e sostenuto*. Lichtenthal (1826, 1:127) associated "*Canto spianato*, otherwise called *Cantabile*" with "the art of threading the notes" (*l'arte di filar i suoni*) and with the sentiment of *nobilità*. In this sense "threading" had nothing to do with the "thread" (*filo*) that served to unify the conduct of a piece, but indicated rather the application of the vocal "swell" or *messa di voce*. Milanese singing professor Francesco Lamperti (1864, 6; 1891, 9), for instance, who explicitly ascribed his method to the *castrati* of the late eighteenth century, defined "threaded notes" (*suoni filati*) as indicative of the fourth, most important and difficult method of singing, which "consists of attacking a note pianissimo, reinforcing it to the full extent of the voice, and then gradually diminishing it, so as to end pianissimo, retaining the same quality of sound in all the gradations of crescendo and diminuendo." Asioli (1832, 3:43) distinguished three types of vocal delivery: *canto declamativo* (declamatory singing), *bel canto* (fine singing), and *di un getto solo* (of a single throw/cast in one way). The precise meaning of the latter term remains elusive, since it is rooted in a mode of performance that has gone largely unrecorded. Asioli's brief observation that in an *aria di un getto solo* "a single phrase in a single tempo dominates from beginning to end" may have referred to a straightforward style of execution, devoid of expressive distortions to the *ritmo* and other embellishments.

In general, the terms *bel canto, canto spianato, canto figurato,* and occasionally *cantabile* were all used to refer to the smooth, expressive, and heavily ornamented style of singing (hence also of melody) of the great eighteenth-century *castrati* or, as they were euphemistically known, "musickers" (*musici*), as inherited and adapted by their successors, the soprano prima donnas who came to the fore in the early nineteenth century as a result of the Napoleonic suppression of castration. Stendhal (1824, 251–52), a champion of the old traditions, traced the origins of *bel canto* very precisely to Bolognese castrato Francesco Pistocchi in the year 1680 and claimed, in an obvious snub to Rossini, that it was perfected in 1778 through the vocal art of Gasparo Pacchierotti. He also affirmed and documented the crucial links between the new schools of soprano singing and their teachers, the great *castrati*. On these connections, see also André (2006, 36–44).

Canto spianato was generally associated with the traditional recitation of poetry, while *bel canto* aspired to a "natural" form of pronunciation. The castrato Girolamo Crescentini (1811, 4), for instance, maintained that his exercises were designed to impart skills in a type of lyric oratory: "Singing should be an imitation of speech" (Il canto deve essere un imitazione del discorso). Maguire (1989, 50–57, 146–76) provides a survey of primary sources that testify to the predominance of poetry over mechanical aspects of singing in the *bel canto* traditions.

By the time of Ritorni (1841), the terms *bel canto* and *spianato* had begun to signify a style of singing associated with the age of Rossini and Bellini. A newer style, associated primarily with

the teachings of García, placed greater emphasis on volume of sound and vocal projection (for instance, by keeping the larynx lowered). The differences between Italian singing styles of the 1820s and 1840s were discussed in the Neapolitan journal *L'Omnibus;* see Maguire (1989, 56). Boucheron (1842, 69) rebranded the *cantabile* style with the more philosophical-sounding term *canto ideale* (ideal singing), which he opposed to *canto declamato* (declamatory singing).

15. Gossett (2006, 290–331) offers an invaluable survey and discussion of the evidence contained in composers' sketches for the practice of vocal performance in Italian opera during the first half of the nineteenth century.

16. Since the present chapter is concerned with the connections between vocal training, melody, and composition, especially as they continued to feature as late as Puccini's works, it bypasses the lengthy discussions on technical aspects of the voice that tended to dominate published vocal "methods" from the time of Mancini (1777) onwards and focuses instead on the notated singing exercises. The descriptive parts of vocal methods usually concerned general observations on the voice and the different voice types and their registers, followed by descriptions of techniques such as the *messa di voce* and the *portamento,* and ornaments such as the *appoggiatura,* trill, and *passaggi.* Most methods included a series of *vocalizzi* or *solfeggi* and sometimes examples of recitatives, arias, and cadenzas.

17. Gervasoni (1800, examples: 9); as discussed above in chapter 4. The method is explained in more detail in Gervasoni (1812, 341–57). Sabbatini (1789–90, 2:66–78) offers another example of the same method: his progressive course of sung counterpoint through scales and leaps culminates in a series of *solfeggi* designed to impart vocal skills such as the trill,

the use of falsetto, and the application of appoggiaturas.

18. According to Mancini (1777, 244, 250), who studied singing with Leo: "Questo grand'uomo costumava di scrivere ogni tre giorni un nuovo solfeggio a ciascun suo scolare, ma con riflessione di adattarlo alle forze ed all'abilità di ciascuno." See also Tosi (1723, 13). Mozart, incidentally, wrote a series of *solfeggi* (K. 393/K.⁶ 385b) for Constanze Weber, an accomplished singer, whom he married on August 4, 1782.

19. As Mancini acknowledged (1777, 254), Padre Martini was renowned for the composition of such duets. A characteristic set may be found in Asioli (ca. 1795). Ledbetter (2009, 36) discusses this traditional teaching method in relation to early eighteenth-century instrumental repertories.

20. According to Maguire (1989, 117), the first such collection published in Paris was *Solfèges d'Italie* in 1772. In Lichtenthal's dictionary (1826, 1:365), Mengozzi was listed as the last singer of the Florentine school worthy of mention.

21. Batiste (1867, 1:vii).

22. Manuel García's researches on physiological aspects of the voice, his treatise on the art of singing (1840, 1847), and his invention of the laryngoscope (1855) did much to encourage this shift away from the inclusive style of musical training typical of the Italian traditions toward the specialized, discipline-specific style of vocal pedagogy that continues to inform conservatory teaching to this day. Although he claimed to have studied briefly with Zingarelli in Naples and traded on his Italian connections, albeit as a Spaniard, the Italians regarded him as a Parisian. Regli's biographical dictionary (1860, 224) described him as a "French singer." His ideas were nevertheless taken up in Italy by Giraldoni (1864) and Delle Sedie (1876). For evidence of the conservative Italian

reaction to the new "Parisian" methods of singing, see Anon. (1852a), Anon. (1854b), Mariotti (1853), Lo Basso (1856), Ruffini (1856), and Meini (1858–59).

23. In 1807 Vaccai gave up law studies in Rome to train with Paisiello in Naples. After some success as an opera composer, he established himself in 1830 as a singing teacher in Paris, venturing into the London market in 1832. He soon returned to Milan to take up a teaching position at the Conservatory, eventually becoming its director. His *Practical Method of Italian Singing* remains in use to this day. See Ghislanzoni (1855) for a contemporary assessment.

24. Mathilde Marchesi de Castrone (née Graumann) studied in her native Frankfurt, in Vienna, and in Paris with García, where, in 1881, she founded an extraordinarily successful school of singing. She trod the boards only once as an operatic mezzo, in Bremen in 1852, subsequently devoting her career to teaching. As García's most active disciple, she promoted his innovative, specialized, physiological approach to vocal training, and occasionally exploited the term *bel canto* for its aura of tradition and authenticity (Rosselli 1992, 109). Incidentally, the chromatic scale for the "emission of the voice" that begins her *Metodo teorico pratico per canto: op. 31* derives from the exercise in *messa di voce* that precedes Bordogni's set of twelve *vocalizzi* (1842).

25. See Florimo (1881–83, 2: 412–13).

26. Paraschivescu (2009, 60). Before arriving in Naples Bellini received musical training from his grandfather, Vincenzo Tobia Bellini (1744–1829), who had studied with Durante and Leo at the Conservatorio di Sant'Onofrio a Porta Capuana during the 1750s. A contemporary account of Zingarelli may be found in De LaFage (1854).

27. De Vecchis (1850, 2: 31): "[Solfeggi] conducono con molto sollecitudine

all'acquisto del buon Canto espressivo, tanto più che in simili Componimenti, il Compositore è libero nell'adop[e]rare quel canto che più aggrada, di tessergli come più gli piace, ed esprimere a suo piacere qualsiasi Affetto." As quoted in Sullo (2009, 99).

28. Countless collected volumes of *solfeggi* were published throughout the nineteenth century—far too many to list here. Hasse's set of twelve were first published after his death as part of a collection purporting to represent the "School of Singing of the Ancient Conservatory of Naples," edited by D. Giuseppe Aprile (1791). They first reached a wider audience as part of a series entitled *Solfeggi d'Italia* (London: Monzani, 1807). A modern "Urtext" edition of Hasse's twelve *solfeggi* may be found in Hasse (1982).

Vittorio Ricci studied composition and singing in his native Florence and later in Paris with Giovanni Sbriglia before taking up a position as singing teacher at the University of Edinburgh. Between 1900 and 1917 he published numerous collections of didactic pieces for vocal practice according to the "Old Italian School," as well as *The Art of Phrasing for the Violin: Melodies of Old Italian Masters* (London: Joseph Williams, 1914).

29. Drabkin (1986, 87); Christen (1978, 99–102).

30. The Italians were in general far less squeamish about parallel fifths and octaves than the Germans, perhaps because of the frequent seeming parallels that arose through practical counterpoint exercises based on the scale. See, for example, Asioli (1832, Examples 1:23), Rossi (1858, 106, 111), and De Sanctis (n.d. [1887?], 141). Passages of parallel root-position triads even occurred from time to time in opera scores, from the passage "Già cade il dì" (or "Voici la nuit") in the opening chorus of act 2 of Rossini's *Guillaume Tell* to Desdemona's

"amava un uom" in Verdi's *Otello* (act 4, RD, m. 4). According to Lauro Rossi's harmony course for the Milan Conservatory (1858, 26), "In the free modern style fifths are just about tolerated ascending and descending by conjunct step in direct motion between the inner parts." In a footnote he elaborated further: "And there is no lack of examples of successions of fifths between the parts and the bass. I am however of the opinion that such licenses should be used as seldom as possible."

31. Gara (1958, 134): "L'atto è composto quasi tutto di *ritorni* logici, salvo il duettino 'Sono andati' e la Zimarra di Colline e poco altro. Mi pare d'aver trovato per il *duettino* un buon principio e la frase culminante è efficace benchè non troppo nuova; ma bisogna poi non sottilizzare tanto—non è vero?"

32. The text from the revised 1905 edition of the opera reproduced in Example 6.4 remained identical to the original libretto of 1889; see Puccini (2002, 16).

33. Mancini (1777, 73–74) described the typical style in which maestros would accompany singing students: "to anyone who understands music, the oldest and most ancient rules by which a Professor of singing accompanies are well known: only a few fingers should be used on the keyboard, [and] the addition of free elaborations is not desirable; rather, a very firm and simple accompaniment is required, so that the singer is not disturbed in any way" (a chiunque conosce la Musica, son note le vecchie vecchissime regole, che per accompagnare un Professore di canto, devonsi adoperare sul Cembalo poche dita, non vi vogliono grazie aggiunte a capriccio, ma richiedesi il più rodo, e semplice accompagnamento, acciò [che] il cantante in verun modo non sia disturbato). See also Perrino (1810, 22).

34. The first version of 1889 contains a number of variants and additional lines; see Puccini (2002, 18).

35. To mention a few of the most obvious examples, see the descending minor scales in second position underlying "Cortigiani, vil razza dannata" from act 2 of Verdi's *Rigoletto* or "Regnava nel silenzio" from act 1 of Donizetti's *Lucia di Lammermoor,* or, in descending third position, "La donna è mobile" from act 3 of *Rigoletto* or Mimì's "Ascolta, ascolta" from Puccini's *La Bohème,* act 3.

36. Basevi (1859a, 24).

37. The original libretto of 1893 omits the line "un gelido mortal" from the beginning of the aria, but is otherwise similar to later versions; see Puccini (2002, 41).

38. Girardi (2000, 124–26). For discussions of the relevance of the "usual" duet form to Puccini's operas, see Powers (2004) and Rosen (2004). It is worth noting that Girardi's fidelity to the cause of rebranding Puccini's style as "international"—by emphasizing its connections with contemporary developments in the supposed mainstream of European musical culture—led him to downplay the conventional elements of this duet scene, even to apologize for them: "It is thus clear how the traditional arrangement of set pieces is no more [!] than the vehicle Puccini used to ensure comprehensibility and emphasize the universality of the message" (p. 126).

39. English translation adapted from Weaver (1966, 33). This section of text, extracted from the vocal score of 1896, corresponds closely to that of the original libretto, with the exception of an additional "e intanto" before "le dirò con due

parole"; see Puccini (2002, 61) and Bernardoni (2008, 217).

40. Translation adapted from Weaver (1966, 35). The original libretto of 1896 set the verses from "Chi son?—Sono un poeta" to "Vi piace dirlo? [Vi piaccia dir]," including these, as seven tercets of *settenari;* see Puccini (2002, 61) and Bernardoni (2008, 218). The final version, reproduced here, added the line "e i bei sogni miei" and the extra "deh! parlate" in the last verse.

41. Translation adapted from Weaver (1966, 35). This final version of the text differs significantly from the original version of 1896; see Puccini (2002, 62) and Bernardoni (2008, 218–19).

42. Translation from Weaver (1966, 188). The original libretto of 1900 differs in significant respects; see Puccini (2002, 94).

43. Dahlhaus (1989, 117–19). In an article published in the last ever edition of the conservative Neapolitan journal *La Musica,* exhorting young composers not to forget their national roots, Florence-trained maestro Gandolfi (1885, 1) chose this same melody to counter the argument that Italian opera relied on bland symmetrical formulas.

44. See Gjerdingen (2007a, 77–88).

45. De Vecchis (1850, 1: 27): "Il Giovane d'ingegno dovrà più presto che potrà, incominciare a dare la forma delle Frasi, e Periodi, alle sue Melodie, per quanto comporterà la natura del Basso delle lezioni, se vuol trar profitto dallo studio del Contrappunto."

PRIMARY SOURCES (BEFORE 1912)

Agricola, Johann Friedrich. 2006. *Introduction to the Art of Singing*. Trans. and ed. Julianne Baird. Cambridge: Cambridge University Press. Orig. pub. as *Anleitung zur Singkunst*, Berlin, 1757.

Algarotti, Francesco. 1763. *Saggio sopra l'opera in musica*. Leghorn: Coltellini.

Andreoli, Guglielmo, and Edgardo Codazzi. 1898. *Manuale d'armonia*. Milan: L. F. Cogliati.

Anon. n.d. [ca. 1707]. *Primi Elementi di Musica prattica per gli Studenti Principianti di tal Professione. A' quali si sono aggiunti alquanti Solfeggi a due voci in partitura, d'eccellente Autore*. Venice: Antonio Bortoli a S. Maria Formosa in Calle Longa.

Anon. n.d. [1760s?]. "Principi di musica con Solfeggi, ed altre Regole che contengano [*sic*] in questo libretto e cadenze per tutti i tuoni." Museo internazionale e biblioteca della musica di Bologna, Ms. II.239.

Anon. n.d. [1772]. *Solfèges d'Italie avec la basse chiffrée composés par Leo, Durante, Scarlatti, Hasse, Porpora, Mazzoni, Caffaro, David Perez &c. Recueillis par les Srs Levesque & Bêche, Ordinaire de la musique de Sa Majesté*. Paris, Versailles: Cousineau.

Anon. 1818. *Regolamento generale per l'educazione delle alunne nel Real Conservatorio Luisa Carlotta in Lucca*. Lucca: Tipografia Reale.

Anon. 1835. "Alexandre Choron." *Supplement to the Musical Library* 10:115. London: Charles Knight.

Anon. 1848. "Della musica in Germania." *L'Italia musicale* 1, no. 47 (June 21): 342–43.

Anon. 1851a. "Polemica." *L'Italia musicale* 3, no. 31 (April 16): 121–23.

Anon. 1851b. "Del dramma lirico." *L'Italia musicale* 3, no. 32 (April 19): 125–26; 3, no. 34 (April 26): 133–34; 3, no. 36 (May 3): 141–42; 3, no. 43 (May 28): 169; 3, no. 44 (May 31): 173–74; 3, no. 50 (June 21): 197–98; 3, no. 53 (July 2): 209–10.

Anon. 1851c. "L'arte è morta?" *L'Italia musicale* 3, no. 93 (November 10): 369–70.

Anon. 1851d. "Della scuola fantastica in musica." *L'Italia musicale* 3, no. 94 (November 22): 373–74; 3, no. 95 (November 26): 377–78.

Anon. 1852a. "Sul metodo di canto della signora Cinti-Damoreau sui metodi pratici di vocalizzazione per le voci di basso, di baritone, e di tenore del professore Gaetano Nava." *L'Italia musicale* 4, no. 43 (May 29): 169–70.

Anon. 1852b. "Le due scuole." *L'Italia musicale* 4, no. 89 (November 6): 353–54.

Anon. 1852–53. "Sguardo allo stato degli studi estetici-musicali." *L'Italia musicale* 4, no. 50 (June 23): 197–98;

4, no. 58 (July 21): 229–30; 4, no. 60 (July 28): 237–38; 4, no. 62 (August 4): 245–46; 4, no. 71 (September 4): 281–82; 4, no. 79 (October 2): 313–14; 4, no. 83 (October 13): 325–26; 4, no. 91 (November 13): 361–62; 4. No. 103 (December 28): 409–10; 5, no. 2 (January 5): 7–8.

Anon. 1853a. "Domanda e desiderio." *L'Italia musicale* 5, no. 33 (April 23): 131–32; 5, no. 34 (April 27): 135–36.

Anon. 1853b. "Schizzi storici. Il canto." *L'Italia musicale* 5, no. 66 (August 17): 263–64; 5, no. 67 (August 20): 267–68; 5, no. 69 (August 27): 275–76.

Anon. 1853c. "La musica in Alemagna." *L'Italia musicale* 5, no. 79 (October 1): 315; 5, no. 85 (October 22): 340; 5, no. 86 (October 26): 343–44; 5, no. 89 (November 5): 355–56; 5, no. 90 (November 9): 359–60; 5, no. 93 (November 19): 371–72; 5, no. 94 (November 23): 375–76; 5, no. 96 (November 30): 383–84; 5, no. 101 (December 17): 403–404; 5, no. 103 (December 24): 411–12; 5, no. 105 (December 31): 419–20.

Anon. 1853–54. "Tradizioni della musica italiana." *L'Italia musicale* 5, no. 23 (March 19): 91–92; 5, no. 26 (March 30): 103–104; 5, no. 31 (April 16): 123; 5, no. 36 (May 4): 143–44; 5, no. 38 (May 11): 151–52; 5, no. 41 (May 21): 163; 5, no. 47 (June 11): 187; 5, no. 57 (July 16): 227–28; 5, no. 70 (August 31): 279–80; 5, no. 73 (September 10): 291–92; 5, no. 82 (October 12): 327–28; 5, no. 83 (October 15): 331; 5, no. 86 (October 26): 343–44; 5, no. 90 (November 9): 359–60; 6, no. 3 (January 11): 9–10.

Anon. 1854a. "Filosofia della musica: Melodia–Ritmo–Armonia." *L'Italia musicale* 6, no. 66 (August 19): 261–62.

Anon. 1854b. "Dei cantanti e dei maestri di canto." *L'Italia musicale* 6, no. 9 (1 February): 33–34; 6, no. 10 (4 February): 37–38; 6, no. 14 (18 February): 53–54; 6, no. 16 (25 February): 61–62.

Anon. [X.]. 1854c. "Ciarle sulla musica del giorno." *Gazzetta musicale di Firenze* 2, no. 11 (August 24): 41–42.

Anon. [X. antiscettico]. 1854d. "Voce, voce, e voce." *Gazzetta musicale di Firenze* 2, no. 15 (September 21): 57.

Anon. [X.]. 1854e. "Zerino." *Gazzetta musicale di Firenze* 2, no. 18 (October 12): 69–70.

Anon. 1854f. "Il Maestro." *Gazzetta musicale di Firenze* 2, no. 27 (December 14): 105–106.

Anon. 1855a. "Sguardo storico sulla scuola napolitana." *La Musica* 1, no. 30 (August 24): 233–35.

Anon. 1855b. "Poetica ad uso dei librettisti." *Gazzetta musicale di Firenze* 2, no. 40 (March 15): 157–58.

Anon. 1856a. "Dei trattati di composizione." *L'Italia musicale* 8, no. 34 (April 26): 133–34; 8, no. 35 (April 30): 137–38; 8, no. 39 (May 14): 153–54; 8, no. 41 (May 21): 161–62; 8, no. 42 (May 24): 165–66.

Anon. 1856b. "Un consiglio ai poeti melodrammatici." *L'Armonia* 1, no. 36 (October 15): 141–42.

Anon. [G. N.]. 1857a. "Delle scuole e dei sistemi in musica." *L'Armonia* 4, no. 1 (January 15): 165–66.

Anon. 1857b. "Studio sul *Pirata* di Bellini." *L'Armonia* 4, no. 19 (May 30): 37–39.

Anon. [C. M.]. 1858a. "Corso elementare completo di lettura musicale, in brevi solfeggi, di R. Boucheron." *L'Armonia* 5, no. 9 (May 15): 129.

Anon. [Pietro Trisolini?]. 1858b. "Intorno all'avvenire dell'arte musicale." *L'Armonia* 6, no. 21 (November 15): 177–78.

Anon. 1861. *Regolamento per li Signori Musici della Capella di San Petronio in Bologna.* Bologna: Tipografia alla Colomba.

Anon. 1876. "Pedagogia musicale: Lo studio dell'armonia in Italia." *La Musica* 1, no. 3 (August 19): 2–3.

Anon. [Michele Ruta?]. 1883. "La Melodia." *La Musica* 4, no. 1 (January 1):

1–2; 4, no. 2 (January 15): 1–2; 4, no. 3 (February 5): 1–2; 4, no. 4 (February 19): 2–3; 4, no. 5 (March 5): 1–2; 4, no. 6 (March 19): 1–2; 4, no. 7 (April 2): 1–3; 4, no. 8 (April 16): 1–2; 4, no. 9 (May 7): 1–2; 4, no. 10 (May 21): 1–2; 4, no. 11 (June 4): 1–3; 4, no. 13 (July 2): 1–2; 4, no. 14 (July 16): 1–2; 4, no. 16 (August 20): 1–2.

Aprile, D. Giuseppe. 1791. *Die Singschule oder Solmisation, dergleichen noch keiner zum Vorscheine gekommen, worinnen die nothwendigsten Regeln und eine Menge musikalische und fugirte Stücke.* Vienna: L. Hohenleitner.

———.1812. *The Modern Italian Method of Singing with a Variety of Progressive Examples, and Thirty-six Solfeggi.* London: Goulding, d'Almaine, Potter and Co.

Arteaga, Stefano. 1783, 1785, 1788. *Le rivoluzioni del teatro musicale italiano dalla sua origine fino al presente.* 3 vols. 2d ed. Bologna: Stamperia di Carlo Palese; reprint of the 1st ed., Sala Bolognese: Arnaldo Forni, 1969.

Asioli, Bonifazio. ca. 1795. *Collection complette des duos avec accompagnement de piano ou de harpe.* Paris: Tipographie de la Syrène.

———.1809. *Primi elementi di canto.* Milan: G. Ricordi.

———.1814. *Trattato di armonia adottato dal Regio conservatorio di musica di Milano.* Milan: G. Ricordi.

———.1824 [1809]. *Principj elementari di musica adottati dall'I. R. Conservatorio di Milano per le ripetizioni giornaliere degli alunni compilati da B. Asioli.* Turin: Giacinto Marietti.

———.ca. 1829. *Dialoghi sul Trattato di armonia composti da Bonifazio Asioli.* 2d ed. Milan: Ricordi.

———.1832. *Il Maestro di composizione, ossia seguito del Trattato d'armonia.* 3 vols. Milan: Ricordi.

———.1836. *Elementi di Contrappunto.* Florence: V. Batelli e figli.

"Avvocato A. G." [Carlo Andrea Gambini?]. 1844. "Cenni sul R. Istituto musicale di Lucca." *Gazzetta musicale di Milano* 3, no. 41 (October 13): 170–71.

Azzopardi, Francesco. 1786. *Le musicien pratique, ou leçons qui conduisent les élèves dans l'art du contrepoint, en leur enseignant la manière de composer correctement toute espèce de musique; ouvrage composé dans les principes des Conservatoires d'Italie et mis dans l'ordre le plus simple et le plus clair.* Trans. M. Framery. Paris: Le Duc.

Bach, Carl Philipp Emanuel. 1949. *Essay on the True Art of Playing Keyboard Instruments.* Trans. William J. Mitchell (*Versuch über die wahre Art, das Clavier zu spielen*, vol. 1, Berlin, 1753). London: Cassell.

Baini, Giuseppe. 1820. *Saggio sopra l'identità de' ritmi musicale e poetico.* Florence: Piatti. Trans. Comte de Saint Leu as *Essai sur l'identité du Rhythme poétique et musical, traduit de l'ouvrage italien de Mr. L'Abbé Joseph Baini.* Florence: Piatti, 1820.

Balbi, Melchiorre. 1845a. *Grammatica ragionata della musica considerata sotto l'aspetto di lingua.* Milan: G. Ricordi.

———.1845b. "Proposta di una definizione del ritmo (Riposta ad un quesito del signor Don N. E. Cattaneo)." *Gazzetta musicale di Milano* 4, no. 5 (February 2): 20–21.

———.1868. *Rudimenti musicali compilati secondo il nuovo sistema proposto dallo stesso e confrontati col presente di B. Asioli adottati dal R. Conservatorio di Milano.* Padua: Prosperini.

Bandini, Uberto. 1888. *Scuola di armonia, contrappunto e composizione.* Milan: Ricordi.

Bàrberi, Americo. 1868. *Scienza nuova delle armonie de' suoni e sue leggi raccolte a codice da Americo Bàrberi professore di acustica sperimentale.* 2d ed. Milan: Paolo de Giorgi editore musicale.

Barbirolli, Luigi. 1857. *Principii di metodica musicale coll'applicazione del metronomo*. Rovigo: Minelli.

Basevi, Abramo. 1853. "Potenza della musica." *Gazzetta musicale di Firenze* 1, no. 23 (November 17): 89–90; 1, no. 24 (November 24): 93–94; 1, no. 25 (December 1): 97–98; 1, no. 26 (December 6): 101–102.

———.1853–54. "La prima opera in musica." *Gazzetta musicale di Firenze* 1, no. 29 (December 29): 114–15; 1, no. 30 (January 5): 118; 1, no. 31 (January 12): 121; 1, no. 32 (January 19): 125–26; 1, no. 34 (February 2): 133.

———.1854a. "Rapporto della declamazione col canto." *Gazzetta musicale di Firenze* 1, no. 45 (April 20): 177–78.

———.1854b. "Dell'effetto." *Gazzetta musicale di Firenze* 2, no. 1 (June 16): 1.

———.1854c. "Il fondo della melodia." *Gazzetta musicale di Firenze* 2, no. 9 (August 10): 33–34.

———.1854d. "Logica della musica." *Gazzetta musicale di Firenze* 2, no. 17 (October 5): 65–66.

———.1854e. "Il compositore ed il critico." *Gazzetta musicale di Firenze* 2, no. 22 (November 9): 85–86.

———.1854f. "Gl'Imitatori." *Gazzetta musicale di Firenze* 2, no. 25 (November 30): 97–98.

———.1855a. "La musica di Meyerbeer." *Gazzetta musicale di Firenze* 2, no. 37 (February 22): 145–46.

———.1855b. "L'esagerazione nella musica." *Gazzetta musicale di Firenze* 2, no. 48 (May 10): 189–90.

———.1855c. "Storia fantastica della melodia." *Gazzetta musicale di Firenze* 3, no. 15 (September 20): 57–59.

———.1855d. "Rassegna dei giornali." *Gazzetta musicale di Firenze* 3, no. 16 (September 27): 62–63.

———.1855e. "Decadenza o risorgimento?" *Gazzetta musicale di Firenze* 3, no. 26 (December 11): 101–102.

———.1856a. "Le riforme." *L'Armonia* 1, no. 1 (January 1): 1–2.

———.1856b. "Della riforma musicale in Germania." *L'Armonia* 1, no. 8 (February 19): 29–30; 1, no. 9 (February 26): 33–35; 1, no. 13 (March 25): 49–50.

———.1856c. "Il poeta il maestro ed il cantante." *L'Armonia* 1, no. 11 (March 11): 41–42.

———.1856d. "Il linguaggio musicale." *L'Armonia* 1, no. 12 (March 18): 45–46.

———.1856e. "La musica istrumentale in Italia." *L'Armonia* 1, no. 14 (April 1): 53–54.

———.1856f. "La melodia antica e moderna in Italia." *L'Armonia* 1, no. 16 (April 15): 61–62; 1, no. 18 (April 29): 69–70; 1, no. 19 (May 6): 73–74; 1, no. 22 (May 27): 85–86; 1, no. 23 (June 3): 89; 1, no. 24 (June 10): 93–94. Reprinted in *Boccherini* 10, nos. 1–10 (January 24–September 30, 1872).

———.1858. "Il Guglielmo Tell di Rossini." *L'Armonia* 5, no. 8 (April 28): 125–27.

———.1859a. *Studio sulle opere di G. Verdi*. Florence: Tipografia Tofani; reprint, Sala Bolognese: Arnaldo Forni, 1978. Originally published in installments in *L'Armonia*, from 4, no. 11 (June 15, 1857) to 6, no. 17 (September 15, 1858).

———.1859b. "Eloquenza musicale." *L'Armonia* 6, no. 7 (April 16): 217–18.

———.1859c. "Della simmetria nella musica." *L'Armonia* 6, no. 8 (May 2): 221–22.

———.1859d. "Del razionalismo nella musica." *L'Armonia* 6, no. 9 (May 31): 225–26.

———.1859e. "Il compositore ed il critico." *L'Armonia* 6, no. 10 (July 6): 229–30.

———.1860. "Sul nuovo R. Istituto musicale di Firenze. Cenno di A. Basevi." *Gazzetta musicale di Milano* 18, no. 19 (May 6): 145–47.

————.1862. *Introduzione ad un nuovo sistema d'armonia.* Firenze: Tipografia Tofani.

————.1874. *Beethoven op. 18: Con analisi dei sei quartetti.* Florence: G. G. Guidi.

Basili, Francesco. 1850. "Musica." *L'Italia musicale* 2, no. 44 (June 29): 173–74.

Batiste, Édouard, ed. 1867. *Méthode de chant du Conservatoire rédigée par L. Cherubini, Méhul, Gossec, Garat, Plantade, Langlé, Richer, and Guichard avec la collaboration de Gingvené, de l'institut, et du Professeur Mengozzi.* 8 vols. 2d ed. Paris: Heugel.

Batteux, Charles. 1773 [1746]. *Les beaux arts réduits à un même principe.* Paris: Chez Saillant et Nyon, Veuve Desaint.

Bazzini, Antonio. 1867. *Turanda: 3 pezzi ridotti per canto e pianoforte.* Milan: F. Lucca and Ricordi.

————.n.d. "I discorsi di Antonio Bazzini." Typescript: Biblioteca del Conservatorio di Milano.

Beethoven, Ludwig van. 1855 [1833]. *Trattato d'armonia e di composizione.* Trans. and ed. F-J. Fétis and L. F. Rossi. Milan: Giovanni Canti. Reprint, Sala Bolognese: Arnaldo Forni, 2007.

Benzo, Giovanni. 1883a. "Criteri musicali." *La Musica* 4, no. 18 (September 17): 1–2; 4, no. 19 (October 1): 1–2; 4, no. 21 (November 5): 1–2.

————.1883b. "Sterilità." *La Musica* 4, no. 22 (November 19): 1–2; 4, nos. 23–24 (December 17): 1–2.

Berardi, Angelo. 1687. *Documenti armonici.* Bologna: Giacomo Monti. Facs. Sala Bolognese: Arnaldo Forni, 1970.

Berlioz, Hector. 1990 [1865]. *The Memoirs of Hector Berlioz.* Trans. and ed. David Cairns. (*Mémoires, comprenant ses voyages en Italie en Allemagne en Russie et en Angleterre,* Paris, 1865.) London: Cardinal.

Bertini, Domenico. 1857. *Principj elementari di musica del m. Domenico Bertini, dettati per uso dei suoi alunni nella scuola comunale di Massa ducale.* Lucca: tipografia Balatresi.

Bertini, Giuseppe. 1814–15. *Dizionario storico-critico degli scrittori di musica e de' più celebri artisti di tutte le nazioni sì antiche che moderne.* 4 vols. Palermo: Dalla Tipografia reale di guerra.

Biaggi, Gerolamo Alessandro. 1847. "Critica musicale. Della musica melodrammatica in Italia." *L'Italia musicale* 1, no. 1 (July 7): 3–5; 1, no. 3 (July 21): 17–20; 1, no. 4 (July 28): 25–26; 1, no. 6 (August 11): 41–43; 1, no. 7 (August 18): 49–50; 1, no. 8 (August 25): 57–59; 1, no. 16 (October 20): 121–22; 1, no. 17 (October 27): 129–30; 1, no. 18 (November 5): 137–38; 1, no 19 (November 10): 147–48; 1, no. 20 (November 17): 155–57; 1, no. 21 (November 24): 161–62; 1, no. 22 (December 1): 169–70.

————.1848. "Storia musicale: La giovane generazione musicale." *L'Italia musicale* 1, no. 29 (January 19): 225–26; 1, no. 30 (January 26): 235–36; 1, no. 31 (February 2): 241–42; 1, no. 32 (February 9): 249–50; 1, no. 33 (February 16): 257–59; 1, no. 35 (March 1): 275–76; 1, no. 37 (March 15): 289–91.

————.n.d. [1850s?]. *Istradamento pratico alla lettura della musica proposto a' giovanetti da G. A. Biaggi.* Milan: F. Lucca.

Bidera, Emanuele. 1853. *Euritmia drammatica-musicale, dichiarata per le leggi fisiche della caduta dei gravi e del quadrato delle distanze.* Palermo: Stabilimento tipografico dell'Armonia.

Blasis, Carlo. 1844. *Studi sulle arti imitatrici.* Milan: Giuseppe Chiusi; reprint, Sala Bolognese: Arnaldo Forni, 1971.

Boito, Arrigo. 1942. *Tutti gli scritti.* Ed. P. Nardi. Milan: Mondadori.

Bonesi, Barnaba. 1806. *Traité de la mesure, ou de la division du temps dans la musique et dans la poesie.* Paris: Chez l'Auteur et H. I. Godfroy.

Bonomo, Girolamo. 1875. *Nuova scuola d'armonia: metodo elementare di partimento.* Palermo: G. Stancampiano.

Bordogni, [Giulio] Marco. 1842. *12 nuovi vocalizzi: sei dei quali con poesia per mezzo-soprano*. Milan: Francesco Lucca.

Boucheron, Raimondo. 1842. *Filosofia della musica o estetica applicata a quest'arte*. Milan: Ricordi.

———.1844. "Sulla proposta fatta dal chiarissimo signor Geremia Vitali di un nuovo mezzo per determinare con esattezza i tempi musicali. Riposta alla lettera dell'egregio Don Nicolò Eustachio Cattaneo." *Gazzetta musicale di Milano* 3, no. 30 (July 28): 126–27.

———.1856. *La scienza dell'armonia spiegata dai rapporti dell'arte coll'umana natura—Trattato teorico pratico*. 2 vols. Milan: Ricordi.

Bovio, Giovanni Michele. 1885. "Donizetti. II." *La Musica* 6, no. 2 (March 16): 1–2.

Brendel, Franz. 1852. *Geschichte der Musik in Italien, Deutschland und Frankreich von den ersten christlichen Zeiten bis auf die Gegenwart. Zweiundzwanzig Vorlesungen gehalten zu Leipzig im Jahre 1850*. Leipzig: Bruno Hinze; reprint, Vaduz, Lichtenstein: Sändig, 1985.

———.*Geschichte der Musik in Italien, Deutschland, und Frankreich von den ersten christlichen Zeiten bis auf die Gegenwart*. 4th ed. Leipzig: Heinrich Matthes, 1867.

Burney, Charles. 1773. *The Present State of Music in France and Italy*. 2d ed. London: T. Becket.

———.1935 [1789]. *A General History of Music from the Earliest Ages to the Present Period*. Ed. Frank Mercer. London: Harcourt Brace.

Calegari, Francesco. 1828. *Elementi generali di musica, raccolti ed esposti con chiarezza ed ordine progressivo da Francesco Calegari per uso degli allievi nei Licei filarmonici*. 2d ed. Bologna: presso la Ditta Cipriani e C., tipografia Marsigli.

Campion, François. 1716. *Traité d'Accompagnement et de Composition selon la règle des Octaves de Musique*. Paris: not specified. Facs. Geneva: Minkoff, 1976.

Canuti, Filippo. 1829. *Vita di Stanislao Mattei*. Bologna: Tipografia di E. dall'Olmo.

Capalti, Francesco da Fossombrone. 1788. *Il Contropuntista pratico, o siano Dimostrazioni fatte sopra l'esperienza da Francesco Capalti da Fossambruno, maestro Romano, al servizio dell'insigne Cattedrale dell'antichissima Città di Narni*. Terni: Antonino Saluzj stampator vescovile.

Caputo, Michele Carlo. 1877. "Le riforme al Collegio di musica in S. Pietro a Maiella." *La Musica* 2, no. 13 (July 7): 2–4.

Carpani, Giuseppe. 1823 [1812]. *Le Haydine ovvero Lettere sulla vita e l'opere del celebre maestro Giuseppe Haydn*. Padua: Tipografia della Minerva; reprint, Sala Bolognese: Arnaldo Forni, 1969.

———.1817. *The Life of Haydn in a Series of Letters Written at Vienna etc.* Trans. Stendhal et al. London: John Murray.

———.1824a. *Le Rossiniane ossia lettere musico-teatrali*. Padua: Tipografia della Minerva.

———.1824b. *Le Majeriane: ovvero lettere sul bello ideale: in riposta al libro "Della imitazione pittorica" del cav. Andrea Majer*. 3d ed. Padua: Tipografia della Minerva.

Casamorata, Luigi Ferdinando. 1846. "Osservazioni, discussioni, proposte. Articolo terzo." *Gazzetta musicale di Milano* 5, no. 11 (March 15): 83–85; 5, no. 13 (March 29): 99–102.

Catel, Charles-Simon. ca. 1825 [1802]. *Traité d'harmonie conforme à l'édition du conservatoire*. Paris: Leduc. Translated as *A Treatise on Harmony Written and Composed for the Use of the Pupils at the Royal Conservatory of Music in Paris*. London: Chappell.

Cattaneo, Nicolò Eustachio. 1828. *Grammatica della musica ossia elementi teorici di questa bell'arte.* Milan: da Candido Buccinelli.

———.1844a. "Della proposta fatta dal chiarissimo signor Geremia Vitali di un nuovo mezzo per determinare con esattezza i tempi musicali. Al chiarissimo signor maestro Raimondo Boucheron." *Gazzetta musicale di Milano* 3, no. 28 (July 14): 116–17.

———.1844b. "Varietà. Il ritmo. Quesito musico-teorico." *Gazzetta musicale di Milano* 3, no. 51 (December 22): 211.

———.1847. *Instradamento all'armonia ossia Introduzione allo studio de' trattati di questa scienza.* Milan: Ricordi.

Celentano, Luigi. 1867. *Intorno all'arte del cantare in Italia nel secolo decimonono: Considerazioni di Luigi Celentano.* Naples: Stabilimento tipographico Ghio.

Cerù, Domenico Agostino. 1871. *Cenni storici dell'insegnamento della musica in Lucca, e dei più notabili Maestri Compositori che vi hanno fiorito.* Lucca: Tipografia Giusti.

Cherubini, Luigi. 1835. *Cours de contrepoint et de fugue.* Paris: Maurice Schlesinger. Trans. as *Corso di contrappunto e di fuga* by Luigi Felice Rossi. Milan: Lucca, 1835.

———.n.d. [1835?]. *Marches d'Harmonie pratiquées dans la composition produisant des Suites Régulières de Consonances et de Dissonances.* Paris: Ménestrel. Translated as *Andamenti d'armonia praticati nella composizione i quali producono successioni regolari di consonanze e dissonanze.* Milan: G. Ricordi, 1880.

Choron, Alexandre-Étienne, and Vincenzo Fiocchi. 1804. *Principes d'accompagnment des écoles d'Italie extrait des meilleurs auteurs.* Paris: Imbault.

———.1808. *Principes de composition des écoles d'Italie. Adoptés par le Gouvernement Français pour server à l'instruction des élèves des Maîtrises de Cathédrales.* 6 vols. Paris: Auguste Le Duc. 2d ed., 3 vols, 1816.

Choron, Alexandre-Étienne, and J.-Adrien De LaFage. 1836–39. *Manuel complet de musique vocale et instrumentale, ou Encyclopédie Musicale.* 3 vols. Paris: Roret.

Coli, Antonio. 1834. *Vita di Bonifazio Asioli da Correggio compilato da D. Antonio Coli e seguita dall'elenco delle opere del medesimo.* Milan: Ricordi.

Colombani, Alfredo. 1900. *L'opera italiana nel secolo XIX.* Milan: Tipografia del Corriere della sera.

Concone, Giuseppe. ca. 1887. *15 Vocalises pour soprano ou mezzo-soprano, op. 12.* Ed. W. H. Cummings. London: Edwin Ashdown.

Corghi, Carlo. 1847. "Istituzioni musicali. Lettura musicale e canto elementare. Metodi Wilhelm e Rossi." *L'Italia musicale* 1, no 10 (September 8): 75–77; 1, no. 11 (September 15): 84–85; 1, no. 12 (September 22): 91–92.

Corio, Lodovico. 1882. *Pietro Metastasio: studio critico.* Milan: Civelli.

———.1908. *Ricerche storiche sul R. Conservatorio di musica di Milano.* Milan: Allegretti.

Corri, Domenico. 1810. *The Singers' Preceptor.* London: Maunder; reprint, New York: Garland, 1995.

Crescentini, Girolamo. 1811. *Raccolta di essercizi per il canto all'uso del vocalizzo.* Paris: Imbault.

Crotti, Ilaria, and Ricciarda Ricorda. 1997 [1910]. "Scapigliatura e dintorni." In *Storia letteraria d'Italia,* vol. 3: *L'Ottocento,* ed. Armando Balduino, 1471–1566. Padua: Piccin nuova libraria.

Dacci, Giusto. 1872. *Trattato teorico-pratico d'armonia semplice e composta.* Milan: Paolo De Giorgi.

———.1886. *Trattato teorico-pratico di lettura e divisione musicale pei dilettanti. Estratto dal trattato completo dello stesso autore.* Milan: F. Lucca.

———.1893 [1881]. *Trattato teorico-pratico d'armonia, istrumenzione, contrappunto e composizione (diviso in 4 libri).* 3d ed. Milan: Paolo De Giorgi.

Dall'Olio, Cesare. 1887. *Lo studio della composizione musicale secondo i principi naturali dell'estetica.* Bologna: Nicola Zanichelli.

Danby, John. 1788. *La guida alla musica vocale. Containing various Examples and Duetts.* London: printed for the author.

D'Anna, Salvatore. 1866. *Nuova sistema musicale: Grammatica riguardante i principi elementari di musica.* Palermo: Tipografia di Michele Amenta.

D'Arenzio, Nicola. 1878. *L'introduzione del sistema tetracordale nella musica moderna.* Milano: Ricordi-Lucca.

De-Champs, Ettore. 1879. "Se sia miglior sistema quello usato anticamente a Napoli, d'iniziare alla composizione, studiando praticamente l'armonia accompagnando sul basso numerato (partimento) ovvero, come oggi da molti ad imitazione dei tedeschi si pratica, studiando prima teoricamente l'armonia." *Atti dell'Accademia del Regio istituto musicale di Firenze* 17: 46–68. Florence: Stabilimento Civelli.

———.1885. *Manuale per l'alunno delle Scuole di Solfeggio—cantato nel R. Istituto musicale di Firenze.* Florence: Galletti e Cocci.

De LaFage, Adriano. 1845. "Studj biografici: Giuseppe Baini." *Gazzetta musicale di Milano* 4, no. 39 (September 28): 166–67.

———.1854. "Niccolò Zingarelli." *Gazzetta musicale di Firenze* 2, no. 6 (July 20): 22–23; 2, no. 8 (August 3): 31–32; 2, no. 10 (August 17): 38.

Delle Sedie, Enrico. 1876. *Arte e fisiologia del canto: trattato.* Milan: Tito di G. Ricordi.

———.1881. *Riflessioni sulle cause della decadenza della Scuola di Canto in Italia.* Paris: Paolo Dupont.

De Macchi, Luigi. ca. 1830. *Grammatica musicale. Teoria dei principj elementari di musica compilata dietro le norme di Asioli e di altri rinominati autori da Luigi De-Macchi.* Novara: Francesco Artaria.

De Rosa, Carlo Antonio (marchese di Villarosa). 1840. *Memorie dei compositori di musica del regno di Napoli.* Naples: Stamperia Reale.

De Sanctis, Cesare. n.d. [1887?]. *La polifonia nell'arte moderna spiegata secondo i principi classici: Libro 1. Trattato d'armonia: approvato e adottato dalla R. Accademia di S. Cecilia e da altri istituti musicali; Libro 2. Appendice di Trattato d'armonia; Libro 3. Trattato di contrappunto e fuga.* Milan: Ricordi.

De Vecchis, Giovanni Battista. 1850. *Compendio di contrappunto della antica e moderna scuola di musica napolitana.* 2 vols. Naples: Domenico Capasso.

Durante, Francesco. n.d. [1730s?]. *Regole.* Biblioteca del Conservatorio di Musica San Pietro a Majella, Naples, MSS 34.2.4 and Oc 3.40. In Gjerdingen (2005)

———.2003 [1730s?]. *Bassi e fughe. Un manual inedito per riscoprire la vera prassi esecutiva della Scuola Napoletana del Settecento.* Ed. G. A. Pastore. Padua: Armelin Musica.

Eximeno, Antonio. 1774. *Dell'origine e delle regole della musica, colla storia del suo progresso, decadenza e rinnovazione.* Rome: Michel'Angelo Barbiellini nel Palazzo Massimi.

Fenaroli, Fedele. 1775. *Regole musicali per i principianti di cembalo nel sonar coi numeri e per principianti di contrappunto.* Naples: Vincenzo Mazzola-Vocola; reprint, Sala Bolognese: Arnaldo Forni, 1975.

———.1814. *Partimenti, ossia Basso Numerato: opera completa di Fedele Fenaroli, per uso degli alunni del Real Conservatorio di Napoli.* Paris: Typographie de la Sirène. 2d ed. Florence and Milan: Giovanni Canti; reprint, Sala Bolognese: Arnaldo Forni, 1978.

Ferro, Cavaliere Giovanni di. 1807–1808. *Delle belle arti: dissertazioni.* 2 vols. Palermo: Solli.

———.1809. *Stabilimenti per l'interno regolamento del Real Conservatorio di musica San Sebastiano in Napoli.* Naples: Treni.

Ferroni, Vincenzo. 1908. *Della forma musicale classica: Brevi appunti ad uso delle Scuole di Composizione.* Milan: Musicale italiana.

Fétis, François-Joseph. 1825. *Traité du contrepoint et de la fugue, contenant l'exposé analytique des règles de la composition musicale, depuis deux jusqu'à huit parties réelles.* Paris: Troupenas. Facs. Osnabrück: Zeller, 1972.

———.1836. *Metodo elementaire e ristretto di armonia e di accompagnamento del basso.* Naples: Girard.

———.1866–75. *Biographie universelle des musiciens et bibliographie générale de la musique.* 8 vols. Paris: Firmin Didot Frères.

Filippi, Filippo. 1860. "Le riforme nell'istruzione musicale." *Gazzetta musicale di Milano* 18, no. 9 (February 26): 65–68; 18, no. 10 (March 4): 73–77.

Florimo, Francesco. 1840–42. *Breve metodo di canto: divise in tre parti.* Milan: Giovanni Ricordi.

———.1876. *Riccardo Wagner ed i Wagneristi.* Naples: not specified.

———.1881–83. *La Scuola musicale di Napoli e i suoi conservatorii.* 4 vols. Naples: V. Morano; reprint, Sala Bolognese: Arnaldo Forni, 2002 [1969].

Forkel, Johann. 1788, 1801. *Allgemeine Geschichte der Musik.* 2 vols. Leipzig: Schwickertschen Verlage; reprint, Laaber: Laaber Verlag, 2004.

Fritelli, Fausto. 1743. *Il modo di solfeggiare all'uso francese, ricavato da due lettere familiari, scritte da uno ad un'altro amico in lingua toscana, introdotti nuovamente in Siena dal M. R. Signore Fausto Frittelli sacerdote sanese maestro di cappella nella metropolitana di Siena.* Siena: nella stamperia del Pub.

Frontorj, Luigi di Cento. 1831. *Le trentatrè giornate musicali, ossia la vera teoria della musica divisa in trentatrè lezioni, di Luigi Frontorj.* Bologna: stamperia di S. Tomaso d'Aquino.

Furno, Giovanni. n.d. [1817?]. *Metodo facile breve e chiaro delle prime ed essensiali regole per accompagnare partimenti senza numeri del Maestro Giovanni Furno per uso degli alunni del Real Conservatorio di musica.* Naples: Orlando Vico. In Gjerdingen (2005).

Fux, Johann Joseph. 1761 [1725]. *Salita al Parnasso, o sia Guida alla regolare composizione della musica con nuovo, e certo Metodo non per anche in ordine sì esatto data alla luce, e composta da Giovanni Giuseppe Fux.* Milan: Carpi.

Galeazzi, Francesco. 1791, 1796. *Elementi teorici-pratici di musica con un saggio sopra l'arte di suonare il violin analizzata, ed a dimostrabili principi ridotta, opera utilissima a chiunque vuol applicar con profitto alla musica e specialmente a' principianti, dilettanti, e professori di violin.* Vol. 1. Rome: Pilucchi Cracas. Vol. 2. Rome: Michele Puccinelli.

Galli, Amintore. 1871. *La musica ed i musicisti dal secolo X ai nostri giorni.* Milan: n.p.; reprint, Sala Bolognese: Arnaldo Forni, 1980.

———.1887 [1877]. *Elementi di armonia.* Milan: Sonzogno.

———.1879. *Trattato di contrappunto e fuga.* Milan: Sonzogno.

———.1884. *Ortofonia: L'armonia e la melodia rese alla intelligenza di tutti.* Milan: Sonzogno.

———.1886. *Partimenti: regole musicali per quelli che vogliono suonare coi numeri e per i principianti di contrappunto.* Milan: Sonzogno.

———.1900. *Estetica della musica.* Milan: Bocca; reprint, Sala Bolognese: Arnaldo Forni, 1975.

————.1902. *Piccolo lessico del musicista.* Milan: Ricordi.

Galli, Amintore, and Alberto Mazzucato. 1870. *Arte fonetica: istituzioni scientifico-musicali.* Milan: Pubblicazione del giornale Euterpe.

Galli, Eugenio. 1840. *Prolusione al corso di contrappunto, detta il 13 dicembre 1839 dal professore Eugenio Galli Maestro di camera e cappella di sua Altezza Reale l'Infante Duca di Lucca, socio dell'I. e R. Accademia fiorentina delle belle arti ecc.* Lucca: tipografia Giusti.

Gamucci, Baldassarre. 1877–78. "Il nuovo sistema d'armonia del Prof. Abramo Basevi." *Boccherini* 24, nos. 6–7 (June 30, 1877): 23–24; 24, no. 8 (August 4): 29–30; 24, no. 9 (September 11): 33–34; 24, no. 10–11 (October 11): 37–38; 24, no. 12 (December 13): 45–46; 25, nos. 1–2 (January 31, 1878): 1–2; 25, no. 3 (March 1): 9–10; 25, no. 4 (March 31): 13–14; 25, no. 5 (May 7): 17–18.

Gandolfi, Riccardo. 1884–85. "Utilità e danno dell'influenza straniera sulla musica italiana." *La Musica* 5, no. 12 (August 4, 1884); 1–2, and 6, no. 3 (April 13, 1885): 1–2.

García, Manuel Patricio Rodríguez (fils). 1840, 1847. *École de García: traité complet de l'art du chant par Manuel García fils.* Paris: Mayence. The 1872 edition of the second part was trans. and ed. by Donald V. Paschke as *A Complete Treatise on the Art of Singing.* Da Capo Press: New York, 1975.

————.1894. *Hints on Singing.* Trans. Beata García. London: E. Ascherberg.

————.1943 [1849]. *Scuola di García: trattato completo dell'arte del canto di Emanuele García figlio, tradotto dal francese da Alberto Mazzucato.* Milan: Giovanni Ricordi.

Gaspari, Gaetano. 1886. *Musica e musicisti a Bologna: ricerche, documenti e memorie riguardanti la storia dell'arte musicale in Bologna.* Bologna: Bibliotheca musica bononiensis; reprint, Sala Bolognese: Arnaldo Forni, 1969.

Gasparini, Francesco. 1708. *L'armonico pratico al cimbalo.* Venice: Antonio Bortoli. Facs. New York: Broude Brothers, 1967. Trans. F. S. Stillings as *The Practical Harmonist at the Keyboard.* New Haven: Yale University Press, 1963.

Gennaro Grossi, Giovanni Battista. 1820. *Le belle arti.* 2 vols. Naples: Giornale enciclopedico.

Gerli, Giuseppe. 1870. *Dialoghi illustrati d'armonia, che insegnano la dottrina degli accordi, la scienza della modulazione e la teoria di armonizzare melodie, etc.* Milan: Lucca.

————.n.d. [1877?]. *L'allievo al primo corso d'armonia applicata al pianoforte: esercizi elementari progressivi in tutti i toni, bassi numerate, preceduti dalle relative scale e dalle cadenze semplice composte e doppie nelle tre posizioni che servono d'introduzione allo studio di partimenti dei classici d'ogni scuola, no. espressamente composti per la scuola d'armonia teorica e pratica del R. Conservatorio Mus.le di Milano.* Milan: F. Lucca.

Gervasoni, Carlo. 1800. *La Scuola della musica, in tre parti divisa.* Piacenza: Niccolò Orcesi; reprint, Sala Bolognese: Arnaldo Forni, 1969.

————.1812. *Nuova teoria della musica ricavata dall'odierna pratica ossia metodo sicuro e facile in pratica per ben apprendere la musica a cui si fanno precedere varie notizie storico-musicali.* Parma: Niccolò Orcesi.

Ghislanzoni, Antonio. 1855. "Brevi cenni sulla vita e le opere di Nicola Vaccai." *Gazzetta musicale di Firenze* 2, no. 33 (January 25): 130; 2, no. 35 (February 8): 138–39; 2, no. 37 (February 22): 146; 2, no. 38 (March 1): 149–50; 2, no. 39 (March 8): 154; 2, no. 40 (March 15): 158–59.

Giovannini, Alberto. ca. 1882. *Corso preparatorio allo studio dell'armonia proposto agli alunni del R. Conservatorio di musica in Milano da Alberto Giovannini professore del conservatorio stesso.* Milan: Alessandro Pigna.

Giraldoni, Leone. 1864. *Guida teorico-pratica ad uso dell'artista cantante.* Bologna: Marsigli e Rocchi.

Gossec, François-Joseph. 1800. *Principes élémentaires de Musique arrêtés par les Membres du Conservatoire pour servir à l'étude de cet établissement; suivis de Solfèges par les Cit. Agus, Catel, Cherubini, Gossec, Langlé, Lesueur, Méhul et Riegel.* 2 vols. Paris: L'imprimerie du Conservatoire.

Grassi Landi, Bartolomeo. 1880. *Descrizione della nuova tastiera cromatica ed esposizione del nuovo sistema di scrittura musicale invenzione des Sac. B. Grassi Landi.* Milan: Tipografia di Roma.

———. 1881. *L'armonia considerata come vera scienza ossia Dimostrazione delle leggi fisiche dell'armonia.* Milan: Calcografia musica sacra.

Guarino, Pietro. 1883. "Rossini e il suo tempo." *La Musica* 4, no. 13 (July 2): 3–4.

Guarnaccia, Emanuele. ca. 1851. *Metodo (nuovamente riformato) de' partimenti, arrichito di schiarimenti e di una completa Imitazione dal maestro Emmanuele Guarnaccia,* 2 vols. Milan: G. Ricordi.

Hasse, Johann Adolf. 1982 [1730s]. *12 Solfeggi für eine Singstimme oder Instrumente (Bläser oder Streicher) und Basso Continuo. 2 Bände.* Ed. Dietrich Knothe and Kurt Janetzky. Heidelberg: Willy Müller.

Hauptmann, Moritz. 1873 [1853]. *Die Natur der Harmonik und der Metrik: Zur Theorie der Musik.* Leipzig: Breitkopf und Härtel. 2d ed. Trans. William E. Heathcote as *The Nature of Harmony and Metre.* New York: Da Capo Press, 1991.

Heinichen, Johann David. 1728. *Der General-Bass in der Composition.* Dresden: Selbstverlag.

Hiller, Johann Adam. 2001. *Treatise on Vocal Performance and Ornamentation.* Trans. and ed. Suzanne J. Beicken. Cambridge: Cambridge University Press. Orig. pub. as *Anweisung zum musikalisch-zierlichen Gesange* (Leipzig, 1774).

Imbimbo, Emanuele. 1821. *Observations sur l'enseignement mutuel appliqué à la musique et sur quelques abus introduits dans cet art; précédées d'une notice sur les conservatoires de Naples.* Paris: Firmin Didot.

Kalkbrenner, Friedrich Wilhelm. 1849. *Treatise on Harmony for the Pianist.* Trans. R. L. Cocks. London: Cocks.

Kiesewetter, Raphael Georg. 1834. *Geschichte der europäisch-abendländischen oder unsrer heutigen Musik. Darstellung ihres Ursprungs, ihres Wachsthums und ihrer stufenweise Entwickelung; von dem ersten Jahrhundert des Christenthumes bis auf unsre Zeit.* Leipzig: Breitkopf und Härtel. Trans. Robert Müller as *History of the Modern Music of Western Europe, from the First Century of the Christian Era to the Present Day.* London: T. C. Newby, 1848.

Kirnberger, Johann. 1771–79. *Die Kunst des reinen Satzes.* 2 vols. Berlin: Decker und Hartung. Facs. Hildesheim: G. Olms, 1988.

———. 1982 [1771–79]. *The Art of Strict Musical Composition.* Trans. D. Beach and J. Thym. New Haven: Yale University Press.

———. 1781. *Grundsätze des General-Basses als erster Linien zur Composition.* Hamburg: Johann August Böhme.

———. 1782. *Anleitung zur Singkomposition mit Oden in verschiedenen Silbenmassen begleitet.* Berlin: G. I. Decker.

Koch, Heinrich C. 1782, 1787, 1793. *Versuch einer Anleitung zur Composition.* 3 vols. Leipzig: A. F. Böhme. Facs. Hildesheim: G. Olms, 2000 [1969].

———. 1983. *Introductory Essay on Composition.* A partial translation of Koch

(1782, 1787, 1793) by N. Baker. New Haven: Yale University Press.

———, and Johann Georg Sulzer. 2006 [1771–74, 1787]. *Aesthetics and the Art of Musical Composition in the German Enlightenment.* Trans. and ed. Nancy Baker and Thomas Christensen. Cambridge: Cambridge University Press.

Kotzbue, August Friedrich von. 1806. *Travels through Italy in the Years 1804 and 1805.* 4 vols. London: Richard Phillips.

Lamperti, Francesco. 1864. *Guida teorico-pratica-elementare per lo studio del canto.* Milan: Tito di Gio. Ricordi.

———.1891. *The Art of Singing.* Trans. by J. C. Griffith. New York: Schirmer.

Lamperti, Giovanni Battista. 1876a. *Solfeggi per baritono.* Milan: Francesco Lucca.

———.1876b. *Vocalizzi per baritono.* Milan: Francesco Lucca.

———.1905. *Die Technik des Bel Canto.* Berlin: Albert Stahl.

Landucci, Luigi. 1905. *Carlo Angeloni: cronistoria.* Lucca: Marchi.

Lavignac, Albert. 1877–94. *Solfège Manuscrit. Complément du Solfège des Solfèges Op. 17.* Paris: Lemoine.

Lichtenthal, Pietro. 1807. *Der musikalische Arzt.* Vienna: Christian Friedrich Wappler und Beck.

———.1826. *Dizionario e bibliografia della musica.* 4 vols. Milan: Antonio Fontana. Facs. of the 1836 ed. Sala Bolognese: Arnaldo Forni, 1970. Trans. Domenique Mondo as *Dictionnaire de musique par le Dr. Pierre Lichtenthal.* Paris: Chez Troupenas, 1839.

———.1831. *Estetica, ossia Dottrina del bello e delle arti belle.* Milan: Pirrotta.

Liverziani, Giuseppe Romano. 1797. *Grammatica della Musica, o sia nuovo e facile metodo per istruirsi nell'intero corso della Musica, non per anche posto in ordine da alcuno, ove premesse le Notizie Istoriche, e le Proprietà della medesima, s'insegnano fin dai più remoti principi le Regole per ben Cantare, e Suonare il Cembalo, indi si procede allo studio del Contrapunto, e Composizione Prattica. Di Giuseppe Liverziani Romano compositore di Musica.* Rome: Nella stamperia Pilucchi Cracas.

Lo Basso, Giuseppe. 1855. "L'accento in rapporto colla musica." *Gazzetta musicale di Firenze* 3, no. 12 (August 30): 46–47.

———.1856. "Principali cagioni della decadenza dell'arte del canto." *L'Italia musicale* 8, no. 18 (March 1): 70; 8, no. 20 (March 8): 78; 8, no. 25 (March 26): 98.

Lussy, Mathis. 1883. *Le Rhythme musical; son origine, sa fonction et son accentuation.* Paris: Heugel.

Luvini, Francesco. 1869. *Trattato completo d'armonia: con una nuova classificazione degli accordi e delle dissonanze basata sui centri armonici.* Turin: Arnaldi.

———.1870. *Armonia e melodia: breve riassunto del Trattato completo d'armonia.* Turin: Arnaldi.

Majer, Andrea. 1821. *Discorso sullu uriglne progressi e stato attuale della musica italiana.* Padua: Minerva.

Mampieri, Alessandro. 1840. *Teoriche elementari di musica proposte dalla Commissione di musica per lo studio degli alunni dei R. stabilimenti e collegi in Napoli, dedicate a S. R. il Cav. D. Felice Santangelo Soprintendente Generale del Real Albergo de' Poveri, e Stabilimenti riuniti da Alessandro Mampieri maestro di contrapunto e di canto nel collegio di musica del real albergo.* Napoli: dalla tipografia del Vesuvio.

Mancini, Giambattista. 1777 [1774]. *Pensieri, e riflessioni pratiche sopra il canto figurato.* Milan: Galeazzi; reprint, Sala Bolognese: Arnaldo Forni, 1970. Trans. and ed. Edward Foreman as *Practical Reflections on Figured Singing.* In *Masterworks on Singing,* vol. 7. Champaign, Ill.: Pro Musica Press, 1967.

Manfredini, Vincenzo. 1775. *Regole armoniche.* Venice: Zerletti.

————.1788. *Difesa della musica moderna e de' suoi celebri esecutori*. Bologna: Trenti; reprint, Sala Bolognese: Arnaldo Forni, 1972.

Marchesi de Castrone, Mathilde. n.d. [1860s]. *Vocalizzi*. Milan: Ricordi.

————.1888. *Metodo teorico pratico per canto: op. 31*. Turin: Giudici e Strada. Trans. as *Bel Canto: A Theoretical and Practical Vocal Method*. London: Enoch and Sons, 1896; abridged reprint, New York: Dover, 1970.

Mariotti, Olimpio. 1853. "Questioni di vocalità." *Gazzetta musicale di Firenze* 1, no. 11 (August 25): 41–42; 1, no. 12 (September 1): 45–46; 1, no. 13 (September 8): 49–50; 1, no. 15 (September 22): 57–59.

Mariscotti, Augusto. 1858. "Giambattista Pergolese." *L'Armonia* 5, no. 7 (April 15): 123.

Marpurg, Friedrich Wilhelm. 1751. *Die Kunst das Clavier zu spielen*. Berlin: Haude und Spener.

————.1753–54. *Abhandlung von der Fuge*. Berlin: A. Haude und J. Spener; reprint, Laaber: Laaber Verlag, 2002.

————.1759. *Kritische Einleitung in die Geschichte und Lehrsätze der alten und neuen Musik*. Berlin: Gottlieb August Lange.

————.1762. *Handbuch bey dem Generalbasse und der Composition: mit zwo-drey-vier-fünf-sechs-sieben-acht und mehreren Stimmen für Anfänger und Geübtere*. Berlin: G. A. Lange.

————.1754–62, 1778. *Historisch-kritische Beyträge zur Aufnahme der Musik*. 5 vols. Berlin: J. J. Schützens Witwe, G. A. Lange.

————.1763. *Anleitung zur Musik überhaupt und zur Singkunst besonders*. Berlin: Bey A. Wever.

Marselli, Niccolò. 1859. *La ragione della musica moderna*. Naples: Albert Detken Librajo.

Martignoni, Ignazio. 1810. "Del bello musicale." In *Del bello e del sublime*, 37–42. 2 vols. Milan: Mussi.

Martini, Giovanni Battista [Giambattista]. 1757. *Storia della Musica. Tomo Primo*. Bologna: per Lelio dalla Volpe Impressore dell'Istituto delle Scienze.

————.n.d. [1760s?]. "Regole per accompagnare su 'l Cembalo o Organo." Museo internazionale e biblioteca della musica di Bologna, Ms. I.50.

————.1761. "Regole per accompagnare del P[ad]re Gio. Batt[ist]a Martini min. Con[ventua]le, e M[aest]ro di Cappella di San Francesco in Bologna. Per uso di Fra Luigi Ant[oni]o Sabbatini Min. Con[ventua]le." Museo internazionale e biblioteca della musica di Bologna, Ms. I.51.

————.1767. *De Usu Progressionis Geometricae in Musica*. Bologna: Istituto delle Scienze; reprint, Sala Bolognese: Arnaldo Forni, 1980.

————.1769. *Compendio della teoria de' numeri per uso di musico di F. Giambattista Martini minor Conventuale*. Bologna: dalla Volpe.

————.1774–75. *Esemplare, o sia saggio fondamentale pratico di contrappunto sopra il canto fermo*. Bologna: Per Lelio dalla Volpe Impressore dell'Istituto delle Scienze. 2 vols. Facs. Ridgewood, N.J.: Gregg, 1975.

Marx, Adolph Bernhard. 1837–47. *Die Lehre von den musikalischen Komposition*. 4 vols. Leipzig: Breitkopf und Härtel.

Masutto, Giovanni. 1882–84. *I maestri di musica Italiani del secolo xix: Notizie biografiche*. Venice: Giovanni Cecchini.

Mattei, Saverio. 1773. *I libri poetici della Bibbia tradotti dall'ebraico originale, ed adattati al gusto della poesia italiana*. Naples: Stamperia Simoniana.

————.1785. *Memorie per servire alla vita del Metastasio*. Colle: Nella stamperia di Angiolo M. Martini, e Comp; reprint, Sala Bolognese: Arnaldo Forni, 1987.

Mattei, Stanislao. 1788a. "Scale, Versetti, Bassi numerati per accompagnare, ridotti ad intavolatura a due violini e viola; come pure Contrapunti a 2. 3. 4. 5. 6. 7. 8. voci sopra la scala ascendente e discendente, con diversi modi di passare da un tono ad un altro, di F. Stanislao Mattei M. Conv.le." Museo internazionale e biblioteca della musica di Bologna, Ms. UU.10 (Olim NN.251).

———.1788b. "Contrappunti a 2, 3, 4, 5, 6, 7, 8 voci sopra la scala ascendente (e discendente) di terza maggiore (e minore)." Museo internazionale e biblioteca della musica di Bologna, Ms. NN.256.

———.n.d. [1790s?]. "Piccolo basso in tutti gli toni per introduzione alli bassi numerati ò siano Partimenti del Padre e Maestro Stanislao Mattei Minore Conventuale." Biblioteca del Conservatorio di Musica San Pietro a Majella, Naples, Ms. Od 2.18. In Gjerdingen (2005).

———.1804. "Principj di musica e di contrappunto compilati nel 1804, allorchè fu instituito il Liceo Comunale di Bologna." Museo internazionale e biblioteca della musica di Bologna, Ms. K.6.

———.ca. 1824–25. *Pratica d'accompagnamento sopra bassi numerati e contrappunti a più voci sulla scala ascendente, e discendente maggiore, e minore con diverse Fughe a quattro, ecc..* Bologna, Florence, and Leghorn: Gasparo Cipriani; reprint, Turin: G. Magrini, 1850.

———.ca. 1827. *Pratica d'accompagnamento e contrappunto del Padre Maestro Stanislao Mattei. Parte seconda: Contrappunti da due a otto parti sopra la scala ascendente e discendente in ambo i modi coll'aggiunta di parecchi contrappunti a 4 parti finora inediti.* Ed. Luigi Felice Rossi. Turin: A. Racca.

———.1850 [1829?]. *Bassi numerati per accompagnare. Ridotti ad intavolatura a due violini e viola.* Milan: F. Lucca; reprint, Sala Bolognese: Arnaldo Forni, 1969.

Mattheson, Johann. 1739. *Der vollkommene Capellmeister.* Hamburg: Christian Herold; reprint, Kassel: Bärenreiter,

1999. Translated by Ernest Charles Harriss as *Johann Mattheson's Der vollkommene Capellmeister: A Revised Translation with Critical Commentary.* Ann Arbor: UMI Research Press, 1981.

Mayr, Giovanni Simone. 1844–45. "Cenni intorno allo stato e coltura progressiva della musica in Germania." *Gazzetta musicale di Milano* 3, no. 44 (November 3, 1844): 182–83; 3, no. 50 (December 15): 205–6; 4, no. 16 (April 20, 1845): 69–70; 4, no. 31 (August 3): 131–32; 4, no. 35 (August 31): 150–51; 4, no. 36 (September 7): 154; 4, no. 42 (October 19): 177–78.

———.1977 [ca. 1800–40]. *Zibaldone, preceduto dalle pagine autobiographiche.* Ed. Arrigo Gazzaniga. Gorle-Bergamo: Gutenberg editrice.

———.1993 [ca. 1800–40]. *Passi scelti dello zibaldone e altri scritti.* Bergamo: banca popolare.

Mazzini, Giuseppe. 1836. "Filosofia della musica." In *Scritti editi ed inediti,* 8: 119–65. 94 vols. Imola: Cooperativa tipografico-editrice Paolo Galeati, 1906–43.

Mazzucato, Alberto. 1851. "Degli elementi tonali: frammenti di un corso di lezioni sulla tonalità." *Gazzetta musicale di Milano* 9, no. 23 (June 8): 107–108 and 9, no. 25 (June 22): 117–18.

Meini, Vittorio. 1858–59. "Considerazioni sull'arte del canto." *L'Armonia* 6, no. 22 (December 1): 181–82; 6, no. 3 (February 15): 201–202.

Melisi, Francesco. 1900. *Catalogo dei libretti per musica dell'Ottocento (1800–1860). Biblioteca del Conservatorio di San Pietro a Majella di Napoli.* Lucca: Libreria musicale italiana.

Melzi, Lodovico. 1878. *Cenni storici sul R. Conservatorio di musica in Milano, dal 10 gennaio 1873 al 10 novembre 1878.* Milan: Ricordi.

———.1880. *Memorie e documenti per servire alla storia di Lucca.* Vol. 12. Lucca: Accademia lucchese di scienze, lettere ed arti.

Mengozzi, Bernardo. 1803. *Méthode de chant du Conservatoire de musique.* Paris: À l'imprimerie du Conservatoire de musique.

Minoja, Ambrogio. 1812. *Lettera sopra il canto.* Milan: Luigi Mussi.

Momigny, Jérôme-Joseph de. 1803–1806. *Cours complet d'harmonie et de composition.* 3 vols. Paris: Momigny and Bailleul.

Momigny, Girolamo-Giuseppe di. 1823. *La sola e vera teoria della musica.* Bologna: n.p.; reprint, Sala Bolognese: Arnaldo Forni, 1969. Translation of *La seule vraie théorie de la musique.* Paris, 1821.

Morigi, Angelo. n.d. [1820s?]. *Trattato di contrappunto fugato di Angelo Morigi già direttore dell'orchestra della real Corte di Parma, pubblicato da B. Asioli e dedicato agli allievi del regio Conservatorio di musica di Milano.* Milan: Ricordi.

Mozart, Wolfang Amadeus. n.d. [1850s?]. *Breve trattato di contrappunto del M.° W. A. Mozart. Prima versione italiana, riveduta dal M.° Cav. L. F. Rossi.* Turin: F. Blanchi.

Napoli, Raffaele. 1857. *Esame critico del trattato di armonia e composizione sul metodo della scuola di musica napoletana pubblicato da Giuseppe dei baroni Staffa.* Naples: Federico Vitale.

Napoli-Signorelli, Pietro. 1813. *Storia critica de' teatri musicali italiani.* 10 vols. Naples: Vincenzo Orsino.

Naumann, Johann Gottlieb. 1762–68. "Lezioni ossia studi di contrappunto fatti sotto il p. Martini in Bologna, cominciando dal 25 aprile 1762 al marzo 1768." Museo internazionale e biblioteca della musica di Bologna, Ms. II.23.

Nava, Gaetano. 1829. *Ventiquattro solfeggi di stile moderno per contralto o basso espresse in ambidue le chiavi con basso numerico.* Milan: Giovanni Ricordi.

———. 1849. *Solfeggi ossiano vocalizzi a tenore e basso concertati con accompa-* *gnamento di pianoforte: op.18.* Milan: Giovanni Ricordi.

———. 1855. *Metodo pratico di vocalizzazione per tenore.* Milan: Francesco Lucca.

———. 1884. *Elementi di vocalizzazione ad uso delle fanciulle.* London: Augener.

Nerici, Luigi. 1857. *La Scuola di Canto Fermo.* Lucca: Giuseppe Giusti.

———. 1872. *Dell'origine della musica moderna.* Lucca: Giuseppe Giusti.

———. 1879. *Storia della Musica in Lucca.* Lucca: Giuseppe Giusti; reprint, Sala Bolognese: Arnaldo Forni, 1969.

Pacini, Giovanni. 1834. *Cenni storici sulla musica e Trattato di contrappunto.* Lucca: Giuseppe Giusti.

———. 1844a. *Corso teorico-pratico di lezioni d'armonia, compendiato dal maestro cav. Giovanni Pacini, direttore del regio Istituto Musicale di Lucca.* Milano: Gio. Ricordi.

———. 1844b. "Alcune parole intorno al ragionamento sulla musica e sulla poesia melodrammatica italiana del secolo XIX del signor maestro Giovanni Battista Rinuccini." *Gazzetta musicale di Milano* 3, no. 32 (August 11): 135.

———. 1845. "Corso teorico-pratico di lezioni d'armonia compendiato dal Maestro Giovanni Pacini, direttore del R. istituto musicale di Lucca." *Gazzetta musicale di Milano* 4, no. 2 (January 12): 5–6; 4, no. 6 (9 February): 24; 4, no. 10 (March 9): 44–45; 4, no. 25 (June 22): 105; 4, no. 28 (July 13): 120–21; 4, no. 29 (July 20): 124.

———. 1849. *Principj elementari di musica e metodo per l'insegnamento del meloplasto.* Lucca: Baroni.

———. 1864. *Nei funerali de Michele Puccini.* Lucca: not specified.

———. 1865. *Le mie memorie artistiche.* Florence: G. G. Guidi.

———. 1875. *Le mie memorie artistiche.* 2d ed. Florence: Le Monnier; reprint, Lucca: Maria Pacini Fazzi, 1981.

Paisiello, Giovanni. 1782. *Regole con ben accompagnare il Partimento, o sia il Basso Fondamentale sopra il Cembalo.* St Petersburg: Napechatano v Tipografii Morskogo Shliakhetskogo Kadetskogo Korpusa. New annotated edition in *Praxis und Theorie des Partimentospiels,* vol. 1. Wilhelmshaven: Noetzel, 2008.

Panofka, Heinrich [Enrico]. 1871. *Voci e cantanti: ventotto capitoli di considerazioni generali sulla voce e sull'altare del canto.* Florence: M. Cellini; reprint, Sala Bolognese: Arnaldo Forni, 1984.

Panseron, Auguste-Mathieu. 1846. *The ABC of Music, or, Progressive Lessons in the Rudiments of Music and Solfeggi.* London: Ditson.

Parisini, Federico. 1879a. *Trattato elementare d'armonia.* Bologna: Società Azzoguidi.

———.1879b. *Principii elementari di Musica.* 3d ed. Bologna: Società Azzoguidi.

Penna, Lorenzo. 1684. *Li primi albori musicali per il principianti della musica figurata.* Bologna: Giacomo Monti; reprint, Sala Bolognese: Arnaldo Forni, 1996.

Perosa, Leonardo. 1864. *Della origine, dei progressi e degli effetti del melodramma in italia.* Venice: Tipografia Antonelli Editrice.

Perotti, Giuseppe A. 1844. "Critica (Due Libri di A. Ferrary Rodigino, *Il progetto di riforma dei teatri musicali d'Italia e Le Convenienze teatrali. Analisi della condizione presente del teatro musicale italiano*)." *Gazzetta musicale di Milano* 3, no. 19 (May 12): 76.

Perrino, Marcello. 1810. *Osservazioni sul canto.* Naples: Stamperia Reale.

———.1814. *Lettera di Marcello Perrino ad un amico sul proposito di una disputa relativa alla musica.* Naples: Angelo Trani.

Persico, Tommaso M. 1883a. "Tradizione e progresso." *La Musica* 4, no. 9 (May 7): 2–3.

———.1883b. "Napoli a teatro." *La Musica* 4, no. 12 (June 18): 1; 4, no. 13 (July 2):

2–3; 4, no. 14 (July 16): 2; 4, no. 15 (August 6): 1–2; 4, no. 16 (August 20): 2–3.

———.1883c. "Pro domo mea." *La Musica* 4, no. 18 (September 17): 1.

Picchi, Ermanno. 1853a. "Emulare non imitare." *Gazzetta musicale di Firenze* 1, no. 6 (July 21): 21–22.

———.1853b. "Dimanda e riposta." *Gazzetta musicale di Firenze* 1, no. 8 (August 4): 29–30.

———.1853c. "Sopra una riforma di solfeggio proposta dal Canonico Alessandro Figlinesi d'Empoli." *Gazzetta musicale di Firenze* 1, no. 9 (August 11): 35–36.

———.1853d. "Se siamo in progresso." *Gazzetta musicale di Firenze* 1, no. 16 (September 29): 61–62.

———.1853e. "Non più contralti." *Gazzetta musicale di Firenze* 1, no. 17 (October 6): 65–67; 1, no. 19 (October 20): 73–74.

———.1853f. "Il Trovatore del Verdi." *Gazzetta musicale di Firenze* 1, no. 18 (October 13): 69–70.

———.1853g. "La Scienza dell'Armonia e le Regole del Accompagnamento brevemente esposte ed applicate alla prima pratica dell'Arte." *Gazzetta musicale di Firenze* 1, no. 27 (December 15): 105–106.

Picchianti, Luigi. 1821. *Memoria di Luigi Picchianti; ai sigg. Professori sopra una questione di musica.* Florence: Nella Stamperia del Giglio.

———.1834. *Principj generali e ragionati della musica teorico-pratica di Luigi Picchianti.* Florence: Tipografia della Speranza.

———.1846–47. "Un manoscritto dell'organista Del Bucine contenente alcuni ricordi per servire ad un esame critico delle regole del contrappunto e della fuga." *Gazzetta musicale di Milano* 5, no. 48 (November 29, 1846): 377–79; 5, no. 49 (December 6): 385–86; 5, no. 52 (December 27): 409–10; 6, no. 1 (January 3, 1847): 3–4; 6, no. 2 (January 10): 11–12; 6, no. 4 (January 24): 27–28.

———.1853. *La Scienza dell'armonia e Le Regole dell'accompagnamento, brevemente esposte, ed applicate alla prima pratica dell'arte, da Luigi Picchianti per uso degli alunni delle pubbliche scuole di musica, annesse alla I. e R. Accademia fiorentina di belle arti.* Florence: Giuseppe Passerai.

Pintado, Giuseppe. 1794. *Vera idea della musica e del contrappunto.* Rome: Stamperia di G. Puccinelli; reprinted as "Vera idea della musica e del contrappunto di D. Giuseppe Pintado. Pubblicato in Roma nel 1794," *La Musica* 1, no. 19 (March 1, 1858) through 2, no. 18 (June 5, 1859).

Planelli, Antonio. 1981 [1772]. *Dell'opera in musica.* Ed. Francesco Degrada. Fiesole: Discanto.

Platania, Pietro. 1872. *Corso completo di fughe e canoni d'ogni genere, etc..* Milan: Lucca.

———.1883. *Trattato d'armonia: seguito da un corso di contrappunto dal corale al fugato e partimenti analoghi divisi in tre fascicoli.* Milan: Lucca.

Poglietti, Alessandro. 1676. *Compendium oder kurtzer Begriff, und Einführung zur Musica, Sonderlich einem Organisten dienlich.* Facs. Kremsmünster: Cornetto, 2008.

Porpora, Nicola. 1858 [1720s?]. *Porpora's Elements of Singing. Adopted by Righini and All Eminent Masters since His Time. Extracted from the Archives at Naples.* Ed. Marcia Harris. London: Addison, Hollier, and Lucas.

Puccini, Michele. 1846. "Corso pratico di contrappunto da Michele Puccini per uso de' suoi allievi." Ms.: Museo Puccini in Celle, Pescaglia.

Quadri, Domenico. 1832. *Lezioni d'armonia scritte da Domenico Quadri per facilitare lo studio della composizione.* Naples: Aniello Tramater.

Raffaelli, Pietro. 1856a. "Il melodramma in Italia." *L'Armonia* 1, no. 1 (January 1): 2–3; 1, no. 3 (January 15): 10–11: 1, no. 4 (January 22): 14–15; 1, no.5 (January 29): 17–18; 1, no. 7 (12 February): 26–27: 1, no. 8 (19 February): 30–31; 1, no. 13 (March 25): 50; 1, no. 14 (April 1): 54–55; 1, no. 15 (April 8): 57–59; 1, no. 16 (April 15): 62–63; 1, no. 17 (April 22): 67–68; 1, no. 18 (April 29): 71–72.

———.1856b. "Sulla riforma del melodramma." *L'Armonia* 1, no. 19 (May 6): 74–75; 1, no. 20 (May 13): 78.

Raimondi, Pietro. ca. 1836. *Bassi imitati e fugati divisi in tre libri.* Naples: Girard.

Ray, Pietro. 1832. *Solfeggi progressivi per soprano: parte prima.* Milan: Giovanni Ricordi.

———.1846. *Studio teorico-pratico di contrappunto compilato per i suoi allievi dal maestro P. Ray professore di composizione e vice-censore del conservatorio di musica in Milano.* Milan: Giovanni Ricordi.

Regli, Francesco. 1860. *Dizionario Biografico dei più celebri poeti ed artisti melodrammatici, tragici e comici, maestri, concertisti, coreografi, mimi, ballerini, scenografi, giornalisti, impresarii ecc., che fiorirono in Italia dal 1800 al 1860.* Turin: Enrico Dalmazzo.

Reicha, Antoine. 1814. *Traité de Melodie: Abstraction faite de ses Rapports avec l'Harmonie.* Paris: J. L. Sherff.

———.1824–26. *Traité de haute composition musicale.* 2 vols. Paris: Zetter.

———,Antonio. 1830. *Trattato della melodia considerata fuori de' suoi rapporti con l'armonia seguito da un supplement su l'arte di accompagnare la melodia coll'armonia quando la prima dev'essere predominante.* Milan and Florence: Ricordi.

———.2000. *Treatise on Melody: Considered Apart from Its Relationship with Harmony, Followed by a Supplement on the Art of Accompanying Melody with Harmony, Where the Former Is Dominant, All Demonstrated by the Best Me-*

lodic Models. Trans. Peter M. Landey. New York: Pendragon Press.

Riccati, Conte Giordano Trivigiano. 1762. *Saggio sopra le leggi del Contrappunto del Conte Giordano Riccati Nobile Trivigiano*. Castel Franco: Giulio Trento.

Ricci, Vittorio. 1900–1902. *Daily Vocal Practice: Consisting of 150 Exercises, Transposed into All Keys*. London: Paterson and Sons.

———. 1908. *25 Solfeggios for Soprano or Tenor by the Most Celebrated Italian Composers of the XVII, XVIII, and XIX Centuries*. London: Joseph Williams.

———. 1912. *The Old Italian School of Singing. Second Series: 20 Solfeggios for Contralto or Bass*. London: Joseph Williams.

Riemann, Hugo. 1884. *Musikalische Dynamik und Agogik: Lehrbuch der musikalischen Phrasirung auf Grund einer Revision der Lehre von der musikalischen Metrik und Rhythmik*. Hamburg: D. Rahter.

———. 1903. *System der musikalischen Rhythmik und Metrik*. Leipzig: Breitkopf und Härtel.

———. 1901. *Geschichte der Musik seit Beethoven (1800–1900)*. Stuttgart: Spemann; reprint, Charleston, S.C.: BiblioBazaar, 2008.

Riepel, Joseph. 1752–68. *Anfangsgründe zur musicalischen Setzkunst*. 5 vols. Regensburg, Frankfurt, or Augsburg: E. F. Bader, J. L. Montag, J. J. Lotter, or J. C. Krippner. Revised and ed. Thomas Emmerig as *Anfangsgründe zur musicalischen Setzkunst: Sämtliche Schriften zur Musiktheorie*. 2 vols. Vienna: Böhlau, 1996.

Rinuccini, Giovanni Battista. 1843. *Sulla musica e sulla poesia melodrammatica italiana del secolo XIX*. Lucca: L. Guidotti.

Ritorni, Carlo. 1841. *Ammaestramenti alla composizione d'ogni poema e d'ogni opera appartenente alla musica*. Milan: Luigi di Giacomo Pirola.

Rossi, Lauro. 1858. *Guida ad un corso d'armonia pratica orale per gli allievi del R. conservatorio di musica in Milano*. Milan: Ricordi.

———. 1864. *Esercizi per canto a complemento dello studio dei solfeggi e dei vocalizzi e come preparazione allo studio complessivo delle partiture di opere teatrali: Serie prima: 12 Esercizi per voce di soprano*. Milan: Tito di G. Ricordi.

———. 1866. *Otto vocalizzi di soprano in classe di perfezionamento*. Milan: Tito di G. Ricordi.

———. 1877. "Ill[ustrissi]mi Componimenti il Consiglio Direttivo del R. Collegio di musica in S. Pietro a Maiella." *La Musica* 2, no. 6 (March 17): 1–2.

Rossini, Gioachino. 1958 [1827]. *Gorgheggi e Solfeggi per rendere la voce agile e imparare il bel canto*. Milan: Tito di G. Ricordi.

Rossi-Scotti, Giovanni Battista. 1860. *Della vita e delle opere del Cav. Francesco Morlacchi di Perugia*. Perugia: Tipografia de V. Bartelli.

Rousseau, Jean-Jacques. 1792–93. *Oeuvres complètes de J. J. Rousseau. Nouvelle édition, classée par ordre de matieres, et ornée de quatre-vingt-dix gravures. Tomes 19–22: Écrits sur la musique*. Paris: Poinçot.

———. 1824. *Oeuvres complètes de J. J. Rousseau, mises dans un nouvel ordre, avec des notes historiques et des éclaircissements; par V. D. Musset-Pathay. Beaux-Arts. Écrits sur la musique*. Paris: P. Dupont.

Rovani, Giuseppe. 1856. "Bellini e Meyerbeer o la musica drammatica secondo le scuole italiana e germanico-francese." *L'Italia musicale* 8, no. 3 (January 9): 9–10; 8, no. 5 (January 16): 17–18; 8, no. 8 (January 26): 29–30; 8, no. 11 (6 February): 41–42; 8, no. 26 (March 29): 101; 8, no. 28 (April 5): 109–10; 8, no. 29 (April 9): 113; 8, no. 37 (May 7): 145–46; 8, no. 38 (May 10): 149–50; 8, no. 43

(May 28): 169–70; 8, no. 46 (June 7): 181–82; 8, no. 57 (July 16): 225–26.

Ruffini, Salvatore. 1856. "Bordogni e Panofka al Conservatorio di musica di Parigi." *L'Italia musicale* 8, no. 48 (June 14): 189–90.

———.1857. "Dello stato attuale del teatro in Italia." *L'Italia musicale* 9, no. 32 (April 22): 125–26; 9, no. 34 (April 29): 133.

Ruta, Michele. 1855. "Ricordi pei giovani compositori. I. La Romanza." *La Musica* 1, no. 9 (March 27): 66–67.

———.1856a. "Pedagogia musicale. Il maestro di composizione." *L'Italia musicale* 8, no. 72 (September 6): 286.

———.1856b. "Pedagogia musicale. Il solfeggio." *L'Italia musicale* 8, no. 80 (October 4): 318.

———.1856c. "Pedagogia musicale. Oltre il solfeggio." *L'Italia musicale* 8, no. 84 (October 18): 334; 8, no. 85 (October 22): 338.

———.1876. "Pedagogia musicale. Lo studio dell'armonia in Italia." *La Musica* 1, no. 3 (August 19): 2–3.

———.1877a. "Ricordi pe' giovani compositori. Il crescendo." *La Musica* 2, no. 3 (3 February): 1.

———.1877b. "Ricordi pe' giovani compositori. L'attacco." *La Musica* 2, no. 20 (October 20): 1.

———.1884. "Considerazioni sulla frase musicale nella pedagogia del canto." *La Musica* 5, no. 3 (18 February): 1–2.

Sabbatini, Luigi Antonio. 1789–90. *Elementi teorici della musica colla pratica de' medesimi, in duetti, e terzetti a canone accompagnati dal basso, ed eseguibili sì a solo, che a più voci, di F. Luigi Antonio Sabbatini de' Minori Conventuali. Parte prima: Elementi di teorica; Parte seconda: Serie delle scale; Parte terza: Solfeggi a due, e tre voci sopra le Scale, e Salti.* Rome: Nella stamperia Pilucchi Cracas, e Giuseppe Rotilj socio. 2d ed. *Elementi pratici della musica formati in duetti a canone accompagnati dal basso sì a solo, che a più voci.* Rome: Nella stamperia Pilucchi Cracas, e Giuseppe Rotilj socio, 1795.

———.1802. *Trattato sopra le Fughe musicali di fra Luigi Antonio Sabbatini M. C. corredato da copiosi saggi del suo Antecessore Padre Francesco Antonio Vallotti dello stesso ordine maestro di cappella nella basilica di S. Antonio di Padova.* Venice: Sebastiano Valle.

Sacchi, Giovenale. 1770. *Della divisione del tempo nella musica nel ballo e nella poesia: Dissertazioni III del P. D. Giovenale Sacchi Barnabita.* Milan: Per Giuseppe Mazzucchelli nella Stamperia Malatesta; reprint, Sala Bolognese: Arnaldo Forni, 1969.

———.1780. *Delle quinte successive nel contrappunto e delle regole degli accompagnamenti.* Milan: per Cesare Orena stamperia Malatesta.

———.1786. *Dell'antica lezione degli ebrei e della origine de' punti dissertazione.* Milan: per Cesare Orena nella stamperia Malatesta.

Saint-Lambert, Michel de. 1702. *Les principes du clavecin.* Paris: Cristophe Ballard. Trans. Rebecca Harris-Warrick as *Principles of the Harpsichord by Monsieur de Saint-Lambert.* Cambridge: Cambridge University Press, 1984.

Sala, Nicola. 1794. "Regole del contrappunto pratico di Nicola Sala napoletano, primo maestro del Reale Conservatorio della Pietà de' Turchini dedicate alla Maestà di Ferdinando IV Re delle due Sicilie." 3 vols. Naples: Stamperia Reale. Biblioteca del Conservatorio di Milano, Mascarello Collection, Ms. TM40.

Santa María, Tomás de. 1565. *Libro llamado arte de tañer fantasia.* Facs. Geneva: Minkoff, 1973; reprint, Valladolid: Maxtor libreria, 2009. Trans. A. C. Howell and W. E. Hultberg as *The Art of Playing the Fantasia.* Pittsburgh: Latin American Literary Review Press, 1991.

Santley, Charles. 1893. *Student and Singer.*
 London: Edward Arnold.
———.1909. *Reminiscences of My Life.*
 London: Isaac Pitman.
Santucci, Marco. 1828. *Sulla melodia,*
 sull'armonia e sul metro: Dissertazioni
 di Marco Santucci, canonico della Metro-
 politana di Lucca, dedicate alla studiosa
 gioventù. Lucca: dalla ducale tipografia
 Bertini.
Sarti, Giuseppe. n.d. [1780s?]. "Trattato
 del Basso Generale del Sig. Giuseppe
 Sarti." Museo internazionale e biblioteca della musica di Bologna, Ms. L.20.
Scarlatti, Alessandro. n.d. [1720s?]. "Principii Del Sigr. Cave. Alessandro Scarlatti." British Library, Ms. Add. 14244.
Schmidl, Carlo. 1887–90. *Dizionario uni-*
 versale dei musicisti, 12 vols. Milan: Ricordi. 2d ed. 2 vols. Milan: Sonzogno,
 1926–29. 3d ed. 2 vols. Milan: Sonzogno, 1936–38.
Scoppa, Antonio. 1803. *Traité de la poésie*
 italienne, rapportée à la poésie française,
 dans lequel on fait voir la parfaite ana-
 logie entre ces deux langues. Versailles:
 L'imprimerie de Jacob.
———.1811–14. *Les vrais principes de la*
 versification développés par un examen
 comparatif entre la langue italienne et la
 française. 3 vols. Paris: V. Courcier.
Scudo, P. 1847. "Storia musicale. Dell'arte
 del canto." *L'Italia musicale* 1, no. 12
 (September 22): 93–94; 1, no. 13 (September 29): 99–101; 1, no. 14 (October
 6): 108–109; 1, no. 15 (October 13):
 117–19.
Selvaggi, Gaspare. 1823. *Trattato di armo-*
 nia, ordinato con nuovo metodo, e corre-
 dato di tavole a dichiarazione delle cose in
 esso esposte. Naples: Raffaele Miranda.
Soffredini, Alfredo. 1901. *Le opere di Verdi:*
 studio critico analitico. Milan: Carlo
 Aliprandi.
Speth, Balthasar. 1823. *Die Kunst in*
 Italien. Vol. 3, 376–451. Munich: J. A.
 Finsterlin.

Staffa, Giuseppe. 1849, 1856. *Metodo della*
 Scuola Napolitana di composizione mu-
 sicale. Parte prima: Trattato d'armonia.
 Naples: Francesco Azzolino; *Parte se-*
 conda: Trattato di composizione. Naples:
 Carlo Lista Vico Gerolomini.
———.1857a. "Esame critico dei sistemi e
 delle opere musicali." *La Musica* 1, no. 1
 (June 1): 4–5.
———.1857b. "Uno sguardo sulla scienza
 e l'arte de' suoni." *La Musica* 1, no. 2
 (June 15): 9–11.
———.1857c. "Parallelo tra una lingua e
 la musica." *La Musica* 1, no. 2 (June 15):
 13–15.
———.1857d. "Elementi della musica."
 La Musica 1, no. 3 (July 1): 20–21; 1,
 no. 4 (July 15): 27–29; 1, no. 5 (August
 1): 35–37; 1, no. 6 (August 15): 43–44;
 1, no. 7 (September 1): 50–51; 1, no. 8
 (September 15): 58–59; 1, no. 9 (August
 15): 66–67.
———.1857e. "A Raffaele Napoli." *La Mu-*
 sica 1, no. 6 (August 15): 41–3.
———.1857f. "Sistemi musicali." *La Musi-*
 ca 1, no. 12 (November 15): 91–92; 1, no.
 13 (December 1): 97–99.
———.1857–58. "Parte Seconda. Elementi
 della esecuzione musicale, comune a
 tutti gli strumenti che si adoperano
 nella musica." *La Musica* 1, no. 14 (December 15, 1857): 107; 1, no. 19 (March
 1, 1858): 150–51; 1, no. 20 (March 15):
 158–9.
———.1859. "Giuseppe Verdi. Simon
 Boccanegra." *La Musica* 2, no. 11 (January 1): 81–83.
Stendhal [Beyle, Marie-Henri]. 1824. *Me-*
 moirs of Rossini. London: T. Hookham.
Tacchinardi, Guido. n.d. [1830s?]. *Saggi di*
 Basso numerato e Contrappunto. Milan:
 Ricordi.
Tartini, Giuseppe. 1754. *Trattato di musica*
 secondo la vera scienza dell'armonia. Padova: Giovanni Manfrè.
Tomeoni, Florido. 1798. *Méthode qui ap-*
 prend la connoissance de l'harmonie et la

pratique de l'accompagnement selon les principes de l'école de Naples, par Florido Tomeoni. Paris: chez l'auteur.

———.1799. *Théorie de la musique vocale, ou règles qu'il faut connaître et observer pour bien chanter, ou pour apprendre à bien juger par soi-même du dégré de perfection de ceux que l'on entend; avec des remarques sur la prononciation des langues françoises et italienne.* Paris: Chez Pougens.

———.1800. *Traité d'harmonie et d'accompagnement selon les principes de Durante et Leo, fondateurs de l'harmonie dans les conservatoires de Naples par Florido Tomeoni, Elève de l'École de Durante.* Paris: Chez l'auteur.

Tomeoni, Pellegrino. 1795. *Regole pratiche per accompagnare il basso continuo.* Florence: Anton-Giuseppe Pagani; reprint, Sala Bolognese: Arnaldo Forni, 2007.

Tosi, Pier Francesco. 1723. *Opinioni de' cantori antichi, e moderni; o sieno osservazioni sopra il canto figurato.* Bologna: Lelio dalla Volpe. Trans. John Galliard as *Observations on the Florid Song; or, Sentiments on the Ancient and Modern Singers.* London: J. Wilcocks, 1743. Facs. London: Travis and Emery, 2009.

Trisolini, Pietro. 1855a. "Della necessità di studiare la storia della musica." *La Musica* 1, no. 16 (May 15): 121–22; 1, no. 17 (May 22): 129–30.

———.1855b. "La lingua italiana è la lingua del canto." *La Musica* 1, no. 33 (September 15): 257–58; 1, no. 34 (September 21): 265–66.

Tritto, Giacomo. 1816. *Scuola di contrappunto.* Milan: Ferdinando Artaria.

———.1821. *Partimenti e regole generali per conoscere qual numerica dar si deve ai vari movimenti del basso.* Milan: Ferdinando Artaria.

Vaccai, Nicola. 1837 [1832]. *Metodo pratico di canto italiano per camera diviso in 15 lezioni, ossiano Solfeggi progressivi ed elementari sopra parole di Metastasio.* Mi-

lan: Ricordi; reprinted with additional manuscript materials, Turin: Zedde Editore, 1999.

Venini, Francesco. 1798. *Dei principi dell'armonia musicale e poetica, e sulla loro applicazione alla teoria e alla pratica della versificazione italiana. Dissertazione dell'Abate Francesco Venini.* Paris: Gio. Claudio Molini.

———.1818. *Saggi della poesia lirica antica e moderna.* 2 vols. Milan: Giovanni Silvestri.

Vicentino, Nicola. 1555. *L'Antica musica: ridotta alla moderna pratica.* Rome: not specified. Facsimile, Kassel: Bärenreiter, 1959. Trans. and ed. Maria Rika Maniates and Claude V. Palisca as *Ancient Music Adapted to Modern Practice.* New Haven: Yale University Press, 1996.

Vissian, Massimino. 1846. *Dizionario della musica ossia Raccolta dei principali vocaboli italiani-francesi co' loro significati . . . preceduto da un trattato italiano e francese sui principj elementari della musica.* Milan: a spese di Massimino Vissian.

Vitali, Geremia. 1844a. "Proposto d'un nuovo mezzo per determinare con essattezza i tempi musicali." *Gazzetta musicale di Milano* 3, no. 20 (May 19): 79–80.

———.1844b. "Intorno al nuovo progetto di misurare i tempi musicali coi minuti. Al chiarissimo signor maestro Raimondo Boucheron." *Gazzetta musicale di Milano* 3, no. 32 (August 11): 134–35.

———.1847. *La Musica ne' suoi principj nuovamente spiegata.* Milan: Ricordi.

———.1850a. *Della necessità di riformare i principj elementari di musica di Bonifazio Asioli.* Milan: Tipografia e libreria di Giuseppe Chiusi.

———.1850b. "Del *Trattato di melodia* di Antonio Reicha." *Gazzetta musicale di Milano* 8, no. 42 (October 20): 180–81.

Wagner, Richard. 1893–99. *Richard Wagner's Prose Works.* Trans. William Ashton Ellis. 8 vols. London: Routledge and Kegan Paul.

Walker, Francis. 1895. *Letters of a Baritone.* New York: Charles Scribner's Sons.

Walther, Johann. 1955 [1708]. *Praecepta der musicalischen Composition.* Ed. P. Benary. Leipzig: Breitkopf and Härtel.

Zambaldi, Francesco. 1874. *Il ritmo dei versi italiani.* Turin: Loescher.

Zarlino, Gioseffo. 1573 [1558]. *Le istitutioni harmoniche.* Venice: Francesco de i Franceschi Senese. 2d ed. Facs. Ridgewood, N.J.: Gregg Press, 1966.

Zingarelli, Nicolò. 1830. *Partimenti del signor maestro don Nicolò Zingarelli, dal medesimo dedicati al suo caro amico e discepolo di contrappunto il Signor Francesco Pollini.* Milan: Gio. Ricordi.

SECONDARY SOURCES

Adami, Giuseppe, ed. 1982 [1928]. *Epistolario Giacomo Puccini.* Milan: A. Mondadori.

Albarosa, Nino, ed. 1984. *Amilcare Ponchielli, 1834–1886: saggi e ricerche nel 1500 anniversario della nascita.* Casalmorano: Cassa Rurale ed Artigiana di Casalmorano.

Allorto, Riccardo, and Claudio Sartori. 1963–64. *Enciclopedia della Musica,* 4 vols. Milan: Ricordi.

Ambìveri, Corrado. 1998. *Operisti minori dell'800 italiano.* Rome: Gremese.

Anders, Micheal F. 1997. "Musical and Dramatic Structure in the Finales of the Operas of Giacomo Puccini." PhD diss., Ohio State University.

André, Naomi Adele. 2006. *Voicing Gender: Castrati, Travesti, and the Second Woman in Early-Nineteenth-Century Italian Opera.* Bloomington: Indiana University Press.

Antolini, Bianca Maria, and Wolfgang Witzenmann, eds. 1993. *Napoli e il teatro musicale in Europa tra Sette e Ottocento: Studi in onore di Friedrich Lippmann.* Florence: Olschki.

Antolini, Bianca Maria, ed. 1999a. *Milano musicale, 1861–1897.* Lucca: Libreria musicale italiana.

———. 1999b. "La musica a Napoli nell'Ottocento nel carteggio dei marchesi Capranica." In *Francesco Florimo e l'Ottocento musicale,* ed. Rosa Cafiero and Maria Marino, 1:365–401. Reggio Calabria: Jason.

Arnold, Frank Thomas. 1965 [1931]. *The Art of Accompaniment from a Thoroughbass: As Practised in the XVIIth and XVIIIth Centuries.* New York: Dover.

Ashbrook, William. 1988. "Boito and the 1868 *Mefistofele* Libretto as a Reform Text." In *Reading Opera,* ed. Arthur Groos and Roger Parker, 268–87. Princeton: Princeton University Press.

Ashbrook, William, and Harold Powers. 1991. *Puccini's Turandot: The End of the Great Tradition.* Princeton: Princeton University Press.

———. 1995 [1968]. *The Operas of Puccini.* Ithaca: Cornell University Press.

Baggiani, Franco. 1982. *Organi e organisti nella cattedrale di Lucca.* Lucca: Maria Pacini Fazzi.

Baker, N. K. 1992. "An *Ars poetica* for Music: Reicha's System of Syntax and Structure." In *Musical Humanism and Its Legacy: Essays in Honour of Claude V. Palisca,* ed. N. K. Baker and B. Hanning, 419–49. Stuyvesant, N.Y.: Pendragon Press.

Balthazar, Scott. 1985. "Evolving Conventions in Italian Serious Opera: Scene Structure in the Works of Rossini, Bellini, Donizetti, and Verdi, 1810–50." PhD diss., University of Pennsylvania.

———. 1988. "Rossini and the Development of the Mid-Century Lyric Form." *Journal of the American Musicological Society* 41, no. 1: 102–25.

———. 1988–89. "Ritorni's *Ammaestramenti* and the Conventions of Rossinian Melodramma." *Journal of Musicological Research* 7: 281–311.

———. 1989. "The *Primo Ottocento* Duet and the Transformation of the Rossinian Code." *Journal of Musicology* 7, no. 4: 471–97.

———.1990. "Analytic Contexts and Mediated Influences: The Rossinian *Convenienze* and Verdi's Middle and Late Duets." *Journal of Music Research* 10: 19–45.

———.1991a. "Mayr, Rossini, and the Development of the Early 'Concertato' Finale." *Journal of the Royal Musicological Association* 116, no. 1: 236–66.

———.1991b. "The Rhythm of Text and Music in *Ottocento* Melody: An Empirical Reassessment in Light of Contemporary Treatises." *Current Musicology* 49: 5–28.

———.1995. "Aspects of Form in the Ottocento Libretto." *Cambridge Opera Journal* 7, no. 1: 23–35.

———.2004. "The Forms of Set Pieces." In *The Cambridge Companion to Verdi*, ed. Scott Balthazar, 49–68. Cambridge: Cambridge University Press.

Barbier, Patrick. 1996. *The World of the Castrati: The History of an Extraordinary Operatic Phenomenon*. London: Souvenir.

Bartel, Dietrich. 1997. *Musica Poetica: Musical-Rhetorical Figures in German Baroque Music*. Lincoln: University of Nebraska Press.

Bassi, Adriano. 1987. *Giacomo Orefice*. Padua: Franco Muzzio.

Battelli, Giulio, ed. 1990. *I Tesori della Musica Lucchese*. Lucca: Maria Pacini Fazzi.

Beiser, Frederick C. 2003. *The Romantic Imperative: The Concept of Early German Romanticism*. Cambridge: Harvard University Press.

Beltrami, Pietro G. 1991. *La metrica italiana*. Bologna: Il Mulino.

———.1996. *Gli strumenti della poesia: guida alla metrica italiana*. Bologna: Il Mulino.

Bent, Ian, ed. 1996. *Music Theory in the Age of Romanticism*. 2 vols. Cambridge: Cambridge University Press.

Berg, Karl G. M. 1991. *Giacomo Puccinis Opern. Musik und Dramaturgie*. Kassel: Bärenreiter.

Bergé, Pieter, ed., William E. Caplin, James Hepokoski, and James Webster. 2009. *Musical Form, Forms, and Formenlehre: Three Methodological Reflections*. Leuven: Leuven University Press.

Bernardoni, Virgilio. 1990. "La teoria della melodia vocale nella trattatistica italiana (1790–1870)." *Acta Musicologica* 62: 29–61.

———.1998. "La drammaturgia dell'aria nel primo Puccini: Da 'Se come voi piccina' a 'Sola, perduta, abbandonata.'" *Studi pucciniani* 1: 43–56.

———.2008. *Verso Bohème: Gli abbozzi del libretto negli archivi di Giuseppe Giacosa e Luigi Illica*. Florence: Olschki.

Berrong, Richard. 1992. *Politics of Opera in Turn-of-the-Century Italy: Letters of Catalani*. Lampeter: Edwin Mellen.

Biagi Ravenni, Gabriella, and Carolyn Gianturco, eds. 1997. *Giacomo Puccini: L'uomo, il musicista, il panorama europeo*. Lucca: Libreria musicale italiana.

Bianconi, Lorenzo, and Giorgio Pestelli, eds. 1998. *Opera Production and Its Resources (History of Italian Opera, Vol. 4)*. Trans. Lydia Cochrane. Chicago: University of Chicago Press.

———, eds. 2002. *Opera on Stage (History of Italian Opera, Vol. 5)*. Trans. Kate Singleton. Chicago: University of Chicago Press.

———, eds. 2003. *Opera in Theory and Practice, Image and Myth (History of Italian Opera, Vol. 6)*. Trans. Kenneth Chalmers and Mary Whittall. Chicago: University of Chicago Press.

Black, John. 1984. *The Italian Romantic Libretto: A Study of Salvadore Cammarano*. Edinburgh: Edinburgh University Press.

Bögel, Hartwig. 1978. "Studien zur Instrumentation in den Opern Giacomo Puccinis." PhD diss., Eberhard Karls Universität, Tübingen.

Bonaccorsi, Alfredo. 1950. *Giacomo Puccini e i suoi antenati musicali*. Milan: Edizioni Curci.

———.1967. *Maestri di Lucca: I Guami e altri Musicisti.* Florence: Olschki.

Bonds, Mark Evan. 1988. "Haydn's False Recapitulations and the Perception of Sonata Form in the Eighteenth Century." PhD diss., Harvard University.

———.1991. *Wordless Rhetoric: Musical Form and the Metaphor of the Oration.* Cambridge: Harvard University Press.

———.2010. "The Spatial Representation of Musical Form." *Journal of Musicology* 27, no. 3: 265–303.

Borgir, Tharald. 1987 [1971]. *The Performance of the Basso Continuo in Italian Baroque Music.* Ann Arbor: UMI Research Press.

Brandenburg, Daniel. 1999. "Francesco Florimo, la vocalità e la didattica vocale dell'ottocento." In *Francesco Florimo e l'Ottocento musicale,* ed. Rosa Cafiero and Maria Marino, 1:163–74. Reggio Calabria: Jason.

———. "Enrico Delle Sedie, la presenza scenica e la cultura vocale dell'Ottocento." In *"Una piacente estate di San Martino": Studi e ricerche per i settant'anni di Marcello Conati,* ed. Marco Capra, 337–48. Lucca: Libreria musicale italiana.

Brofsky, Howard. 1987. "Martini's Music School." In *Padre Martini: musica e cultura nel Settecento europeo,* ed. A. Pompilio, 305–13. Firenze: Olschki.

Brown, Clive. 1999. *Classical and Romantic Performing Practice, 1750–1900.* Oxford: Oxford University Press.

Budden, Julian. 1987. "Wagnerian Tendencies in Italian Opera." In *Music and Theatre: Essays in Honour of Winton Dean,* ed. N. Fortune, 299–332. Cambridge: Cambridge University Press.

———.1989. "The Genesis and Literary Source of Giacomo Puccini's First Opera." *Cambridge Opera Journal* 1, no. 1: 79–85.

———.1992 [1973, 1978, 1981]. *The Operas of Verdi.* 3 vols. Oxford: Oxford University Press.

———.2002. *Puccini: His Life and Works.* Oxford: Oxford University Press.

Buelow, George J. 1992. *Thorough-Bass Accompaniment According to Johann David Heinichen.* Rev. ed. Lincoln: University of Nebraska Press.

Burton, Deborah. 1995. "An Analysis of Puccini's *Tosca:* A Heuristic Approach to the Unifying Elements of the Opera." PhD diss., University of Michigan.

———.1996. "Michele Puccini's Counterpoint Treatise." *Quaderni pucciniani,* 173–86.

Busch, Hans. 1978. *Verdi's* Aïda: *The History of an Opera in Letters and Documents.* Minneapolis: University of Minnesota Press.

———.1988. *Verdi's Otello and Simon Boccanegra (Revised Edition) in Letters and Documents.* 2 vols. Oxford: Oxford University Press.

———.1997. *Verdi's* Falstaff *in Letters and Contemporary Reviews.* Bloomington: Indiana University Press.

Cafiero, Rosa. 1993a. "La didattica del partimento a Napoli fra Settecento e Ottocento: Note sulla fortuna delle Regole di Carlo Cotumacci." In *Gli affetti convenienti all'idee: Studi sulla musica vocale italiana,* ed. Rosa Cafiero, Maria Caraci Vela, and Angela Romagnoli, 549–80. Naples: Edizioni Scientifiche Italiane.

———.1993b. "Una biblioteca per la biblioteca: la collezione musicale di Giuseppe Sigismondo." In *Napoli e il teatro musicale in Europa tra Sette e Ottocento: Studi in onore di Friedrich Lippmann,* ed. B. M. Antolini and W. Witzenmann, 299–367. Florence: Olschki.

———.1999a. "Metodi, progetti, e riforme dell'insegnamento della 'scienza armonica' nel Real Collegio di musica di Napoli nei primi decennia dell'Ottocento." *Studi musicali* 28: 425–81.

———.1999b. "Istruzione musicale a Napoli fra decennio francese e restaurazione borbonica: il Collegio di musica delle donzelle (1806–1832)." In *Francesco Florimo e l'Ottocento musicale,* ed. Rosa Cafiero and Maria Marino, 753–825. Reggio Calabria: Jason, 1999.

———. 2001. "Teorie armoniche di scuola napoletana ai primi dell'Ottocento: Cenni sulla fortuna di Francesco Durante fra Napoli e Parigi." In *Giacomo Francesco Milano e il ruolo dell'aristocrazia nel patrocinio delle attività musicali nel secolo XVIII,* ed. Gaetano Pitorresi, 171–98. Reggio Calabria: Laruffa.

———. 2005. "Conservatories and the Neapolitan School: A European Model at the End of the Eighteenth Century?" In *Musical Education in Europe (1770–1914): Compositional, Institutional, and Political Challenges,* ed. Michael Fend and Michel Noiray, 1:15–29. Berlin: Berlin Wissenschafts Verlag.

———. 2007. "The Early Reception of Neapolitan Partimento Theory in France: A Survey." *Journal of Music Theory* 51: 137–59.

———. 2009. "La formazione del musicista nel XVIII Secolo: il 'modello' dei Conservatori napoletani." *Rivista di Analisi e Teoria Musicale* 15, no. 1: 5–25.

Cafiero, Rosa, and Marina Marino, eds. 1999. *Francesco Florimo e l'Ottocento musicale.* 2 vols. Reggio Calabria: Jason.

Caplin, William. 1981. "Theories of Harmonic-Metric Relationships from Rameau to Riemann." PhD diss., University of Chicago.

———. 1998. *Classical Form.* Oxford: Oxford University Press.

Capra, Marco, ed. 2000. *"Una piacente estate di San Martino": Studi e ricerche per i settant'anni di Marcello Conati.* Lucca: Libreria musicale italiana.

Caswell, Austin B. 1989. *Embellished Opera Arias.* 8 vols. London: A-R Editions.

Celletti, Rodolfo. 1991 [1983]. *A History of Bel Canto.* Oxford: Oxford University Press.

Cesari, Francesco. "L'intricata vicenda del preludio all'atto IV di *Edgar.*" *Quaderni pucciniani,* 83–108.

———. 1993. "Genesi di *Edgar.*" In *Ottocento e Oltre,* ed. Francesco Izzo and Johannes Streicher, 451–69. Rome: Pantheon.

Cerquetelli, Giuseppe. 1923. *Guida teorico-pratica-dimostrativa per la risposta alla fuga: corredata di norme osservazioni ed esempi per uso dei giovani contrappuntisti.* Milan: Sonzogno.

Cesari, Gaetano, and Alessandro Luzio, eds. 1913. *I Copialettere di Giuseppe Verdi.* Milan: Tipografia Stucchi Ceretti.

Chirico, Teresa. 1999. "La musica nel Reale Albergo dei Poveri di Napoli e negli istituti dipendenti (1817–61)." In *Francesco Florimo e l'Ottocento musicale,* ed. Rosa Cafiero and Maria Marino, 1:827–59. Reggio Calabria: Jason.

Christen, Norbert. 1978. *Giacomo Puccini: analytische Untersuchungen der Melodik, Harmonik, und Instrumentation.* Hamburg: Karl Dieter Wagner.

Christensen, Thomas. 1992. "The *Règle de l'Octave* in Thorough-Bass Theory and Practice." *Acta Musicologica* 64: 91–117.

———. 1993. *Rameau and Musical Thought in the Enlightenment.* Cambridge: Cambridge University Press.

———, ed. 2002. *The Cambridge History of Western Music Theory.* Cambridge: Cambridge University Press.

———. 2008. "Fundamenta Partiturae: Thorough Bass and Foundations of Eighteenth-Century Composition Pedagogy." In *The Century of Bach and Mozart: Perspectives on Historiography, Composition, Theory, and Performance,* ed. Sean Gallagher and Thomas Forrest Kelly, 17–40. Cambridge: Harvard University Press.

Churgin, Bathia. 1968. "Francesco Galeazzi's Description (1796) of Sonata Form." *Journal of the American Musicological Society* 21: 181–99.

Chusid, Martin, and William Weaver. 1979. *The Verdi Companion*. New York: W. W. Norton.

———, ed. 1997. *Verdi's Middle Period*. Chicago: University of Chicago Press.

Colas, Damien. 2002. "I critici francesi e le strutture dell'opera italiana dell'ottocento: Problemi di terminologia." *Musica e storia* 10, no. 1: 271–90.

Conati, Marcello, ed. 1984. *Encounters with Verdi*. Trans. R. Stokes. Ithaca: Cornell University Press.

———. 2004. "*Il tabarro* ovvero la 'solita' insolita forma." *Studi pucciniani* 3: 265–82.

Conati, Marcello, and Mario Medici, eds. 1994. *The Verdi–Boito Correspondence*. Trans. William Weaver. Chicago: University of Chicago Press.

Corsi, Domenico. 1958. "La 'dinastia' dei Puccini—Antonio Puccini ed alcuni suoi carteggi." In *Giacomo Puccini nel centenario della nascita*. Lucca: Lorenzetti and Natali.

Dahlhaus, Carl. 1982. *Esthetics of Music*. Trans. William Austin. Cambridge: Cambridge University Press.

———. 1984. *Die Musiktheorie im 18. und 19. Jahrhundert. Erster Teil. Grundzüge einer Systematik*. Darmstadt: Wissenschaftliche Buchgesellschaft.

———. 1989. *Nineteenth-Century Music*. Trans. J. Bradford Robinson. Berkeley: University of California Press.

———. 1990 [1968]. *Studies on the Origin of Harmonic Tonality*. Trans. Robert Gjerdingen. Princeton: Princeton University Press.

Dallapiccola, Luigi. 1979. "Words and Music in Italian Nineteenth-Century Opera." In *The Verdi Companion*, ed. Martin Chusid and William Weaver, 193–215. New York: W. W. Norton.

Damerini, Adelmo. 1942. *L'istituto musicale "Giovanni Pacini" di Lucca*. Florence: Le Monnier.

Damschroder, David, and David Russell Williams. 1990. *Music Theory from Zarlino to Schenker: A Bibliography and Guide*. New York: Pendragon.

Damschroder, David. 2008. *Thinking about Harmony: Historical Perspectives on Analysis*. Cambridge: Cambridge University Press.

Darcy, Warren, and James Hepokoski. 2006. *Elements of Sonata Theory: Norms, Types, and Deformations in the Late-Eighteenth-Century Sonata*. Oxford: Oxford University Press.

Davis, Andrew. 2010. *Il Trittico, Turandot, and Puccini's Late Style*. Bloomington: Indiana University Press.

De Angelis, Marcello. 1978. *La musica del Granduca. Vita musicale e correnti critiche a Firenze, 1800–1855*. Florence: Vallecchi.

Deathridge, John. 2008. *Wagner: Beyond Good and Evil*. Berkeley: University of California Press.

DelDonna, Anthony R., and Pierpaolo Polzonetti, eds. 2009. *The Cambridge Companion to Eighteenth-Century Opera*. Cambridge: Cambridge University Press.

Del Fiorentino, Dante. 1952. *Immortal Bohemian*. London: Gollancz.

Della Corte, Andrea, ed. 1933. *Canto e bel canto*. Turin: Paravia.

Della Seta, Fabrizio. 1998. "Some Difficulties in the Historiography of Italian Opera." *Cambridge Opera Journal* 10, no. 1: 3–13.

———, ed. 2000. *Giuseppe Verdi: La traviata. Schizzi e abbozzi autografi*. Parma: Ministero per i beni e le attività culturali, Comitato nazionale per le celebrazioni verdiane; Istituto nazionale di studi verdiani.

———. 2004. "New Currents in the Libretto." In *The Cambridge Companion to Verdi*, ed. Scott Balthazar, 69–87. Cambridge: Cambridge University Press.

De Napoli, Giuseppe. 1936. *Amilcare Ponchielli (1834–1886): La vita, le opera, l'epistolario, le onoranze.* Cremona: Società Editorale Cremona Nuova.

De Nardis, Camillo. 1942 [1895]. *Partimenti dei Maestri Cotumacci, Durante, Fenaroli, Leo, Mattei, Platania, Sala, Scarlatti, Tritto, Zingarelli.* Milan: Ricordi.

De Van, Gilles. 1998. *Verdi's Theater: Creating Drama through Music.* Trans. Gilda Roberts. Chicago: University of Chicago Press.

Di Benedetto, Renato. 1982. "Lineamenti di una teoria della melodia nella trattatistica italiana fra il 1790 e il 1830." *Analecta musicologica* 21: 421–43.

Di Giacomo, Salvatore. 1924. *I quattro antichi Conservatorii di musica di Napoli. Il conservatorio di Sant'Onofrio a Capuana e quello di S. Maria della Pietà dei Turchini.* Palermo: Sandron.

———. 1928. *I quattro antichi Conservatorii di musica di Napoli. Il conservatorio dei Poveri di Gesù Christo e quello di S. Maria di Loreto.* Palermo: Sandron.

Dirksen, Pieter. 1997. *The Keyboard Music of Jan Pieterszoon Sweelinck.* Utrecht: Koniklijke Vereniging voor Nederlandse Muziekgeschiedenis.

Dodds, Michael R. 2006. "Columbus's Egg: Andreas Werckmeister's Teachings on Contrapuntal Improvisation in *Harmonologia musica* (1702)." *Journal of Seventeenth-Century Music* 12, no. 1.

Döhring, Sieghart, and Wolfgang Osthoff. 2000. *Verdi-Studien: Pierluigi Petrobelli zum. 60 Geburtstag.* Munich: Ricordi.

Drabkin, William. 1986. "The Musical Language of *La Bohème*." In *Giacomo Puccini: La Bohème,* ed. Arthur Groos and Roger Parker, 80–101. Cambridge: Cambridge University Press.

Dreyfus, Laurence. 2004. *Bach and the Patterns of Invention.* Cambridge: Harvard University Press.

Duey, Philip A. 1951. *Bel Canto in Its Golden Age: A Study of Its Teaching Concepts.* New York: Oxford University Press; reprint, New York: Read Books, 2007.

Dunstan, Harry. 1989. "Performance Practice in the Music of Giacomo Puccini as Observed by Luigi Ricci." PhD diss., Catholic University of America.

Elias, Norbert. 2000. "Sociogenesis of the Antithesis between *Kultur* and *Zivilisation* in German Usage." In *The Civilizing Process,* 5–30. London: Blackwell.

Elphinstone, Michael. 1992a. "Errata corrige: un errore di datazione della prima di *Edgar* a Ferrara." *Quaderni pucciniani,* 109–14.

———. 1992b. "Le prime musiche sinfoniche di Puccini: quanto ne sappiamo." *Quaderni pucciniani,* 115–162.

Fabbri, Paolo. 2003. "Metrical and Formal Organization." In *Opera in Theory and Practice, Image and Myth,* ed. Lorenzo Bianconi and Giorgio Pestelli, 151–220. Chicago: University of Chicago Press.

———. 2007. *Metro e canto nell'opera italiana.* Turin: EDT.

Fairtile, Linda B. 1996a. "Giacomo Puccini's Operatic Revisions as Manifestations of His Compositional Priorities." PhD diss., New York University.

———. 1996b. "Verdi's First 'Willow Song': New Sketches and Drafts for *Otello.*" *Nineteenth-Century Music* 19, no. 3: 213–30.

———. 1999. *Giacomo Puccini: A Guide to Research.* New York: Garland Science.

Fellerer, Karl. 1937. *Giacomo Puccini.* Potsdam: Athenaion.

———. 1940. *Der Partimento-Spieler.* Leipzig: Breitkopf and Härtel.

Fishman, Lisa. 2001. "'To Tear the Fetter of Every Other Art': Early Romantic Criticism and the Fantasy of Emancipation." *Nineteenth-Century Music* 25, no. 1: 75–86.

Fraccaroli, Arnaldo. 1925. *La vita di Giacomo Puccini.* Milan: Ricordi.

Frank, Manfred. 1989. *Einführung in die frühromantische Ästhetik.* Frankfurt: Suhrkamp.

Fubini, Enrico. 1986. *Musica e cultura nel settecento europeo.* Turin: EDT.

———. 1994. *Music and Culture in Eigh-teenth-Century Europe: A Sourcebook.* Trans. Bonnie J. Blackburn. Chicago: University of Chicago Press.

Gallarani, Marina Vaccarini. 1999. "Aspet-ti e problemi della didattica musicale a Milano nell'ultimo ventennio dell'otto-cento." In *Milano Musicale,* ed. Bianca Maria Antolini, 351–53. Lucca: Libreria musicale italiana.

Gara, Eugenio, ed. 1958. *Carteggi puccinia-ni.* Milan: Ricordi.

Garibaldi, Luigi Agostino. 1931. *Giuseppe Verdi nelle lettere di Emanuele Muzio ad Antonio Barezzi.* Milan: Treves.

Gatti, Carlo, ed. 1941. *L'abbozzo del Rigo-letto di Giuseppe Verdi.* Milan: Ministe-ro della cultura populare.

———. 1953. *Catalani: La Vita e le Opere.* Milano: Garzanti.

———. 1955. *Verdi.* Trans. E. Abbott. Lon-don: Gollancz.

———. 1964. *Il Teatro alla scala nella sto-ria e nell'arte (1778–1963).* 2 vols. Milan: Ricordi.

Giger, Andreas. 2008. *Verdi and the French Aesthetic: Verse, Stanza, and Melody in Nineteenth-Century Opera.* Cambridge: Cambridge University Press.

Gingras, Bruno. 2008. "Partimento Fugue in Eighteenth-Century Germany: A Bridge between Thoroughbass Lessons and Fugal Composition." *Eighteenth-Century Music* 5: 51–74.

Giovannetti, Gustavo. 1958. *Giacomo Puc-cini nei ricordi di un musicista lucchese.* Lucca: Baroni.

Girardi, Michele. 2000. *Puccini: His Inter-national Art.* Trans. Laura Basini. Chi-cago: University of Chicago Press.

Gjerdingen, Robert O. 1986. "The Forma-tion and Deformation of Classic/Ro-mantic Phrase Schemata: A Theoretical Model and Historical Study." *Music Theory Spectrum* 8: 25–43.

———. 2005. *Monuments of Partimenti.* http://faculty-web.at.northwestern.edu/ music/gjerdingen/partimenti/index .htm.

———. 2007a. *Music in the Galant Style: Being a Treatise on Various Schemata Characteristic of Eighteenth-Century Music for Courtly Chambers, Chapels, and Theaters, Including Tasteful Passages of Music Drawn from Most Excellent Chapel Masters in the Employ of Noble and Noteworthy Personages, Said Music All Collected for the Reader's Delectation on the World Wide Web.* New York: Ox-ford University Press.

———. 2007b. "Partimento, que me veux-tu?" *Journal of Music Theory* 51: 85–135.

———. 2009. "The Perfection of Craft Training in the Neapolitan Conserva-toires." *Rivista di Analisi e Teoria Musi-cale* 15, no. 1: 26–49.

Gossett, Philip. 1970. "Gioacchino Rossini and the Conventions of Composition." *Acta Musicologica* 42: 48–58.

———. 1974–75. "Verdi, Ghislanzoni, and *Aida:* The Uses of Convention." *Critical Enquiry* 1: 291–334.

———. 1985. *"Anna Bolena" and the Artis-tic Maturity of Gaetano Donizetti.* Ox-ford: Oxford University Press.

———. 2001. "Der kompositorische Prozeß: Verdis Opernskizzen." In *Giu-seppe Verdi und seine Zeit,* ed. Markus Engelhardt, 169–90. Laaber: Laaber Verlag.

———. 2004. "Compositional Methods." In *The Cambridge Companion to Rossini,* ed. Emanuele Senici, 68–84. Cambrid-ge: Cambridge University Press.

———. 2006. *Divas and Scholars.* Chi-cago: University of Chicago Press.

Greenwald, Helen. 1991. "Dramatic Expo-sition and Musical Structure in Pucci-ni's Operas." PhD diss., City University of New York.

———. 1993. "Recent Puccini Research." *Acta Musicologica* 65, no. 1: 23–50.

———. 1998. "Puccini, *Il Tabarro,* and the Dilemma of Operatic Transposition."

Journal of the American Musicological Society 51, no. 3: 521–58.

Groos, Arthur, and Roger Parker, eds. 1986. *Giacomo Puccini: La Bohème.* Cambridge: Cambridge University Press.

———, eds. 1988. *Reading Opera.* Princeton: Princeton University Press.

Groos, Arthur, and Luca Zoppelli. 1996. "The Twilight of the True Gods: *Cristoforo Columbo, I Medici,* and the Construction of Italian History." *Cambridge Opera Journal* 8, no. 3: 251–69.

Guidotti, Fabrizio. 1990. "La Biblioteca di casa Puccini e il suo catalogo: Il Repertorio di Musica di Antonio Puccini (1818)." In *I Tesori della Musica Lucchese,* ed. Giulio Battelli, 38–44. Lucca: Maria Pacini Fazzi.

Haböck, Franz. 1927. *Die Kastraten und ihre Gesangskunst: eine gesangsphysiologische, kultur- und musik-historische Studie.* Leipzig: Deutsche Verlags-Anstalt.

Hansell, Kathleen Kusmick. 1997. "Compositional Techniques in *Stiffelio:* Reading the Autograph Sources." In *Verdi's Middle Period,* ed. Martin Chusid, 45–97. Chicago: University of Chicago Press.

Hasty, Christopher F. 1997. *Meter as Rhythm.* Oxford: Oxford University Press.

Hatten, Robert S. 2004. *Interpreting Musical Gestures, Topics, and Tropes: Mozart, Beethoven, Schubert.* Bloomington: Indiana University Press.

Heartz, Daniel. 2003. *Music in European Capitals: The Galant Style, 1720–1780.* New York: Norton.

Hegel, Georg Wilhelm Friedrich. 1998 [1806]. *Aesthetics: Lectures on Fine Art.* 2 vols. Trans. T. M. Knox. Oxford: Oxford University Press.

Hepokoski, James. 1983. *Giuseppe Verdi: Falstaff.* Cambridge: Cambridge University Press.

———. 1986–87. "Compositional Emendations in Verdi's Autograph Scores: *Il Trovatore, Un Ballo in Maschera,* and *Aïda.*" *Studi verdiani* 4: 87–109.

———. 1987. *Giuseppe Verdi: Otello.* Cambridge: Cambridge University Press.

———. 1989. "Genre and Content in Mid-Century Verdi: 'Addio, del passato.'" *Cambridge Opera Journal* 1, no. 3: 249–76.

———. 1997. "*Ottocento* Opera as Cultural Drama: Generic Mixtures in *Il Trovatore.* In *Verdi's Middle Period,* ed. Martin Chusid, 147–96. Chicago: University of Chicago Press.

Heriot, Angus. 1980 [1956]. *Castrati in Opera.* London: Calder.

Hibberd, Sarah. 2009. *French Grand Opera and the Historical Imagination.* Cambridge: Cambridge University Press.

Hobsbawm, Eric, and Terence Ranger, eds. 1983. *The Invention of Tradition.* Cambridge: Cambridge University Press.

Holtmeier, Ludwig. 2007. "Heinichen, Rameau, and the Italian Thoroughbass Tradition: Concepts of Tonality and Chord in the Rule of the Octave." *Journal of Music Theory* 51: 5–49.

Houle, George. 2000. *Meter in Music, 1600–1800: Performance, Perception, and Notation.* Bloomington: Indiana University Press.

Hudson, G. Elizabeth. 1993. "Narrative in Verdi: Perspectives on His Musical Dramaturgy." PhD diss., Cornell University.

Huebner, Steven. 1992. "Lyric Form in *Ottocento* Opera." *Journal of the Royal Musicological Association* 117, no. 1: 123–47.

———. 2004. "Structural Coherence." In *The Cambridge Companion to Verdi,* ed. Scott Balthazar, 139–53. Cambridge: Cambridge University Press.

Izzo, Francesco. 2001. "Verdi's *Un giorno di Regno:* Two Newly Discovered Movements and Some Questions of

Genre." *Acta Musicologica* 73, no. 2: 165–88.

Izzo, Francesco, and Johannes Streicher, eds. 1993. *Ottocento e oltre: Scritti in onore di Raoul Meloncelli*. Rome: Pantheon.

Jensen, Luke. 2004. "An Introduction to Verdi's Working Methods." In *The Cambridge Companion to Verdi*, ed. Scott Balthazar, 257–68. Cambridge: Cambridge University Press.

Kaufman, Thomas G. 1990. *Verdi and His Contemporaries: A Selected Chronology of Performances with Casts*. New York: Garland.

Kaye, Michael. 1987. *The Unknown Puccini*. Oxford: Oxford University Press.

Kerman, Joseph. 1982. "Lyric Form and Flexibility in *Simon Boccanegra*." *Studi verdiani* 1: 47–62.

Kimbell, David R. 1981. *Verdi in the Age of Italian Romanticism*. Cambridge: Cambridge University Press.

———. 1998. *Vincenzo Bellini: Norma*. Cambridge: Cambridge University Press.

Lacombe, Hervé. 2001. *The Keys to French Opera in the Nineteenth Century*. Trans. Edward Schneider (*Les Voies de l'opéra français au XIXe siècle*, Paris, 1997). Berkeley: University of California Press.

Larue, C. Steven. 1995. *Handel and His Singers*. Oxford: Oxford University Press.

Latham, Alison, and Roger Parker, eds. 2001. *Verdi in Performance*. Oxford: Oxford University Press.

Lawton, David. 1973. "Tonality and Drama in Verdi's Early Operas." PhD diss., University of California at Berkeley.

Ledbetter, David. 1990. *Continuo Playing According to Handel*. 4th ed. Oxford: Oxford University Press.

———. 2009. *Unaccompanied Bach: Performing the Solo Works*. New Haven: Yale University Press.

Le Guin, Elizabeth. 1996. *Boccherini's Body: An Essay in Carnal Musicology*. Berkeley: University of California Press.

Lester, Joel. 1992. *Compositional Theory in the Eighteenth Century*. Cambridge: Harvard University Press.

Lippmann, Friedrich. 1966. "Die Melodien Donizettis." *Analecta musicologica* 3: 80–113.

———. 1969a. "Verdi e Bellini." In *Atti del I congresso internazionale di studi verdiani 1966*, 184–96. Parma: Istituto di studi verdiani.

———. 1969b. "Rossinis Gedanken über die Musik." *Die Musikforschung* 22: 285–98.

———. 1969c. *Vincenzo Bellini und die italienische Opera Seria seiner Zeit: Studien über Libretto, Arienform, und Melodik*. Cologne and Vienna: Böhlau.

———. 1973–75. "Der italienische Vers und der musikalische Rhythmus: Zum Verhältnis von Vers und Musik in der italienischen Oper des 19. Jahrhunderts, mit einem Blick auf die 2. Hälfte des 18. Jahrhunderts." *Analecta Musicologica* 12 (1973): 253–369; 14 (1974): 324–410; 15 (1975): 298–333. Translated by Lorenzo Bianconi and revised as *Versificazione italiana e ritmo musicale: i rapporti tra verso e musica nell'opera italiana dell'Ottocento*. Naples: Liguori, 1986.

———. 1977. "Belliniana." In *Il melodramma italiano dell'ottocento*, ed. Giorgio Pestelli, 281–317. Turin: Giulio Einaudi.

London, Justin. 1990. "Riepel and *Absatz*: Poetic and Prosaic Aspects of Phrase Structure in Eighteenth-Century Theory." *Journal of Musicology* 8, no. 4: 505–19.

———. 2000. *Hearing in Time: Psychological Aspects of Musical Meter*. Oxford: Oxford University Press.

Luzio, Alessandro, ed. 1935–47. *Carteggi verdiani*. 4 vols. Bologna: Forni.

Maehder, Jürgen. 1983. *Esotismo e colore locale nell'Opera di Puccini: Atti del I Convegno Internazionale sull'Opera di Giacomo Puccini*. Pisa: Giardini.

————.1988. "The Origins of Italian *Literaturoper: Guglielmo Ratcliff, La figlia di Iorio, Parisina,* and *Francesca da Rimini*." In *Reading Opera,* ed. Arthur Groos and Roger Parker, 92–128. Princeton: Princeton University Press.

————, and Lorenza Guiot, eds. 1993. *Ruggero Leoncavallo nel suo tempo: Atti del I Convegno Internazionale di Studi su Ruggero Leoncavallo.* Milan: Casa musicale Sonzogno.

————.1995. "Giacomo Puccinis Schaffensprozess im Spiegel seiner Skizzen für Libretto und Komposition." In *Vom Einfall zum Kunstwerk,* ed. Hermann Danuser and Gunter Katzenberger, 35–64. Laaber: Laaber Verlag.

————.2003. "Drammaturgia musicale e strutture narrative nel teatro musicale italiano della generazione dell'ottanta." In *Alfredo Casella e L'Europa: Atti del convegno internazionale di studi,* ed. Mila De Santis, 223–48. Florence: Olschki.

Maguire, Simon. 1989. *Vincenzo Bellini and the Aesthetics of Early Nineteenth-Century Italian Opera.* New York: Garland.

Mallach, Alan. 2007. *The Autumn of Italian Opera: From Verismo to Modernism, 1890–1915.* Boston: Northeastern University Press.

Mamy, Sylvie. 1988. "L'importation des solfèges italiens en France à la fin du XVIII siècle," in *L'opera tra Venezia e Parigi,* ed. M. T. Muraro, 1:67–89. Florence: Olschki.

————.1994. *Les grands castrats napolitains à Venise au XVIIIe siècle.* Liège: Mardaga.

Mandelli, Alfredo. 1992. "Le varianti in Puccini, le versioni di Edgar e il 'Preludio di Madrid.'" *Quaderni pucciniani,* 75–82.

Manén, Lucie. 2004 [1987]. *Bel Canto: The Teaching of the Classical Italian Song Schools: Its Decline and Restoration.* Oxford: Oxford University Press.

Mann, Alfred. 1986 [1958]. *The Study of Fugue.* New York: Dover.

Marchetti, Arnaldo. 1973. *Puccini com'era.* Milan: Curci.

Marchetti, Leopoldo, ed. 1968. *Puccini nelle immagini.* Lucca: Museo di Torre del Lago.

Marino, Marina. 1999. "Lauro Rossi ed un suo mancato progetto di riforma del Conservatorio di Music 'San Pietro a Maiella' di Napoli (1877) attraverso le pagine del periodico *La Musica.*" In *Francesco Florimo e l'Ottocento musicale,* ed. Rosa Cafiero and Maria Marino, 1:861–910. Reggio Calabria: Jason.

Markstrom, Kurt Sven. 2006. *The Operas of Leonardo Vinci, Napoletano.* London: Pendragon.

Masotti, Roberto. 2000. *Le siècle de feu de l'opera italien.* Paris: Chene.

Menichini, Maria. 1993. *Alfredo Catalani alla luce di documenti inediti: Con il catalogo dei manoscritti dell'istituto musicale "Luigi Boccherini" di Lucca.* Lucca: Maria Pacini Fazzi.

Mioli, Piero. 1993. *Manuale del Melodramma.* Milan: Rizzoli.

————.2006. *Padre Martini: Musicista e musicografo da Bologna all'Europa (1706–84).* Lucca: Libreria musicale italiana.

Miragoli, Livia. 1924. *Il melodramma italiano nell'ottocento.* Rome: Maglione and Strini.

Moindrot, Isabelle. 1993. *L'opera seria ou le règne des castrats.* Paris: Fayard

Mompellio, Federico. 1941. *Il R. Conservatorio di musica "Giuseppe Verdi" di Milano.* Florence: Felice Le Monnier.

Monaldi, Gino. 1925. *Giacomo Puccini e la sua opera.* Rome: Selecta.

Monelle, Raymond. 2000. *The Sense of Music: Semiotic Essays.* Princeton: Princeton University Press.

————.2006. *The Musical Topic: Hunt, Military, and Pastoral.* Bloomington: Indiana University Press.

Montemorra Marvin, Roberta. 1997. "Aspects of Tempo in Verdi's Early and Middle-Period Italian Operas." In *Verdi's Middle Period,* ed. Martin Chusid, 393–411. Chicago: University of Chicago Press.

———, and Hilary Poriss, eds. 2010. *Fashions and Legacies of Nineteenth-Century Italian Opera.* Cambridge: Cambridge University Press.

Moreen, Robert Anthony. 1975. "Integration of Text Forms and Musical Forms in Verdi's Early Operas." PhD diss., Princeton University.

Morelli, Giovanni. 1994. *Arrigo Boito: Atti del convegno internazionale di studi dedicato al centocinquantesimo della nascita di Arrigo Boito.* Florence: Olschki.

Moreno, Jairo. 2000. "Challenging Views of Sequential Repetition: From 'Satzlehre' to Melodielehre.'" *Journal of Music Theory* 44, no. 1: 127–69.

Musco, Gianfranco. 1989. *Musica e Teatro in Giacomo Puccini,* vol. 1: *La formazione giovanile.* Cortonoa: Calosci.

Nello Vetro, Gaspare. 1993. *L'allievo di Verdi: Emanuele Muzio.* Parma: Edizioni Zara.

Neubauer, John. 1986. *The Emancipation of Music from Language: Departure from Mimesis in Eighteenth-Century Aesthetics.* New Haven: Yale University Press.

Nicolaisen, Jay. 1977. *Italian Opera in Transition, 1871–1893.* Michigan: UMI Research Press.

Nicolodi, Fiamma, and Paulo Trovato, eds. 1994. *Le parole della musica,* vol. 1: *Studi sulla lingua della letteratura musicale.* Florence: Olschki.

Nuti, Giulia. 2007. *The Performance of Italian Basso Continuo: Style in Keyboard Accompaniment in the Seventeenth and Eighteenth Centuries.* Aldershot: Ashgate.

Osborne, Charles. 1971. *The Letters of Giuseppe Verdi.* London: Gollancz.

Osborne, Richard. 2007. *Rossini.* Oxford: Oxford University Press.

Pagannone, Giorgio. 1996. "Mobilità strutturale della *lyric form:* Sintassi verbale e sintassi musicale nel melodramma italiano del primo Ottocento." *Analisi* 7, no. 20: 2–17.

———.1997. "Aspetti della melodia verdiana: 'periodo' e 'barform' a confronto." *Studi verdiani* 12: 48–66.

———.2004a. "Dal libretto alla musica (e viceversa): Sul rapporto tra forme musicali e forme testuali nell'opera italiana del primo Ottocento." In *Il teatro di Donizetti: Atti dei convegni delle celebrazioni 1797, no. 1997–1848, no. 1998, II, Percorsi e proposte di ricerca. Venezia 22–24 maggio 1997,* ed. Paolo Cecchi and Luca Zoppelli. Bergamo: Fondazione Donizetti.

———.2004b. "Puccini e la melodia ottocentesca: L'effetto 'barform.'" *Studi pucciniani* 3: 201–26.

Paraschivescu, Nicoleta. 2009. "Una chiave per comprendere la prassi del partimento: la sonata 'Perfidia' di Francesco Durante." *Rivista di Analisi e Teoria Musicale* 15, no. 1: 52–67.

Parker, Roger. 1989. *Studies in Early Verdi, 1832–44: New Information and Perspectives on the Milanese Musical Milieu and the Operas from Oberto to Ernani.* London: Taylor and Francis.

———.1997. *Leonora's Last Act: Essays in Verdian Discourse.* Princeton: Princeton University Press.

———.2006. *Remaking the Song: Operatic Visions and Revisions from Handel to Berio.* Cambridge: Cambridge University Press.

Pasquini, Elisabetta. 2004. *L'esemplare, o sia saggio fondamentale pratico di contrappunto: Padre Martini teorico e didatta della musica.* Florence: Olschki.

———.2007. *Giambattista Martini.* Palermo: Società editrice L'Epos.

Pestelli, Giorgio, ed. 1977. *Il melodramma italiano dell'ottocento: Studi e ricerche per Massimo Mila.* Turin: Giulio Einaudi.

Petrobelli, Perluigi. 1994. *Music in the Theater: Essays on Verdi and Other Composers.* Trans. Roger Parker. Princeton: Princeton University Press.

———. 2004. "Remarks on Verdi's Composition Process." In *The Cambridge Companion to Verdi,* ed. Scott Balthazar, 48–74. Cambridge: Cambridge University Press.

Phillips-Matz, Mary J., and William Weaver. 2002. *Puccini.* Boston: Northeastern University Press.

Pompilio, Angelo, ed. 1987. *Padre Martini: musica e cultura nel Settecento europeo.* Florence: Olschki.

Potter, John, ed. 2000. *The Cambridge Companion to Singing.* Cambridge: Cambridge University Press.

Powers, Harold. 1987. "'La solita forma' and 'The Uses of Convention.'" *Acta Musicologica* 59: 65–90.

———. 2000. "Basevi, Conati, and *La Traviata:* The Uses of Convention." In *"Una piacente estate di San Martino": Studi e ricerche per Marcello Conati,* ed. Marco Capra, 215–35. Lucca: Libreria Musicale Italiana.

———. 2004. "Form and Formula." *Studi pucciniani* 3: 11–49.

Puccini, Giacomo, et al. 2002. *Le prime: Libretti della prima rappresentazione.* Milan: Ricordi.

Puccini, Simonetta, ed. 1994. *The Puccini Companion.* New York: Norton.

Ranum, Patricia. 2001. *The Harmonic Orator: A Guide to the Phrasing and Rhetoric of the Melody in French Baroque Airs.* London: Pendragon Press.

Ratner, Leonard. 1980. *Classic Music: Expression, Form, and Style.* New York: Schirmer.

Rehding, Alexander. 2003. *Hugo Riemann and the Birth of Modern Musical Thought.* Cambridge: Cambridge University Press.

Renwick, William. 2001. *The Langloz Manuscript: Fugal Improvisation through Figured Bass.* Oxford: Oxford University Press.

Ricci, Corrado. 1995. *Farinelli: Quattro storie di castrati e primedonne fra Sei e Settecento.* Lucca: Libreria musicale italiana.

Ricci, Luigi. 1954. *Puccini interprete di se stesso.* Milan: Ricordi.

Ricci, Vittorio. 1923. *Il bel canto: Florilegio di pensieri, consigli, e precetti sul canto.* Milan: Ulrico Hoepli.

Ricoeur, Paul. 1983. *History and Truth.* Trans. Kathleen McLauchlin and David Pellauer. Chicago: University of Chicago Press.

Robinson, Michael F. 1972. *Naples and Neapolitan Opera.* Oxford: Oxford University Press.

Rosen, David. 2004. "*La solita forma* in Puccini's Operas?" *Studi pucciniani* 3: 179–200.

Rosenberg, Jesse. 1993. "Notes on Raimondi's Triple Oratorio." In *Ottocento e oltre: Scritti in onore di Raoul Meloncelli,* ed. Francesco Izzo and Johannes Streicher, 319–38. Rome: Pantheon.

———. 1995. "The Experimental Music of Pietro Raimondi." PhD diss., New York University.

———. 1999. "Il 'leista' Raimondi contro il 'durantista' Bellini." In *Francesco Florimo e l'Ottocento musicale,* ed. Rosa Cafiero and Maria Marino, 1:75–98. Reggio Calabria: Jason.

———. 2000. "Analyses of Verdi's Music from *La scienza nuova d'armonia* of Americo Bàrberi (1861)." In *"Una piacente estate di San Martino": Studi e ricerche per i settant'anni di Marcello Conati,* ed. Marco Capra, 237–60. Lucca: Libreria musicale italiana.

———. 2002. "Abramo Basevi: A Music Critic in Search of a Context." *Musical Quarterly* 86, no. 4: 630–88.

Ross, Peter. 1980. "Studien zum Verhältnis von Libretto und Komposition in den Opern Verdis." PhD diss., Universität Bern.

———.2004. "Die multidimensionale Szenenstruktur in der italienischen Oper am Ende des 19. Jahrhunderts." *Studi pucciniani* 3: 151–78.

Rosselli, John. 1984. *The Opera Industry in Italy from Cimarosa to Verdi.* Cambridge: Cambridge University Press.

———.1988. "The Castrati as a Professional Group and a Social Phenomenon, 1550–1850." *Acta Musicologica* 60: 143–79.

———.1991. *Music and Musicians in Nineteenth-Century Italy.* London: Batsford.

———.1992. *Singers of Italian Opera.* Cambridge: Cambridge University Press.

———.1998. "Opera Production, 1780–1880." In *Opera Production and Its Resources,* ed. Lorenzo Bianconi and Giorgio Pestelli, 81–164. Chicago: University of Chicago Press.

Rutherford, Susan. 2006. *The Prima Donna and Opera, 1815–1930.* Cambridge: Cambridge University Press.

Salvetti, Guido. 1992. "Edgar di Puccini nella crisi degli anni ottanta." *Quaderni pucciniani,* 69–74.

———.1993. *Aspetti dell'opera italiana fra Sette e Ottocento: Mayr e Zingarelli.* Lucca: Libreria Musicale Italiana.

———, ed. 2003. *Milano e il suo conservatorio, 1808–2002.* Milan: Skira.

Salvetti, Guido, and M. G. Sità, eds. 2003. *La cultura dei musicisti italiani nel Novecento.* Milan: Guerini.

Sanguinetti, Giorgio. 1997. "Un secolo di teoria della musica in Italia: Bibliografia critica (1850–1950)." *Fonti Musicali Italiane* 2: 155–248.

———.1999. "I travagli del 'celeste impero': La teoria della composizione a Napoli nell'Ottocento fra tradizione e innovazione." In *Intersezioni: Quattro studi di teoria e analisi musicale,* ed. Giorgio Sanguinetti, 137–83. Cosenza: Università della Calabria.

———.2000. "La vera analisi delle melodie: la teoria 'meloarmonica' di Abramo Basevi." In *"Una piacente estate di San*

Martino": Studi e ricerche per Marcello Conati, ed. Marco Capra, 261–86. Lucca: Libreria Musicale Italiana.

———.2005. "Decline and Fall of the 'Celeste Impero': The Theory of Composition in Naples during the Ottocento." *Studi musicali* 34: 451–502.

———.2007. "The Realization of Partimenti: An Introduction." *Journal of Music Theory* 51: 51–83.

———.2008. "L'eredità di Fenaroli nell'Ottocento." In *Giuseppe Martucci e la "caduta delle Alpi,"* ed. Paologiovanni Maione and Francesca Seller. Lucca: Libreria musicale italiane.

———.2009. "La scala come modello per la composizione." *Rivista di Analisi e Teoria Musicale* 15, no. 1: 68–96.

———.In press-a. "Diminution and Harmony-oriented Counterpoint in Late Eighteenth-Century Naples: Vincenzo Lavigna's Studies with Fedele Fenaroli." In *Schenkerian Analysis— Analyse nach Heinrich Schenker,* ed. Oliver Schwab-Felisch, Michael Polth, and Hartmut Fladt. Hildesheim: Olms.

———.In press-b. *The Art of Partimento in Naples: History, Theory, and Practice.* New York: Oxford University Press.

Santi, Piero. 1992. "Il rapporto col libretto al tempo dell'Edgar." *Quaderni pucciniani,* 41–54.

Sapienza, Annamaria. 1998. *La parodia dell'opera lirica a Napoli nell'ottocento.* Naples: Guida.

Sartori, Claudio. 1942. *Il Regio Conservatorio di Musica "G. B. Martini" di Bologna.* Florence: Le Monnier.

———.1958. *Casa Ricordi, 1808–1958.* Milan: Ricordi.

———.1959. *Giacomo Puccini.* Milan: Ricordi.

———.1959. *Dizionario Ricordi della Musica e dei Musicisti.* Milan: Ricordi.

———.1978. *L'avventura del violino: l'Italia musicale dell'Ottocento nella biografia e nei carteggi di Antonio Bazzini.* Turin: ERI.

Satragni, Giangiorgio. 2000. "Parola cantata e parola declamata ne *La bohème* di Puccini." *Nuova rivista musicale italiana* 33, no. 1: 7–25.

Scherr, Suzanne. 1993. "National and International Influences on the Formation of Puccini's Early Compositional Style." *Rivista de musicologia* 16, no. 6: 3206–15.

Schickling, Dieter. 1989. *Giacomo Puccini: Biographie*. Stuttgart: Deutsche Verlags-Anstalt.

———. 2003. *Giacomo Puccini: Catalogue of the Works*. Kassel: Bärenreiter.

Senici, Emanuele, ed. 2004a. *The Cambridge Companion to Rossini*. Cambridge: Cambridge University Press.

———. 2004b. "Words and Music." In *The Cambridge Companion to Verdi*, ed. Scott Balthazar, 88–110. Cambridge: Cambridge University Press.

Serafin, Tullio, and Alceo Toni. 1958. *Stile, tradizioni, e convenzioni del melodramma italiano del Settecento e dell'Ottocento*. Milan: Ricordi.

Sessa, Andrea. 2003. *Il melodramma italiano, 1861–1900: Dizionario bio-bibliografico dei compositori*. Florence: Olschki.

Simms, Bryan Randolph. 1971. "Alexandre Choron (1771–1834) as an Historian and Theorist of Music." PhD diss., Yale University.

———. 1975. "Choron, Fétis, and the Theory of Tonality." *Journal of Music Theory* 19: 112–38.

Smart, Mary Ann. 2000. "In Praise of Convention: Formula and Experiment in Bellini's Self-Borrowings." *Journal of the American Musicological Society* 53, no. 1: 25–68.

Smith, Martin Dennis. 1979. "Antoine Joseph Reicha's Theories on the Composition of Dramatic Music." PhD diss., Rutgers University.

Smith, Patrick J. 1971. *The Tenth Muse: A Historical Study of the Opera Libretto*. London: Gollancz.

Specht, Richard. 1931. *Giacomo Puccini: das Leben—der Mensch—das Werk*. Berlin: Max Hesses.

Staël-Holstein, Anna Luisa. 1816. "Sulla maniera e la utilità delle traduzioni." *Biblioteca italiana,* January, 9–18.

Stark, James. 1999. *Bel Canto: A History of Vocal Pedagogy*. Toronto: University of Toronto Press.

Stefan, Paul, and Franz Werfel, eds. 1973. *Verdi: The Man in His Letters*. Trans. Edward Downes. New York: Vienna House.

Stella, Gaetano. 2007. "Partimenti in the Age of Romanticism: Raimondi, Platania, and Boucheron." *Journal of Music Theory* 51: 161–86.

———. 2009. "Le 'Regole del contrappunto pratico' di Nicola Sala: Una testimonianza sulla didattica della fuga nel Settecento napoletano." *Rivista di Analisi e Teoria Musicale* 15, no. 1: 116–38.

Strohm, Reinhard. 1997. *Dramma per Musica: Italian Opera Seria of the Eighteenth Century*. New Haven: Yale University Press.

Sullo, Paula. 2009. "I Solfeggi di Leo e lo studio della forma nella scuola napoletana del Settecento." *Rivista di Analisi e Teoria Musicale* 15, no. 1: 97–115.

Surian, Elvidio. 1983. "Musical Historiography and Histories of Italian Opera." *Current Musicology* 36: 167–75.

———. 1998. "The Opera Composer." In *Opera Production and Its Resources (History of Italian Opera, vol. 4)*, ed. Lorenzo Bianconi and Giorgio Pestelli, trans. Lydia Cochrane, 291–344. Chicago: University of Chicago Press.

Tarasti, Eero. 1994. *A Theory of Musical Semiotics*. Bloomington: Indiana University Press.

Taruskin, Richard. 1995. *Text and Act: Essays on Music and Performance*. New York: Oxford University Press.

———. 2009a. *The Danger of Music and Other Anti-Utopian Essays*. Berkeley: University of California Press.

————.2009b. *The Oxford History of Western Music: Music in the Nineteenth Century.* Oxford and New York: Oxford University Press.

————.2010. *The Oxford History of Western Music: Music in the Seventeenth and Eighteenth Centuries.* Oxford and New York: Oxford University Press.

Tomlinson, Gary. 1986. "Italian Romanticism and Italian Opera: An Essay in Their Affinities." *Nineteenth-Century Music* 10, no. 1: 43–60.

Unger, Hans-Heinrich. 1941. *Die Beziehungen zwischen Music und Rhetorik im 16.–18. Jahrhundert.* Würzburg: K. Triltsch.

Verdi, Giuseppe. 1985a. *The Works of Giuseppe Verdi. Series I: Operas. Vol. 5/1: Ernani.* Ed. Claudio Gallico. Chicago and Milan: University of Chicago Press and Ricordi.

————.1985b. *The Works of Giuseppe Verdi. Series I: Operas. Vol. 5/2: Ernani: Critical Commentary.* Ed. Claudio Gallico. Chicago and Milan: University of Chicago Press and Ricordi.

————.2005a. *The Works of Giuseppe Verdi. Series I: Operas. Vol. 10/1–2: Macbeth.* Ed. David Lawton. Chicago and Milan: University of Chicago Press and Ricordi.

————.2005b. *The Works of Giuseppe Verdi. Series I: Operas. Vol. 10/3: Macbeth: Critical Commentary.* Ed. David Lawton. Chicago and Milan: University of Chicago Press and Ricordi.

Vial, Stephanie. 2008. *The Art of Musical Phrasing in the Eighteenth Century.* Rochester, N.Y.: University of Rochester Press.

Wagner, Hans-Joachim. 1999. *Fremde Welten: Oper des italienischen Verismo.* Stuttgart: Metzler.

Walker, Frank. 1951. *A Chronology of the Life and Works of Nicola Porpora.* London: Italian Studies.

————.1962. *The Man Verdi.* London: Dent.

Weaver, William. 1966. *Puccini Librettos, in New English Translations by William Weaver.* With the original Italian. Garden City, N.Y.: Anchor Books.

Webster, James. 1987. "To Understand Verdi and Wagner We Must Understand Mozart." *Nineteenth-Century Music* 11, no. 2: 175–93.

————.1991. "The Analysis of Mozart's Arias." In *Mozart Studies 2,* ed. Cliff Eisen, 101–99. Oxford: Oxford University Press.

Wedell, Friedrich. 1995. *Annäherung an Verdi.* Kassel: Bärenreiter.

Williams, Peter. 1970. *Figured Bass Accompaniment.* 2 vols. Edinburgh: Edinburgh University Press.

Wilson, Alexandra. 2007. *The Puccini Problem: Opera, Nationalism, and Modernity.* Cambridge: Cambridge University Press.

Winterhoff, Hans-Jürgen. 1973. *Analytische Untersuchungen zu Puccinis Tosca.* Regensburg: Gustav Bosse.

Woodring Goertzen, Valerie. 1996. "By Way of Introduction: Preluding by 18th- and Early 19th-Century Pianists." *Journal of Musicology* 14, no. 3: 299–337.

Yeston, Maury. 1976. *The Stratification of Musical Rhythm.* New Haven: Yale University Press.

Zurletti, Michelangelo. 1982. *Catalani.* Turin: Edizioni di Torino.

A NOTE ON ONLINE RESOURCES
A comprehensive catalog of music manuscript material held in Italian libraries and archives is maintained by the National Library Braidense in Milan. It can be accessed at *www.braidense.it/urfm*.

Since 2007 the Ministero per i Beni e le Attività Culturali has maintained the Biblioteca digitale italiana (Italian Digital Library) at *www.bibliotecadigitaleit aliana.it,* which enables online access to a large collection of music manuscripts. The vast resource of Italian *partimenti* is gradually being transcribed, studied, and made available by the "Monuments of Partimenti" project hosted by Northwestern University under the direction of Robert Gjerdingen (see Gjerdingen [2005] above). The database may be accessed at *faculty-web.at.northwestern .edu/music/gjerdingen/partimenti/index .htm.*

The Centro Studi Giacomo Puccini in Lucca, in collaboration with L'Istituto Musicale L. Boccherini, the Museo Puccini, Celle di Pescaglia, and four local archives, is in the process of making available to scholars over six thousand documents and overseeing the publication of complete critical editions of the correspondence, the music, and the opera production books. Details may be found at *www.puccini.it* and at *www .progettopuccini.it.*

Some relevant primary sources have been transcribed and made available through the Saggi Musicali Italiani database, directed by Andreas Giger at Louisiana State University. They can be accessed at *www.chmtl.indiana.edu/smi/index.html.*

The Retrospective Index to Music Periodicals / *Répertoire international de la presse musicale* (RIPM) is one of four international cooperative bibliographic undertakings in music, alongside *Le Répertoire international des sources musicales* (RISM), *Le Répertoire international de littérature musicale* (RILM), and *Le*

Répertoire international d'iconographie musicale (RIdIM). The RIPM is in the process of making available, online at *www.ripm.org,* annotated indexes and full texts of many nineteenth-century journals, such as the *Gazzetta musicale di Milano* and *Gazzetta musicale di Firenze.*

The *Lessico della letteratura musicale Italiana 1490–1950* (*LesMu*), or *Lexicon of Italian Music Literature* (Florence: Cesati, 2007), is a large historical dictionary of the Italian language of music and music criticism, edited by Fiamma Nicolodi and Paolo Trovato in collaboration with Renato Di Benedetto, with the assistance of Luca Aversano, Elisabetta Marinai, and Fabio Rossi. Available on CD-ROM or as a full-text databank, it provides a valuable tool for research involving Italian musical terminology. Further details are available at *www .disas.unifi.it/CMpro-v-p-160.html.*

A detailed online catalog of the collection of the Museo internazionale e biblioteca della musica di Bologna— an essential resource for research on Martini, Mattei, and the Franciscan school—may be accessed at *www.mu- seomusicabologna.it/biblioteca.htm.*

Since 2007, the Biblioteca del Conservatorio G. Verdi di Milano has embarked upon a project to digitalize a selection of its holdings, including treatises by Asioli and Sala, early editions of operas by celebrated and not-so-celebrated maestros, and early-nineteenth-century promotional materials. They are available online at *www.consmilano.it.*

abbozzo (continuity draft), xiv–xv

accento (accent), xvii–xviii; *accento comune* (common or principal verse accent), see *desinenza; accento grammatico, oratorio,* and *patetico* (grammatical, oratorical, and pathetic accents), 323n18; *accento musicale* (musical speech-accent, or inflection of the voice), 71–78, 86, 94, 105, 107, 114, 120, 134, 139, 140, 216, 239, 250, 263, 302, 309; *obbligati* (obligatory or principal) and *casuali* (casual or subsidiary) accents, 81, 113

addizione (chordal addition), 154, 170–71, 179

affetto (affect), xviii, 19, 83, 188–89, 197–99, 202–203, 222, 338n5, 339n11, 339n14, 339n18, 342n43; *affetto dominante* (dominant affect), 73, 91, 108, 126, 190–94, 203–205, 207, 211, 232, 235, 283–86, 294, 304

anapesto (anapest). See *piedi poetici*

andamento (progression): as contrapuntal progression, see *movimento, movimento regolare del basso;* as extended fugue subject, 168

anfibraco (anfibrach). See *piedi poetici*

antecedent (*Vordersatz*) and consequent (*Nachsatz*), 96, 118, 209, 216, 280–82, 300

antifone (antiphon), 258

apocopation, 77, 275

appendice (appendix), 207, 212, 281–82

approssimazione (approximation of a standard chord voicing), 153

armonia (harmony or accompaniment), ix, 3, 5, 145–46, 149–60

attacco (attachment): as connecting passage, 336n80; as melodic attachment, 147, 168–69, 175, 177–79, 181, 242, 259–62

bass motion. See *movimento, movimento regolare del basso*

basso fondamentale (fundamental bass) and *basso sensibile* (perceived bass), 154–55, 163, 297

battuta (beat or bar), xix, 66–74

bel canto (fine singing). See *canto*

cabaletta, 204, 205, 206, 226, 283, 342n50

cadenza (cadence), 57–60, 85–86, 118, 148, 171; cadential progressions, 57–58, 148–49; *cadenza aritmetica* and *cadenza armonica* (arithmetic or plagal, and harmonic or perfect cadences), 320n43; *cadenza composta* (compound cadence), 57–60; *cadenza de' tuoni naturali* (cadence of natural tones), 57–60; *cadenza doppia* (double cadence), 57–60, 160; *cadenza finale* (final cadence), 127, 215, 232–34, 239, 251, 253, 273, 278, 282, 284, 293, 300; *cadenza maggiore* ("major" or half cadence), 215; *cadenza media* (central cadence), 206; *cadenza minore* ("minor" or imperfect

Adler, Guido (1855–1941), xiii
Agricola, Johann Friedrich (1720–74),
257, 348n4, 349n6, 355
Alembert, Jean le Rond d' (1717–83), 54
Andreoli, Guglielmo (1862–1932), 21,
162, 334n56, 355
Anfossi, Pasquale (1727–97), 11, 53, 56
Angeloni, Carlo (1834–1901), 47, 56, 97,
165, 335n66, 366
Arnim, Ludwig Achim von (1781–1831), x
Arteaga, Esteban de [Stefano] (1747–99),
53, 69, 97, 322n10, 324n34, 357
Ashbrook, William, 183, 315n8, 318n44,
337n96, 342n50, 376
Asioli, Bonifazio (1769–1832), 50, 52,
134, 238, 242, 250, 258, 260, 276, 304,
309, 316nn23–24, 319n27, 323n19,
326nn86–87, 350nn13–14, 352n19,
353n30, 357, 361–62, 369, 375, 391;
on affect and imitation, 192–93, 196,
198–202; on conduct, 206, 210, 213,
219, 227–28, 230–31, 233–34, 339n14,
339n20, 342n43, 342n50, 343n58,
345n79, 345n81, 346n98, 347n119,
348nn129–30, 348n134; and the Conservatorio di Milano, 3, 17–20, 25–26,
27, 61; on harmony and counterpoint,
144–45, 147, 149, 153–57, 161, 163–64,
177–81, 184, 331nn41–43, 331nn45–
46, 332n25, 334n52, 334n55,
334nn61–64, 335n65, 336n82, 336n89,
337nn90–91, 337n99; on melodic and
harmonic *ritmi*, 68, 71, 77–78, 82, 84,

91, 93, 98–105, 321n5, 322n12; on
musical phrases and poetic meters,
105–26, 327n94, 328n100, 328n102,
329n113, 330n119
Azzopardi, Francesco (1748–1809), 357

Bach, Carl Philipp Emanuel (1714–88),
190, 338n7, 339n8, 357
Bach, Johann Christian (1735–82), 11
Bach, Johann Sebastian (1685–1750),
x–xi, xiii, 22, 190, 315n12, 326n82,
336n79, 336n88, 350n12
Baïf, Jean-Antoine de (1532–89), 322n12
Baini, Giuseppe (1775–1844), 29, 70–71,
96–97, 107, 321n6, 322n12, 325n75,
357, 362
Balbi, Melchiorre (1796–1879), 20, 30,
124, 316n33, 324n37, 357
Balthazar, Scott, 4, 207–208, 210, 216,
315n8, 342n47, 342nn50–51, 343n60,
344n66, 376–77, 380, 383–84, 387,
389
Bandini, Uberto (1860–1919), 26, 357
Barbirolli, Luigi (fl. 1830–60), 191, 358
Barezzi, Antonio (1787–1867), 48, 382
Basevi, Abramo (1818–85), 3–4, 29,
32–33, 37, 64, 73, 90–91, 182, 190, 204,
207, 210, 281, 314n8, 317nn33–35,
318n43, 342n47, 342n50, 343n61, 358,
364, 387–88
Basili [Basily, Basilj], Francesco (1767–
1850), 52, 319n27, 359
Batiste, Édouard (1820–76), 264, 359

Raimondi, Pietro (1786–1853), 2, 12, 52, 371, 387
Rameau, Jean-Philippe (1683–1764), 8, 16, 25, 54, 140, 144–46, 151–55, 164, 215, 333n36, 379, 383
Ray, Pietro (fl. 1830–50), 11, 256, 371
Reicha, Antoine [Anton] (1770–1836), ix, xviii, 17, 19, 23, 26, 50, 145, 273, 288, 303, 371, 375, 376, 389; on modulation, 152–53, 163, 334n59; theory of dimensions, 205, 208, 222, 227, 228–31, 233, 237–38, 247, 248, 250, 345n83, 346n106, 347n109, 347n121, 348n127; theory of rhythm, 71, 78, 98–101, 118, 123–24, 326n78
Riccati, Count Giordano (1709–90), 54, 372
Ricci, Luigi (fl. 1915–55), 241, 381, 387
Ricci, Vittorio (1859–1925), 266–67, 353n28, 372, 387
Richter, Ernst Friedrich (1808–79), 30
Riegel [Rigel], Henri-Jean (1770–1852), 264, 365
Riemann, Hugo (1849–1919), ix, xii, 16, 30, 33, 79, 82, 91, 302, 310, 372, 387
Riepel, Joseph (1709–82), 86, 150, 218, 324n50, 372, 384
Ritorni, Count Carlo (1786–1860), 71, 107, 113, 123, 192, 204–205, 210, 214, 322n12, 326n87, 328n99, 330n119, 342n43, 342n47, 351n14, 372, 376
Rodio, Rocco (ca. 1535–1615), 1
Ronchetti Monteviti, Stefano (1814–82), 64
Rosen, David, 315n8, 342n50, 354n38, 387
Rosenberg, Jesse, 4, 9, 140, 335n76, 387
Ross, Peter, 315n8, 387
Rossi, Lauro (1812–85), 5, 19–20, 32, 61, 94, 144, 151, 157, 162, 257, 314n8, 318n42, 337n99, 348n3, 353n30, 372, 385
Rossini, Gioachino (1792–1868), ix, xi, xii, xiv, 3, 5, 26, 29, 44, 48, 51–52, 56, 60, 140, 167, 263, 265, 302, 314n6, 342n50, 343n52, 350n14, 353n30, 358, 360, 365, 372, 374, 376–77, 382, 384,

386; Armida (1817), 182; Mosè in Egitto (1818), 120–21; Semiramide (1823), 113–14
Rota, Andrea (1553–97), 2
Rousseau, Jean-Jacques (1712–78), 53, 54, 229, 344n70, 372
Rustici, Giuseppe (1813–56), 54, 320n34
Ruta, Michele (1826–96), 13, 33–34, 78–79, 216, 314n7, 321n6, 323n30, 331n4, 336n80, 343n54, 346n87, 347n123, 356, 373

Sabbatini, Luigi Antonio (1732–1809), 2, 15, 25, 53, 147, 151, 167, 182, 258, 260, 315n5, 332n18, 349n6, 351n17, 367, 373
Sacchi, Giovenale (1729–89), 69, 71, 97, 373
Sacchini, Antonio (1730–86), 11, 53, 229
Sala, Nicola (1713–1801), 9, 11, 12, 25, 53, 57, 140, 147, 165–66, 256, 258, 335n75, 373, 381, 389, 391
Saladino, Michele (1835–1912), 62
Sand, Georges [Amantine, Baronne Dudevant] (1804–76), xii
Sanguinetti, Giorgio, xv, 4, 9, 57, 140, 142–43, 147–48, 150, 316n17, 317n34, 317n41, 331n3, 334n53, 388
Santa María, Tomás de (ca. 1510–70), 8, 373
Santucci, Marco (1762–1843), xix, 3, 29, 46, 52, 53–55, 97, 165, 202, 350n14, 374
Sarti, Giuseppe (1729–1802), 2, 14, 147, 167, 175, 374
Scarlatti, Alessandro (1660–1725), x, 1, 8–11, 53, 56, 265, 355, 374, 381
Scarlatti, Domenico (1685–1757), 331n4
Schenker, Heinrich (1868–1935), xiii, 85, 126, 275
Schlegel, August Wilhelm von (1767–1845), x, 195
Schlegel, Friedrich (1772–1829), x
Schoenberg, Arnold (1874–1951), xiii, 35
Schulz, Johann Peter (1747–1800), 91

NICHOLAS BARAGWANATH is Director of Postgraduate Studies and Associate Professor of Musicology at the University of Nottingham and was formerly Dean of Research and Enterprise at the Royal Northern College of Music. He has published widely on Italian opera, critical theory, and the music of Wagner, Mahler, and the Second Viennese school, winning the Westrup Prize in 2006.

This book was designed by Jamison Cockerham at Indiana University Press, set in type by Cathy Bailey, and printed by Sheridan Books, Inc.

The text face is Arno, designed by Robert Slimbach in 2007, and the display face is Cantoria, designed by Ron Carpenter in 1986, both issued by Adobe Systems.